Your Body Knows

D1552400

Your Body Knows provides the foundation actors need to move with ease and power. It is a practical guide to movement starting at the very beginning: knowing your body and experiencing how it works.

Through the work of F.M. Alexander, Rudolf Laban, and Michael Chekhov, this book offers basic training in movement fundamentals. Its step-by-step process supports the actor's work in any acting or movement training program and as a working professional. The book focuses on three main areas of exploration:

- Body facts – Know your body and its design for movement. Let go of misinformed ideas about your body. Move more freely, avoid injury, and develop a strong body-mind connection.
- Movement facts – What is movement? Discover the movement fundamentals that can serve your art. Explore new ways of moving.
- Creative inspiration – Connect your body, mind, and imagination to liberate authentic and expressive character movement.

Your Body Knows: A Movement Guide for Actors is an excellent resource for acting students and their teachers, promoting a strong onstage presence and awakening unlimited potential for creative expression.

Meade Andrews, PhD, is an internationally recognized, senior teacher of the Alexander Technique. She is a certified member of the American Society for the Alexander Technique (AmSat) and Alexander Technique International (ATI). She teaches Movement for Actors to students and professionals, and has served as a movement coach for over 40 theatrical productions. She is a certified teacher of the Michael Chekhov Acting Technique and has also done an extensive study of the work of Rudolf Laban and Irmgard Bartenieff with Carol Boggs, CMA. Former director of the Dance Program at American University in Washington, DC, Meade also taught at the Studio Theatre in Washington, DC for 20 years, offering classes in acting, improvisation, and Alexander Technique. With her colleague, Jeanne Feeney, she won the Helen Hayes Award for choreographing the Studio Theatre's 30th anniversary revival of *HAIR*. She currently teaches and coaches performers at Rider University, and the Westminster Choir College, located in Princeton, NJ. She has taught numerous workshops in the Alexander Technique for actors, dancers, singers, and musicians throughout the US, Europe, and Asia.

Jana Tift, MFA, has taught movement for actors in academic and professional settings for over 20 years. Certified to teach the Alexander Technique, the Michael Chekhov Acting

Technique, and Amrit Yoga, she has led workshops and coached actors and singers throughout the US and abroad. Ms. Tift taught movement in the graduate Acting program at Florida Atlantic University for ten years. She also served on the faculty at New World School of the Arts. A student of Rudolf Laban's work for many years, Ms. Tift is a founding member of the Labanites of South Florida, a collective of movement specialists dedicated to the study and promotion of Laban's work. An award-winning director, she has been a Hendrix-Murphy Foundation Artist-in-Residence at Hendrix College and an artist-in-residence at The Ragdale Foundation. She is a teaching member of Alexander Technique International (ATI) and a proud member of the Stage Directors and Choreographers Society. Ms. Tift holds an MFA in Theatre from Florida State University.

Your Body Knows

A Movement Guide for Actors

Meade Andrews and Jana Tift

Routledge
Taylor & Francis Group

NEW YORK AND LONDON

First published 2020
by Routledge
52 Vanderbilt Avenue, New York, NY 10017

and by Routledge
2 Park Square, Milton Park, Abingdon, Oxon, OX14 4RN

Routledge is an imprint of the Taylor & Francis Group, an informa business

Library of Congress Cataloging-in-Publication Data
Names: Andrews, Meade, author. | Tift, Jana, author.
Title: Your body knows : a movement guide for actors / Meade Andrews, Jana Tift.
Description: New York, NY : Routledge, 2020. | Includes bibliographical references and index.
Identifiers: LCCN 2019043318 (print) | LCCN 2019043319 (ebook) |
ISBN 9780367258818 (hardback) | ISBN 9780367258825 (paperback) |
ISBN 9780429330568 (ebook)
Subjects: LCSH: Movement (Acting)
Classification: LCC PN2071.M6 A53 2020 (print) | LCC PN2071.M6 (ebook) |
DDC 792.02/8–dc23
LC record available at https://lccn.loc.gov/2019043318
LC ebook record available at https://lccn.loc.gov/2019043319

MEDICAL DISCLAIMER: The following information is intended for general information purposes only. Individuals should always see their health care provider before administering any suggestions made in this book. Any application of the material set forth in the following pages is at the reader's discretion and is his or her sole responsibility.

ISBN: 978-0-367-25881-8 (hbk)
ISBN: 978-0-367-25882-5 (pbk)
ISBN: 978-0-429-33056-8 (ebk)

Typeset in Univers
by Swales & Willis, Exeter, Devon, UK

Printed in Canada

Dedication

To our students

whose curiosity and commitment inspired us and shaped our work

Contents

PART II
Elements of Expression   **199**

Acknowledgments

Many, many people – friends, family, teachers, students – were instrumental in the writing of this book. We are so grateful to:

John Shamburger, our amazing, gifted illustrator, who was willing, dedicated, and patient throughout the process. John read our minds and created beautiful illustrations even when words failed us. And also, we are grateful to David Schulz for his dynamic cover illustrations.

Our teachers in the Alexander Technique:

> Marjorie Barstow
> Elisabeth Walker
> Martha Hansen Fertman, who read our manuscript and offered valuable feedback
> Barbara Conable and Carol Boggs, who offered invaluable advice and insights
> John Nicholls, Jessica Wolf, Bill Conable, Bruce Fertman, Michael Frederick, Marie-Francoise Le Foll, and the teachers and students of the Philadelphia School for the Alexander Technique

Our teachers in the Chekhov Technique:

> Joanna Merlin, Ted Pugh, Fern Sloan, Lenard Petit, Mala Powers, Ragnar Freidank, Mark Monday, Lavinia Hart, Lionel Walsh, Cathy Albers, John McManus, Jessica Cerullo. Special thanks goes to Joanna and Fern who read material and offered their insights. And to Jessica, who assisted us with locating sources, permissions, and generously provided material for the cover illustrations

Our Laban/Bartenieff Movement Analysis teachers:

> Peggy Hackney, Karen Studd, Bill Evans, Carol Boggs

Alexander Technique Colleagues:

> Melody Schaper and Robert Lada, who read the manuscript and offered valuable insights

Betsy Polatin and Carolyn Serota, who read and recommended our proposal
Robert Rickover, alexandertechnique.com, who offered much-needed assistance in locating sources
Judy Stern, Lyn Charlsen, Lucia Walker, Joan Schirle, Ty Palmer, Susan Dorchin, Jan Baty, Cynthia Mauney, Teresa Lee, Glenna Batson, Mio Morales, Michael Gelb, Jean M.O. Fischer, Ted Dimon

Laban/Bartenieff Movement Analysis Colleagues:

The "Labanites" of South Florida: Clarence Brooks, Toranika Washington, Juliet Forest, Dale Andree, Deborah Kahan, Lauren Palmieri, and most especially:
Daniela Wancier, who generously read our manuscript and provided valuable feedback

Michael Chekhov Technique Colleagues:

Missy Barnes, Susan Cato-Chapman, Ariana Cato-Chapman, Hugh O'Gorman, Trent Blanton, Robb Maus, Matt Davis, Connie Rotunda

Our colleagues from our 20+ years of teaching at Florida Atlantic University and Rider University, where we developed this material, in particular, Des Gallant, Matthew Wright, Kathryn Johnston, Lynn McNutt, Bridget Connors, Jean Louis-Baldet, Trent Blanton, Rebecca Simon, Mariann Cook, James Jordan

Our students from American U, FAU, Rider, especially those who allowed us to use their writings about their movement experiences: Brianna Handy, Scott Wells, David Meldman, Sean Patrick Gibbons, Colby Dezelick, Michael Empson, Taylor Darden, Elizabeth Price, Jack Gerhard, Connor Padilla, Clifton Adams, Melissa St. Amand. Also, a special thanks to Gaby Tortoledo for her assistance with the cover image.

Our editor, Stacey Walker, and assistant editor, Lucia Accorsi, whose patience and guidance gave us confidence and the space we needed to create. Also, our infinitely patient and knowledgeable copy-editor Sarah Davies, creative and resourceful production managers Colin Morgan and Alison MacFarlane, and Diana Taylor, permissions coordinator for Taylor & Francis.

Our editorial assistant, Elizabeth Price, who tirelessly pursued permissions, organized material, and took care of so many details we don't even know what they all are! Also, Scott Wells, who was so resourceful in tracking down rights and truly went the extra mile in contacting the authors' estates for permissions.

The Author's Guild – 9,700 members strong – offered invaluable advice on navigating the legal aspects of publishing our work. Also, thanks to Chris Sherman, who offered insights and legal advice.

We gratefully acknowledge the permission to quote from: "MOVE ON" from *SUNDAY IN THE PARK WITH GEORGE*. Words and Music by Stephen Sondheim. (c) 1984 RILTING MUSIC, INC. All Rights Administered by WC MUSIC CORP. All Rights Reserved. Used by Permission. *Reprinted by Permission of Hal Leonard LLC*

Jana wishes to thank Tom, Madison, and Nelson, who read chapters, offered insights, formatted footnotes, encouraged, and supported throughout the long process of birthing *YBK*. You three are the light of my life, and I am so thankful for you!

Meade wishes to thank colleagues at the Studio Theatre, Washington, DC: Joy Zinoman and Jeanne Feeney. Also, most especially, Melody Schaper, Martha Fertman, Naima Prevots, and Carol Boggs, for your continuous support, inspiration, and deep friendship.

Introduction

A little over seven years ago, Meade saw students perform a play at a prestigious university. She became concerned as she saw the students moving in ways that could injure them – straining their bodies and voices. Excess tension clogged their ability to communicate the story of the play to the audience. Their obvious talent was masked by a lack of connection to their bodies.

As the two of us talked about her experience, we agreed that, if those students had known just a few facts about their bodies and how they move, they would have been more comfortable and more effective onstage. And the experience of the audience would have been much more enjoyable! That was when this book was conceived.

For many actors, expressive movement onstage seems like an insurmountable challenge. Actors, even working professionals, tell us they feel stiff, they don't know what to do with their hands, they don't know how to fill the void between themselves and the audience. However, Your Body Knows. Your body – in partnership with your mind and imagination – is a treasure trove of creative inspiration and expression. The aim of this book is to teach you to reconnect with it. You can experience movement as an expression of your whole self: body, mind, and being.

Your Body Knows is based on a simple premise: expressive movement can lead you to inspired acting. If your primary task as an actor is to communicate a story to an audience, your body is the primary communicator. As you develop your body's potential for inspired communication, you connect your physical life with your mental and emotional life. Your breath, imagination, voice, and intelligence are reflected in your body and your movement choices.

Famed acting teacher Larry Moss put it this way,

> *... you must deeply understand the material you are acting and begin to see your body as an exquisite conduit directly connected to the audience's guts. You want to heat up the minds and feelings of the audience, and nothing does that better than unique, idiosyncratic, specific human physicality.*[1]

Beautiful, inspiring words, it's true. What actor wouldn't want their body to be "an exquisite conduit?" But how? Is there a path to "specific human physicality?" Yes, there is. Movement training opens the channels between your body, mind, and imagination. This creative trio becomes the powerhouse behind your artistic inspiration.

Your Body Knows (*YBK*) is a practical guide to movement starting at the very beginning: knowing your body and experiencing how it works. Our purpose is not to teach you a particular movement system, like Laban or Alexander, but to offer you "basic training" in movement fundamentals. Through a step-by-step process, you can discover and **experience** your potential for creative physical expression. The material in *YBK* offers support to your work in any acting or movement training program and as a working professional.

The process takes you through three main areas of exploration:

- **Body facts** – Know your body and its design for movement. Release old, misinformed ideas about your body, move more freely, and avoid injury. Your body and mind work together to support your **physical** presence as a performer.
- **Movement facts** – What is movement? Know the movement fundamentals that can serve your art. Discover new ways of moving.
- **Creative inspiration** – Connect your body, mind, and imagination – your terrific trio – to liberate authentic, expressive character movement.

You've probably discovered that you can't force creativity; you can't even coax it to appear. You have to feed it and make space for it to arise in the moment. Movement training teaches you to open up your body and make room for creative impulse to express itself. The Practices in this book teach you to recognize your body, mind, and imagination as a coordinated whole, a source of creative inspiration and communication.

Your Body Knows is based in the work of three great movement pioneers, which we have studied and taught for many years: F.M. Alexander (1869–1955), Rudolf Laban (1879–1958), and Michael Chekhov (1891–1955). Their passion for the creative possibilities of the human body revolutionized movement study. Their work also transformed every aspect of our personal and artistic lives:

> Meade was a dancer, who had no idea that she was using her body in ways that led to injury. Misinformation about movement caused her to force and manipulate her body when rehearsing and performing. Through the work of F.M. Alexander, Rudolf Laban, and his student Irmgard Bartenieff, she discovered how to change her approach to movement. She moved out of pain and into freedom.

> Jana had a limited movement background. She was teaching in a small college theatre department when she noticed movement problems in her acting students. She felt powerless to help them – and set out to find solutions. Laban and Alexander opened a whole new world of physical expression for her and her students.

Michael Chekhov's unique approach to acting closely connects movement and an actor's creative imagination. We found that it built perfectly on Laban's and Alexander's work to support our students as they develop a character's physical life.

Laban, Alexander, Chekhov, and other movement pioneers have given us and our students a path to freedom of movement onstage and so much more: authenticity, creativity, and presence. Their work taught us that our bodies are only one part of our whole self, the visible aspect of our artistic life. Our bodies are always in partnership with our minds and imaginations. This was a revelation that liberated our creativity and empowered our students to be the best actors they can be.

Now after more than 50 years' teaching experience between us, we have seen this work inspire scores of students, as their movement training transforms the way they think, move, and feel. That is the experience we hope you discover in the pages of this book. Your Body Knows – and it is longing to tell you.

How to Use This Book

Your Body Knows is not a sit-on-the-couch-and-read sort of book, but a get-up-and-try-it-out kind of book. Think of it as a workbook filled with practical movement knowledge.

When it comes to movement training, experiencing information with your body is essential to learning. So, *YBK* offers you Practices that help you ground the concepts and principles in your body, mind, nervous system, and imagination. Your whole self participates in every Practice, and your experience is your laboratory.

Our approach may be quite different than the kind of movement you have encountered before. We believe that Your Body Knows much more than we give it credit for. If we push, prod, and force it to comply with a predetermined set of expectations, we are literally blocking our creative potential. We want to dispel the idea that your body is separate from your mind and your imagination. All of you participates in developing creative movement.

So, unlock your artistic curiosity, and give yourself permission to experience a different way of approaching your physical life. Below, we offer some tips, so you can get the most out of your practical explorations in *YBK*.

Pause to Discover

Our culture seems to be built around hurry, time management, getting there – wherever "there" is. We invite you to become counter-cultural. Your creative body, mind, and imagination work best when you give them time to expand and explore.

- Be willing to slow down as you explore the Practices, so you can sense what is happening in your body as you work.

- We ask you to Pause a lot. Embrace this part of the process. Pausing gives you the mental and physical space to be present before beginning an activity, and Pausing allows you to process what you experienced when you've completed a Practice.
- At first, you may feel resistance to pausing and slowing down. Be patient. Your body and mind will thank you for it. We promise!
- You may want to take more than one session to work through the Practices in a chapter, especially in Part I. If you feel like you are on "sensory overload" or overwhelmed, stop. Come back and finish the other Practices at another time.
- Give yourself a chance to fully explore each chapter. It is best to limit a movement session to one chapter at a time, or even explore longer chapters over several sessions.

Experience Movement

The Practices are not result-oriented. **Your** experience and **your** discoveries are most important.

- Commit to your movement experience in each Practice.
- Explore with a spirit of curiosity. Often you will see a question before the Practice: "I investigate." You can allow this question to guide your exploration or develop your own question.
- Your **experience** of movement terms is more important than memorizing them. The terms describe concepts that already exist in your body. You can know them from the inside out!
- Visit and re-visit the Practices – each time, your experience can deepen, change, and grow.

Practice Non-judgment

You are working with your living body and mind, which can change at any moment. Remind yourself often: A Practice that seems challenging today may become the movement foundation you rely on tomorrow.

- Start with where you are. Your unique experience and discoveries matter.
- Let go of preconceived ideas and approach the Practices with an open mind.
- Avoid self-judgment: *Fire the Judge, Hire the Witness*.
- Let go of trying to "get it right." There is no wrong or right – only exploration and your own discoveries about your movement.
- If you are in a class, avoid comparing yourself with others. Everyone experiences the material in their own way.
- The Practice you detest the most is usually the one you need the most. Go deep! Commit to discovering your movement potential in every Practice.

- When you encounter a Practice that is challenging for you, revisit it a day or two (or a week) later. Often, your mind and body need time to make a connection for a new skill, and your exploration will yield new information the second time around.

Prepare, Play, Then Process

The Practices follow a three-part progression: Preparation, Play, Process.

When you pause, you are preparing your body and mind to play and experience the Practice.

Our students say that when they approach a Practice as play, they are less likely to judge themselves or feel self-conscious. Have fun!

- Each Practice offers a moment of preparation before you begin your exploration. Fully honor this moment. The rewards are great.
- Play through the Practice, without analyzing or describing your experience while you're moving. No reason to split your focus. Then when the Practice is complete, you can:
  - *Spy back* (Key Word). This term is a basic concept in the Michael Chekhov Acting Technique. It is a moment to look back on an exploration and describe your experience. It allows you to process after the Practice, so you aren't trying to move/create and analyze at the same time.
- If you are in a group, you can share your experience and learn from the experiences of others as you *spy back* together. Listen to your classmates' experiences. They can offer you new insights into the Practice.
- *PAUSE TO PROCESS*! The Practices are meant to be experienced and savored. We encourage you to take your time with them; pause often and journal or share with a friend or classmate to process your experience. The Practices can unlock long-held tension and, sometimes, long-held emotion. As you delve deeper into movement, take time to articulate the changes you are experiencing, and the meaning and impact they have in your work and daily life. *PAUSE TO PROCESS* is a Key Practice (*KP*).

Practical Information

We want *Your Body Knows* to be as accessible as we can make it. Below is some practical information that will help you as you work – or rather, play – your way through the book.

- *YBK* is a survey course: movement basics that can serve you in any movement or acting training.
- We affirm that there is no separation between body, mind, and spirit; each influences the others and they interact seamlessly as part of a cohesive whole. When we refer to your body, please look and think beyond the limitations of language. Your body is

the part of you that is seen by the audience; however, all parts of your being shape your movement.

- This book is a step-by-step progression. Each Practice prepares you for the next. Be aware that the Practices in Part II are best explored after you have completed Part I, and the same with Parts II and III.
- The Practices give step-by-step instructions. It is best to read them through before you begin, unless you have a teacher or guide directing the Practice. If you are working alone, record them, so you can give your full attention to movement.
- Revisit Practices often: your experience will deepen as you become more and more familiar with your creative instrument.
- We've designated the most-used words and phrases as *Key Words*, like *Spy back*. The Key Words (KW) are useful for communicating about and describing movement, and they help connect your body and mind.
- We've also designated a few *Key Practices*, like *PAUSE TO PROCESS*. These elemental Practices ground the most important concepts in your body, and they can be practiced again and again to support your body and mind as you prepare for rehearsal or performance.
- We offer you "Real-life Stories" sprinkled throughout the book, most of which have been altered slightly – names and play titles – to protect our students' and friends' privacy. We've also included some of our students' journal entries, used with permission.
- As you are learning about your body, it's helpful to have a model skeleton as a study aid – as it is 3-D, and you can (gently) move it.
- Appendix I offers more Practices, building on and expanding the Practices in the chapters.
- We offer examples from three study plays, *Three Sisters*, *The Laramie Project*, and *The Glass Menagerie*. We recommend that you read them before beginning Part II.
- We have chosen to use gender neutral language – they, them, their – except when referring to a specific person and their gender.

Since *Your Body Knows* is a survey, we offer you a taste of various movement modalities. You can visit Appendix II to learn more about the movement pioneers whose work so deeply influenced *YBK*. Also, there are resources for further study there, if you would like to know more.

Keep in mind that you are developing new skills! Most of us have had many years of education, in which we sat at a desk, developed our intellect, and shut down our natural desire to move. Be gentle with yourself as you begin the process of developing your movement awareness.

> "If you approach this work not just as an actor, but also as a human, you will gain so much more. I think that is so important to remember."
>
> Connor, acting student, Florida Atlantic University[2]

We hope you will find *Your Body Knows* informative, practical, and inspiring. Enjoy!

Key Word: *Spy back*

Key Practice: *PAUSE TO PROCESS*

Notes

1   Moss, Larry. *The Intent to Live*. New York: Bantam Books p.123, 2005.
2   From a student journal. Used with permission.

Know Your Instrument (So You Can Really Play)

PART I   KNOW YOUR INSTRUMENT

Introduction to Part I

All performers – actors, musicians, dancers – spend many hours in training. They work on the technical aspects of their art form, rehearse the material, and ultimately, perform in a public situation before an audience. All of these elements – working with their instruments, developing their skills, sharpening their performance – unite to create the performer's unique artistic quality.

As an actor, you are your primary instrument of expression. Musicians navigate the relationship between two instruments – such as the cello or the piano – and themselves. Actors engage in an artistic dialogue with only one primary instrument: themselves.

When your instrument is not in tune, it becomes challenging – in fact, impossible – to make beautiful art. One of the authors of *YBK* experienced this distressing situation first-hand. Here is her story:

> *As a young actor, I wanted so badly to be seen as a truthful and sincere actor. I can still recall my desperate feelings of frustration in the scene from Chekhov's play, The Seagull, where Masha confesses her love for Constantin. I was unable to make any emotional connection with my lines. Many years later, I can still visualize and sense that moment with distinct clarity.*
>
> *Now, after studying Alexander Technique and other movement disciplines, I can describe this experience as a classic example of performance anxiety and excess muscular tension. I was literally choking on my words, constricting my breath, and compressing my whole body while trying to contact some shred of emotional responsiveness. The flow of my inner impulses was significantly distorted and disrupted.*

Today, when we work with actors, we relate this experience as a cautionary tale, and as an example of why a well-balanced, finely-tuned instrument – body, mind, and spirit – is so crucial for artistic expression.

Knowing your body and how it works is the ground-floor for building a dynamic physical presence onstage. We live in our bodies. We think we know them. But for many of us, our movement potential is blocked by misconceptions and misinformation. Like the actress in the story above, our choices are limited by self-imposed restrictions we have placed on our bodies.

However, there is good news: Your Body Knows! Part I: *Know Your Instrument (So You Can Really Play)* introduces you to the **facts** of your body's design for movement and some little-known aspects of your physical life that may be unfamiliar to you. Through the Practices in each chapter, you can connect your body and mind – seamless communication that supports your creative inspiration – and you can discover your body's design for movement from the inside out.

Exploration is key to uncovering your body's potential for movement. Allow yourself to be surprised as you get to know your body and expand your movement vocabulary. We hope that, at the end of Part I, you will be in harmony with your body, mind, and the environment in which you move.

The Starting Place

We are always moving. Right now, though you may be sitting "still" as you read these words, hundreds of muscles are working in your body. Tiny muscles are moving your eyes left to right. As you breathe, your diaphragm is constantly moving downward, then rising upward, causing the muscles in your ribs and torso to expand and contract – all the way down to your pelvis. Perhaps you are drumming your fingers on the table or tapping your foot. We are dynamic beings, always changing in relationship to ourselves, others, and the world. We move!

On the stage, your movement assumes a heightened state. The audience absorbs not only the words you say, but the way you move your body, your gestures, and the way you occupy space. If you drum your fingers on the table or tap your foot, you are conveying important details about the character. Through your movement choices, you communicate a wealth of information to the audience.

YBK provides a practical and artistic foundation for enlivening your onstage presence. It offers a learning process designed to build your self-awareness, body knowledge, and ultimately, the ability of your body and mind to respond to the action of the play. Each time you encounter a new concept or principle, you are invited to practice it in a simple exercise. In this way, you can begin to expand your "movement vocabulary," both mentally and physically.

A beautiful two-way street joins the mental and the physical: You **know your body** and you **embody your knowledge**. When you practice *Body-Mind Communication* (KW), information is constantly flowing from your body to your mind and back again. This seamless relationship serves your imagination and supports your performance as you create compelling characters and a powerful presence on stage.

In this first section, *The Starting Place*, you can explore fundamentals that support all movement: *kinesthetic sense*, *3-dimensional body*, and breath. No matter what the physical demands of the role may be, these elements provide the underpinning for every movement choice you make as an actor and as a human being.

Key Word: *Body-Mind Communication*

Your Motion Detector

Your Body Knows! Your body has a natural balance that supports ease of movement, yet most of us are unaware of it. We lack awareness and knowledge to recognize and access this balance. Though we have a choice about the way we move, many of us are not making use of the wealth of movement potential available to us.

This section introduces you to movement awareness, the conscious ability to sense ourselves as we move. With movement awareness as a foundation for your physical presence, you are free to create! You can learn to shed excess tension that interferes with fully expressive movement. You can also learn to completely embody a character, as well as respond easily to the play, the other actors, and the audience.

As you approach the explorations below, allow yourself to enjoy moving – let go of preconceived ideas, and welcome new possibilities!

PRACTICE 1.1 LET'S GET MOVING

This Practice is all about "giving permission." Let go and let yourself move!

I investigate: What is it like to move for fun without judging myself?

- Stand. Close your eyes. Sense your body. Notice where your attention is drawn: you may sense a twinge in your shoulder, the pressure of your feet against the floor, the weight of your arms. Let go of any need to "get it right." Quietly observe your body and your sensations as they are right now. Pause.
- Just for fun, put on some music you like that might inspire you to move or dance. (We like Michael Jackson's "The Way You Make Me Feel" or Ottmar Liebert's "Barcelona Nights.") Just let your body move. You can work with your eyes open or closed.
- Let go of thinking about how to move, how you look, or "what am I supposed to get out of this?" Let the music inspire you. Follow your impulses. Play!

- When the music ends, pause. Stand. Close your eyes. Sense your body. Notice where your attention is drawn. Quietly observe yourself.
- *Spy back.* What did you experience? What was it like to move just for fun? How did you feel – physically, emotionally? What was your experience of standing and observing before the exercise? And after? Were the sensations different?

In this Practice, you allowed your body to begin to move freely from inner impulse in response to a stimulus, the music. This is an essential ingredient in moving freely onstage. You've also practiced pausing and observing your movement sensations using your *kinesthetic sense*.

Your Motion Detector: The *Kinesthetic Sense*

Each of us has a built-in movement monitor: the *Kinesthetic Sense* (KW). Through this amazing motion detector, we can get to know our bodies, our movement, and the space around us from the inside out. Your *kinesthetic sense* invites you to experience life in a deeper way – not just intellectually, but viscerally, with your muscles, bones, organs, and nerves. It opens you to an endless array of movement options.

What is the *kinesthetic sense*? What does it do?

The *kinesthetic sense* is "the sensation of movement in the muscles; muscle memory; the awareness of the relationship of the body to itself."[1]

The *kinesthetic sense* is our "spatial and muscular sense." Like the other senses – taste, touch, smell, sight, and hearing – it is at work 24/7, and like the other senses it can function unconsciously or consciously. When we bring the *kinesthetic sense* into our awareness, we can make informed movement choices.

The *kinesthetic sense*:

- Informs us about **relationships within the body**, i.e., how the various body parts relate to one another.
- Tells us how much pressure or strength is needed, **the amount of effort** required, to lift a heavy object, or execute a pirouette.
- Informs us **when and how the body needs to move**, such as standing and stretching after sitting at the computer for a long period of time or initiating a movement in a gentle way for stroking a puppy, or a firm way for massaging a sore muscle.
- Perceives the **sensation of movement in the muscles, tendons, and joints**, including excess tension.
- Tells us the **speed of a movement**, the difference between fast and slow.
- Is a factor in remembering movement so that it can be repeated: **muscle memory**.
- **Recognizes our relationship with the space around us** and influences the way our body interacts with it.*

---

* Physicians may employ other names for this important sensory information, such as *proprioception* and *exteroception*. In teaching movement for the stage, we choose to combine these somatic terms under one sensory umbrella: *The Kinesthetic Sense*.

The *kinesthetic sense* is always working, yet most of us are unaware of its existence. In fact, for many of us, it is shut down. Sometimes, modern life requires that we ignore the *kinesthetic sense*. For instance, a growing six-year-old isn't meant to sit in a desk for hours at a time, but most of us did it in first grade. We had to ignore our *kinesthetic sense* and its message: time to move!

As actors, we must reawaken our *kinesthetic sense*, because it is the foundation on which all movement relies. We can't make informed movement choices without aware-ness of what we are doing **as we are doing it**. Most importantly, the *kinesthetic sense* takes us out of our head and into our body. Then we are free to follow the impulse to move, as you did in Practice 1.1 above.

In the Practices below, you can become more familiar with *kinesthetic sensing*, while exploring simple, familiar movements; this develops your *Kinesthetic Awareness* (KW). This Key word refers to light, gentle attention to movement sensations throughout your body, as well as an awareness of your body in space. *Kinesthetic awareness* opens a communication pathway between your body, your brain, and the space around you.

Awakening Your Kinesthetic Sense

PRACTICE 1.2 **WHERE IS MY HAND?**[2]

This is a simple Practice for tuning in to the spatial relationship of one part of your body to another. When practicing *kinesthetic awareness*, avoid heavy concentration, or "laser focus," which tends to cause excess tension or even interfere with your breathing. Remember to give "light, gentle" attention to sensation, **all** sensation, not just in one area.

I investigate: What can I learn from *kinesthetic awareness*?

- Stand. Pause. Use your *kinesthetic awareness* to "tune in" to the sensations of your breath and body.
- Place one hand where you can't see it, and where it isn't touching anything.
- Tune in to the sensations in your body as you notice your hand. Use *kinesthetic awareness* to sense your hand and arm, and the distance between your hand and your body.
- Where is your hand? You can sense that your hand is at the end of your arm, and your arm is connected to your whole body.
- Can you also sense if it is higher than your head? Or is it lower than your knees? Is it 3 inches away from your body – or 12 inches? Ask someone to val-idate your observation or look in a mirror to confirm. You are using your *kines-thetic sense* to define **relationships within your body**.
- If you also wiggle your fingers, and move at your wrist joint, you can experience *kinesthetic sensation* as well.
- Return your hand to its usual relationship with your body.

- Pause. Notice your hand, arm, and whole body.
- Explore this sequence with your other hand/arm, in a different position. Follow the steps above.
- Pause.
- *Spy back.* How did you know where your hand was? What were the sensations? Were you aware of your breath? In what way? What did you discover about the difference between strong, focused attention and light, gentle attention?

You can practice this simple exploration often, playing with light *kinesthetic awareness*. You can sense the differences in your body if you slip from *kinesthetic awareness* into heavy concentration, shutting out the space around you. For many of us, *kinesthetic awareness* is a new skill, so give yourself the opportunity to play with it a bit, as you will do in the Practice below.

PRACTICE 1.3 THROWING AND CATCHING

In this Practice, enjoy noticing the stream of information from your *kinesthetic sense*, while playing a simple game of catch with an imaginary ball.

I investigate: Write your own investigative question. What are you curious about as you approach throwing and catching?

Part I

- Stand. Pause. Notice yourself, your breathing, your balance, the room around you.
- Using an imaginary ball, practice throwing the ball up in the air and catching it. Notice that your body knows exactly what to do, and how to time the actions: **muscle memory**.
- Use *kinesthetic awareness* to notice the **sensations in your muscles and joints** as you throw; sense the subtle movements happening under your skin.
- Give yourself permission to pause and notice the sensations in your body before you throw.
- Practice throwing the ball lightly. Throw it hard. Your *kinesthetic sense* tells you **how your body needs to move**, and **the amount of effort required** to accomplish a task in a particular way.
- After a few minutes, pause. Notice yourself standing in the room.
- *Spy back.* What was the experience of placing your attention on sensation while moving? How did the sensations differ when throwing softly or hard? What did you notice in your Pause before the Practice? After the Practice?

When you are performing familiar movements, your *kinesthetic sense* offers you feedback about effort, sensation, body and spatial relationships, and timing. By revisiting this practice, you can continue to develop your awareness of this important sensory information.

Part II

- Repeat the Practice with a partner.
- *Spy back.* What did you learn about your ability to pay attention to your *kinesthetic sense* while also responding to a partner? What did you notice about your breath? How might this information serve you as an actor?

This Practice gives you the opportunity to explore your *kinesthetic sense* in a low-stakes situation (no audience, no pressure to catch a real ball). Yet, it has elements of performance, because you are responding to another performer and your imagined circumstances.

Kinesthetic awareness is your essential movement guide. The next Practice invites you to strengthen your *body-mind communication.*

> If you like, *PAUSE TO PROCESS* before continuing to the next Practice. Notice how *kinesthetic awareness* can inform your movement as you take a walk, drive your car, or brush your teeth. Journal or discuss your new awareness with a classmate or friend.

PRACTICE 1.4   KINESTHETIC SENSING (KP)

This Key Practice quiets your nervous system; it invites your mind to quiet, as the *kinesthetic sense* becomes your primary focus. Your brain is invited to **receive** kinesthetic sensation, without trying to analyze or describe it. You are strengthening kinesthetic communication from *body* to *mind*.

I investigate: What happens when I allow my brain to take in information from my body?

- Stand. Close your eyes. Sense your body. Take a pause. Tell your analytical brain to take a back seat for the next few moments and listen to the information your *kinesthetic sense* is offering.
- Notice the sensations of breathing.
- Slowly make a simple movement, like raising your arm high above your head. Place your attention, not on the action of doing, but on the sensations as you are moving your arm. Your brain may want to describe or analyze the sensation, but instead, simply feel **the sensation of movement in the muscles, tendons and joints.**
- When your arm has reached its full length above your head, pause for a moment. Continue to focus on the sensation of having your arm in this position – notice any sensation in other parts of your body as well – shoulder, back, neck, legs, your other arm, etc.
- Now lower your arm, using *kinesthetic awareness* to notice the sensations in your body as you move your arm.
- Pause. Notice the sensations in your arm. Resist the temptation to describe or analyze your sensations.

- Repeat all the steps above with your other arm.
- Pause. Notice any new sensations in your arms.
- *Spy back.* What was your experience of receiving kinesthetic sensations without analyzing or describing them? Did you notice changing sensations as you moved your arm? Describe them. How did your body and mind respond to *kinesthetic sensing*?

If you did not notice much change in sensation, be patient with yourself. After years of educating your mind, awakening to your body's intelligence is a new experience. Give yourself time to become reacquainted with this part of you. *Fire the Judge! Hire the Witness!*

Try this again tomorrow and see what you discover. Each time you explore this Practice, *Kinesthetic Sensing*, you can make new discoveries, so revisit it often. Each Practice included in *YBK* can offer you something new each time you explore it.

Kinesthetic sensing can be practiced in a number of ways, in any activity. Many of our students report that they experience a calming effect when they practice it. They feel their muscles lengthen, their body and mind are in tune, and they are more responsive to the world around them.

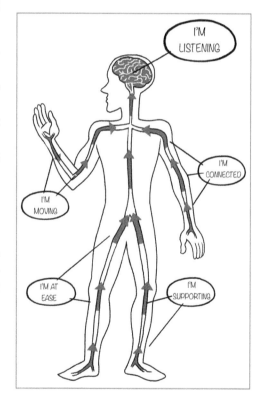

In most Practices in *YBK*, you will be asked to take a *Kinesthetic Moment* (KP) during or after your exploration. *Kinesthetic moment* gives you time (and space!) to practice *kinesthetic sensing*: it is a moment to give your body permission to "speak" to your mind by placing light attention on sensation – without trying to describe it.

Then, through *Spy back*, your brain can turn your sensory experience into information. You can put words to what you experienced, as your mind completes the feedback loop. The *kinesthetic moment* awakens your *kinesthetic sense* and helps strengthen *body-mind communication*.

You can also take a *kinesthetic moment* at the beginning of a Practice. It is a moment to sense your body in space, your feet on the floor, and *kinesthetic sensation*. You are in the present moment and ready to explore.

Figure 1.1 In a *kinesthetic moment*, your brain quiets and takes in sensations from your body, without analyzing or describing them.

The movement concepts in *YBK* rely on your *kinesthetic sense* to support you as you move. The more you practice *kinesthetic awareness*, the more available it will be when you are onstage. Just as you unconsciously absorb what you see and hear, you can absorb and utilize kinesthetic information, as you are rehearsing or performing.

As you may have discovered, *kinesthetic awareness* requires a *body-mind* partnership. Your *kinesthetic sense* sends sensory signals to your conscious mind, which trans-lates the signals into information that then informs your movement. Your *body-mind* feedback loop is essential to discovering movement that supports your creative impulses.

You can continue to awaken your *kinesthetic sense* by bringing this delicate, yet dynamic, form of sensing into your daily life. In the exploration below, you can connect your body and mind as you practice *kinesthetic sensing* in a simple activity.

PRACTICE 1.5   THE MIRACLE OF SMALL MOTOR MOTION AND INCLUSIVE ATTENTION

This Practice expands your connection between your body and your mind, as you gather information about the way you move in a familiar activity.

Part I

* Sit at a table with a piece of paper and a pen in front of you.
* Pause. Breathe. Take a *kinesthetic moment*.
* Notice any sensations that are drawing your attention.
* Prepare to write your name on the piece of paper. Notice yourself, your *kinesthetic sensations*, as you reach for the pen and prepare to write.
* Sense your fingers/hand/wrist moving as you write, and more subtly, **sensations in your muscles and joints**. Note that your hand forms the letters automatically; there is no need to tell it how to move.
* Be aware of the miracle of your **muscle memory**.
* Pause.
* *Spy back*. What were the sensations you felt as you wrote? Were there any sur-prises? What were they? **How much effort is needed** to complete the task of writ-ing your name? How much effort did you actually use?
* Practice again and play with changing the amount of effort you use as you write your name. You can also play with the **speed of the movement**. After your explor-ation, pause.
* *Spy back*. What was your experience in this exploration? If we apply the saying, "The way you do anything is the way you do everything," to this Practice, how could your discoveries about effort serve you in your everyday activities? As an actor?

As you saw in this Practice, *kinesthetic awareness* helps you discover valuable information about your movement. However, your movement relies on more than *kinesthetic sensing*. Your body does not exist in isolation – it is in relationship with everything around it. *Inclusive Attention* (KW) invites you to notice your whole self and the world around you simultaneously.[3] You can receive information from all your senses, such as sight, hearing, touch, and of course, your *kinesthetic sense*.

Part II

* Repeat Part I, with this change: This time, practice *inclusive attention* as you write your name. In addition to your *kinesthetic sense,* be aware of your other senses, and the room around you.
* Practice awareness of your whole body as you write your name.
* Sense the chair under your legs, your feet on the floor, sounds in the room. See the paper, the table; note your peripheral vision as you continue to write.
* Notice your breath as you expand your awareness.
* Play with the amount of effort you use to write. Notice what happens to breath, body, vision, and your awareness of space as you increase and decrease effort. Notice what happens if you change the speed with which you write.
* Put down the pen.
* Pause. Take a *kinesthetic moment*.
* *Spy back.* How did *inclusive attention* affect the simple action of writing your name?

Becoming aware of the amount of effort you use to complete simple tasks may offer you a clue about your habitual movement patterns. Patterns of misuse or excess tension can limit the creative movement that is available to you. When you develop and refine your "motion detector," you can recognize and take advantage of a wider range of choices.

Conscious choice is at the heart of lively, vibrant movement. Awakening your *kinesthetic sense*, and learning to include it in your awareness, is the gift that keeps on giving. It gives you a choice about how you move onstage and in everyday life.

PAUSE TO PROCESS Journal or talk with someone about your discoveries. Give yourself time to integrate *kinesthetic awareness* and *inclusive attention* into your daily activities.

Key Words: *Kinesthetic Sense, Kinesthetic Awareness, Inclusive Attention*

Key Practice: *Kinesthetic Moment, Kinesthetic Sensing*

Notes

1 "kinesthesia (kinesthetic sense)". *Merriam-Webster.com.* Merriam-Webster, 2018. Web.
2 Conable, Barbara and Conable, Bill. *How To Learn The Alexander Technique*. Portland, OR: Andover Press, 1991. Print. p. 19
3 Conable, Barbara. Personal correspondence. July 10, 2012. *Inclusive Attention* is a concept developed for the Andover Educators teacher training course in *Body Mapping*.

Your 3-Dimensional Body

As actors, we are communicators. We share our whole self – body, mind, and imagination – with the audience. However, most of us are limited by a lack of awareness. For instance, we are conscious of the parts of our body that we can see, but what about the rest of it? Your 360° body is a source of support for your creative process.

You can develop awareness of your *3-dimensional body* (KW) through your *kinesthetic sense*. By using all of your body as you perform, you give yourself more movement options. You can move beyond the ordinary to the excitement of the heightened reality that is required onstage.

Limited awareness of your *3-D body* can trigger excess tension, which interferes with breathing and your ability to move easily. Each of the dimensions – vertical, horizontal, and sagittal – is always and equally at play in your coordinated body.

Each of the three dimensions is composed of two counterbalancing directions. The **vertical dimension** consists of **height**: up in relation to down. The **horizontal dimension** is composed of **width** – from side to side, left and right. And the **sagittal dimension** gives us **depth** from front to back. When we say the directions counterbalance, we mean that each direction balances its opposite direction with an equal weight or force. Front counterbalances back, left counterbalances right, up counterbalances down, and vice versa.

The three dimensions, all six directions, join together to support the rounded shape of our body. There are no straight lines in our bodies: arms, head, torso, legs, even fingers and toes, are rounded shapes. We are truly 360° actors.

When your body can move in any direction, you are free to follow your impulses. Cultivate your three dimensions, release unwanted tension, and act with your whole body – supported by your mind and imagination. In the Practices below, discover the possibilities for movement inspired by the interplay of these directions.

PRACTICE 2.1   DIMENSIONAL AWAKENING

In *How To Learn The Alexander Technique*, master teacher Barbara Conable explains that your other senses provide support for your *kinesthetic sense.*[1] In this Practice, your sense of touch and your visual sense assist your *kinesthetic sense* in developing your 3-dimensional awareness.

Your body itself is 3-dimensional. It has length, width, and depth. Each of these dimensions is a direction in your body. Rather than imposing the dimensions on your body, you can sense the dimensions from **within** your *3-dimensional body*.

Figure 2.1a & b The rounded shape of your body is supported by the three dimensions.

I investigate: What can I learn about movement from exploring my *3-dimensional body?*

Part I: Sensing Breath

- Stand in the space. Pause.
- Lightly place your hands on the sides of your ribs and sense the movement of your ribs under your hands as you breathe. Don't try to create movement. Just allow breathing to happen.
- After a minute or two, place one hand in back, resting on your lower ribs (the back of your hand will be touching your back), and place the other hand in front, again using your sense of touch to help you become aware of movement as you inhale and exhale.
- After a minute or two, place one hand on your chest and another on your abdomen. Sense the changing shape of the length of your torso as you inhale and exhale.

- After a few minutes, take your hands away.
- Pause. Take a *kinesthetic moment*.

Part II: Sensing Vertical

- Take a walk around the space. Practice *inclusive attention* as you sense yourself and see the room. Note the sensation of your feet against the floor, the air against your skin. After a few minutes, pause.
- Bring light attention to your vertical dimension. Sense the height of your whole body, from head to toe, as you stand, easing upward and releasing downward.
- Lightly place the fingers of one hand on top of your head. Let this light touch help you sense your vertical dimension.
- Feel the pressure of the floor against your feet. Accept the support of the ground.
- Sense your vertical connection, from the top of your head to your feet, and from your feet to the top of your head, **through** your whole body. Avoid "pulling up" or "pressing down": Up and Down are happening simultaneously; they counterbalance each other.
- Move through the room or remain stationary, as you continue this tactile/kinesthetic/visual exploration.
- You can stand on your tiptoes or crouch down, and still connect to the counterbalance inherent in your vertical dimension.
- When you have thoroughly explored your vertical dimension from head to toe, have another walk without putting your hand on top of your head. Use your visual and *kinesthetic senses*. Practice *inclusive attention*.
- After a few minutes, pause.

Part III: Sensing Horizontal

Now bring your attention to your horizontal dimension.

- Sense the width of your body as you stand. Bring light awareness to your whole body and its width. Move your attention from side to side, sensing the width of each part of your body, including each limb.
- Lightly place your hands against the sides of your pelvis, palms inward. Let your hands and fingers help you sense the width of your pelvis. Sense that the width continues *through* your body, from one side to the other, between your hands.
- Move your hands to another part of your body and continue to clarify your width by moving your hands along your sides. Explore the width of each shoulder, leg, foot, the sides of your head, etc.
- Feel free to move through the space or remain stationary, as you continue this tactile/kinesthetic/visual exploration.
- Move any way you like, placing your hands on the sides of your body to help you sense your horizontal dimension.

- When you have thoroughly explored your width in every part of your body, have another walk without using your tactile sense. Practice *inclusive attention* as you explore the width of your body and the 360° room around you.
- After several minutes, pause. *Take a kinesthetic moment.*

Part IV: Sensing Sagittal

- Last, but not least, repeat Part II with attention on the sagittal dimension. Explore your depth with hands on your back and front, from your head to your feet. Include your arms and hands.
- Placing one hand on your forehead and the other hand at the back of your head can give you a sense of the rounded shape of your skull!
- If you find it difficult to place a hand on your back, stand against a wall or use a towel, as if you were drying your back after a swim.
- Pause. Take a *kinesthetic moment.*

Part V: Your 360° Body

- Practice *inclusive attention* as you stand in the space. Notice your *3-dimensional body* and your 3-dimensional breath. Sense the connection of your three dimensions with each other, as they support the rounded shape of your body.
- Walk around the space, enjoying the freedom and fullness of your three dimensions.
- Feel free to use your hands to assist you in awakening any dimension that is out of your awareness.
- Continue walking and try turning in a new direction. Notice that all three dimensions are working together simultaneously as you turn.
- At some point, let go of your thoughts about 3-dimensionality. Continue to move any way you like (stand, sit, crawl, turn, leap), and sense the fullness of the movements. You can also pause at any time to contrast your *3-D body* in movement and in stillness.
- Recognize and celebrate that 3-dimensionality is not something you **do**, it is who you **are**.
- Pause.
- *Spy back.* What did you discover about your movement and your dimensionality? In what ways did your awareness of your dimensions change as you explored? How did awakening the dimensions affect your movement?

You can revisit this Practice any time. Dimensional awakening can assist you in moving from feeling "stuck" or "stiff" to a sense of lively possibilities for expressive movement. The three dimensions are always at play in your body.

Out of the Movement Box

Most of us do not make the most of our three dimensions in daily life, except, possibly, when we are exercising. We carry out our daily activities in a "movement box." When we sit at the computer, brush our teeth, drive, text, read, cook, eat, wash dishes – we use the same limited range of movement over and over.

The box does not invite us to use our full vertical dimension, from the top of our heads to the bottoms of our feet. We may forget about our backs and our sides, as we tune out any part of the body that isn't directly involved in carrying out these familiar tasks.

We may also feel restricted because of social norms. Some of us feel self-conscious about letting our hips sway side-to-side, for instance. If we feel too tall, we may restrict our use of our upward direction. We may be unaware that we have created a mental "movement box."

What can we do to get out of our movement box? First, remember that you **are** 3-dimensional. It's not a concept or tool: it is a fact of the way you are made. Just because parts of you are not directly involved with an activity, doesn't mean they can't participate and support your movement.

Next, begin to cultivate dimensional awareness: sensing your *3-D body* can support and "fill out" your movement, even when you are working within the confines of "the box." If your hands are on the computer keyboard or the steering wheel in

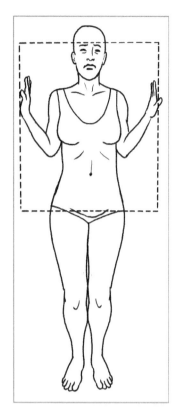

Figure 2.2 The movement box can limit your choices.

front of you, bring your awareness to the counterbalancing direction through your body, all the way to your back. See how full and awake your body can be, as you bring all three dimensions into this familiar activity.

Just as you awakened your *kinesthetic sense* in Chapter 1, you can develop your 3-dimensional awareness. You can give yourself permission to make conscious choices about allowing your more "unfamiliar" dimensions to fully participate in your movement.

The exploration below offers you the chance to awaken the fullness of all three of your lively, balanced, supportive dimensions. Through this Practice you can discover that you have many choices for how and where you move.

PRACTICE 2.2 REVISIT LET'S GET MOVING (IN THREE DIMENSIONS!)

With a lively *kinesthetic awareness* of your *3-dimensional body*, revisit Practice 1.1 from Chapter I, with this added focus.

- Follow the directions for Practice 1.1 (Let's Get Moving), being particularly aware of the expressive possibilities of each dimension.

- Play with moving through your vertical dimension. Sense the counterbalancing of up and down. With your arms above your head – can you simultaneously sense your feet on the floor?
- Explore the possibilities of moving through your vertical dimension, such as rising and sinking.
- Repeat the above step exploring your horizontal dimension: open your arms to the side. Sense left counterbalancing right and right counterbalancing left. Express yourself: explore the range of possibilities in moving side-to-side.
- Repeat the above step exploring your sagittal dimension: try a forward lunge, then shift backward and forward. Remember: forward counterbalances backward and vice versa. How many ways can your body move front to back and back to front?
- Play with moving from dimension to dimension; connect them all seamlessly, exploring the possibilities in 3-D movement – circles, diagonals, spirals, etc. – as you respond to the music.
- Pause at the end and take a *kinesthetic moment*. Have a walk around the room.
- Pause.
- *Spy back*. What was it like to explore your three dimensions? How did this Practice differ from your experience in Practice 1.1? Did you notice differences in your movement choices? What were they? How might this information serve you as an actor?

Now that your three dimensions are more "awake," you can take your discoveries into your everyday activities. You can learn to let go of the mental and physical restrictions of your movement box.

Real-life Story: The Power of Counter-balancing Directions

Julia often felt uncomfortable on stage. She felt her movement was "flat," as if she were a piece of cardboard. Standing in one place was worse than moving; her shoulders, arms, and shins always felt tense and tight.

As Julia began to explore her three dimensions, she realized that her legs were pulling upward, away from the floor, and her shoulders were lifted to take the place of the floor's support. She could sense the "up" in her vertical dimension, but she recognized she was lacking "down."

Julia decided to make a change. She began to practice sensing "up and down" in her body, through simple everyday movements, like reaching up to take a book off a shelf. As she reached up, she took care to sense her feet on the floor. When she stood, she found that if she sensed the bottoms of her feet meeting the floor, her legs did not pull up away from the floor: "down" began to balance "up." With the counterbalance of both directions through her body, she felt more supported. Her shins and her shoulders softened, as she sensed up and down counterbalancing each other.

With balance in her vertical dimension, Julia felt her other dimensions were more available as well. Far from feeling like a piece of cardboard, Julia was becoming a 360-degree actor.

In the next Practice, enjoy playing with what you've learned as you explore the 3-dimensionality that's at the heart of the *Cupid Shuffle*.

PRACTICE 2.3   THE CUPID SHUFFLE

Play with your dimensionality: "The Cupid Shuffle," by Cupid,[2] opens and enlivens your three dimensions. You can find it on YouTube. The original music video is wonderful, and the simple instructions are in the song.

If you don't already know "The Cupid Shuffle," there are instructional videos on YouTube as well. We like *How To Do The Cupid Shuffle/Kids Hip Hop Moves* on YouTube:[3] the teacher is very clear in his instructions, and he is connected to his *3-D body*!

- Pause. Stand. Notice yourself and any sensations in your body.
- Have fun as you follow the simple steps in the "Cupid Shuffle." As you move in each direction, be aware that the connections between *all* of your dimensions support each movement.
- After you dance your way through the song, pause to notice yourself in the space. Give yourself a *kinesthetic moment* to enjoy the sensations in your body.
- *Spy back*.

Each time you revisit these fun, energetic movements, bring your *kinesthetic awareness* into the picture. Practice *inclusive attention* and enjoy the support of your 360° body.

When you fully awaken your *3-dimensional body*, you can move in any direction, and you can become more specific and creative in your physical expression of a character. You also free your breath, and open your resonating chambers, liberating your voice. In the next chapter, you can practice *kinesthetic sensing* and dimensional awareness as you explore your 3-dimensional breath.

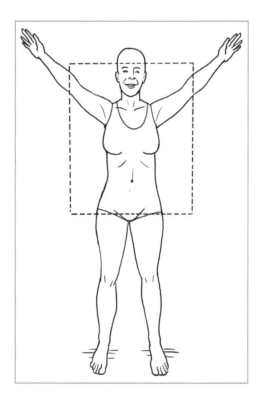

Figure 2.3 You can move beyond the movement box.

> *PAUSE TO PROCESS* Journal or discuss your discoveries with someone. Practice awareness of your *3-D body* in your daily life.

Key Word: *3-dimensional (3-D) body*

Notes

1 Conable, Barbara and Conable, Bill. *How to Learn the Alexander Technique*. Portland, OR: Andover Press, 1991. Print, p. 25

2 Bernard, Bryson. *The Cupid Shuffle*. Performed by Cupid. Asylum: Atlantic Records, 2006.

3 Howcast. *How To Do the Cupid Shuffle/Kids Hip-Hop Dance Moves*. Performed by Jeff Cowans. YouTube. July 13, 2013. www.youtube.com/watch?v=5_srg-18Fz0.

Your Moving Breath

CHAPTER 3

Movement rides on the flow of the breath.

Irmgard Bartenieff[1]

Breathing is the most fundamental, and the most significant movement we make. Our lives depend on the support of our breath, as we inhale oxygen from our surroundings and exhale carbon dioxide. Fortunately, we don't have to think about breathing, because it is completely ongoing, day and night. Our breathing provides our fundamental support for speaking, singing, walking, running, and every other activity in our daily lives. Breathing is Life!

Sometimes we hold our breath. And then we say, "I forgot to breathe!" When we hold our breath, our "most significant movement" has been stopped. We interrupt the natural flow that coordinates our body and all our body's systems. Our whole torso becomes rigid, and our arms and legs tighten and pull inward. When breathing returns to its regular rhythm, our body is restored to its natural balance. Movement truly does "ride on the flow of the breath."

Breathing is an "inside job," resulting from the expansion and contraction of your diaphragm, a large muscle which rhythmically guides your inhale and exhale. Breathing is also a duet form, a dance occurring between the movement of your dome-like diaphragm with your ribs.

When you inhale, your diaphragm moves down and spreads out inside your ribs, which respond by gently expanding. On the exhale, your diaphragm returns to its dome-like shape, and your ribs are restored to their resting state. Your movable spine supports the diaphragm–rib dance, as your lungs fill with oxygen and release CO_2. In fact, your whole body is constantly and subtly moved by the rhythms of breathing.

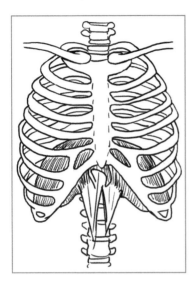

Figure 3.1 Shape of diaphragm, spine, and ribs at rest.

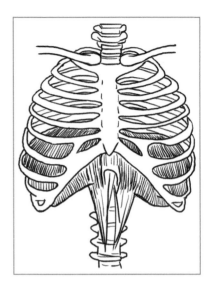

Figure 3.2 Shape of diaphragm, spine, and ribs inhaling.

Get to know your breath from the inside out! Through the explorations in Part I below, you can become better acquainted with the movement of your breath. Then in Part II, you can discover how the flow of your breath supports your movement.

Part I: Your Flowing Breath

Even though your breath is powerful, it is delicate. It gently and constantly moves through you. In order to know your breath better, pause and listen to it. These next Practices invite you to get acquainted with this foundational support for all movement.

PRACTICE 3.1 SENSING THE MOVEMENT OF YOUR BREATH

In this exploration, you can give yourself time to notice your breathing while lying down. We will invite you to move into a supportive relationship with the floor called the *Balanced Resting State* (KP). Your *kinesthetic sensing* and *inclusive attention* will serve you as you sense the movement of your breath in this restful Practice.

I investigate: What is my experience of movement when I breathe?

* Pause. Stand. Take a *kinesthetic moment*. Using your *kinesthetic sense*, notice any sensations in your body, including the sensation of breathing.
* Continue noticing yourself as you have a walk around the room.
* Pause.

- Lie down on the floor on your back with legs and arms extended. Place a book or folded towel under your head to relieve any neck pressure.
- Pause.
- Let your body rest. Accept the support of the floor.
- Notice the movement of your breath.
- On an exhale, slide one heel toward your sit bone, allowing your knee to ease upward. Your foot will rest on the floor and your knee will point toward the ceiling.
- On your next exhale, send your other leg on the same journey.

Figure 3.3 The *balanced resting state*.

- As your feet receive the support of the floor, sense the gradual spreading of your whole back into its natural length and width. Allow your pelvis to receive the support of the floor as well.
- Allow your hands to rest palms down on your body, below your ribs and above your pelvis.
- Take some time to rest in *inclusive attention* as your breathing calms itself.
- Sense the rhythmic movement of your breathing. This is a process of allowing, rather than trying to "make something happen."
- You may notice small internal movements, movements under your hands, or the changing sensations of your back against the floor.
- Notice any sensations of movement in your whole body as you inhale and exhale.
- After several minutes, pause. (But keep breathing, of course!)
- When you are ready, let your breath be your guide as you roll onto your side and use your hands to bring yourself to sitting.
- Allow your breath to support your return to standing.
- Pause. Notice any sensations in your body, including your breathing.
- Continue to notice yourself as you have a walk around the room.
- Pause.
- *Spy back*. Were you able to accept the support of the floor? How was your breath affected? What differences did you notice in your body/breath sensations before, during, and after the lying-down Practice?

Breathing: Just the Facts

- Your "springy," trampoline-like diaphragm attaches around the insides of your lower ribs and is also anchored along the sides of your lower spine.
- The 24 movable vertebrae of your spine lengthen and gather in response to the rhythmic action of your diaphragm.
- The interplay between the joints of your ribs, your diaphragm, and your spine creates a rhythmic pulse that supports the 3-dimensional movement of breathing.
- Your ribs expand in all three dimensions as you inhale, and they return to their resting state on the exhale. Your sternum responds to the movement of your ribs and goes along for the ride.
- Your lungs simply fill and empty as your diaphragm expands and contracts. You do not have to "take a breath."
- Like your lungs, your nose is a passive participant in breathing. It allows breath to come into and go out of your lungs. You do not need to sniff or gasp to breathe.
- Your diaphragm is almost constantly in motion. At the completion of your inhale, there is a momentary pause, before your diaphragm reverses its direction. And another pause, usually slightly longer, occurs at the end of your exhale.
- The ongoing movements of breath gently move the bony structures and muscles of your torso. Because of this, breath deeply supports the natural balancing and rebalancing of your whole coordinated body.

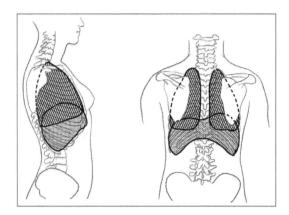

Figure 3.4 Relationship of lungs, diaphragm, spine, and ribs.

PRACTICE 3.2   BREATH AWARENESS, THREE DIMENSIONS

One of the ways we can sense our dimensionality is through awareness of our breath. Your 3-dimensional breath can create a sense of expansiveness in the torso and calm your mind and nervous system.

Refine your awareness as you sense expansion and release in all six directions with each inhalation and exhalation.

- Begin with standing. Notice your whole body. Notice your breath. Pause.
- Move to the floor and lie down in the *balanced resting state*.
- Notice the floor beneath you, take a moment to note all the parts of you that are touching the floor: head, elbows and upper arms, parts of the back, pelvis, and feet. Note that you are supported by the floor, and you cannot fall. You can safely give your weight to the floor.
- Pause.
- Bring your attention to your breath. Notice the movement of your back against the floor, your belly under your hands, shoulders, rib cage, spine, and even your lower abdomen. Don't try to breathe in order to make them move, just breathe and observe what **is** moving.
- Bring attention to the horizontal dimension of your breath; feel your torso expand to the sides as you inhale, and feel it fall back toward center as you exhale; repeat several times. Practice *inclusive attention* by including your horizontal dimension within your awareness of your whole body and the room around you.
- Pause, return your attention to the fullness of the breath's cycle.
- Bring awareness to the sagittal dimension of your breath; feel your torso expand toward the mat and toward the ceiling as you inhale and release toward center as you exhale. Repeat several times. Remember that your breath affects all of you, so include your whole body in your awareness.
- Pause, return your attention to the fullness of the breath's cycle.
- Bring awareness to the vertical dimension of your breath; feel the expansion of your whole torso – toward your head and down to your pelvic floor – as you inhale, and feel your body return to balance as you exhale. Repeat several times, remembering to include your whole body in your awareness.
- Sense the interplay of all three dimensions and the cylindrical shape of your body. Feel the liveliness and spaciousness of these six counterbalancing directions as you breathe.
- Pause. Bring awareness to your whole body.
- Rise from the floor and stand. Notice any differences in your body after this exploration.
- Have a walk about the space to allow your body to integrate this information. Enjoy your 3-dimensional breath and body as you move.
- *Spy back.* What did you discover about the movement of breath in your body? What differences did you notice in your body when you stood at the beginning and at the end of the exploration?

Perhaps you have been told by someone, such as a voice teacher, not to lift your chest to breathe. Pulling your chest and shoulders up as you inhale restricts your breathing. The fact is, there is a natural, 3-dimensional expansion of your whole torso that occurs as your ribs accommodate the movement of your diaphragm and lungs. Like the other parts of your torso, your chest moves slightly in response. Be certain that you are allowing, but not forcing, movement in all six directions as you inhale and exhale.

PRACTICE 3.3 ALLOWING THE NATURAL BREATHING CYCLE

You may be surprised to learn that many of us interfere with our natural breath cycle. Although this is not a conscious decision, of course, it is a common problem among performers. For instance, excess muscular tension can make it difficult to inhale fully. Another interference is inhaling before the natural movement of the exhale is complete.

This Practice invites you to become aware of your breath as a cycle – a continuous motion, like a wheel turning.[2] Give yourself permission to allow the cycle to happen without interference. Your body knows how to breathe. You can trust it, and when you do, you will find that breath is available to support any activity you undertake.

- Repeat the steps for Practice 3.1 above with this added focus: each time you exhale, pause and wait for your intelligent body to take the next inhale.
- Avoid "pressing" the air out. Just allow each exhale to come to completion and wait for your body to take the next breath. Trust the breathing cycle, riding the exhale to its natural conclusion.
- Using *kinesthetic awareness*, notice any tension in other parts of your body as the inhale begins. Recognize these interferences and let them go. Let "your body breathe you."
- Once you have returned to standing, pause. Then have a walk around the room. Pause again.
- *Spy back.* What did you notice about your breath as you practiced allowing the natural cycle? Were you able to let your body breathe you? Did you notice any impulse to make something happen? If so, what did you do in response? What did you experience when you stood and walked around the room at the end of the Practice?

After these Practices, you may find that your breath feels freer, and your torso (chest, back, shoulders, belly), and even your mind feel more at ease. When your breath follows its natural pattern, overly tense muscles can take a vacation. You can experience an even easier flow of air in and out of your body. This is the calming power of your breath.

This Practice can be repeated often as you learn to trust your natural breathing process. If you found it challenging to let go of tension as you inhaled or exhaled, continue practicing over a few days, and give your body and mind a chance to return to their natural balance.

After exploring the Practices above for a day or two, move on to Part II, *Movement Rides on the Flow of Your Breath*. That way, your calm 3-dimensional breath will be available to support you as you experience the next set of Practices.

PAUSE TO PROCESS Now is a good time to take a pause. Let your *body-mind* absorb the work of these three Practices. You may not be aware of it, but your nervous system received a lot of information through these explorations. Your body, brain, and being need time to absorb and notice any changes that are taking place. Notice if your breath changes as a result of your new awareness: in your classes, rehearsals, the gym, and daily life. Journal, draw, and discuss those differences.

Real-life Story: David Discovers the Joys of Breathing

This is an excerpt from David's journal in movement class, as he explored the movement of breath:

Breath is our most natural right, perhaps among the first free actions we take in the world: emerging from the womb … we prepare for our first free action, a declaration of self, a good, free breath. The breath and the pulse are the time pieces of all our acts; they are the natural measure to put all activity upon. When I rediscovered … simple, mindful being, it was a homecoming; a homecoming to balance, to juncture, to plasticity. A haiku:

Pull off the Armor.
Breathe in, sitting peacefully.
Enemies can wait.

At the pauses between inhale and exhale, that the door of our being rotates around, in that juncture is our home … There, if we look closely, we can see it in the great recesses of the mighty pause … ourselves. As we breathe again, we must leave. But we will return. At heart all of us are nomads. All of us are home, and then gone … and then home again.

Thus ends this stage of the journey. The next one starts at the next breath.[3]

Part II: Movement Rides on the Flow of Your Breath

Dr. Carl Stough, an expert on coordinated breathing, says that our breath is "the balance wheel of the body."[4] In the Practices below, you can explore your movement as it "rides on your breath."

PRACTICE 3.4   **MOVEMENT FLOW**

Now that you have experienced the natural flow of your breath, explore what happens when movement and breath work (and play!) together.

I investigate: Write your own question. What are you curious about as you explore the connection between breath and movement?

Part I

* Pause. Stand in the space. Sense your whole body. Note the floor's support.
* Practice the simple movement of raising your arm.
* Release your arm. Pause.
* Bring your attention to your breath. Sense the changing shape of your torso as you inhale and exhale. Notice the subtle 3-dimensional movement from the inside out.
* On your next exhale, raise your arm again. Continue breathing as your arm rides the flow of your breath and returns to your side.
* Pause. Continue to notice the sensations of breath.
* Now, see what happens if you hold your breath and practice the same movement.
* When your arm has returned to your side, pause.
* Experiment with other simple movements, allowing the ongoing cycle of breath to support you as you move. Remember that your body is 3-dimensional and so is your breath.
* Bring your conscious attention to the flow of your breath, as it coordinates with your movement.
* Pause. Take a *kinesthetic moment*.
* *Spy back*. What was your experience of paying no attention to your breath, holding your breath, and "riding your breath?" How might this information serve you as an actor?

Part II

* Observe your breath throughout the day. Notice if you hold your breath or interfere with the natural rhythm of breath. Remember breath is your most constant movement.
* Begin to bring *inclusive attention* to everyday activities. Sense your whole self and see the space around you. Give yourself permission to follow your natural breath rhythms and allow your movement to flow with your breath.
* If you are in a stationary position for a long time, like sitting at a computer or reading, check in. Are you breathing? You can experiment with a simple movement, like raising your arm on the flow of your breath. Sitting does not mean that the flow of movement and breath stops!
* Movement and breath are partners. Have fun exploring this friendly duet.

- *Spy back*. What did you learn about the flow of your breath during your day? Did you notice times that your breath did not flow? What were they? How might this information serve you as an actor?

Be curious about your breath. Get to know yourself at this fundamental level.[5] What happens when you notice "breath interference?" Experiment with allowing your breath to breathe you, and see how this affects your movement throughout the day.

PRACTICE 3.5   EXPLORING YOUR BREATH RHYTHMS

Your body knows how to breathe when you speak or sing, and how much air is needed at the appropriate time. You can allow your body to inhale and exhale naturally, as opposed to forcing a breath, even when speaking on cue. Your breath adjusts to each occasion, because your body and mind are an integrated whole, responding seamlessly to your needs and the world around you.

I investigate: What is my experience as I allow my words to ride on the flow of my breath?

Part I

- Pause. Stand. Take a *kinesthetic moment*. Notice the space around you.
- Sense your *3-D body* and the subtle, 3-dimensional movements of breath.
- Now lie down on the floor in the *balanced resting state.*
- Continue to notice the movement of your 3-D breath. Give yourself time to experience the movement, and to accept the support of the floor, as your back spreads into its full length and width.
- Have a thought that you would like to speak: "My name is _____." Notice what happens in your body and to your breath as you have this thought, but do not speak.
- Pause. Return your attention to the movement of your breath.
- On your next inhale, have the thought that you would like to speak, and allow yourself to speak "My name is _____" on the flow of the exhale.
- Pause. Notice if you are still accepting the support of the floor.
- Repeat this sequence several times. Practice *inclusive attention* as you alternate between (1) simply having the thought to speak and (2) actually speaking. If other words or phrases arise, continue to allow the words to ride on the flow of your breath.
- Notice any unnecessary tension associated with speaking. Continue to place your attention on your breath, rather than speaking, and notice what happens.
- You may find it helpful to start the exhale before you start speaking. Let your body do the breathing for you. Avoid "taking a breath."
- After a couple of minutes, pause. Take a *kinesthetic moment*.

- Flowing with your breath, gently roll to one side and sit up. Continue to be aware of your breath as you come to standing.
- Notice yourself, the subtle movements of your breath, and your *3-D body*. Practice *inclusive attention* as you sense yourself and see the room around you.
- Have a walk around the space.
- *Spy back.* What did you discover about your body and breath when you prepared to speak? When you simply thought about speaking, what happened? What happened when you spoke on the flow of your breath?

Jessica Wolf, author of *The Art of Breathing* and professor at Yale School of Drama, says, "The key to coordinated breathing is an easy exhalation that prompts a full and easy inhalation."[6] Explore Part I several times before moving on to Part II.

Part II

This Practice invites you to repeat Part I while standing. You may want to return to Practices 1.1–1.3 before beginning this exploration.

- Stand. Pause. Take a *kinesthetic moment*. Notice your breath.
- Have a walk around the room. Practice *inclusive attention*.
- Pause.
- Practice Part I above, but continue standing, instead of lying down.
- *Spy back.* How were breathing and speaking different when you were standing than when you were lying down? What is your experience of having the thought to speak, but not speaking? Of speaking on the flow of your breath? How might this serve you as an actor?

We hope you will revisit these Practices often. Little by little, you can discover any interferences with your natural breathing and speaking process. Remember that breath is your most constant and significant movement. By placing your attention on your natural breathing cycle, you can release unnecessary tension, and return to moving on the flow of your breath.

Your *3-dimensional body*, along with your *kinesthetic sense* and breath are foundations for all movement. They are also a part of you from birth. As actors, we want to awaken them, cultivate our awareness of them, and allow them to work as they are designed to work. With these three foundations as The Starting Place, you are ready to explore the principles and Practices in the next Section: You Are Designed for Movement.

PAUSE TO PROCESS Give yourself time and space to absorb and process Section I: The Starting Place. This is significant work, and your *body-mind* needs time and space to integrate this information.

Processing Section I may include journaling, drawing, talking, or moving. Discover how you process best: it may be sharing with another person or you might explore some creative movement as a response to your discoveries with a Key Word or

Practice. For example, you can create a movement "vignette" or story (alone or in a group): You can define a concept, express something you've learned, feelings that have arisen, or explore changes you've noticed in your movement. If you are in a class, you can share your creative expressions with each other.

When you process these concepts, they "live" in you, and you will have a firm foundation as you move on to Section II.

When you are ready, you can also visit Appendix I: *Practices for Further Exploration.* Here you will find more Practices for deepening your understanding of the ideas, experiences, and concepts explored in Chapters 1–3.

On the next page, you can Take a Restful Break.

Key Practice: *Balanced Resting State*

Notes

1 Bartenieff, Irmgard with Dori Lewis. *Body Movement, Coping with the Environment.* New York: Routledge, 2002. Print. p. 232.
2 Stough, Carl and Reece. *Dr. Breath.* New York: William Morrow Company, 1970, p. 125.
3 Student journal. Used with permission.
4 Stough, p. 125.
5 Park, Glen. *The Art of Changing.* London: Ashgrove Publishing, 2000. Print. p. 30.
6 Wolf, Jessica. *Jessica Wolf's Art of Breathing: Collected Articles*, 2013, p. 4. Used with permission.

A Restful Break

Constructive Rest #l

In our daily lives, we often find ourselves rushing around non-stop, and then collapsing at the end of the day. We rarely allow ourselves time to pause and rest. If you observe animals, particularly cats, you will see that they alternate periods of intense activity with times of rest and recuperation. Our bodies and minds need to experience both of these phases throughout each day.

One aspect of the Alexander Technique includes lying down in the *balanced resting state* and bringing awareness to your body-mind coordination. You pause to let your body **rest**. You allow your body to receive **constructive** thoughts designed to release old movement patterns. Many teachers refer to this Practice as *Constructive Rest* (KP).[1]

As you move into the *balanced resting state*, be sure that the book or towel supports the balance of your head with the rest of your body. If the head support is too low, your head will fall backward, causing tension in the back of your neck and spine. If the support is too high, your head will tilt forward, causing tension in the front of your neck.

- Move into the *balanced resting state*. Pause. Breathe.
- Give your attention to the relationship of your feet and pelvis. If your heels are too close to your sit bones, you will feel a shortening in the back of your pelvis and spine. If your heels are too far from your sit bones, your pelvis will rock forward, also compressing your spine.
- Play with these relationships between your legs and your back until you sense an even distribution of weight through your whole body.
- Your thighs release from your pelvis, your knees point up toward the ceiling, and your lower leg releases down toward your ankles. Sense an even distribution of weight in your feet.
- Notice your arms widening across your collarbones and shoulder blades and lengthening from there down to your hands and fingers. Allow your arms to rest on the floor. Pause.

- Gently bring your hands to rest on your ribs or upper abdomen. Allow your elbows to ease sideways and rest on the floor and find a comfortable place to rest your whole arm.
- Take a moment to sense the complete connection from your hands through your arms to the resting of your collarbones and shoulder blades.
- Give yourself time to breathe. The muscles of your body soften into their natural length, width and depth. The weight of your bones invites your whole body to release into the support of the floor.
- Sense the parts of you that are touching the floor: feet, elbows and upper arms, back, and head. Allow your body to accept the support of the floor. Breathe.
- After you have given yourself time to rest, expand your awareness to your whole *3-D body*.
- When you feel ready, you can gently roll on to one side, ease up to sitting and then standing. Pause.
- Have a walk around the space, practicing *inclusive attention* and *kinesthetic awareness*. Pause.
- *Spy back*.

Key Practice: *Constructive Rest*

Note

1 Though the phrase *constructive rest* has been adopted by many in the Alexander Technique community, this term was developed by Lulu Sweigard, author of *Human Movement Potential*. Boggs, Carol. "To Use or Not to Use: *The Term* Constructive Rest." *AmSAT Journal*, Fall, 2015, Issue 8, pp. 13–14.

You Are Designed for Movement

When we meet with our students on the first day in Movement for the Actor class, we stand together in a circle and pose the following question: "How do we know we are alive?"

Here are their three consistent answers: (1) We are breathing. (2) Our hearts are beating. (3) Our weight is shifting from place to place in our bodies. Each answer reveals their innate ability to sense movement happening somewhere inside their bodies.

Movement is the core of life, the foundation for living fully in each moment. Our hearts rhythmically expand and contract, pumping blood through our body. We sense our breath, and we move with its dynamic rhythms. We walk, we run, we dance. These essential movements are part of the ongoing flow of our daily lives.

All movement involves the coordinated "dance" between our brain and nervous system, muscles, and bones. When these systems are in sync, we experience a sense of liveliness in our movement. And when we move our bodies through space, we fully experience our whole self in action: we know we are alive!

Many of us carry wrong or misinformed ideas about our bodies. This can interfere with our ability to respond to movement impulses onstage. Misinformation can also result in injury. As performers, body-knowledge is essential to our creativity and our well-being.

In this section, You Are Designed for Movement, you can learn the **truth** about how your body moves, and you can **experience** your anatomy by exploring it with your moving body.

Carl Rogers, the pioneering psychologist, said, "The facts are always friendly. Every bit of evidence one can acquire, in any area, leads one that much closer to what is true."[1] When you discover the *Friendly Facts* (KW) of your body's design, you free your movement from misinformed ideas. Interfering tensions fall away, allowing you to move more safely and effectively.

In addition, the *friendly facts* can lead you "that much closer" to a more truthful performance. Your body-knowledge provides a strong foundation for your movement work: your body, mind, and imagination are in sync, and your emotions and deepest creative instincts arise naturally and effortlessly.

In the last chapter of this section, we build on your knowledge by exploring how movement cycles through your whole coordinated body: where it begins and how it travels and comes to completion. Through your understanding of your true design and functioning, you receive a priceless gift: the ability to choose how you move.

The process is simple yet powerful: Observe, Explore, Discover the *friendly facts* of your body's design for movement.

Key Word: *Friendly Facts*

Note

1 Excerpt from *The Carl Rogers Reader*, edited by Howard Kirschenbaum and Valerie Land Henderson. Copyright © 1989 by Howard Kirschenbaum and the Estate of Carl Rogers. Reprinted by permission of Houghton Mifflin Harcourt Publishing Company. All rights reserved. p. 26.

Get to Know Your Joints

We are designed for movement. You might believe this, and yet move in ways that interfere with your body's natural design. We move according to the way we **think** about our body, and our thoughts can help or hinder our movement, depending on the accuracy of our *Body Map* (KW).

According to Barbara and Bill Conable, authors of *How to Learn the Alexander Technique*, our *body map* is our "self-representation of our body's structure in our own brain." It is our movement map. If the map is accurate, we move easily and efficiently. If it is faulty, movement is inefficient, and even harmful.[1]

Each part of your body has a specific role to play in moving your whole body. No part moves in isolation, because all parts of our body are interconnected in many ways, including joints, tendons, and muscles. These connections allow specific, fluid relationships between each body part. Sensing the joint connections in your body – each *Part Within the Whole* (KW) – is essential to dynamic movement.

In this chapter, and the ones that follow in this section, we explore joint movement and joint relationships through your body's major movement connections. You will not only learn about your joints in more detail, but you will **experience** your anatomy through movement.

Touch, sight, breath, and your *kinesthetic sense* help you in exploring joint action and movement connections. These senses also help your brain develop an accurate *body map*. This is *body-mind communication* at work!

Know Your Joints: Anatomy and Practice

Joints are formed by the joining of the ends of two bones with each other, creating a multitude of unique movement possibilities. Joints do not hinge, bend, or fold. Instead, they rock, roll, glide, slide, and spiral. Each of our many joints is structured to allow for a wide range of ever-changing, ever-adjusting, 3-dimensional movement possibilities.

The range of movement in your joints is wide: from micro-movements occurring when we are standing and balancing with gravity, to the larger movements involved in walking or running. Joints and muscles work together to create a lively movement dialogue throughout our whole body. Via this inner flow, our bodies are never "locked" in place. Instead, we are poised for action. As Alexander Technique teacher Marie-Francoise Le Foll says, We are "ready for anything, and prepared for nothing."[2]

Meet Your Joints

- Joints are formed where the rounded end surfaces of two bones meet.
- Each joint has a certain degree of "play" available in its movement; the amount of play is determined by the size and shape of the joint.
- Freely movable joints, like your hip joint, have a wide range of movement: the rounded, ball-shaped end of one bone fits into a curved joint socket, which allows sliding, gliding, rocking, rolling, and spiraling to occur.
- Slightly movable joints, such as the 24 vertebrae of your spine, subtly slide and glide in relation to each other.
- Joints are surrounded by a membrane of tissue (joint capsule) which contains synovial fluid. This fluid acts as a lubricant for joint action, creating smooth, supple movement within each joint.
- Movement happens at the joints because the **rounded** end surfaces of the bones interact with each other (Figure 4.1). Bones do not stack like bricks!

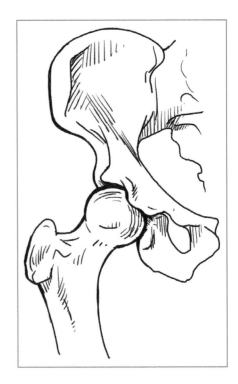

Figure 4.1 Rounded surfaces slide, glide, and roll at the hip joint.

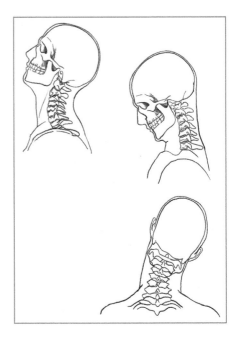

Figure 4.2 Vertebral joints give your spine mobility.

- When you move, the weight of your body transfers from one bone to another via your joints.

We are fans of *Hamilton* by Lin-Manuel Miranda, especially the song, "The Room Where It Happens." Your joints are the "room" where movement happens. When we have faulty ideas about how joints work or where they are, we can't be in the place where it happens. The door into our movement life is locked. So, get to know your joints. Unlock the door to your joints, and enter the room where movement happens!

Observe, Explore, Discover: The Practices below and in the next few chapters help you "get to know your joints" through location, sensing, and range of movement. This process connects you with your body's amazing gift of "dynamic play" at each joint. In this way, you can develop an accurate *body map*, a map that reflects your body's true design for movement. You can enter the room where it happens, a room that is full of more easeful, energized, and varied movement possibilities.

PRACTICE 4.1   MOVING THROUGH YOUR JOINTS (KP)

Take a "movement tour" of the multiple possibilities for unique joint action throughout your body.

Put on some lively instrumental music and enjoy moving and sensing the connections of your bones at your joints. We like "I Like It Like That" by Pete Rodriguez.[3] Play with movement possibilities for each joint, and focus on the flow of movement from joint to joint via kinesthetic sensing (rather than repetitive movements for exercise you may be accustomed to doing at the gym.)

I investigate: What can I discover about the movement of my joints?

- Take a walk through the space and tune in to where you are today in your body, before beginning the Practice.
- Stand. Pause. Breathe. Take a *kinesthetic moment*.
- Begin to move your fingers and thumbs, with the intention of warming the fluid inside your joints and linking up the parts of your hand. Practice *kinesthetic sensing* as movement flows through each joint in your hand.
- Explore wrist movement. Note the sliding and gliding possibilities as you warm your wrist joints.
- Continue this exploration through your elbows, shoulder joint, collarbones (collarbones have a joint at your breastbone).
- Explore the joints of your jaw through small movements. Be gentle with yourself. See if you can sense the sliding action of your jaw, side to side, up and down, and forward and back.
- With small movements, gently explore the rolling and gliding action of your head way up at the top of your spine. Note the sensations in your joints as your spine responds to these movements.
- Warm the joints as the movement travels through the many joints of your spine – from your head to your pelvis. Include the rib joints. Start at the top and work your

way down. Take your time – find all the individual movements and warming possibilities for each vertebra. Include your many rib joints in your exploration.

- On to the hip joints, where your legs meet your pelvis – feel free to place a hand on the wall or the back of a chair for balance, as you explore the roundness of the joint where the pelvis meets the thigh. Lift a leg and enjoy the movement possibilities in many directions. Then repeat with the other leg.
- Sit or lie down to explore the full range of movement in your knees. Then move the joints of your ankles, feet, and toes. Explore each one before going on to the next. Remember to focus on feeling sensation and flow, rather than repetitive movements.
- Pause. Lie down and allow your feet to rest on the floor with your knees pointing toward the ceiling. Take a *kinesthetic moment*.
- Roll on to one side and move to standing. Take your time.
- Cycle back through your whole body, warming the synovial fluid, sensing the flow of movement from joint to joint.
- Pause. Take a *kinesthetic moment*. Notice your breath.
- Take a walk through the space, with awareness of your joints as you move through the room.
- If you find yourself tightening as you walk, pause and move through your joints again.
- You can jump, hop, or skip through the space to explore the play in your joints!
- *Spy back*. What was the experience of sensing the flow of movement through your joints? How does this differ from repetitious exercises, like those in a gym class? Did your walk at the beginning differ from your walk at the end? How? How might this Practice serve you as an actor?

Through this Practice, you can become more familiar with your balanced body, and its many movement possibilities.

Your Balanced Body and Your Breath

Now that you are familiar with the way that movement travels through your joints, you are ready to sense the subtle joint actions created by your breath.

The Practice below gives you permission to explore the movement of breath while you are standing. Permission may seem like a strange word to use, but most of us are not accustomed to paying attention to such subtle movements. However, the movements of breathing support your body's dynamic balance. It is well worth your time and attention to explore this natural process.

PRACTICE 4.2 A MOVEMENT DUET – JOINTS AND BREATH

This introductory breathing Practice prepares you to sense subtle movements in your body. It is an opportunity to sense movement internally: the rhythm of your breath, and the subtle movements that occur in your body at your joints, as you stand and breathe.

The 3-dimensional shape of your torso changes with every inhalation and exhalation. Ride these changes as you explore your moving breath.

- Stand. Pause. Take a *kinesthetic moment*. Close your eyes.
- Sense your *3-dimensional body*.
- Using your *kinesthetic sense* notice the gentle rhythms of your breathing.
- Notice the subtle shape changes in your body as you breathe.
- Allow each exhale to come to its natural completion. Then, allow your body to naturally inhale. Let your body breathe you.
- Notice the subtle joint actions in your torso as you breathe.
- See if you can sense subtle balancing and rebalancing of your whole body in response to the movements of your breath. Allow unnecessary tensions to melt away with these subtle movements.
- After a few minutes, pause. Take a walk around the room, noticing the connected movements of all your joints as you ride on the flow of your breath.
- Pause. Take a *kinesthetic moment*.
- *Spy back*. What was your experience of giving attention to the movement of your breath? How did your breath affect movement at your joints? What surprised you as you paid attention to the movements of breath?

Your whole torso is constantly moving, changing its shape in response to your breath. Your joints allow it to expand with your inhale and return to its resting balance with your exhale. Because your arms and legs connect to your torso, they are also affected by this gentle movement. And since your head poises on the top of your moving spine, it, too, is influenced by your breath.

This is great news! Our bodies are never static or stuck, because there are always small movements of your body balancing and rebalancing with your breath. Though this process may not be visible to the outside observer, your *kinesthetic sense* can tell you if you are restricting or allowing your body's natural movement in response to your breath.

The rhythms of your breath create a readiness in your body, and an overall receptivity for movement. The freedom that you experience with these subtle movements offers you a sense of wholeness, preparing you for the joint explorations that follow.

Now that your joints are wide awake, you are ready to explore specific joints, their unique design, and the connections between the joints. Enjoy the ongoing creative play of your joints and their lively, artistic possibilities.

Note: In the chapters that follow, you can "get to know your joints" from the inside out, by sensing them. Though our illustrations are helpful, you may want to investigate further. We highly recommend *Albinus on Anatomy* by Hale and Coyle. If you have access to a model skeleton, you can see the bones and joints in three dimensions. Be aware that illustrations you find on the internet may not be accurate representations.

Key Words: *Body Map, Part Within the Whole*

Key Practices: *Moving Through Your Joints*

Notes

1 Conable, Barbara and Benjamin. *What Every Musician Needs to Know About the Body*. Portland, OR, Andover Press, 2000. Print. p. 5.

2 Le Foll, Marie-Francoise. Alexander Class: Guest Artist Series. Teacher Training Weekend. The Alexander Foundation, Philadelphia. April 7, 1992. Lecture. Marie-Francoise often uses this phrase in her classes to describe the sense of readiness we feel when our bodies are in balance and at ease. From our naturally balanced body, we recognize that we are not braced in anticipation, but ready to respond to any stimulus or impulse that arises.

3 Pabon, Tony and Rodriguez, Manny. "I Like It Like That." Performed by Paul Rodriguez, Alegre, 1967.

CHAPTER 5

Joint Connections in Your Head–Spine–Pelvis

In the early part of the 20th century, an Australian actor, F.M. Alexander, sought a cure for hoarseness which plagued him onstage. Through long and persistent exploration, he discovered that the balance of his head with his spine was critical to his vocal health. Even more important, he noted that when his head was in balance, pressure was relieved from his whole spine, freeing the movement of his entire body. After making this discovery, Alexander solved not only his vocal problems, but developed the Alexander Technique, which has supported generations of actors in building a dynamic physical presence.

As you read *YBK*, you will encounter many of Alexander's principles and practices, which help you access the *friendly facts* of your body's design for movement. Your body knows these practical facts, which relieves you of the burden of struggling to "learn" them. Instead, you can **experience** them. Enjoy exploring the many movable joints in your torso, neck, and head, as you begin your own journey of discovery.

The Central Core of Your Body

Your body is organized around your spine, which provides a powerful yet flexible support for balanced movement. Your head–spine relationship, including your brain and spinal cord, is the center of your body's anatomy; it is a key to movement in your torso, arms, and legs.

In this chapter, you can learn and experience the facts of your head–spine–pelvis relationship. This all-important connection, from your head to your pelvis, is at the core of your movement design. Enjoy exploring the supple, movable joints from your head to your pelvis, and discover more balance and ease in your whole body!

Your Atlanto-Occipital Joint (A-O Joint)

The delicate and subtle balance of your head with your spine has a dynamic effect on the coordination of movement throughout your entire body.

Where It Is

- The atlanto-occipital joint is located behind your nose and between your ears.
- Your whole head is 3-dimensional; it has a back, sides, top, bottom, and a front. Your face is one part of your whole head, which rests on the A-O joint.

Where It Isn't

- In the neck at chin level. As you notice in Figure 5.2, your jaw is not part of your skull, and the joint between your head and spine does not move from the middle of your neck.
- Your head does not balance on a single point of your spine, like a ball on a stick. Your movable head connects with your first vertebra at your A-O joint (see Figure 5.3).

How It Moves

- On the underside of your head are two rockers that rest in two grooves on your first vertebra, the atlas.
- Your skull can slide, glide, rock, and roll on the A-O joint, supported by your whole spine.
- Your head turns side to side through the action of the 1st and the 2nd vertebra, the axis, as your whole spine responds.
- When your head tilts from side to side, the A-O joint and the axis work together, and the rest of your spine responds (Figure 4.2).

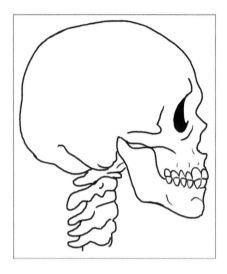

Figure 5.1 Your head meets your spine at your Atlanto-Occipital (A-O) joint.

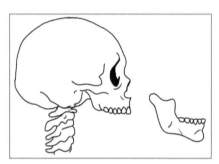

Figure 5.2 Your lower jaw hides your A-O joint from view.

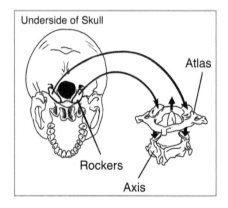

Figure 5.3 Your skull's rockers rest on two grooves on your atlas.

EXPERIENCING YOUR TOP JOINT

Allow your *kinesthetic sense* and *inclusive attention* to guide you while practicing these explorations. They will heighten your awareness of your head/spine relationship, your joint actions, and your sensations of whole-body movement.

I investigate: Where is my top joint and how does it move?

Experience #1

As you explore these movements, remember that your jaw is not part of your skull, and it can freely and easily ride along with the motions of your head. Also, remember: much of your head extends back behind your ears!

- Pause. Stand. Take a *kinesthetic moment*. Breathe.
- Sense your whole head. You can use your hands to help you sense its size and shape.
- Gently put your index fingers in your ears and imagine an axis running from fingertip to fingertip.
- Nod your head up and down (just say "yes"), and imagine it rotating around the axis. Notice the sensations as you move.
- Turn your head side to side (just say "no").
- Your head can also subtly rotate side to side around the axis of your nose ("maybe").
- Pause. Can you sense the subtle balancing and rebalancing of your whole head on your A-O joint?

Experience #2

- Take a *kinesthetic moment*. Sense the relationship of your whole head to your whole body.
- Run the tip of your tongue along the roof of your mouth to the place where your bony hard palate meets your soft palate. Above that spot, level with your nose, is where your head and spine meet.
- Begin some small movements with your head – "yes," (nodding) "no" (turning right and left) – as you explore the A-O joint's rolling, sliding, gliding actions.
- You can also try tilting, circling, and moving your head backward and forward. Remember, these are small, gentle movements.
- Practice *inclusive attention* as you sense your spine, especially the vertebrae of the neck, responding to these movements.
- Pause and sense the dynamic balance of your head at the top of your spine.
- Have a walk around the space. Notice the movability of your whole head/spine/body.
- *Spy back*. What changes for you when your head is gently poised on your spine? What did you discover about the ways your head can move on your top joint? Were you surprised about where you sensed movement as you explored? How does your whole body respond to the balance of your whole head?

As you go about your day, keep in mind that there is no "perfect position" for your head (or any other part of you!). Your head is movable, always balancing and re-balancing in relation to your spine and your whole body.

As you explore your joint connections, you are discovering more movement options and refining your *body map*. Through these Practices, your mind and body work together as a dynamic duo.

Your Spine–Pelvis Connection

The two halves of your pelvis cradle the base of your spine and provide stability for your whole movable spine.

Where the Connections Are

• Your spine is designed with four counterbalancing, forward and backward curves – cervical, thoracic, lumbar, and sacrum/coccyx. Your four curves balance around the vertical line of gravity.

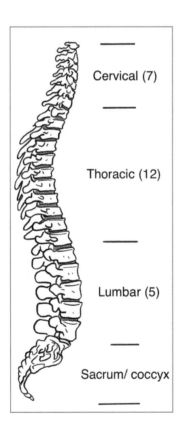

Figure 5.4 The four counterbalancing curves of your spine.

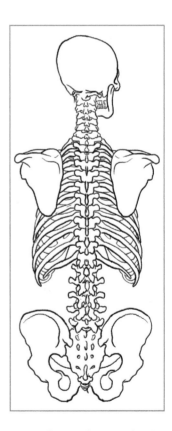

Figure 5.5 Twenty-four individual vertebrae plus your sacrum and coccyx connect your head, neck, torso, and pelvis.

- Most of your spine is composed of a series of 24 vertebrae, with spongy, fluid-filled discs between each vertebra, extending from your A-O joint to your sacrum.
- The vertebrae have a sturdy weight-bearing front, and spines on the back and sides.
- Your spinal cord runs through the hollow center of the vertebrae.
- The sacrum and coccyx are the lowest part of the spine – the sacrum joins with the lowest (lumbar) vertebra at its top, and the coccyx (tailbone) at its bottom.
- Your pelvis nestles on either side of the sacrum at two slightly movable joints, the sacroiliac joints.
- The rounded rockers (your sit bones) that form the bottom of your pelvis complete the length of your torso.

Where They Are Not

- The spine is not a series of bumps along your back, ending at the waistband of your pants!

How They Move

- Each vertebra can move individually – forward, backward, side to side, and rotate at its joints.
- Each vertebra's sliding, gliding movement ripples through all the other vertebrae. Even the coccyx can move at its joint with the sacrum.
- Your spongy discs cushion the movement at each joint.
- The 12 thoracic vertebrae are attached to the 24 ribs. They don't have as much freedom as the vertebrae of the neck or lumbar spine, but they can still move individually.
- Your pelvis can move forward and back, up and down, and side to side.
- Your pelvic bones are in two halves that are joined in the front by cartilage, and in back by the sacrum. These joints are "slightly movable," with enough range of motion to allow for small, easeful adjustments.

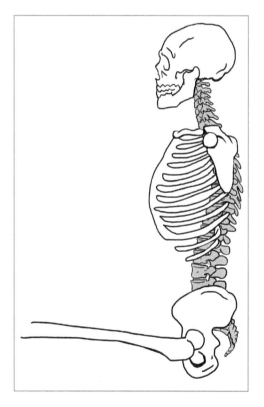

Figure 5.6 Your torso balances around the four curves of your spine.

PRACTICE 5.2 EXPLORING YOUR PELVIS–SPINE–HEAD CONNECTION

"Don't think of back bending, but think, 'Your head leads into a backward arc …!'"

Rudolf Laban[1]

Using your *kinesthetic sense* and *inclusive attention*, Observe, Explore, Discover the many joint connections of your spine, ribs, pelvis, and head. The movements in this exploration are 3-dimensional; enjoy the fullness of each fluid motion.

I investigate: Can I discover something new about the connection between my spine and pelvis?

Part I

In yoga, this Practice is often called "Cat-Cow." By changing your shape, you can give your flexible spine a chance to play.

- Stand. Pause. Take a *kinesthetic moment*. Breathe.
- Kneel on all fours, with your hip joints balanced over your knees, your thighs perpendicular to the floor, and your wrists under your shoulders. Pause. Tune in to your breathing.
- Sense the length of your spine. Let your eyes move toward the ceiling, allow your neck to soften, and your head to rotate back and up via your A-O joint. Follow your gaze and allow each vertebra, down to the sacrum and coccyx, to subtly ease into the movement, one after the other. Your belly drops toward the floor, and your back hollows.
- Now reverse this process: your eyes move toward the floor, your head rotates forward on the A-O joint as it follows your eyes. Your back arches upward and your tailbone releases.
- Sense the flow of movement from joint to joint, from your head all the way through your long, flexible spine.

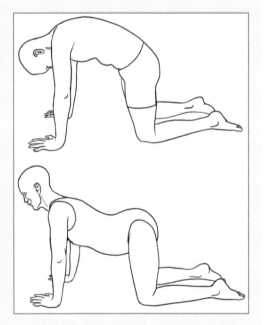

Figure 5.7 Cat-Cow: your flexible spine moooooves!

- Your 24 ribs connect to the mid-spine; allow them to follow along as well!
- Practice this sequence several times. Allow the movement of your breath to support your *3-dimensional body* in this exploration.
- Pause.
- *Spy back.* What did you discover about your movement design: the relationship of head–neck–spine to your whole body?

There is a strong head–tail connection in your body, and your spine is the link between them. When your head rolls back, it's important to maintain length in your spine – particularly your neck – so the connection to your tail isn't broken. You can sustain freedom of movement through your vertebrae in whatever movement you make. You can practice awareness of this connection in Part II below.

Part II

- Pause.
- Move to all fours.
- Return to Cat-Cow for a few moments, exploring your juicy head–tail connection.
- Pause and take a *kinesthetic moment*.
- Now, play with other head–spine–pelvis movements: side to side, rotation, forward and back. Enjoy exploring the 3-dimensional possibilities of your head–tail connection.
- Let these movements take you into other body shapes and movements, like lying down, rolling, crawling. Let your head–spine–tail connection guide you. This is free play.
- Explore the wide range of movement available, from tiny to large.
- Allow your whole body to be affected by each part. No movement happens in isolation!
- Bring your exploration to completion. Pause. Take a *kinesthetic moment*.
- Come to standing. Notice the full length of your spine.
- Take a walk around the room, enjoying the joint connections throughout your body. Pause. Take a *kinesthetic moment*.
- *Spy back.* What did you discover about your body connections? What new movement possibilities did you discover through this exploration? How does awareness of your head–spine–pelvis connection affect the way your body feels and moves?

You might think of your head–spine relationship as your body's "central organizing power." This *friendly fact* is at the heart of the Alexander Technique and a foundation for the information and Practices throughout *YBK*. Alexander recognized that Your body knows how to move when you do not interfere with its natural balance. "Standing up straight" or collapsing on your spine are two ways that we can interfere with the freedom you just experienced in the Practices above.

> The idea of spinal fluidity is refreshing and interesting. I think that we may get the false idea ... that a correct spine is a very erect one. But a fluid spine does not mean a slouch. I'm an organism, not a block of wood.[2]
>
> Taylor, acting student, Florida Atlantic University

In the exploration below, you can experience the natural movements of your spine and their effect on your whole body.

PRACTICE 5.3 **EXPERIENCING THE FULL LENGTH OF YOUR SPINE**

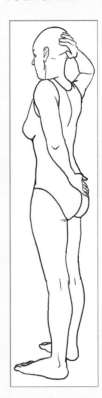

- Pause. Stand. Breathe. Take a *kinesthetic moment.*
- Bring one hand to the fat part of the **back** of your head, place the **back** of your other hand on your sacrum.
- Sense your whole spine, with its movable vertebrae, which runs between your two hands. Feel free to move through the joints of your spine a bit to get a sense of this. You can also sense movement under your hands.
- Walk around the space, with your hands still on your skull and on your sacrum. Sense the movement that happens throughout your body, and particularly through the many joints of the spine. (If your arms tire, switch your hands, or lower them for a time and put them back.)
- After a couple of minutes of doing this, take your hands away and see what it's like to walk through the space with *kinesthetic awareness* of your whole body, with your long, movable spine at the center of your torso.
- It is important to let your eyes take in the room around you, as you sense your body: *inclusive attention.* Breathe.

Figure 5.8 Your hands can bring your attention to your long spine from head to tail.

- Pause. Breathe. Take a *kinesthetic moment*.
- *Spy back*. Celebrate the length of your movable spine!

As you can see – and sense – your head–spine–pelvis connection and its many joints play a central role in your movable body. All movement emerges from and leads back to this central core. Because of the lively relationships between the muscles, bones, and joints of your spine, you are always ready to respond to the world around you. You are ready for change and new possibilities for movement.

When you use your body according to the facts of your design, you might compare the experience to riding in a Rolls Royce. Its suspension system gives you a ride that is smooth, cushioned, lively, grounded, yet buoyant. Riding in your body when it is excessively tight – or the opposite, collapsed – creates a bumpy, disjointed journey. Your body is designed with a high-quality suspension system like a Rolls Royce. Treat it like one; don't drive it like an old Chevy pickup.

As you continue to explore your movable spine, you can, like Alexander, discover your body's perfect design for movement.

PAUSE TO PROCESS Before continuing to Chapter 6, pause. Have a conversation with someone or journal about your experiences, as you explored your joints and your movable spine.

Take time to explore the unique movement possibilities of your head. How do these movements affect your spine? Your pelvis? Repeat: explore the unique qualities of your spine and then, your pelvis. Sense each of these *parts within the whole* as you play. Pause between each exploration.

You can say, "Yes," with your head, or "No." What else can your head communicate? What can your pelvis say that your head cannot? How about your spine? Play.

Put on some music and enjoy sensing your head–spine–pelvis connection as your whole body moves in different directions through space. Allow your eyes to be a lively part of these changes in direction. Play with tempo and have fun!

PAUSING TO PROCESS allows you to make connections with the discoveries you've made in Chapters 1–5 Carry your new awareness with you as you go about your daily activities, and as you explore Chapter 6.

Notes

1 As quoted in Bartenieff, Irmgard. *Body Movement: Coping with the Environment.* New York: Routledge, 2002. Print. p. 229.
2 From a student journal. Used with permission.

Joint Connections in Your Arm Structure

Your arm structure has many moving parts! Included are your fingers, hands, wrists, lower arms, elbows, upper arms, shoulder joints, collarbones, and shoulder blades, to name a few.

Because your collarbones and shoulder blades rest on your ribs, your arms receive strong support from your whole torso (including your spine). This support, which is quite movable, allows your arms to have more mobility than any other part of your body. This movable connection links your supportive shoulder girdle to your whole arm all the way to your fingertips.

In this chapter, you can learn the facts about the design of your arm structure and experience your joint connections from the inside out. Your *kinesthetic sense* will serve you as you explore your movable arms and the way your whole body supports them.

Shoulder Blades and Collarbones to the Fingertips

Where the Connections Are

- Your wrist, hand and fingers have 27 bones. Each finger has three joints, the thumb has two.
- The long bones of your hand form joints with the fingers at one end and intersect the eight bones of the wrist at the other.
- Your wrist has eight small bones that slide and glide with each other. They allow your hands to have mobility and your lower arm to have stability.
- Your lower arm is made up of two bones that meet the wrist bones on one end and the upper arm at the other. The joint formed by the upper and lower arm bones is the elbow.
- The two lower arm bones also have joints with each other at both ends, creating the radioulnar joint. (Figure 6.3)

- Your upper arm meets the shoulder blade, forming a ball and socket joint, at the side of your torso.
- The shoulder girdle is completed by the collarbone, which forms a joint with your breastbone at one end and your shoulder blade at the other.
- Your shoulder blades and collarbones provide major support for your arm structure. Your shoulder blades rest (and move in many directions!) on your back ribs, allowing the rest of your arm structure to emerge "from your back." Your arms rest buoyantly on your whole torso.

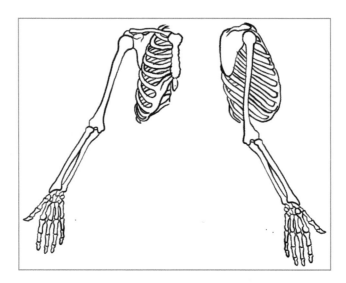

Figure 6.1 The bones and joints of your supported arm structure.

Where the Connections Aren't

- The knobby bones that are often referred to as "wrist bones" are actually the bottom of the two lower arm bones. Your wrist joints are between the knobby bones and the long bones of your hand.
- Your arms don't connect to your torso in the front of your body or near your neck. The socket is in the outer edge of your shoulder blade (See Figure 6.1).
- Your shoulder girdle (collarbones/shoulder blades) doesn't lift to move your arm. It responds to your arm, providing support for any direction you may move.

How They Move

- As your fingers roll toward your palm, your finger joints slide and glide. With the help of the hand bones and joints, your fingers open, close, extend, spread, and circle.
- Your thumb has only two bones that move like the finger bones. Its third bone meets your thumb bones at one end and forms a joint with your wrist at the other. This joint offers a wide range of movement options.
- Wrists flex and extend, move side to side, and rotate.

- Your elbow joint has a rolling action. It extends – moving the lower arm away from the upper arm – and flexes – moving the lower arm close to the upper arm.
- Your radioulnar joints are located at the wrist and elbow. Your radius rotates around your ulna. In response, your hand turns over, moving your thumb toward or away from center.
- The ball of your upper arm (humerus) rolls in every direction in its socket, moving your arm up, down, out, in, forward, and back.
- Your shoulder blades ride over your ribs. They rise, fall, and move in, out, forward, and back to accommodate the movements of your arm. The shoulder joint enjoys the largest range of motion in your body.

You have an incredible array of possibilities for movement in your arm joints. As you explore the Practices below, you can develop and refine the way you use your movable arms.

Note: you have many joints to explore in this chapter. Remember to *PAUSE TO PROCESS* if you get overloaded. Return to the next Practice – or part of a Practice – another day.

PRACTICE 6.1   EXPLORING THE JOINTS IN YOUR HAND/ARM/SCAPULA/ COLLARBONE

As you practice the explorations below, begin with small, gentle movements. That way you can sense the changing relationships in your body from the inside out. Use your *kinesthetic sense* and *inclusive attention*. Remember: your whole body supports each of these movements. Each joint is a connected *part within the whole*.

Give yourself the gift of pausing after each exploration: take a walk around the space and allow your arms and hands to move within their relationship to your whole body. Feel free to follow impulse as your arms and hands explore new possibilities.

I investigate: What can I discover about my hand/arm/shoulder blade/collarbone connection that I didn't know before?

Experience 1: Joints of Your Hands and Fingers

- Pause. Stand or sit. Using your *kinesthetic sense*, notice yourself, your breath, and the space around you.
- Explore the many directions your fingers and thumb can move, curling toward the palm, extending, spreading. Place your attention on sensing the movements in the joints.
- Move each finger individually. Explore all three joints of each finger, and the full range of motion of your thumb.
- Make circles with your fingers and thumb. Notice the mobility of each joint.
- Notice that your whole body and whole arm provide support for these movements.
- Pause. Take a *kinesthetic moment*.
- *Spy back*. What did you discover about your hand and finger joints?

Experience 2: Wrist

When exploring wrist action, stabilize your elbow by resting it on a table or in your other hand. In this way you can refine your wrist action without interference from the elbow or shoulder joints.

- Pause. Stand or sit. Using your *kinesthetic sense*, notice yourself, your breath, and the space around you.
- Place your fingers and thumb of your right hand on your left wrist. Through your *kinesthetic sense* and your sense of touch, note the rolling action as you move it.
- Repeat with the other wrist.
- Pause. Take a *kinesthetic moment*.
- Let your right elbow rest on a table or in your left hand with your fingertips pointing toward the ceiling (see Figure 6.2).
- Gently explore your wrist joints by alternately moving the palm of your hand toward the floor and then toward the ceiling. Your wrist joint rolls and glides to accommodate this movement. Fingers are soft; they follow the hand.
- Note the sensation of movement in your joints. Repeat several times, slowly, so you can feel the action of the joint.
- Pause. Take a *kinesthetic moment*. Notice any difference in sensation between your right wrist, hand, and arm and your left.
- Repeat with your left hand and wrist. Pause.
- Now, continuing to stabilize your elbow, explore other wrist actions, such as side-to-side motion and circles.
- Practice *inclusive attention*. Remember your focus is on the sensation of movement in your joints, supported by your whole body. Practice on both sides.
- Pause. Take a *kinesthetic moment*.
- *Spy back*. As you explored the possibilities of wrist action, what did you discover? How did your whole arm and your whole body respond to this exploration?

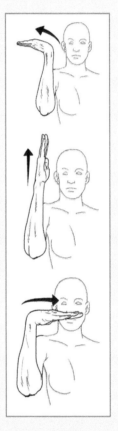

Figure 6.2 Flexing, resting and extending through the wrist joint.

Before going on to Experience 3, have a walk around the space. As you move, sense your fingers, hands, and wrists as part of your whole body. Breathe.

Experience 3: Elbow

Part I: Extending and Flexing

- Pause. Stand or sit. Use *inclusive attention* to notice yourself, your breath, and the space around you.

- As in Experience 2 above, let your right elbow rest on a table or in your left hand with your fingertips pointing toward the ceiling. The palm of your right hand faces you.
- Explore the rolling action that happens at the elbow when you lower your whole lower arm and hand toward the table (or floor) and raise it again. You can bring your hand all the way to your shoulder. Breathe.
- Using your *kinesthetic sense*, notice not only movement in the joint, but also sensation elsewhere in your arm and whole shoulder structure. Practice the movement several times.
- Pause and rest your arm at your side. Take a *kinesthetic moment.*
- Repeat with the left arm. Pause.

Part II: Circling

- Stabilizing your right elbow with your left hand, make circles with your lower right arm and hand.
- Explore the circular actions of your elbow joint, as well as the sensations you experience as you move.
- At some point reverse the circles. Bring awareness to your whole arm all the way to your shoulder girdle. Practice *inclusive attention.*
- Notice: are you breathing? Pause.
- Rest your arms at your sides. Take a *kinesthetic moment.*
- Repeat on the other side.
- Pause.
- *Spy back.* What did you discover when you explored your elbow joint? How does your elbow joint affect movement in other parts of your arm?

Experience 4: Radioulnar Joints

You can practice this action at a table or on the floor.

- Sit at a table or on the floor. Pause. Take a *kinesthetic moment.*
- Place the side of your whole right forearm and hand on the table (or floor) with your pinky and the side of your hand against the table. Your arm is slightly folded at the elbow joint, your palm facing left, and the back of your hand facing the right.

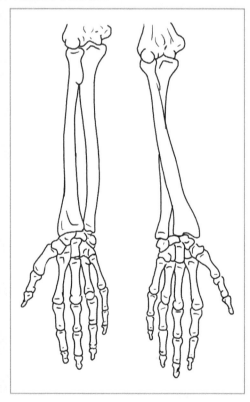

Figure 6.3 Your hand turns over, palm down, as your radius rotates and crosses over your ulna.

- Pause and use your *kinesthetic sense* to notice the relationship of your whole body to your whole arm structure. Breathe.
- With the pinky side of your hand against the table, open your palm and bring the back of your hand to rest against the table.
- Reverse this and rotate around the pinky side of the hand until the palm of your hand rests against the table. You are exploring the rotation of the radioulnar joint. Repeat this motion several times. Breathe as you explore.
- Pause and take a *kinesthetic moment*.
- Repeat on the left side.
- Pause.
- *Spy back.* What do you know now about the action of your radioulnar joint that you didn't know before?

> *PAUSE TO PROCESS* before exploring the rest of your arm structure. Journal, share with a classmate, or allow your whole body to support your lower arm/ hand as you play:
>
> You can investigate the special qualities of your lower arms, hands, and fingers. Put on some music and play with these connections one at a time, then all together. Sense the *parts within the whole* as you play!
>
> Your fingers, hands, and lower arms each move in unique ways. Can you use a finger to say, "Come here?" Can you say it with your hand? Your whole lower arm? Repeat this, saying "Goodbye." What can your fingers communicate? How about your hands? Lower arms? Play with both your left and right sides.

When you are ready, you can continue to Experience 5.

Experience 5: Sensing the Joints in Your Arm, Shoulder Blade and Collarbone

In this Practice, if you have a partner, you can let them place a hand on your shoulder blade to help you sense its movement, rather than using the wall.

- Stand in the space. Pause. Take a *kinesthetic moment*.
- Stand with your back against the wall with your palm facing out. Do not press into the wall.
- Letting your fingers lead the way, raise your whole left arm by sliding it along the wall, noting the mobility of your shoulder joint and sensing the movement of your shoulder blade against the wall.
- Let your awareness include your whole body, especially the connection of your head–neck–spine, as it supports your arm movement. When your arm rises to its fullest height, sense the connection of your arm and shoulder girdle to your whole torso.
- Reaching your fingers out toward the left, slowly lower your arm, sensing the rolling action in the joint and the movement of your shoulder blade against the wall. Pause.

- Repeat with your right arm. Pause.
- Repeat. Play with pausing on the journey upward or on the return – on a diagonal or to the side, etc. Remember your whole body supports your arm movement. Pause.
- Step away from the wall.
- Repeat a couple more times with this addition: place your non-working hand on your collarbone to assist with awareness of its movement as you raise your arm.
- Play with your entire range of movement in your arm/shoulder girdle. Enjoy the support of your whole body for the movement from your collarbone and shoulder blade to your fingertips.
- Pause and take a *kinesthetic moment*.
- Repeat on the other side. Pause.
- *Spy back*. What did you discover about the connections within your arm structure? With your whole body?

Experience 6: Sensing Your Shoulder Joint, Collarbones, Shoulder Blades as the Completion of Your Whole Arm

- Stand. Sense the ground supporting you. Notice your 3-dimensional breath.
- Become aware of your arm structure from your hand to your elbow, then include your upper arm and shoulder joint in your awareness. This is the starting place.
- Allow your whole arm to rotate from the shoulder joint, as you turn the backs of your hands inward toward your legs. After a moment, return to the starting place.
- Now, open your whole arm, turning from the shoulder joint. Allow the palms of your hands to open outward.
- Pause. Sense your collarbones and shoulder blades and give yourself permission to gently "shrug" them up and down. This movement awakens and eases the connection between your arm structure and your sternum and ribs.
- Allow your collarbones and shoulder blades to move easily and gently.

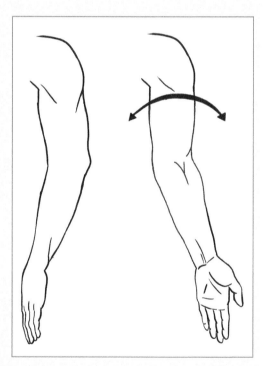

Figure 6.4 Your whole arm can rotate from your shoulder joint, gently turning your lower arm and hand.

- Pause and notice your whole arm structure now, from your fingers all the way to your collarbones and the two small joints at your sternum.
- Begin to rotate your hands outward and inward again, noticing the effect of this movement rippling through your whole arm.
- The next time you rotate your hands outward, allow them to lead your arms sideward and upward, as you lift your arms toward the ceiling. Continue to move your fingers upward and toward each other, creating a circular shape above and slightly forward of your head. Notice that your shoulder blades and collarbones have become part of the shape of this movement as well.
- Letting your fingertips lead, reverse this movement, bringing your arms down by your sides.
- Pause. Notice how your whole arm structure is now buoyantly resting on the support of your whole body. Your body is supported by the ground.
- Have a walk around the room, noticing the freedom available to your whole arm structure.
- Pause. Take a *kinesthetic moment.*
- *Spy back.* After exploring your entire arm structure, what did you discover about the many joints in your arms and how they can move? What surprised you? How can this information serve you as an actor?

Congratulations! You now have a firsthand experience (pun intended!) of the joints in your whole arm structure, from your fingertips to your shoulder blades and collarbones! Your arm structure is highly movable and 3-dimensional, and it is supported by your whole 3-dimensional body.

Your 3-Dimensional Arm Structure

If you look back at Figure 6.1, you may notice a helpful anatomical fact. The collarbones and shoulder blades are oriented toward the horizontal dimension, while your arms, when they are at rest, hang vertically. This strong horizontal support system allows your upper torso to expand and widen, even when your arms are at your sides. When you reach forward with your arms, your ribs and shoulder blades counterbalance the movement in the sagittal dimension, allowing your whole body to support your movement.

You can keep your *3-D body* in your awareness as you experience Arm Joint play below.

PRACTICE 6.2   **ARM JOINT PLAY**

Now that you are familiar with your hand–arm–shoulder joints, enjoy playing with their multiple movement possibilities in all three dimensions.

You are discovering not only the **range of motion**, but also the **sensation** of the joint action, so move gently. Practice *kinesthetic awareness*.

I investigate: In playing with the joints in my arm structure, how many movement possibilities can I discover? What is my experience of sensing the rolling, sliding actions of my joints?

Part I

- Pause. Stand. Breathe. Take a *kinesthetic moment*.
- Sense the support of your whole spine, with your head balancing at the top.
- Notice the support of the collarbones and shoulder blades as your arms rest at your sides.
- Take a walk around the space. Take note of your lively, 3-dimensional arm structure and all its joints.
- Noticing the support of your whole body, play with arm movement as you are walking, standing or sitting (Figure 6.5). Practice *kinesthetic awareness* as you note the sensations in joints and muscles as you move.
- Pause. Take a *kinesthetic moment*. Let your arms rest at your side.
- Still standing, begin to gently "draw" a figure eight in space, as if you were tracing it on the floor. This is a small movement near your side. Your fingers lead this movement, and it travels up your arm all the way to your shoulder blade and collarbone.
- After a few moments, gently make figure eights in the air with your fingers, then your hands, lower arms, then your whole arm,

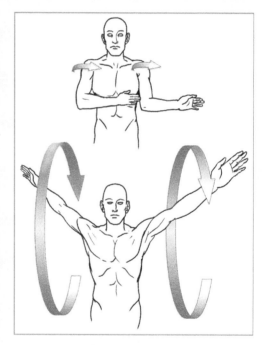

Figure 6.5 Your arm can rotate from your shoulder joint in many directions.

noticing all the ways that each joint in your movable arm structure participates in this movement.

- The figure eights can be any size and move anywhere. You may start to feel like you are conducting an orchestra!
- Pause. Take a *kinesthetic moment*.
- Have a walk around the room, noticing the support of your whole body and the buoyancy of your arm structure.
- Pause.

Part II

- Play with your arm's mobility and 3-D support by practicing the imaginary ball toss from Chapter 1 (Practice 1.3). Give particular attention to the movement in your joints as you play.
- You can throw the ball in any direction you like; try juggling, or throw and catch with a partner. Be sure to use both arms – explore these 3-dimensional movements with your whole body.
- Pause. Take a *kinesthetic moment*.
- Explore other ways of moving from your shoulder joints.
- *Spy back*. What did you discover about your movable arms in these Practices? Could you sense 3-dimensional support from your whole body for the movements? If so, how does this inspire your creative options?

When you play with the options for movement and support within your arm structure, you can discover the role of each *part within the whole*. Every connection supports every other connection. Every relationship supports every other relationship. Your whole body is balanced and ready to respond to whatever arises.

Moving according to your body's true design gives you specificity and freedom onstage and in your everyday life.

PRACTICE 6.3   ARM WAVE

Enjoy practicing the joint connections in your whole arm structure through the Hip Hop Arm Wave. A slower song is best; Mobb Deep's *Infamous Instrumentals* album has some great cuts – like "Quiet Storm."[1] With no lyrics to distract you, you can give special attention to joint connections as the wave moves from joint to joint through your whole arm.

If you don't know how, you can learn! Visit YouTube. We like "How to Arm Wave" (Hip Hop Dance Moves Tutorial) Mihran Kirakosian.[2] Have fun!

- Stand. Pause. Breathe and sense your arm structure and the support of your whole body. Take a *kinesthetic moment*.
- As you dance and practice arm waves, note the wavy, spiraling connection from fingers to wrist to elbow to shoulder joint to collarbone, across to the other collarbone, and through the shoulder joint, elbow, down to the wrist and fingers.
- Let your whole body support this movement. Avoid tightening your neck or jaw. Just play!
- Pause. Take a *kinesthetic moment*.
- *Spy back*. What did the arm wave teach you about your arm joints and their connections? How does the support of your whole body serve you as you play with these movements?

The balanced relationship between your head, spine, and torso provides core support for your arm structure. In a way, every part of you, from the ground up, forms the support for your collarbones, shoulder blades, and arms. This movable structure offers you so many possibilities for expression. Now that you are aware of your movement options, take this information with you into your everyday life and your creative work.

With your new awareness of your supportive head–tail connection and your collarbone/ shoulder blade/hand connection, you are ready to explore your leg/torso connection. Chapter 7 introduces you to joint connections from your toes up to your pelvis. Experiencing the mobility of the joints of your leg structure gives you both support and freedom to move!

PAUSE TO PROCESS, as you did earlier in this chapter, before continuing to Chapter 7. Explore the special qualities of your whole arm structure, supported by your whole body!

Notes

1 Mobb Deep. "Quiet Storm." *The Infamous Instrumentals.* Green Streets Entertainment, 2008.
2 Kirakosian, Mihran. "How to Arm Wave (Hip Hop Dance Moves Tutorial)." *YouTube*, February 15, 2017. www.youtube.com/watch?v=VCX1mNfTnx0.

Joint Connections in your Feet, Legs, and Pelvis

Your legs and feet provide support plus mobility – their many joints make it possible for you to move easily through space. They are perfectly designed to allow you to walk, jump, leap, hop, turn, kick, and also provide balanced support when you stand in place. Your versatile legs and feet receive support from the ground up, freeing you to move anywhere.

In this chapter, you can discover the joint connections within your supportive leg structure. Your legs are both movable and strong.

Your Foot–Pelvis Connection: Foot–Ankle–Lower Leg

Where the Connections Are

- Each foot contains 26 bones and 30+ joints[1]: they are strong and very movable!
- The long bones of your foot stabilize your very movable toes.
- The long bones of your foot form a subtle curving arch and offer dynamic support for standing and walking. Your arch extends from your heel to the ball of your foot.
- Your foot is connected to your lower leg bones by your ankle joint.
- Your ankle joints are located forward and up from your heels. Your heels release back and down, while making a connection with the supportive floor.
- The talus is the rounded foot bone that meets your leg bones at the ankle joint. Your talus rests on top of your heel bone.

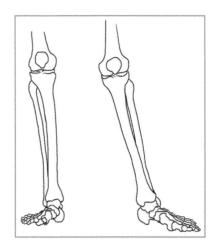

Figure 7.1 Joint relationships: feet and lower legs.

- Your lower leg consists of two long bones, the tibia and fibula, which connect to your talus at the ankle joint.

Where They Are Not

- Your ankle is not the two large bones at the bottom of your lower leg. Though we usually call these our "ankle bones," these are the ends of your leg bones. Much like the wrist joints we described in Chapter 6, your ankle joint is located below these sturdy leg bones.
- Your ankle is not at the sides of your foot or leg; it is a 360-degree joint.

How They Move

- Your toes can lengthen, spread, and extend through the gliding, rolling action of their many joints.
- The sturdy bones and many joints of your arch provide stability when you are standing. When you are moving, the sliding and gliding action of your joints provide flexibility.
- The inward curve at the bottom end of your main lower leg bone (tibia) rests on the sturdy rounded talus, which allows for a rolling motion in your ankle joint.
- Your toe, foot, and ankle joints allow your foot to flex, roll, circle, and extend. When you are on your feet, these actions work with your other leg joints to move you through space.
- When you are standing, the multiple joints of your toes, foot, and ankle are subtly shifting as they balance and rebalance your weight. If you allow your body to work as it is designed, you are never really "standing still."

PRACTICE 7.1   **EXPLORING TOE, FOOT, AND ANKLE ACTION**

Before exploring these joints further, take a walk around the room. At the end of the exploration, you will walk again, noting any differences in sensation or awareness of these joint actions.

In this Practice, you are discovering not only the **range of motion**, but also the **sensation** of the joint action, so move gently. Practice *kinesthetic awareness*.

Work with the first three steps in a seated position – on the floor or in a chair. As you explore, remind yourself that each joint is a *part within the whole*. Practice *inclusive attention*.

- Pause. Take a *kinesthetic moment*. Sit in a chair or on the floor.
- Begin to move your toes with *kinesthetic awareness*; each toe has three joints, except for the big toe, which has two. Enjoy the sensations of these rolling, sliding, and gliding joints: spreading, flexing, extending. Discover the possibilities. See if you can move each toe individually!

- You may sense movement in your foot as well. Yay! Your foot is responding to toe movement.
- Pause.
- Slide your hands down your lower leg past the knobby lower end of your leg bones and feel the soft tissue of the ankle, just below them. With your hands on the front, back, and sides of your ankle (not your leg or your heel), move your foot up and down, side to side, round and round. Use your tactile and *kinesthetic senses* to help you discover ankle joint action.
- Notice the fluid motion in your ankle.
- After a few moments, take your hands away, and allow your *kinesthetic sense* to inform you, as you explore other movement possibilities for your ankle.
- After you have explored both ankle joints, pause. Take a *kinesthetic moment*.
- Stand. Notice your feet meeting the floor and sense the movability in your ankle joints.
- Gently let your weight move forward toward your toes, then back toward your heels. Your toes lift slightly as your weight moves back, and then, as your weight comes forward, your heels lift slightly, creating a gentle rocking motion.
- Enjoy the subtle movements of the bones of your foot, ankle joints, and toes. Sense the fluid movement of the more than 30 joints in your foot and ankle!
- You can also have fun shifting the weight on your feet from side to side, noticing the subtle movements in your arches, ankles, and feet.
- Continue these explorations and expand your attention to your whole leg, whole body, and your breath. Remember that each movement connects each *part* to the *whole*.
- Pause. Take a *kinesthetic moment*.
- Take a walk and notice the sensations of your movable feet, ankles, and legs. Practice *inclusive attention*.
- Pause. Take a *kinesthetic moment*.
- *Spy back.* What did you discover about your movable ankles and feet through these explorations? What changed in your walk from the beginning to the end of the Practice?

For many of us, ankles and feet have been out of our awareness: we are in brand new territory. These first steps (pun intended!) are about experiencing the *friendly facts* and discovering what movements are possible. Be gentle with yourself (and your feet and ankles!) as you explore. Revisit these Practices often.

Your Foot–Pelvis Connection: Lower Leg, Knee, Hip Joint, Pelvis

Your **hip joints, knee joints**, and **ankle joints** work together whether you are walking, dancing, or standing still. These joints are the **Big 3**, because they are key to support and mobility in your whole body.

Where the Connections Are

- The tibia (your main lower leg bone) has a wide top, with two shallow grooves on either side. It provides support for your thigh bone (femur). The lower end of the thigh bone has two curving shapes, which rest into the two grooves of the tibia. This is the main part of your knee joint.
- Your movable kneecap glides over this joint, as it interacts with the femur.
- Inside the knee joint, cushioning cartilage keeps the joint springy and smoothly movable.
- Your upper leg bone (femur) meets your pelvis at the *hip joint*, between the pelvic crest and the sit bone.
- Your pelvis balances on your legs via your hip joints (the joining of the deep sockets at the sides of your pelvis with the balls at the top of your thigh bones).
- Your sit bones are a part of your pelvis. They are located at the bottom of your pelvis below your hip joint.

Where They Are Not

- Your knee is a joint, not a separate bone between the upper and lower leg. It is not the kneecap, and it isn't above the kneecap.
- Your thigh bone does not meet (or move from) the top of the pelvic crest. It swings freely from your hip socket at the lower part of your pelvis.
- When we reach down to pick up an object off the floor, we move from the hip, knee, and ankle joints. There is no "waist" joint. (see Figures 7.4a and b)

How They Move

- The top of your thigh bone is round like a ball; it fits into a concave

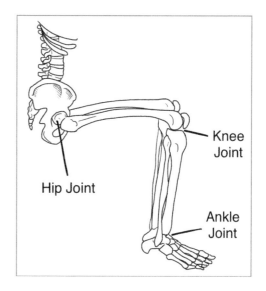

Figure 7.2 The ankle, knee and hip joints.

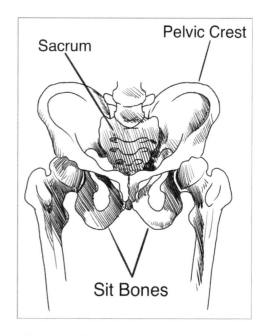

Figure 7.3 Pelvis/leg relationship: the rounded top of your thigh bone rests in the curved hip socket at the side of your pelvis.

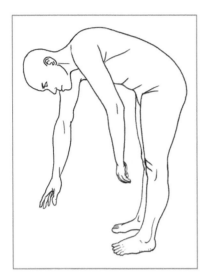

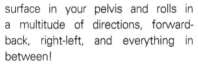

Figure 7.4a You lose your head–spine–pelvis connection when you reach for the floor from "the waist."

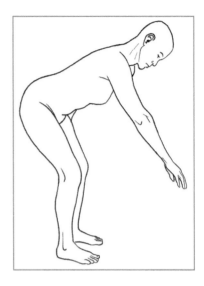

Figure 7.4b You maintain your head–spine–pelvis connection when you reach for the floor and activate your Big 3.

surface in your pelvis and rolls in a multitude of directions, forward-back, right-left, and everything in between!

- Sometimes your pelvis rotates around the thigh bone, as when you are standing and bending over. At other times, your pelvis provides stability as your thigh bone rotates, like when you raise your leg.
- When you are standing, the curved surfaces of the bones allow subtle balancing actions at your Big 3. Standing does not require stiffening or "locking" your legs at your joints.
- What we call "bending" at the knee is actually a rolling action. When your knee joint is activated, your thigh does not press down into your lower leg, and your lower leg does not press down into your foot. The motion of your leg is *forward*, via the rolling action at your ankle, knee, and hip joints.

Figure 7.5 Your rolling knee joint releases forward of your body when activated.

- When it is not bearing weight, your lower leg can rotate in a circle via the rolling action of your knee joint.

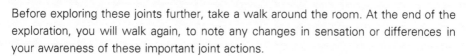

PRACTICE 7.2   **EXPLORING YOUR KNEE AND HIP JOINTS**

Before exploring these joints further, take a walk around the room. At the end of the exploration, you will walk again, to note any changes in sensation or differences in your awareness of these important joint actions.

Remember that your upper and lower leg meet to form your knee joint. Their rounded ends glide and roll as your move.

You are discovering not only the **range of motion**, but also the **sensation** of the joint action, so move gently. As you explore, remind yourself that each joint is a *part within the whole*. Practice *kinesthetic awareness* and *inclusive attention*.

Knee Joint

I investigate: As I explore my knee joint, I am curious about _____ (Fill in the blank).

Part I

- Pause. Take a *kinesthetic moment*. Breathe.
- Sit on a chair. With your sit bones on the chair, your four spinal curves are free to balance your torso and head over your pelvis. Notice the connections of your whole torso to your hip, knee, and ankle joints.
- Tilting forward from your hip joints, place your hands on your right lower leg. Let your fingers and thumbs encircle your leg. Slide them up until they reach the soft tissue just below your kneecap and in the back of your knee. Take a moment to recognize that your hands are on your 360° knee joint.
- With your hands still on the knee joint, extend your lower leg up and away from you, then let it fold back toward you. Using your *kinesthetic* and tactile senses, explore the movement of extending and flexing your lower leg at the knee joint.
- Pause. Place both feet on the floor. Sit and breathe. Take a *kinesthetic moment*.
- Repeat with your left leg. Pause.
- Stand. Pause and notice the gentle sense of balance in your Big 3. Notice any impulse to overtighten muscles around your knee, which could "lock" your knee. Sense a subtle, fluid motion through your whole leg.
- Practice the rolling action at your knee joints by allowing your upper and lower leg bones to move forward, releasing your knee joint. (Before you learned about the design of this joint, you might have called this action "bending at the knee," as in Figure 7.5.)
- Sense how the Big 3 leg joints activate to support this movement: your thigh and lower leg bones are rolling and gliding at the hip and ankle joints, and your whole body is responding.

- Practice *inclusive attention*.
- Pause. Take a *kinesthetic moment*.

Part II

In this Practice, you will be asked to stand on one leg. We recommend that you stand near a wall (your side to the wall) or table, so that you can steady yourself if necessary. Avoid **leaning** into the wall, as it restricts your movement and interferes with your body's natural balance.

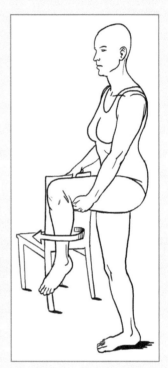

- Stand on your right leg and lift your left thigh. Clasp your hands under your thigh to support your raised leg. Let your knee joint release, and your foot dangle toward the floor.
- Gently swing your lower leg forward and back; sense the rolling action of the knee as you make this movement. Pause.
- Begin to draw a small circle with your foot, exploring your knee joint's rotating action. Allow easy movement through the joint; avoid tightening in your thigh or lower leg. Sense the ease of the movement. Pause. Reverse the direction. Pause.
- Place your foot on the floor. Take a *kinesthetic moment*, sensing your whole leg and your whole body.
- Explore these actions with the other leg.
- *Spy back*. What is your experience of your whole leg as your bones roll and rotate at your knee joint? How do these Practices help you make the foot–pelvis connection?

Figure 7.6 Your lower leg can rotate at the knee joint.

Hip Joint

To find your hip joint, stand on one leg and lift your other thigh until it is parallel to the floor. Release your knee joint and let your lower leg and foot drape loosely toward the floor. Look down and see the crease in your pants at the top of your leg. Your pelvis and leg meet in that area, at the rolling/gliding hip joint.

I investigate: What can I discover about the movement of my legs and their connection with my whole body?

Part I: Sitting

- Sit on a chair. Pause. Bring your attention to your whole body. Breathe.
- Notice your sit bones on the chair, and your thighs releasing out of your hip joints, the ease of your knees and ankles, and your feet resting on the floor.
- Take a *kinesthetic moment.*
- Notice your sit bones as they meet the chair. Recognize that your whole torso is receiving support from the chair. Practice *inclusive attention.*
- Begin to gently shift your weight side to side, rocking on your sit bones.
- After a few moments, pause. Take a *kinesthetic moment.*
- Begin to shift your weight forward and back. Notice that this movement activates a rolling action at your hip joints. Notice your **range of motion** and *kinesthetic sensation.*
- Spend a few moments exploring these movements and others that may occur to you.
- Pause. Take a *kinesthetic moment.*

Part II: Standing

Discover hip joint action. Remember that the wall is a steady support if you need it. Avoid leaning.

- Stand with your right side near a wall or table. Pause. Sense your feet meeting the floor. Breathe.
- Lift your left leg so that your thigh is parallel to the floor, your knee is released, and your foot hangs toward the floor. You can place your right shoulder next to the wall for support.
- Place the fingers of your right hand on the crease of your pants at the hip joint. Put the other hand on your buttock, directly behind the hand in front. Put your foot back on the floor. Raise and lower your leg several times, sensing movement of the joint using your *kinesthetic* and tactile senses.
- Take your hands away and sense the movement kinesthetically.
- Pause. Place your left foot on the floor. Notice any differences in sensation between your right and left legs.
- Repeat with the right leg (left side toward the wall).
- Pause.
- Take a walk around the room, noticing the Big 3 leg joints in action.
- Pause.

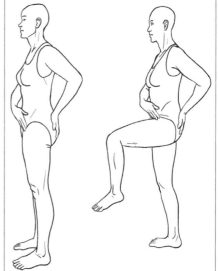

Figure 7.7 Sensing hip joint action.

Exploring Hip Joint Action

- Stand with your right side near a wall or table. Pause. Breathe.
- Place your right hand on the wall for balance. Explore gently swinging your left leg forward and back, enjoying the rolling action in your hip joint.
- Place your left leg on the floor. Pause. Take a *kinesthetic moment*.
- Turn your left side to the wall.
- Pause. Take a *kinesthetic moment*.
- Standing on your right leg, place the ball of your left foot on the floor.
- Turn your left leg inward and outward, sensing the rotation in the hip joint.
- Pause.
- You can use your tactile sense (place a hand on your buttock and/or the crease of your pants) and your *kinesthetic sense* to feel the action of the ball of the thigh bone as it rolls in its supportive hip socket.
- Remove your hand(s) and continue to explore your hip joint's rolling/rotating action, with your foot on or off the floor. Use your *kinesthetic sense* to perceive the sensations of the full range of movement.
- Expand your awareness to include your whole body. No part moves in isolation – all participate and support in subtle ways.
- Pause. Stand. Notice any differences between your two legs.
- Repeat with your left leg.
- Pause. Take a *kinesthetic moment*.
- Have a walk around the room noticing the spacious, fluid movement of the joints of your whole leg and its relationship to your whole body.
- Let your whole body support and respond to the action of your legs and their movable joints. Release any tendency to grip in your legs or torso. Let your spine be long and celebrate the fluid motion through *all* your joints.
- Practice *inclusive attention*. If your eyes are on the floor, pause, and make another choice. See the room around you and sense your whole body as you walk.
- Pause and breathe. Take a *kinesthetic moment*.
- *Spy back.* What have you discovered about the movement of your leg joints? How was walking affected by these explorations? How does knowing your body's true design affect movement in your legs and your whole body?

As you go through your day, enjoy your movable leg joints and the connections of your feet, legs, and pelvis with your whole body.

Now that you're acquainted with your leg joints and the movability of your leg structure, it's a good time to connect the Big 3 leg joints with each other and your whole body. To do this, you can **take a walk**.

Walking

At the end of each Practice we ask you to walk through the room. We do this, because walking connects your whole body and helps your nervous system to process the experience. Walking integrates your discoveries and connects your body and mind.

Here are some *friendly facts* about walking that can help you get the most out of these explorations.

- Walking is a whole-body activity.
- When you take a step, all the joints of your feet and legs are in motion.
- Your thigh bones swing freely from your hip joints.
- Your buoyant spine connects your head, ribs, and pelvis.
- Your eyes can be receptive to the room and the space around you as you move.
- Your arms "go along for the ride," gently swinging in response to the movement from your feet, up through your legs and torso, all the way to your head.
- Now **take a walk**, exploring these *friendly facts* as you move.

As you have discovered, walking involves much more of you than just your legs. Your whole *3-D body* organizes to coordinate this essential movement.

PAUSE TO PROCESS before continuing. Journal or talk with someone about your discoveries. We depend on our legs for so much: standing, walking, running, leaping, jumping, squatting. Take a few moments to explore their expressive qualities.

You can investigate the special qualities of your feet, legs, and pelvis. Put on some music and play with these connections. Sense these *parts within the whole* as you play!

Your feet, legs, and pelvis each move in unique ways. What can your foot communicate that your legs cannot? Can you say "hi" with your foot? (Feel free to sit or lie down.) What else can you say? What can you communicate with other parts of your leg?

Enjoy the sensations in your Big 3 leg joints as you walk through space. Play with allowing your feet to lead your legs, pelvis, and whole body. Let your thighs lead; let your pelvis lead. Play with creating silly walks, fast walks, slow walks, walks with different rhythms. A character may emerge: Enjoy!

By exploring your joint connections, you have gained knowledge and experience of your true design for movement. Yet, when you are onstage, you are not always moving. Here is the good news about that: your joint connections also support dynamic stillness.

In almost every Practice in *YBK*, you begin and end with standing. The heightened awareness of your joint connections gives you a sense of wholeness and ease, no matter what you are doing. In the Practice below, you are invited to use your body-knowledge to experience your lively balance and support when standing.

Standing

When you are standing, your torso balances over your legs. But how, you ask?

Like everything else about your body's design, standing is not a static relationship, but a movable one. Here are some helpful tips about your pelvis–leg–foot relationship when you are standing.

- When standing, your feet should not be outside the width of your pelvis, as soldiers do when they are given the "at ease," command. It is very challenging to keep your hip joints free and movable in that relationship.
- Your feet rest on the floor under your hip joints. There is a throughline of connection from your hip joints, through the long bones of your thighs to your knee joints, to your lower leg, to your ankle joints, and through your feet to the support of the floor.
- Your strong, weight-bearing pelvis is a bridge between your upper body and your legs. Your sit bones aim toward the floor, and your pelvis balances on your legs via your movable hip joints.
- The rounded surfaces of your hip, knee, and ankle joints create a dynamic balance that is always "ready for change." Remember, you are not stacked like bricks. This is a **movable** relationship!

In the exploration below, you can discover the dynamic balance of your head, arms, and upper torso with your pelvis, legs, and feet: your "home base."

PRACTICE 7.3   FINDING "HOME BASE"

As you practice, remember that your leg joints are movable. When you lift one leg, practice sensing the balance and the connections between the joints in your standing leg. Your awareness of the *friendly facts* will help you avoid "locking" your leg joints.

- Stand. Pause. Sense the connection of your feet and legs to your whole body. Breathe.
- Begin a "joint journey" through your left leg. Roll through your foot by lifting your heel. Allow your foot, ankle, knee, and hip joints to respond to this movement. Your toes remain on the floor.
- Play with this movement, changing how much you lift your heel each time. Pause.
- Practice with the other foot and leg. Pause. Sense both feet on the floor, and their connection to your whole body. Pause.
- Repeat the movement of rolling through your left foot by lifting your heel, and allow your toes to rise a little bit off the floor. Your hip, knee, and ankle joints are released, and your foot dangles toward the floor.
- Remember your standing leg and allow those joints to maintain an easy balance with each other.
- Then put your foot back down again. Pause.
- Notice the connection and relationship of your foot, ankle, knee, hip, whole body. Sense the support of the floor.
- Repeat with your right foot and leg. Pause. Take a *kinesthetic moment.*
- As you explore this Practice several times, notice where your foot **wants** to fall in relationship to your hip, knee, and ankle joints. Discover "home base:" the

balanced relationship of your feet on the floor with your hip joints. This may be a new relationship for you.
- As you play with home base, remember that your Big 3 are gently balancing and rebalancing. This is not a "position."
- Pause. Take a *kinesthetic moment*.
- Have a walk around the space. Notice the freedom and ease of your legs and your whole body. Practice *inclusive attention*.
- Practice pausing, sensing home base, then resume your walk. After a few minutes, pause, return to home base, and take a *kinesthetic moment*.
- *Spy back*. What did you discover about the balance and connectivity of your legs to your whole body when standing? When walking? What new awareness have you gained through your exploration of the joint connections throughout your body? How might this serve you as an actor?

Learning how your body really works offers you **Connection**, **Support**, and **Movement**. **Connection**: your body knows that your feet are connected to your pelvis through your whole leg. **Support**: Your sturdy bones and your movable joints support your whole body from the ground up. **Movement**: These are the facts of your design, and they give you many choices about the way you move.

Isn't it wonderful to move when your joints are free? Your whole connected body supports every movement you make. As you become more familiar with the *friendly facts*, old, unneeded tensions fall away, and your coordinated body responds more spontaneously to the world around you. Onstage, you are free to create.

PRACTICE 7.4   **REVISIT *MOVING THROUGH YOUR JOINTS***

Through your explorations in the last four chapters, you have developed a more accurate *body map*. In addition, you've cultivated your *kinesthetic awareness* of your major joints and their connections with each other. Allow this new information to support you, as you revisit Practice 4.2: Moving Through Your Joints.

Your mind, body, and *kinesthetic sense* work together as you warm your joints, explore their movement, and make connections.

- Each part always moves in connection with the whole – nothing happens in isolation.
- Revisit Practice 4.2. You now have new knowledge of the *friendly facts* of your design. Bring this awareness of your joints, their location, their connections, and their actions to this exploration.
- Following the Practice, take a *kinesthetic moment*.
- Have a walk through the space, using your *kinesthetic awareness* to notice sensation and the *parts within the whole*.
- Pause.

- *Spy back.* What did you notice about your body before, during, and after moving through your joints? How was this Practice different from the first time you experienced this exploration?

Now that you've explored individual joint connections in Chapters 4–7, you can take time to reconnect all your joints within the structure of your whole body. Now is the perfect time to introduce a familiar Practice to many, the *roll-down*. Even if you have practiced the *roll-down* before, allowing all your joints to participate with their own rolling, sliding, gliding actions can be a useful and informative (not to mention, it feels great!) experience.

PRACTICE 7.5   **THE ROLL-DOWN (KP)**

The *roll-down* is a full-body movement sequence, which has become a daily warm-up Practice for actors, dancers, singers, and musicians. The specific origin of the *roll-down* is unknown, but it has been passed down from one generation of performers to another and continues to this day.

The *roll-down* releases excess tension and, ultimately, re-balances all your joints within your whole body. As you move downward toward the floor, and then back upward, you are following a lively pathway of movement, stretching your muscles, and preparing yourself for dynamic movement choices.

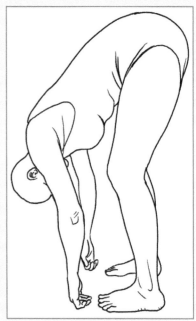

Figure 7.8 As your thighs free, your knees come forward and your spine lengthens in the *roll-down*.

- Pause. Stand. Breathe. Take a *kinesthetic moment.*
- Bring your attention to your whole body, allowing the ground under your feet to offer you lively support in standing.
- Your head begins the *roll-down* with a subtle, arc-like, rolling action, initiated from the A-O joint.
- As the crown of your head aims toward the floor, each vertebra of your spine follows with its own small rolling action.
- The sequential movement of your head and spine allows your pelvis to rotate at the hip joint, with your legs, feet, and the ground as a continuing support.
- Your Big 3 leg joints release as your upper and lower leg release slightly forward at your knee and ankle.
- Your feet continue to receive the support of the ground.

- As you roll down, your arms and hands "go along for the ride."
- Pause, breathe, and continue to sense the support of the floor.
- To initiate your return to standing, take a moment to sense your connection from the crown of your head to your sit bones and tailbone.
- With a sense of your whole body and the support of the floor, allow your pelvis to return to its upright balance, as your sit bones release downward toward the floor.
- Your legs will respond to this movement by gradually returning to their balanced relationship with your pelvis and feet.
- The roll-up will then continue naturally and spontaneously as your vertebrae follow one another in returning your whole torso to upright balance.
- Your arms ride up with your torso, and your head returns to its poise at the top of your spine.
- Pause. Take a *kinesthetic moment*.
- Practice *inclusive attention* as you take a walk around the space. Pause.
- If you like, repeat the practice one or two more times.
- *Spy back*. The *roll-down* awakens a sense of connection through your whole body. How did your sense of connection change from the beginning of the Practice to the end? How does your awareness of your joints foster a sense of connection? What did you notice about your whole self as you walked at the end of the Practice?

Moving through your joints and the *roll-down* are Key Practices. Because they awaken and enliven the whole body, our students often include them in their preshow or pre-rehearsal warm-up.

The explorations in Chapters 4–7 have led you to a clearer understanding of your body's *friendly facts*. You have observed and experienced your movable joints, as you explored their location and their range of movement. You have sensed joint action from the inside out, heightened your awareness of body connections, and discovered your body's natural balance.

Through learning about your joint connections, you have experienced a deeper knowledge of your body and how it works: you studied the facts, and you explored them through movement. In the next chapter, you can discover how your muscles work together as a team with your bones and joints. With a clear and well-defined *body map*, your body and mind are in sync. You have a foundation that will serve you in all your movement choices, and reward you with a powerful, responsive onstage presence.

"I have found the work spilling over into my everyday life as well. My back troubles are almost nonexistent. My joints do not hurt or pop as much as they have in the past. Most importantly, though, the openness I feel in class and my acting work is making me more aware of the world around me. I see and feel more than I ever have in my memory. I feel more available to my family and friends. The movement work we are doing in class is helping me discover the 'real me' in the 'real world.'"[2]

Mike, acting student, Florida Atlantic University

PAUSE TO PROCESS before continuing to Chapter 8. Journal or talk with someone about your discoveries. As you move through your day, notice your movable, supportive legs and their relationship to your whole body.

Key Practice: *Roll-Down*

Notes

1 Hale, Robert Beverly and Coyle, Terence. *Albinus on Anatomy*. Mineola: Dover Press, 1980. pp. 142–145.
2 From a student journal. Used with permission.

Strong Bones, Dynamic Muscles

Man moves in order to satisfy a need. He aims by his movement at something of value to him.

Rudolf Laban[1]

Muscles respond to our needs: walking, sitting, bending, grasping, chewing are all responses to human need. When you see something you want or react to a situation, your muscles respond to your needs by moving your bones.

Your joints provide the fluid motion that allows bones and muscles to interact. When we have a desire, such as "I want a drink of water," our whole *body-mind* coordinates to fulfill that desire. Movement happens, because our highly sensitive sensory organs – our muscles – respond to our needs.

Know Your Muscles*

Whether you are sitting, standing, or moving, the rounded surfaces of your joints are constantly balancing and rebalancing. This means that your responsive muscles are always moving too, supporting your needs, whether you are stationary or in motion.

Here are some basics about how your muscles work within your body's structure:

- Bones and muscles work together to move your body and to support its weight.
- Muscles are constantly changing. They respond to **gravity**, your **weight**, and your **needs**, whether you are standing in one place, seated, or moving through space. They are not designed to stiffen your body into a rigid position.

---

* We refer here to your movement muscles, known as skeletal muscles.

- Tendons attach your muscles to your bones.
- Your bones bear weight, and they provide stability for your muscles. Bones also slightly stretch your muscles, which encourages them to lengthen when they are at rest.
- Your bones rely on your muscles to move them.
- By lengthening and contracting, muscles shift and balance weight throughout your body. This is an almost constant process when you are upright.
- Most muscles connect one bone with another. When they contract, muscles move your bones by pulling them, and this activates movement in your joints. Muscles cannot push your bones.
- Muscles are made up of fibers that can distribute weight throughout a muscle or concentrate it in a specific area to support movement and balance.
- When a muscle is chronically tightened, it is no longer moving weight and sharing weight with bones and other muscles. It does not return to its resting state when it is not needed.
- Chronic tension can interfere with the connections between your joints by hindering their sliding, gliding, rolling action. A tight muscle can disrupt the natural flow of movement through your joints.
- Muscles are arranged in layers. The deepest muscles, the ones closest to the bones, act mainly as support muscles. These muscles sustain your balance in response to gravity. The superficial muscles (closer to your skin) move your bones, responding to your needs and the world around you.

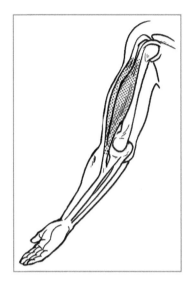

Figure 8.1 Your bicep muscle reaches from the top of your upper arm, past your elbow, to your lower arm.

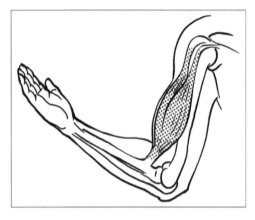

Figure 8.2 When your bicep contracts, it activates your elbow joint.

Your muscles constantly send information to your brain, and vice versa: two-way *body-mind communication*. In his book, *Neurodynamics*, Dr. Ted Dimon puts it this way: "Muscles are not just motor organs, but highly sensitive sensory organs … and the information they provide is crucial to even the most conscious and deliberate movements."[2]

Each time you move, your muscles and your *kinesthetic sense* provide information about how much effort is needed, your balance, and much more. Your muscles respond not only to your changing needs, but to the force of gravity.

Your Muscles and Bones Work With Gravity

When astronauts spend long stretches of time in outer space, their muscles atrophy. Why? They are weightless. Muscles need gravity to work. Our muscles do not fight gravity; they work **with** it. Without gravity, our muscles are no longer responding to our weight, and they literally waste away. Our bodies are perfectly designed to move on planet Earth.

Your skeleton bears your weight passively. Your muscles have a different relationship to weight: they bear weight by actively responding to it. Your fibrous muscles process weight, distributing it where it is needed. When you lift a heavy object, your muscles can move weight through your whole arm and into your torso for added support.

Muscles share your body weight with each other. They balance and support your skeleton and keep you upright in response to the force of gravity. When your muscles pull (contract) against the supportive, stable resistance of your bones, you move.

The Practice below is a gentle investigation into muscle action, weight, and our ability to balance in gravity.

PRACTICE 8.1 **SENSING THE MOVEMENT OF YOUR MUSCLES**

This exploration revisits *kinesthetic sensing*, Practice 1.4.

Kinesthetic sensing refines your ability to discern movement in your muscles. As you raise your arm, weight transfers into your shoulder and torso. And it transfers again, as you lower it. See if you can sense changes in your muscles as they contract and lengthen to produce this simple movement.

Before you begin the Practice, have a walk around the room. What sensations do you notice today? Do you feel sluggish? Lively? What do you notice about your joints as you move? If you are in a class, share your impressions with a partner.

Part I

- Stand. Pause. Breathe. Take a *kinesthetic moment*.
- Follow the steps for Practice 1.4. Practice *inclusive attention* as you slowly raise your arm.
- Give particular attention to the sensation of lengthening and contracting muscles and the changing distribution of weight in your body.
- Give attention to all three of your dimensions as you move.
- Pause.
- *Spy back*. What did you discover about the sensation of weight and movement in your muscles?

Part II

Continue to practice *kinesthetic sensing*, as you enjoy the fluid movement of weight through your body. Allow these gentle movements to unfold naturally and easily. As weight transfers from place to place in your body, it is sometimes helpful to think of your weight as water flowing to fill and empty (and spread) as you move.

Here is a useful mantra for this Practice: no pushing, no pressing, no tightening, no stressing.

- Stand. Pause. Breathe. Take a *kinesthetic moment*.
- Practice *inclusive attention* and *kinesthetic sensing* as you begin to shift your weight toward your right leg, just slightly. Then shift back to center.
- Repeat toward the left. Return to center. These are very small movements. Take your time.
- Repeat a few more times.
- Pause. Take a *kinesthetic moment*.
- With an awareness of kinesthetic sensation, shift your weight slowly and gently toward the front, allowing movement through your Big 3. Avoid pressing into your feet. Let your joints and dynamic muscles work for you.
- Shift your weight back into center, then toward the back, then to center again. Pause. Take a *kinesthetic moment*.
- Play with slightly shifting your weight in every direction (front, back, side). Notice the sensations of weight shifting through your feet and legs, up into your pelvis. Notice the responses of your torso, head, and arms.
- Take note, especially, of the movement through your Big 3 and up into your whole body, as your muscles contract and lengthen to produce these gentle movements.
- Breathe.
- Feel free to change the relationship of your feet – widen your stance, lunge, etc. – as you continue to explore shifting your weight. Simply enjoy the sensation of change, as your muscles provide balance, while serving your need to move!
- As you bring this Practice to a close, return to home base, standing with your feet under your hip joints. Continue to shift your weight in smaller and smaller movements until you are the only one who knows that you are moving. Enjoy the balance of your dynamic body.
- Pause. Take a *kinesthetic moment*.
- Practice *inclusive attention* as you take a walk around the space. Notice the lively movement of your muscles as weight travels through your whole body.
- Pause.
- *Spy back.* What did you discover about your body's ability to process weight through your muscles? What sensations did you notice that seemed new or different? How was your last walk different from your walk at the beginning? How might this information serve you as an actor?

Sensing your weight helps you make a kinesthetic connection between your muscles and bones. This gives you the ability to recognize and release unwanted tension, which interferes with freedom of movement and stifles authentic impulse.

By exploring the lively relationship between your muscles, your bones, and gravity, you open the door to a constant and unending array of movement possibilities.

Your Body's Response to Gravity

You may be wondering why, with the pressure of gravity, we don't slither along the ground like worms. The answer lies in basic physics. Newton's Third Law of Motion states that for every action, there is an equal and opposite reaction.[3] Though you experience the force of gravity, your body is designed to respond to it. So, we can stand on two legs instead of crawling on our bellies!

This Law of Motion is always at play, giving your muscles upward buoyancy that allows you to be upright. This natural force creates constant, dynamic movement in your body.

Ground Reaction Force (KW)

Our muscles are responding to gravity, even when we are standing or sitting "still." As we stand or sit, our deepest muscles, the ones that provide the most support to our skeleton, are "twitching." The muscle fibers are contracting and expanding, as they receive, and slowly respond to, our body weight.

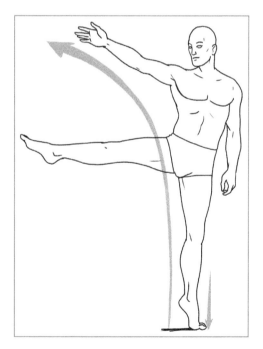

Muscles also respond to gravity through the force of pressure against external objects, like the floor or a chair. This is known as *ground reaction force (GRF)*. Your body exerts a force equal to your weight on the ground, and at the same time an equal and opposite force is exerted by the ground on your body. When your foot meets the ground in walking, for instance, the weight of your body is a force on the ground, and the ground meets your foot with an equal force. This upward force moves through your 3-dimensional muscles and bones, providing support for your whole *3-D body*.

Ground reaction force is part of your design for movement. Your muscles are activated to release the pressure of *GRF* by "sharing the load," which gives your body upward direction, a natural, built-in buoyancy.

Figure 8.3 *Ground reaction force* gives us "upward mobility."

PRACTICE 8.2 **PARTNERING WITH THE FLOOR**

When we were babies, we knew all about *ground reaction force*, as we learned to move from place to place by using our weight against the floor. We scooted, we rolled, we slithered, we crawled.

In this Practice, use the floor as your partner as you move across the room. Explore all the ways you can move – without walking or moving on your feet (walking, jumping, running, or leaping). Let your weight meet the floor and let *GRF* provide the energy for moving. Get up close and personal with the friendly floor and the weight of your body.

- Stand at one end of the room. Pause. Notice your body and its weight. Sense the pressure of your feet against the floor and the sensations in your feet, ankles, legs, and whole body.
- Take a *kinesthetic moment*.
- Move to the floor and sit. Place your hands on the floor and begin to play with putting weight into your arms and hands and pushing away from the floor. Play with the amount of force you use against the floor. Let your whole body respond to these movements.
- You can move your hands anywhere you like on the floor: beside you, behind you, on either side. You can use your hands one at the time as you explore the ways *GRF* can ignite movement through your arms, torso, and whole body.
- At some point let the *GRF* carry your body over toward one side, and then move to lying down on the floor, in whatever way feels comfortable to you.
- Pause.
- Give yourself permission not to use your hands and feet as you explore ways to partner your weight with the floor's supportive force. Use this partner to make your way from one end of the room to the other.
- If your room is small, practice moving from one end to the other several times.
- The last time you travel the room, you can use your hands and/or feet. Practice *inclusive attention*.
- Pause. Take a *kinesthetic moment*.
- Gently move to standing. Notice your feet meeting the floor and allow your whole body to respond to *GRF*.
- Now practice walking to the other end of the room, noticing *GRF*, and the natural buoyancy of your body.
- Pause. Take a *kinesthetic moment*.
- *Spy back*. What did you discover about your body's resilience and its ability to move as your weight meets the ground?

In the Practice above you may have noticed that weight does not move through your body in a straight line. It follows the shapes of the bones and muscles. Whether you are moving or stationary, weight flows through your muscles, the four curves of your spine, up into your head, forward, backward, from side to side. *GRF* affects our bodies in all three dimensions.

As you become reacquainted with *GRF*, recognize that there is a natural give and take between up and down. Our bodies absorb the pressure of gravity and turn it into a force for activating our 3-dimensional muscles. When we allow our bodies to respond to *GRF*, we have a natural "up."

This interplay – between the weight of your body and the upward force of *GRF* – is import- ant when it comes to *Grounding* (KW) your body. When our bodies feel supported by the ground, when we feel connected to the ground, we have a stable foundation from which to move. When we are grounded, we allow our weight to move through us. *Grounding* is not downward pressure toward our feet. Instead, down and up balance each other out, and your *3-D body* is supported and movable. We can be grounded and buoyant at the same time.

Your foot has two counterbalancing qualities: *grounding* and buoyancy.

* The *grounding* aspect of your foot is a weight-bearing triangle: about 50% of your weight balances in your heels, 30% in the ball at the base of your big toe, and 20% in the ball at the base of your little toe.
* The arch of your foot rises from this triangle of support to offer you buoyancy in your foot/leg connection.
* The relationship of your foot to the ground and your whole body is a wonderful example of *ground reaction force* at work.

PRACTICE 8.3   ACCEPTING THE SUPPORT OF THE GROUND

As you practice, remember that your leg joints are movable. When you lift one leg, your joints in your standing leg remain balanced and connected. Your awareness of the *friendly facts* will help you avoid "locking" your leg joints.

Allow your standing foot and leg to support this action without *Over-efforting* (KW). This key word describes what happens when we interfere with the flow of move- ment through our muscles and joints.

When we *over-effort* we substitute tension and strain for allowing our muscles to work together. We literally use too much effort for the movement we want to make. As you practice, maintain an easy sense of connection with your bones and joints, and allow your weight to distribute throughout your standing leg.

* Stand in the space. Take a *kinesthetic moment*. Notice your whole body. Pause.
* Notice your feet in relation to the floor.
* Notice the 50/30/20 triangle of support in each foot and its relationship to the dome-like arch.
* Sense the way your heel, with its padding of soft tissue, releases back and down from your ankle, while your ankle eases forward and up. Your heel connects with with the arch of your foot.

- Working with one foot, roll through all the bones of your foot as you did in Practice 7.3, from your heel through your ankle, through the long bones of your toes. Enjoy the sensation of rolling to the tips of your toes, and back down to your heel.
- Notice that your leg is responding to this action, from your ankles to your knees to your hip joints. Practice several times.
- Pause. Switch to the other foot.
- Pause. Take a *kinesthetic moment*.
- Lift one heel, and rotate your foot and leg, turning your toes inward, as your heel moves outward, and then reverse, turning your heel inward and your toes outward. Experience the spiraling movements that link your ankles, knees, and hip joints.
- After several moments, pause and sense your whole leg and foot.
- Repeat on the other side. Pause.
- Sense the support of the ground through your whole buoyant foot, up into your ankle, leg, knee, thigh, pelvis, torso, arms, and head. Notice the interplay between gravity and the balanced support of your muscles and bones. Pause.
- From here, you are ready for anything. What would you like to do? Speak? Perform? Walk? Skip? Do "the Twist?" Experiment. Anytime you feel unsupported, pause and renew your sense of connection with the ground through your whole body.
- Pause. Take a *kinesthetic moment*.
- *Spy back*. What is it like to connect with the ground through your legs and feet while sensing buoyancy at the same time? How do *grounding* and buoyancy, as complementary qualities, support your whole body? How might this serve you as an actor?

PAUSE TO PROCESS floor support, *GRF*, and *grounding* before continuing to explore the rest of the chapter. Journal or talk with someone about your discoveries.

You can notice *GRF* in your daily activities: in my life, when do I feel most *grounded*? Ungrounded? Can I sense the movement of my muscles in simple activities?

Experiment with *grounding* and *GRF* as you speak or sing. Choose something simple, like a few lines from a poem or a children's song, such as "Row, row, row your boat." You may sense that the easy movement of weight through your whole *3-D body* will allow unwanted tension to fall away – freeing your breath and your whole creative self.

When you are grounded, and there is an easy exchange of weight between your feet and the floor, your whole-body benefits from *GRF*. You are a connected, supported whole. You also experience the dynamic power of *tensegrity*.

Tensegrity (KW)

Fluid movement is a result of the lively interaction of your muscles, tendons, and bones. As you know, from your Practices with your joints in this section, your body is not stacked like building blocks in a wall. A house is structured with static walls fixed on a foundation below, and the bottom of each wall bears significantly more weight than the top of the wall.

Your body, on the other hand, functions like a *tensegrity* structure.[4] Your bones act as stabilizers, and your elastic muscles, tendons, and ligaments counterbalance each other as you move. Your weight distributes throughout your body, and your movements are strong, yet springy.[5]

Tensegrity, a term coined by Buckminster Fuller, combines the words *tension* + *integrity*.[6] In your body, the bones provide a structure that both stretches and stabilizes the muscles. The *tension* of your tendons and muscles maintain the *integrity* of the bony structure. Bones and muscles cooperate to provide "effortless upright support."[7]

When we have a sense of *tensegrity* in our bodies, we can recognize that no movement happens in isolation – there is always a response from other muscles, however subtle. Effort is distributed throughout your whole body, as demonstrated by Figure 8.4.

This is great news! Your full weight is not bearing down on your feet, and you don't have to stack all your body parts and then hold them in place. Your body is dynamic, always changing! In fact, the idea that your body is static when you are standing actually interferes with creating a lively presence onstage (or anywhere else for that matter!). Our bodies are not designed to fight gravity by holding a stiff, forced posture. We are meant to respond to gravity by expanding into dynamic 3-dimensional upright balance.

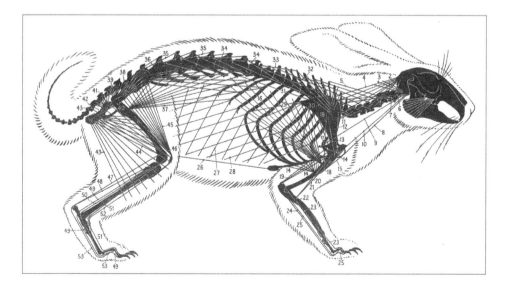

Figure 8.4 Tensegrity provides both stability and springiness.
Credit: Oxford University Press[8]

In the Practice below, the focus is on sensations in your muscles as you make simple movements. As you sense muscle movement, long-held tension can begin to fall away. Your muscles, bones, tendons, and joints are free to balance each other.

PRACTICE 8.4   **SENSING MUSCLE MOVEMENT**

The flow of your movements can be hindered or helped, depending on whether your muscles are holding weight or allowing it to move through your body.

This Practice awakens your kinesthetic sensitivity to muscular sensation. As you move your arms remember that no movement happens in isolation! Your muscles not only initiate movement, but balance and process changes in weight as you move. When you practice awareness, you can prevent unnecessary tension that might interfere with this natural flow.

I investigate: What can I discover about *tensegrity* and muscle movement?

- Pause. Stand. Take a *kinesthetic moment*. See the room around you. Breathe.
- Noticing the sensations as you move, bring your palms and fingers together in front of your chest. In yoga this is called "prayer position."
- Gently press your palms together. Allow the pressure to evenly distribute through your whole arm, shoulder, chest, torso. Give particular attention to letting movement happen through your arm joints. Your whole body supports this action. Breathe!
- Release your arms. Move them back to your sides. Pause. Take a *kinesthetic moment*.
- Move your hands together in front of your pelvis and loosely interlace your fingers, palms facing up (Figure 8.5). Pause.
- If you like, repeat this movement a few times, slowly. Sense the movement of the muscles through your whole arm and even into your back and chest. See if you can sense muscles lengthening, moving weight, and/or contracting to support these movements.
- With fingers still interlaced, slowly rotate your hands to turn your palms down toward the floor (Figure 8.5). Sense the changes in the muscles and joints throughout your whole arm structure and in other parts of your body as you make this movement. Breathe.
- Practice *inclusive attention* as you move.
- On an exhale, gently press your hands away from you, extending your arms (Figure 8.5). Sense your muscles lengthening as you stretch your hands away. Avoid tensing or *over-efforting*. This is a gentle movement.
- Practice *kinesthetic awareness*. Notice the sensations in your back and shoulders as well as your arms, as your muscles, tendons, and bones interact to support this movement. This is *tensegrity* at work.
- With your fingers still interlaced, raise your arms in front of you, then above your head, palms toward the ceiling (Figure 8.6). Using your *kinesthetic sense*, you may notice the muscles of the arms and upper torso lengthening or contracting as you move your arms higher.

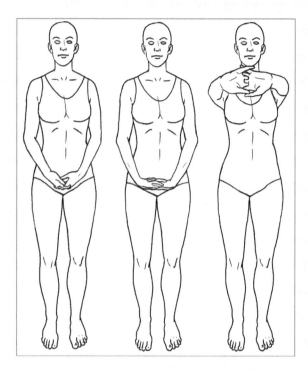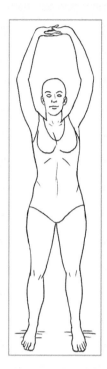

Figure 8.5   Figure 8.6

- Allow your whole body to participate in this movement. Allow the weight of your arms to spread through your whole arm, your shoulders, back, and chest and even into your torso and legs. Sense the length of your spine and the muscles surrounding it, as they activate to support your movements. Breathe.
- Allow your hands to separate and open your arms wide as you lower them until your hands rest at your sides. Notice the change in weight in your shoulders and torso, as you allow weight to redistribute through the muscles of the torso, shoulders, and arms.
- Pause. Note the sensations in your body.
- Repeat these movements a few times.
- Pause. Walk around the room, practicing *inclusive attention*.
- *Spy back.* You may have noticed that some parts of your body stabilize other parts as they move. What did you notice about the relationship of stability vs. movement in your body? What did you notice about your breath as you moved? How can awareness of *tensegrity* affect your movement?

In this exploration, you may have noticed that a movement can begin with your hands and move through your arms into your body. Rather than tightening your whole arm at once, the movement can "pass" from muscle to muscle through your joints. As you interlace your fingers and move your hands away from you, your arms follow.

Reverberation (KW)

When you move your body in a sequence like the one above, your whole body *reverberates* as your muscles, bones, and joints respond to support or yield to the movement. "*Reverberation* is ... the shimmer of action through the body ... [like] ripples [circling] out from a pebble dropped in a pond."[9]

GRF, *tensegrity*, and *reverberation* support your body's natural buoyancy, if you allow them to. This means that you can trust these natural forces to balance your weight. It isn't necessary to pull down to ground yourself or lift your weight to hold yourself upright. Instead, weight shifts easily through your body, as your strong bones and dynamic muscles provide just the right blend of tension and support.

When you allow *reverberation*, your muscles "give and take," as they share the effort required for movement, and release the effort as the movement reaches its natural conclusion. Cultivate *reverberation* by allowing movement to "ripple" through your body.

PRACTICE 8.5   **EXPLORE REVERBERATION**

Every movement *reverberates* throughout your whole body, so you can practice every time you move.

- Walking is a particularly reverberant activity. As your legs take and release weight, the action of your freely moving leg joints – the Big 3 – encourage movement to ripple through your legs, up into your torso, and down to the ground.
- You can observe *reverberation* in the natural world – trees and plants moving in the breeze, a prowling cat. There are great videos of animals in their natural habitat on YouTube.
- Placing your attention on *reverberation,* revisit Practices from previous chapters, such as throwing an imaginary ball (Practice 1.3) from Chapter 1. Play.
- Design your own Practice. Any time your muscles activate and release, you have the opportunity to experience *reverberation*.

Explore *reverberation* in your daily activities. Learn to recognize how much muscle effort you need – when your muscles need to work, and when they can rest. Each time you Pause, you can allow your muscles to recuperate from active exertion. Then, when the need arises, they – and every part of you – are ready to work efficiently and easefully.

Discover freedom of movement through the constant dance of gravity with your muscles, tendons, bones, and joints. You can learn more about this dance in Chapter 9.

PAUSE TO PROCESS Before continuing to Chapter 9, journal, discuss, and apply what you've learned as you go about your daily activities.

Key Words: *Grounding, Ground Reaction Force (GRF), Over-effort, Reverberation, Tensegrity*

Notes

1 Laban, Rudolf. *The Mastery of Movement.* Fourth Ed. Alton: Dance Books, Ltd. *1980,* 2011. p. 1. Print.

2 Dimon, Theodore. *Neurodynamics: The Art of Mindfulness in Action.* Berkeley: North Atlantic Books, *2015.* Print. p. 97.

3 Newton, Isaac, 1642–1727. *Newton's Principia: The Mathematical Principles of Natural Philosophy.* New York: Daniel Adee, 1846. Print. p. 83.

4 Dimon, p. 7.

5 Dimon, p. 7.

6 Fuller, Buckminster. *Synergetics: Explorations in the Geometry of Thinking.* New York: Macmillan Publishing Co. Inc, 1975, 1979. Print.

7 Dimon, p. 8.

8 Young, J.Z. *The Life of Mammals.* London: Oxford University Press, 1957. Figure 63. p. 135. Used with permission.

9 Pierce, Alexandra and Roger. *Expressive Movement: Posture and Action in Daily Life, Sports, and the Performing Arts.* New York: Plenum US, *1989.* Print. p. 141.

Connecting Your Joints and Your Whole Body

Movement can begin anywhere and travel anywhere throughout your body. When you allow movement to travel freely, you use less effort. Your movement becomes more fluid, clear, and nuanced. You move according to your body's design.

When you don't allow movement to flow, you interfere with your design. You can *over-effort*, and your movements can be disjointed and awkward, rather than flowing easily through your muscles and joints.

It's up to you. You can choose where a movement begins and how it travels through your connected body. In this way, you can honor your body's design for movement, and you allow *GRF*, *tensegrity*, and *reverberation* to work for you.

A Coordinated Whole

Everything you've learned in *YBK*, from Chapter 1 to this point, has led you to one fact: you are a coordinated whole. You can do anything from walking down the street to break-dancing, because your coordination is built-in and perfectly designed for movement.

The more you know about your actual design, the more you can move from a true place, and you can trust your *body-mind* to inform you. Even if the circumstances require a high degree of effort, like stage combat, your coordinated *body-mind* knows how to support you – the right amount of effort to use and the movement pathways that lead to a fully realized performance.

So far, we've looked at the parts that contribute to your coordination. You've learned about, and experienced, the *friendly facts* of your design, including 3-dimensionality, *kinesthetic sense*, joint action, head–spine relationship, breath, *GRF*, *tensegrity*, among many other aspects of your movement design.

But your coordinated *body-mind* is more than the sum of these parts. When every part of your *body-mind* works together, making movement choices becomes effortless: impulses arise that you never dreamed of, and you are free to create.

You are a single *body-mind* package, a coordinated whole.

Initiation and Sequencing

Every movement has a starting point. This is called *Initiation* (KW). Once a movement begins, it follows a pathway through your body. This is *Sequencing* (KW). For example, a movement can *initiate* at your hand and travel through your whole arm into your collarbone, shoulder blade, and torso. This *sequence* connects the parts of your arm and integrates the movement with the rest of your body.

Movement travels through your body in a variety of pathways and patterns. As it travels, you are connected with a sense of your whole-body coordination.

Movement Flows from Joint to Joint

In previous chapters you've explored the location, sensation, and unique range of movement in your joints. You have "inside knowledge" of your body's design for movement. Now you are ready to explore more about the interaction between your muscles, bones, and joints.

Initiation and Sequencing: Where Movement Begins and Where It Travels

- *Initiation*. Movement can begin anywhere in your body. You make the choice. When you clarify *initiation,* you become more specific in your physical life.
- *Sequencing*. Once a movement is initiated, it can travel along a specific pathway in your body. *Tensegrity*, *GRF*, *reverberance* ease the way for this natural flow.
- *Initiation* options can be from the edges of your body (such as head, hands, feet) toward the center, or from the center, outward. Many other options are possible.
- *Phrasing* (KW). Every movement has a beginning (*initiation*), middle (*sequencing*), and end (natural conclusion): a complete *phrase*. Then a new movement can be *initiated*, and the process can be repeated.
- Breath – all movement rides on the flow of your breath, which is also expressed in *phrases*!

Your body knows how movement *initiates* and *sequences*. Tune in. Listen to what your body "wants" to do: allow movement to *sequence* through your body in connected pathways. You may be tempted to try to work really hard to get it right, but remember: there are a lot of possibilities, and your body knows them all. You don't have to "make something happen."

Carolyn Adams, one of the great modern dancers of her generation, was a long-time member of the Paul Taylor Dance Company. In an interview at American University, she was asked how she sustained the unusual longevity of her career. Her reply: "I would rather MOVE than do any step right."[1] We can all take Carolyn Adams's advice when we explore movement. There are so many more possibilities when you don't try to "do it right."

Keep this advice in mind as you approach the Practices below. Sense your movement traveling the natural pathways through your body. Allow your coordinated *body-mind* to guide and support you.

PRACTICE 9.1   DISCOVERING MOVEMENT PATHWAYS

Though this Practice is gentle, the results are powerful. Sometimes we might associate strength with effort or tension. Many in our culture believe that if we aren't straining, we aren't working. (The "no pain, no gain" mentality.) Turn to martial artists and modern dancers as examples of lightness, ease, and strength. Recognize the strength and support you unleash when your movement sequences freely through your body.

As you approach this exploration, remember that your rolling, sliding, gliding joints and fluid muscles connect your bones. As each part is gradually included, you can sense the connections throughout your whole body.

I investigate: How do *initiation* and *sequencing* create ease in a simple movement?

Part I: Connecting Through Your Arms to Your Whole Body

Recognize that you have all the time you need to explore these movements. Work slowly and gently. Get to know your movement and your coordination on this fundamental level.

Practice *inclusive attention* and *kinesthetic sensing*. Recognize that the movements you make are supported by your whole body.

- Stand. Pause. Take a *kinesthetic moment*. Breathe.
- With your arms at your sides, turn the palm of one hand toward the front of the room.
- The next step is preparation for movement. Read through the whole instruction before moving.
- In a moment, you are going to bring your fingers to your shoulder through the rolling, gliding action of your wrist, elbow, and shoulder joints. Notice if any part of your arm starts to tighten as you think about moving. Pause, and let go of excess tension. Go back to the first step if you need to.
- Begin to move your fingers toward your shoulder. Let each part of your arm follow this movement: fingers, hand, wrist, lower arm, elbow, upper arm. Bring your fingers up to rest on your shoulder.
- Notice how joint action accommodates this movement. You do not need to lift your shoulder or tighten your neck to make this movement.
- Sense motion through the joints and muscles as you move. Pause when the upward movement reaches its natural conclusion with your fingers resting

gently on your shoulder. If it is comfortable for you, allow your elbow to rise toward the ceiling. You decide when the *phrase* is complete.

- After a moment, *initiate* a movement at your elbow joint, and *sequencing* from muscle to muscle and joint to joint, return your arm to your side. Pause.
- Repeat two more times. Notice that the *sequence* does not stop at your shoulder joint. Sense the connection down into your torso and the support of your whole body.
- Remember to complete each *phrase* before *initiating* a new movement. Check in. Practice *inclusive attention*.
- Repeat on the other side.
- If you like, try both arms at once. Pause.
- Have a walk around the space and let your arms be at ease as you move. Notice how they are connected to and supported by your whole body.
- *Spy back*. What was your experience as you allowed your movement to have a beginning, middle, and end? What was it like to choose an *initiation* point? How cooperative was your body with your choice? Did you notice any parts of your body wanting to take over the *initiation* or move out of *sequence*? In what way? How did your effort change when a part moved in sequence or interrupted the *sequence*?

Remember that all "parts" work together within your whole arm structure, and your arm structure is part of your whole body. Your head and neck remain free, and your whole body – your perfect design – organizes to support your movement.

Part II: Connecting Through Your Legs to Your Whole Body

This Practice focuses on the relationship of your feet, legs, pelvis, and whole body. From the ground up, your foot/leg/pelvis connection serves as a powerful support system for the rest of your body. We will explore each of these connections separately, and then link them together as one movement.

As you practice, remember Carolyn Adams's advice, "I would rather MOVE than do any step right."

Preparation: Body-Mind

This exploration invites you into the *balanced resting state*. If you like, place a book or towel under your head before you begin.

- Lie on your back with your legs extended, your arms resting on the floor. Take a *kinesthetic moment*.
- Breathe. Follow the directions below, as you allow this simple *sequence* to support you as you move into the *balanced resting state*: on your exhalation, let your abdomen soften, as you slide one foot/heel toward your sit bone, allowing your knee to ease upward, and your foot to rest on the floor.
- Do the same with your other foot/leg.
- Now your feet are resting on the floor and your knees point toward the ceiling. Pause. Breathe.

- Sense the connection of both feet with the floor, your knees released upward, and the weight of your upper leg releasing down into your hip joints and pelvis, easing your lumbar spine.
- Notice that this relationship of your legs to your body allows your whole back to release into its full length and width, receiving more support from the floor.
- Take time to rest and breathe.

Clarifying: Legs and Pelvis[2]

This exploration continues from the Practice above. It allows you to experience the movement of your legs and pelvis as they interact. You are clarifying this important relationship, so that each part can play its specific role as you move. Allow your joints and muscles to be in tune with each other as the movement *sequences* through your body.

This Practice prepares you for the two Practices that follow.

- Continuing from the Practice above: Pause.
- *Initiating* with your heel, slide your right foot away from your body until your whole leg lengthens to rest on the floor. Pause.
- Return to the *balanced resting state*, initiating the movement at your right heel. Sense the back of your thigh lengthening as your knee rises toward the ceiling and your heel slides along the floor.
- Repeat with the left leg. Remember to allow these movements to "ride on the flow of your breath." As your foot slides up, sense the continuous rolling and folding at your hip joint.
- Let your lower back release into the floor, as your muscles lengthen in response to these movements. As you move, continuously sense the changing connections through the muscles and joints of your whole leg.
- Continue to practice, alternating legs. Use your *kinesthetic sense* to awaken your experience of sensation. Enjoy the sensation of folding/unfolding at the hip, knee, and ankle as the movement *sequences* through your whole leg. Broaden your awareness to include your whole body.
- After several rounds, pause.

Connections: Pelvis, Feet, Legs, and Body

In this Practice, you build on the preparation above, *initiating* a subtle movement from your feet, that moves through your legs to your pelvis. Your whole body *resonates* with this movement.

If you have a book under your head, remove it for this practice.

- Continuing to rest and breathe, notice the floor under your feet, and your whole back and head resting on the floor.
- Gently pressing your feet against the floor, allow subtle movement to *sequence* upward through your leg joints, causing your pelvis to roll slightly. Your pubic

bone eases upward toward your navel, and your pelvis eases toward the floor. This is not a lift away from the floor, just a slight rolling motion.

- Release the pressure in your feet and allow your whole body to return to a *balanced resting state*.
- Pause.
- Repeat this movement several times. Allow *ground reaction force* to work for you. This is a *sequence* that *initiates* with your feet pressing gently against the floor, and *reverberates* through your legs into your pelvis, causing your pubic bone to roll upward toward your navel.
- You will begin to notice a small, easy rocking motion in your pelvis, as you alternately press and release your feet against the floor.
- Pause. Take a *kinesthetic moment*.

Initiation and Sequencing: A Slight Roll-Up

This movement may be familiar to yoga practitioners. Though it is similar to the bridge pose, this *sequence* only brings your sacrum and pelvis away from the floor, while your upper lumbar and thoracic spine lengthen along the floor. Approach this Practice with "beginner's mind."

- Continue to rest and breathe with your feet, pelvis, and whole body resting on the floor.
- Once again, easily press your feet into the floor, and allow the movement to go through your legs in an upward direction toward your pelvis.
- As your pelvis rolls back, pubic bone toward your navel, allow your pelvis and lower spine to roll up from the floor. If your ribs come off the floor, you've gone too far.
- This is a subtle movement that ripples through your spine as it moves away from the floor.
- Release the movement and rest your whole back on the floor. Breathe.
- Explore this movement several times. It involves a continuous flow of movement from your feet through your legs, pelvis, and lower spine.
- Rest and breathe. Play with gently pressing your feet into the floor and allowing that *initiating* movement to ripple upward through your legs, pelvis, and lower spine.
- Repeat several times, noticing the rippling and rocking motions of your feet, pelvis, spine.
- Pause. Take a *kinesthetic moment*.
- To rise from the floor, roll to your side and gently press your hands on the floor to come to sitting. Move to standing, maintaining an awareness of your whole leg within your whole body. Pause.
- Walk through the space and celebrate the freedom and connection through your legs and body. Practice *inclusive attention*.
- *Spy back*. What did you discover about your legs? The *part within the whole*? Could you experience connection from your heel to your pelvis and into your torso? Describe your experience.

These simple movements give you the opportunity to experience joint action and connection through your whole leg without the added burden of bearing weight or balancing while standing. You are waking up these *parts within your whole* body. If they have been "asleep" for a long time, you may have found the movements challenging and the connections elusive. Revisit this Practice in a day or two, and note if your experience has changed, as you continue to awaken your *kinesthetic sense* and your *body-mind connection*.

> *PAUSE TO PROCESS* Practice *constructive rest*, journal, or take a walk before continuing. For creative Practices in *initiation* and *sequencing*, visit Appendix I, Practice 9.8 and 9.9.

In the next Practice, you can enjoy a whole-body *initiation* and *sequencing* experience.

PRACTICE 9.2   SEQUENCING THROUGH HEAD–SPINE–PELVIS

Part I

- Stand. Pause. Breathe. Take a *kinesthetic moment.*
- Sense your top joint, the A-O joint, behind your nose and between your ears. Gently nod your head, as if you are saying "yes." If it helps, put your index fingers in your ears.
- Lower your hands if you were using them. Gently turn your head side to side.
- Make small circular movements with your head, sensing the rolling, sliding, gliding action of your A-O joint.
- Pause. Sense your long, flexible spine; allow your head to gently rest on the A-O joint.
- Let your eyes gently move right, allowing your head to follow, and then your spine and pelvis.
- As your whole torso spirals to the right, your legs will follow, and turn to the right as well. Continue this *sequence*, until you turn all the way around and you are facing front again.
- Pause. Breathe. Take a *kinesthetic moment.*
- Repeat the *sequence* to the left.
- Pause. Breathe. Take a *kinesthetic moment.*
- Repeat several times. Pause after each *phrase.*

Part II

In this Practice, your rocking, rolling joints allow *initiation* and *sequencing* to support a powerful pathway of full body movement.

- Pause. Stand. Take a *kinesthetic moment.* Breathe.
- Sense the support of the ground.
- *Initiate* a *roll-down* with a subtle, arc-like rolling action at your A-O joint.

- As your head leads, your spine and pelvis follow in *sequence*, followed by your Big 3 leg joints.
- Your arms go along for the ride.
- Continue to accept the support of the ground for these movements.
- The crown of your head is now facing the floor. Your whole body is connected from your head to your sit bones. Breathe.
- To *initiate* your return to uprightness, become aware of the floor under your feet. Allow GRF to support your *sequential* movement as your pelvis, spine, head, and arms return to balance.
- Your whole body has followed a natural *sequential* pathway, and you are standing upright.
- Pause and breathe.
- Have a walk through the space. Enjoy sensing the *sequence* of movement through your whole connected body. Pause.

Part III

- Have a walk around the room, enjoying the central role of your spine as you move.
- As a variation on the Practice above, you can make turns, circles, and spirals by continuing the *sequence*: eyes, head, spine, torso, whole body. Enjoy the experience of "head leads, and body follows."
- Pause. Take a *kinesthetic moment*.
- *Spy back.* How does an awareness of *initiation* and *sequencing* affect your movement? What did you discover about *sequencing* through your head–spine–pelvis? What did you learn about your spine's central role in movement?

This whole-body Practice is always available to you, opening up your joint connections and the pathways that allow movement to *sequence* through your body.

Now you can explore a wider range of movement, *initiating* from anywhere in your body. From rolling and gliding, to rotating and spiraling, you can sense the connected pathways throughout your body, and experience its creative possibilities.

PRACTICE 9.3 MOVEMENT CAN BEGIN ANYWHERE AND GO ANYWHERE

Give your body free reign. Put on some flowing music, like Mark O'Connor's "Appalachia Waltz,"[3] and gently explore *initiation* and *sequencing* possibilities.

- Have a walk around the room. Notice yourself, your breathing, your movement.
- Come to pause. Stand. Breathe. Sense the floor, and the surrounding space of the room. Take a *kinesthetic moment*.
- *Initiate* a movement with a fingertip, letting it move anywhere you like. Allow the hand, wrist, arm, then shoulder, and each part of your body (even your toes!) to respond in a fluid *sequence*, following the movement pathway of the finger. You may find yourself turning, rising, dropping, leaning, as you follow this *sequence* through to its natural end.

- You can begin to *initiate* movement from anywhere in your body, allowing the *sequencing* pathway to unfold. One part of your body **leads** and then the other parts follow. When you sense the ending of one *sequential* pathway through your body, find another part of your body to *initiate* a movement – a new *Body Lead* (KW) – and continue the journey.
- Play with different *body leads*: hands, feet, head, pelvis, spine, elbows – whatever occurs to you – and allow that movement to *sequence* through your body. If you lead with your head, for example, the *sequence* will take you through your spine, ribs, arms, pelvis, legs, and feet. Be an explorer – discover the pathway movement wants to take, as each *part within the whole* "follows the leader."
- After exploring several *sequences*, or when the music ends, pause. Take a *kinesthetic moment*.
- Have a walk through the space. Practice *inclusive attention*.
- *Spy back.* What did you discover when you initiated movement from different places? Were you able to let movement "begin anywhere and go anywhere?" What was that like? Was your walk at the end of the Practice different than at the beginning?

When you pause at the end of this exploration, you may experience that stillness is also dynamic. Your bones and joints are adjusting; your resilient muscles are responding as they make connections and support your upright body. From this lively stillness, you are ready to follow any movement impulse. As your body follows its natural movement pathways, old restrictions fall away. New choices can emerge.

You are **designed for movement!** Through the *friendly facts* and the Practices, you've experienced in this Section, you have developed a deeper understanding of your body, its amazing design, and how it moves:

- Every aspect of your skeletal system is connected from joint to joint.
- Your muscles activate continuous *sequential* movement through your body.
- Your body is perfectly designed for balanced support in response to gravity.
- All parts of you have a specific role to play within your whole coordinated *body-mind*. (And they love to play together!)

When you walk through your day, you are practicing your body knowledge with each step. Through *phrasing* you can develop clarity and refinement in your movement. *Initiation* and *sequencing* create easeful, connected movement in your everyday life and onstage.

With the support of a more accurate *body map*, you have strengthened your *body-mind connection.* Embrace the incredible design of your living, breathing, moving body: you have the physical support you need to dive into new creative territory.

In Section III, you can discover more connections between your thoughts and your movement.

- Take all the time you need as you move your attention up through your body. Use your *kinesthetic awareness* as you sense your feet … ankles … lower legs … knees … upper legs … pelvis … back … stomach … chest … arms … wrists … hands … neck … head … jaw.
- Allow your *kinesthetic awareness* to inform you about sensations and relationships in the body. Notice each *part within the whole*.
- Pause and take a *kinesthetic moment*. Breathe.
- Noticing the effect of these gentle thoughts on your body, broaden your awareness to include the space around your body – above you, beside you, in front of you, under and between your legs.
- Be aware of your whole body in the space, as you gently roll to your side, press your hands against the floor, and bring yourself to sitting.
- Pause and see the room. Sense your *3-D body* and the space around you.
- Gently come to standing. Take a *kinesthetic moment*.
- Take a walk, noticing the effects of this Practice. Pause.
- *Spy back.*

Ideally, you can practice Constructive Rest three times a day, most particularly before bed at night. We cannot emphasize strongly enough how this Practice can free you from unwanted tension and give you freedom to move. You can take this sense of ease into your daily activities, and most importantly, into rehearsal and performance.

Helpful tip: if you would like details on why this position puts your back at rest, read Dr. Theodore Dimon's chapters on "Muscles and the Role of Awareness" and "Directing and the PNR System" in his excellent book, *Neurodynamics* (Berkeley: North Atlantic Books, 2015).

Many Alexander Technique teachers have written about and recorded directions for *Constructive Rest*. Here are a few resources for further study:

Imogen Ragone, Constructive Rest, a guided talk-through http://bodylearning.buzzsprout. com/382/70686-alexander-technique-constructive-rest-guided-talk-through.

Glen Park, *The Art of Changing*. London: Ashgrove Publishing, 2000. Ms. Park also has a CD with a guided constructive rest practice. https://glenpark.uk/

Michael Gelb, *Body Learning*. New York: Henry Holt and Company, 1994.

What You Think Is What You Get

In our bodies, there are so many enemies which stop our creative process, very often in such secret ways that we do not know why we cannot act a certain part. But if the body is free, then I am free to forever act.[1]

Michael Chekhov

Any thought, every thought, affects our movement and how we relate to the world. We have a thought, "I'm too hot," and we move to turn on the fan. Simple thought, simple movement response. On another, less obvious level, thoughts about our work, relationships, and self-image influence our bodies, our breath, and the way we stand, sit, walk, and play.

You are a whole person. Your body and mind are seamlessly intertwined, and your ideas about beauty and body image are strong movement influences. Sometimes, our thoughts subscribe to cultural bias about our bodies. We are unconscious that ideas, like "buns of steel," and "no pain, no gain," can become part of our movement life and actually interfere with our ability to move.

When we want to move, our brain sends signals to our body and our body responds. However, as you may have discovered in Section II, if your brain is misinformed, your body may not move according to its design. The way we think about our anatomy, accurate or not, determines our movement.

In this section, you can explore the connection between thought, movement, and change. Just as knowing your anatomy increases your movement choices, recognizing limiting thoughts can also expand your options. Margaret Goldie, who trained as a teacher with Alexander, put it this way, "People don't recognize the power of thought. They think that they cannot change, and they go on doing their own thing and they do not change. They do not realize that what you think is what you get."[2]

Body-mind wholeness requires *Dynamic Thinking* (KW). These thoughts support your movement, because they are receptive to your *kinesthetic sense,* and they are grounded in the truth about your body and how it moves. Your body and mind are in sync: you have permission to move, instead of holding fixed positions.

The two-way street between your body and mind offers more than a simple understanding of your body's anatomy and function. *Dynamic thinking* clarifies your movement impulses and gives them "somewhere to go." The power of your *body-mind connection* can unleash a flood of creative expression that goes beyond mere intelligence or physical ability.

As Michael Chekhov says, when you free your *body-mind*, "then the talent feels it is free."[3]

Key Word: *Dynamic Thinking*

Notes

1 M.G. "Chekhov on Acting: A Collection of Unpublished Materials (1919–1942)." *The Drama Review: TDR*, vol. 27, no. 3, 1983, p. 69. *JSTOR*, www.jstor.org/stable/1145460. © Michael Chekhov Studio. Used with permission of the Deirdre Hurst du Prey Estate.

2 Goldie, Margaret. In Robb, Fiona. *Not to Do*. London: Camon Press, 1999, p. 94.

3 Chekhov, Michael. *Lessons for the Professional Actor*. New York: Performing Arts Journal Publications,1985, p. 116.

Your Body-Mind Connection CHAPTER 10

We sit and walk as we think.

Mabel Todd, from her book, *The Thinking Body*[1]

Every thought you have produces a movement *Response* (KW) in your body, and your thoughts are informed by your physical sensations. Your *body-mind connection* is essential to making movement choices.

Sometimes your thoughts and movement are *stimulated* by something that is happening around you: you see a speeding car coming toward you, and you jump to get out of the way. Sometimes you *respond* to an internal *Stimulus* (KW): you feel dizzy and decide you need to lie down and rest. Every movement we make is a *response* to a *stimulus*.

In this chapter, you can become aware of the ways in which thought *stimulates* a *response* in your body. You can expand your ways of thinking and open the door to a wider variety of movement choices.

Thought Creates Movement: Stimulus and Response

Your thoughts determine the world you see, and your body *responds* to that world. How you carry yourself – your sense of freedom or restriction, ease or struggle – is determined by your thinking.

Your thoughts define your *Body Image* (KW), the way you see and understand your body: its abilities, how it moves, the way it looks, and others' perceptions of it. Thoughts like, "I'm just a klutz," can define your movement and even become a self-fulfilling prophecy. Misinformation and a limiting *body image* can result in restricted movement and cause injury as well.

Limiting thoughts can also lead to dull acting. Your restrictive thinking becomes an internal *stimulus* for making the same choices over and over. In fact, you aren't really making choices at all; you are at the mercy of your habitual thoughts and movements.

However, as you learned in Section II, your well-informed *body-mind* and the *friendly facts* can clear up these limiting factors, promote *dynamic thinking* and expand your movement options. Awareness is key: if we don't know, we can't make another choice.

As you explore the Practice below and the ones that follow, *dynamic thinking* can be your guide. You can free your whole self from limiting thoughts and become the mover you were born to be.

PRACTICE 10.1 THREE THOUGHTS/THREE BODIES

You can experiment with these three thoughts on your own or within a group setting under the guidance of a leader.

Part I: Inner Response

Sit in a chair or lie on the floor, close your eyes, and take time to notice your kinesthetic responses to each thought.

Close your eyes when each thought is introduced, and notice your inner, kinesthetic responses in your body. These internal responses are the focus of this Practice, rather than larger movement responses.

Warm up by moving through your joints and practicing *kinesthetic sensing* before beginning this Practice.

1st thought

- Pause. Breathe. Take a *kinesthetic moment*.
- Allow yourself time to notice your first responses to this thought: **"I've got to do it fast and get it right."**
- What do you notice about your breathing? Do you sense any changes in the rhythm of your breathing?
- Are you experiencing any increased tension in your body? If so, where?
- Are you experiencing emotions? What are they?
- Take another moment to breathe and release this thought.
- Open your eyes. *Spy back.* Share your experience with the group.

2nd thought

- Pause. Breathe. Take a *kinesthetic moment*.
- Allow yourself time to notice your first kinesthetic response to this thought: **"I'll never get it right, and I give up."**
- Do you notice changes in the rhythm or the depth of your breathing?
- Is the level of tension in your body increasing? Decreasing?
- Are you experiencing emotions? What are they?

- Take another moment to breathe and release this thought.
- Open your eyes. *Spy back.*

3rd thought

- Pause. Breathe. Take a *kinesthetic moment*.
- Allow yourself time to notice your first kinesthetic response to this thought: "I'm at ease with myself, and I have time."
- What changes do you notice about your breathing?
- What kinesthetic sensations do you notice in your body?
- Are you experiencing emotions? What are they?
- Take another moment to breathe and release this thought.
- Open your eyes. Pause. Take a *kinesthetic moment*.
- *Spy back.* Can you describe any differences between your experience after this thought, and the two thoughts you previously experienced? How did your thoughts affect your breathing, emotions, and muscle tension?

Each of the thoughts in this Practice is a *stimulus*, and your body's reaction to it is your *response*. Note that these happen almost simultaneously. That's because they aren't separate! Your body and mind respond as a unified whole.

The first two thoughts lead to a type of thinking that is "result-oriented." It leads to movement that is based on the outcome of the activity – in particular, "getting it right." This is *End-gaining* (KW), placing our attention on results, rather than process.

With the third thought, you open the door to a new level of awareness, one that offers an inclusive sense of yourself and the world around you. Your *body-mind connection* is the underpinning for this experience in *dynamic thinking*.

As actors, we must recognize that *end-gaining* is the opposite of *dynamic thinking*. When we *end-gain*, we are more likely to fix our thoughts on a desired result. We lose our sense of the moment-to-moment unfolding of the action of the play. Our thoughts of getting to the goal have taken over, and our *stimulus* is no longer what is happening onstage at each moment. Instead, we are *responding* to an expectation. *Body-mind communication* is disrupted, and we are left with a disconnected mind that is trying to manufacture a performance, instead of responding with our whole self to events as they occur.

Practicing *dynamic thinking* interrupts the *end-gaining* cycle. You can explore this relationship in the Part II below.

Part II: How I Think Is How I Move

In this Practice, you can recognize how your thinking affects the way you perform a simple activity: crossing the room.

As each thought is introduced, notice your physical response, and let it inform your choices.

Thought I

- Stand. Pause. Notice the room around you. Breathe. Take a *kinesthetic moment*.
- As the thought is introduced, take a moment to notice your physical response. Allow the thought to inform the way you cross the room. Follow your impulse.
- **I have to cross the room fast and I have to get it right.** Follow the impulse created by this thought and cross the room.
- When you reach the other end of the room, pause. Allow the thought to release.
- Breathe. Take a *kinesthetic moment*.
- *Spy back.* What did you experience?

Thought II

In this Practice, two different thoughts will be introduced. After the first thought, simply notice the response created in your body, but do not move. Then with the second thought, follow the impulse created by the thought and cross the room.

- Stand. Pause. Notice the room around you. Breathe. Take a *kinesthetic moment*.
- First thought: **I have to cross the room fast and I have to get it right.** Notice your internal response to this thought, but do not cross the room.
- Pause. Release this thought. Stand and breathe.
- Second thought: **I can sense myself and the space around me as I cross the room.** Cross the room.
- When you reach the other end of the room, pause. Allow the thought to release.
- Breathe. Take a *kinesthetic moment*.
- *Spy back.* What did you experience?

Thought III

- Stand in the space. Pause. Notice yourself and the room around you. Breathe. Take a *kinesthetic moment*.
- When you receive the first thought, notice your internal response, but do not cross the room.
- First thought: **I have to cross the room fast and I have to get it right.**
- Pause. Release this thought. Stand and breathe.
- Second thought: **I'm free to choose my own way of crossing the room.** Cross the room any way you like.
- When you reach the other end of the room, pause. Allow the thought to release.

- Breathe. Take a *kinesthetic moment*.
- *Spy back*. What differences did you notice when crossing the room with Thought I, Thought II, and Thought III? What was your experience of replacing one thought with another? How might this Practice serve you as an actor?

This Practice allows you to experience the difference between *end-gaining* and *dynamic thinking*. Your thoughts create your world, and you move within that world. If your thoughts are limited, your movement world is limited. Each time you recognize your thought and notice your response, you have a choice about how you think and how you move. Through your *dynamic thinking*, you always have options.

Your *body-mind connection* leads you toward *dynamic thinking* and away from *end-gaining*. In Chapter 11, you can put your *dynamic thinking* to work as you address *body myths*.

"I have overcome this idea of being 'right' and have allowed myself to just indulge in the 'process' of this art form. That, in itself, has allowed me to be freer in many of the roles that I have done this semester from Bernick to Hamlet, Dromio, and Imogen. I have loved merging my body with these roles and can't wait to see what next semester brings."[2]

Clifton, acting student, Florida Atlantic University

PAUSE TO PROCESS Journal, discuss, and practice in your daily life.

Key Words: *Stimulus, Response, Body Image, End-gaining*

Notes

1 Todd, Mabel. *The Thinking Body*. New York: Horizons Press, 1937, p. 1.
2 From a student journal. Used with permission.

Body Myths vs. Anatomical Facts

CHAPTER 11

"The Truth will set you free"[1]

In Section II, you learned that your understanding of your body's anatomy influences the way you move. If your *body map* is clear, then you move according to your design. Movement sequences cleanly through your body, and you move with fluidity and ease.

In addition to our *body maps*, cultural bias also influences our movement. For instance, a heavily muscled body is a symbol of strength in our culture. However, big muscles do not necessarily translate to power onstage. In fact, they can interfere with your movement, the balance of your body, and limit the array of roles that are available to you as an actor.

You can clear up misinformation through the *friendly facts* of your design and by recognizing the difference between what is real and what is cultural bias. Ask yourself: what is my true design? How can it serve me in the creation of a variety of roles?

In the Practice below, we explore the limitations of old, unworkable ideas about how we move, and replace them with freedom, the freedom of choice available from our true design. As Alexander Technique teacher Aileen Crow says, "To achieve [performance] goals, it is necessary to tune in specifically to the body's intelligence, to value it, and to listen to what it is saying."[2]

PRACTICE 11.1 VARIATION: THREE THOUGHTS/THREE BODIES: TO TELL THE TRUTH

The way we think we are *supposed* to move can interfere with our body's natural balance. The exploration below illustrates how our thinking can influence movement choices, and how our movement choices can also influence our thinking.

With the group standing in a circle, the leader suggests the following thoughts, one at a time, allowing each person to have a kinesthetic experience of each before adding the next one.

Although this Practice is designed to be experienced within a group setting, with a little imagination, you can explore it on your own as well.

Thought #1

As you follow the leader's directions, allow yourself to experience the physical sensation resulting from each individual thought, as they add up to a whole-body experience.

- Stand. Pause. Breathe. Take a *kinesthetic moment*. Notice the ground under your feet.
- "Hold your head up high"; then add
- "Lift your chest and pull your shoulders back"; now add
- "Straighten your spine"; add
- "Tuck your pelvis"; add
- "Grip the floor with your feet."
- Take this whole pattern into walking. You may need to subtly soften the pattern in order to move.
- Meet others and shake hands.
- Pause. Release the pattern and return to balance. Take a *kinesthetic moment*.
- Look around the room. If you like, take a walk around the space. Breathe.
- *Spy back*. What was your experience of moving into this pattern, and what was it like to relate to other people from this pattern? Was anything familiar to you about this pattern?

This pattern of interference with your body's natural balance, shortens your muscles, puts pressure on your joints, and stiffens your spine. It illustrates what happens when your thoughts cause you to over-tighten your muscles and brace yourself into an upright position.

Thought #2

- Stand. Pause. Breathe. Take a *kinesthetic moment*. Notice the ground under your feet.
- "Let your head feel heavy"; then add
- "Drop your chest"; now add
- "Let your arms feel heavy"; add
- "Let your legs become heavy."
- Take that whole pattern into walking, meeting others and shaking hands.
- Pause. Release the pattern and return to balance. Take a *kinesthetic moment*.
- Look around the room. Take a walk around the space. Pause. Breathe.
- *Spy back*. What was your experience of moving into this pattern? What was it like to relate to other people from this pattern? Was anything familiar to you about this pattern?

This pattern illustrates a moment of collapse, which creates pressure on your rib structure and interferes with your breathing and the balancing curves of your spine.

Thought #1 and #2, bracing and collapsing, are two basic postural patterns that are widespread in our culture. These thoughts create postural patterns that interfere with your body's natural buoyancy. In your daily life, see if you can recognize these patterns, or parts of the patterns, in yourself and others.

Experience #3

As you follow the leader's directions, sense the physical *response* resulting from each suggestion, as they add up to a whole-body experience. Unlike the previous two thoughts, stay with each suggestion for a couple of minutes before moving on to the next one.

- Pause. Notice yourself and the ground under your feet. Breathe.
- Begin to juggle imaginary balls (choose your own color).
- Next, juggle wooden pins.
- Complete the experience by juggling fire torches.
- Pause, and take a *kinesthetic moment*.
- Take this experience into walking and greeting others in any way you choose. Pause.
- *Spy back*. How was this experience different from the first two? What did you notice about your ability to make choices with Thought #1 and #2 and Experience #3?

This third experience is different from the others. Thoughts #1 and #2 interfered with the *friendly facts* of your design. Your thinking put your body in a fixed position, making it hard to move. By contrast, in Experience #3, your thoughts created a series of imagined circumstances. The act of juggling invited your whole body into a lively balance, and your body responded to the moment.

Dynamic thinking places your attention on your creative process, not results or fixed ideas: you are free to create in the moment. Then, everything you have explored and discovered about your body's design is effortlessly available to you, supporting every choice you make.

Recognizing Our Body Myths

> When you stop doing what you have always done, then you are ready to make a change.[3]
>
> Marjorie Barstow, Master Teacher of the Alexander Technique

Change is possible when we recognize our harmful ideas about how we move. Through the explorations of joints, muscles, and *initiation/sequencing*, you've discovered so much about the truth of your body's design. Now, you can apply it, as you learn to recognize *Body Myths* (KW): cultural or personal beliefs about your body that interfere with freedom of movement. You have the power to change the way you move.

> "Stand up straight"
> "Hold your head up high"
> "Shoulders back"
> "Lift your chest"
> "Tuck your pelvis under"
> "Grip the floor with your feet"

Sound familiar? Growing up, many of us heard these postural myths from well-meaning parents and teachers. From these fixed positions, it's hard to move, as you discovered in Practice 11.1 above. Here's the good news: there are other options. Read on!

"Stand Up Straight" and "Hold Your Head Up High" vs. The Dynamic Poise of Your Head with Your Spine

"Stand up straight" and "Hold your head up high" interfere with the dynamic support of your whole body. These are *body myths*, because many, many people believe this is how they are supposed to move, though the truth is, they are actually interfering with their body's natural balance. These *body myths* require you to lock your body into a position and hold it there, and they isolate and separate parts of your body. *Body myths* do not honor the *part within the whole*.

Here are some reminders of the *friendly facts* of your "design for movement." If you want to refresh your memory, revisit Chapter 5.

* The four curves of your spine counterbalance each other, supporting an even distribution of weight through your whole spine and torso.
* Your head balances delicately on the two sturdy grooves in your top vertebra, the atlas. The A-O joint is located behind your nose and between your ears.
* The spongy, fluid-filled discs in between each vertebra create flexibility and buoyant movement in your whole spine.

"Hold your head up high," and its equally misinformed cousin, "Imagine a string pulling up from the top of your head," severely restrict the balance of your head at the A-O joint. It interferes with your sense of *3-dimensionality*. If you are pulling upward, the counterbalancing direction, down, doesn't function. The power of the other dimensions – sagittal and horizontal – are diminished as well.

The thought, "Stand up straight," will cause your back muscles to shorten and over-work, compressing the vertebrae, the spongy spinal discs, and the spinal nerves. The shortened muscles will pull your head back, causing it to add even more downward pressure on your spine.

The facts: The poise of your head and the flexibility of your spinal curves promote a lively balance and ease in your movement. The weight of your head is distributed throughout your whole, movable spine. These facts, plus your *dynamic thinking*, allow you to choose how you stand, without stiffness or excess tension.

The Practice below offers you an experience of the true relationship of your head and spine with your whole body. With these *friendly facts* as your foundation, your body can be upright and balanced when standing. You can let go of the *body myth*: "stand up straight."

Approach the explorations throughout this chapter with courage and an open mind. As Alexander Technique teacher and creative thinker Michael Gelb writes, "Be willing to experience something beyond habit."[4] Observe, Explore, Discover: enjoy the rewards of challenging *body myths*.

PRACTICE 11.2 **YOUR BUOYANT HEAD AND SPINE**

Your spine and your whole body are buoyant, because of your built-in *tensegrity* and the natural force of *GRF*. Your head balances delicately on the A-O joint, with the support of your whole spine.

It is also helpful to remember that your body is about 60% fluid! Enjoy the flow, as you practice "seaweed spine."

- Stand. Close your eyes. Sense the ground under your feet. Breathe.
- Sense the full length of your spine and your head balancing easily at your A-O joint. Remember that your A-O joint slides, glides, rocks, and rolls.
- Expand your awareness to include your whole body.
- Think of your spine as a piece of seaweed underwater. The wavelike action of the water is moving your "seaweed spine."
- Your head and other parts of your body also respond to this wavelike action.
- Allow the waves to gently move your spine side to side.
- Then forward and back.
- Then rotate to the left and to the right.
- Notice how your head rides easily on top of your spine, and your movement rides on the flow of your breath. Allow these movements to affect the rest of your body.
- See if you can sense the individuality of each vertebra as it moves. Notice the springy quality of your spinal discs and the *part within the whole*.
- You can allow a "wave" to affect your head and let the movement *sequence* through your spine.
- Play with *initiating* various places: the "wave" can begin anywhere and go anywhere.
- Pause. Take a *kinesthetic moment*.

- Open your eyes and allow your head to "poise" on top of your movable spine. Sense the dynamic relationship of your whole head, your whole spine, and your whole body. Accept the support of the floor.
- Take a walk around the room. Practice *inclusive attention*.
- *Spy back*. What did you notice about your spine as you moved in this way? Your spine in relationship to your whole body and your breath? Were you able to sense the *part within the whole*? In this experience, what did you notice about your thinking, and how is it different from "stand up straight?"

> "The day I discovered I didn't have to 'Stand up straight' anymore was one of the great days of my life. It felt like taking off a straitjacket, and I could finally move."
> Anne, dancer and Alexander student, American University[5]

Your spine provides both a powerful support system for your whole body, and a wide range of movement possibilities. Our *dynamic thinking* about our head/spine relationship connects us to its amazing movability and strength.

"Shoulders Back" vs. Your Movable Arm Structure

As you remember from Section II, the multiple joints in your arm and shoulder structure offer a wide range of movement possibilities, supported by your whole body. If you need to refresh the *friendly facts* of your design, revisit Chapter 6.

- Your arms connect with your collarbones and shoulder blades, which rest buoyantly on your ribs, and receive support from your whole body.
- Your arm joints – from your collarbones and shoulder blades to your fingertips – are among the most highly movable and expressive structures in your body.

"Pressing your shoulders back" (or down) creates excess tension and pressure in your spine and ribs, restricts your arm movement and breathing, and causes imbalance in your whole body.

In the Practice below, let your *dynamic thinking* and your true *body map* guide the way to an experience of the buoyant relationship of your arms with your ribs, spine, and whole body.

PRACTICE 11.3   YOUR BUOYANT ARM STRUCTURE

As you explore the action of your collarbones, shoulder blades, and arms, be sensitive to the way you are *initiating* the movements. Avoid over-tightening your muscles and be specific about where each movement begins.

Part I: Waking up Your Shoulder Blades and Collarbones

• Stand. Pause. Sense your feet against the floor. Sense your buoyant, supportive spine and your whole body. Take a *kinesthetic moment.* Breathe.
• Take a walk around the room. Practice *inclusive attention.* Pause.
• Bring your attention to your whole arm structure, from your collarbones and shoulder blades through your arm all the way to the tips of your fingers and thumb.
• Begin a very small, slow pulsing movement, *initiating* with your collarbones and shoulder blades, near your shoulder joints. Gently "shrug your shoulders," allowing this pulsing motion to travel along your collarbones and shoulder blades, softening your neck muscles and releasing excess tension in the muscles.
• Continue to practice *inclusive attention.*
• If you find your neck or shoulders are becoming tight, try a smaller, slower movement, and remember to allow the movement to sequence through your shoulders, neck, back, and chest.
• Explore moving each shoulder one at the time.
• Experiment with a little swing forward with a shoulder and then back. Your arms go along for the ride.
• Now explore easy circular motions (forward, up, back, down). See if you can sense your bones moving; this encourages your muscles to do less. Practice *inclusive attention.*
• Are you breathing?
• Pause and sense the liveliness of your shoulder structure and its relationship to your torso, arms, and whole body.

Part II: Connecting Your Whole Arm Structure

The simplicity of this Practice, which you first encountered in Chapter 6, offers you the time and space to experience the *sequential* connections through your whole arm structure. As you practice, remember that your arm structure is supported by your whole body and your thinking.

• Pause. Stand. Notice your feet on the floor and the room around you. Take a *kinesthetic moment.* Breathe.
• Bring your attention to your whole arm structure, including your hands and fingers. Your arms are at your sides.
• Slowly and gently *initiate* a movement at your hand, turning your palm to face the front of the room. This rotation will *sequence* in a spiraling motion through your radioulnar joints, your elbows, and your shoulder joints.
• Allow this *sequence* to include your collarbones and shoulder blades. No movement happens in isolation.
• Now reverse this movement and rotate your palms inward to face the back of the room, letting the rotation *sequence* through your entire arm/shoulder structure.

- Spend a few moments exploring this spiraling *sequence* through your whole arm structure. Notice how these movements affect your whole coordinated body.
- Savor the subtle, gentle flow of these movements, as they are supported by your body. Practice *inclusive attention*.
- Pause and sense the relationship of your movable arms to your whole body.
- Once again, rotate your palms outward, allowing the movement to spiral through your whole arm to your shoulder joints. Allow your fingertips to *initiate* a movement through space, toward the side, to bring your arms up toward the ceiling.
- Sense the movement *sequence* from your hands through your whole arm and shoulder girdle, into your whole body.
- After a moment, allow your fingertips to lead as you open your arms out to the side and return your them to your sides. Allow your arms to rest. Pause.
- Letting your fingertips lead, gently explore other directions and possibilities for your movable arm-shoulder structure. Pause.
- Take a walk around the space. Practice *inclusive attention*. Pause.
- *Spy back*. What did you discover about your arm structure? Your arm structure to your whole body? How is this experience different from "shoulders back?" How might this experience change your thinking about your arm structure?

The thought, "shoulders back," isolates your arm/shoulder girdle from the rest of your body; your arms are no longer supported. The *truth* of your design connects your whole arm structure with your whole coordination. Far from slouching, your buoyant arm and shoulder structure expands and comes into easy balance with your body.

PAUSE TO PROCESS before continuing to "Lift your Chest." Take a walk, dance, journal, draw, or have a conversation with a friend about your discoveries in Practices 11.1–11.3.

"Lift Your Chest" vs. The Poise of Your 3-Dimensional Rib Structure

Your rib structure – spine, ribs, and sternum – has over 40 joints. This design offers you an amazing range of movement possibilities. If you need a refresher on ribs, revisit Chapter 3, "Your Moving Breath."

- Your 24 beautifully rounded ribs are jointed with your thoracic spine in the back, and most of them connect with your sternum in the front.
- Rib movement supports your breath.

"Lift your chest" causes restriction in your spine and ribs, and interferes with the ongoing, active rhythm of your breath. It also immobilizes your arm structure and stiffens your spine.

PRACTICE 11.4 YOUR BUOYANT, 3-DIMENSIONAL RIB STRUCTURE

In this Practice, you can sit on a chair, stool, or exercise ball. Sit toward the front of the chair to leave space for movement.

Remember the balance of your pelvis, and your supportive sit bones on the seat of the chair. If you need a refresher about sitting, revisit Practice 7.2.

- Sit with your hands on your thighs. Close your eyes. Breathe.
- Take a *kinesthetic moment* to notice movement between your ribs and spine as you inhale and exhale. Your arms will also respond to this movement.
- Revisit the wavelike movement of your "seaweed spine." Notice how your ribs also move in all directions.
- Allow yourself to enjoy this oceanic experience of your rib, spine, whole-body connection.
- Pause. Notice the gentle movement created by your breathing.
- Gently come to standing. Notice the buoyancy of your rib structure and its relationship with your whole body.
- Have a walk around the space. Practice *inclusive attention*. Pause.
- *Spy back*. What did you notice about your rib structure? Were you able to sense the *part within the whole*? How is this experience of standing different from "lift your chest?"

Knowing and experiencing your movable ribs frees your whole torso to balance and breathe. As your thinking becomes more accurate, your movement becomes freer and more connected to the whole.

"Tuck Your Pelvis Under" vs. The Balance of Your Pelvis with Your Legs

Your pelvis is at the "geographic center" of your body, halfway between the top of your head and the soles of your feet. To refresh your memory about the pelvis-leg connection, revisit Chapter 7.

- Your pelvis balances in an upright direction with your sit bones directed toward the ground.
- It links your torso with your legs via your hip joints, which are at the side of your pelvis.
- At the hip joints, your legs roll in relation to your pelvis, and your pelvis rolls in relation to your legs; they support each other.
- Your pelvis supports and balances your upper body. Your feet and legs support your pelvis and your whole body from the ground up.

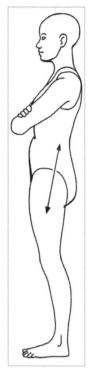

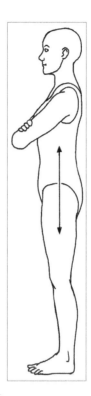

Figure 11.1a Tucking your pelvis flattens your spinal curves and interferes with the balance of your hip joints.

Figure 11.1b Your balanced pelvis is supported by your legs and your spine's natural curves.

To "tuck your pelvis under," is to shorten and tighten the deeper muscles of your pelvis, which then interferes with freedom and poise in your hip, knee, and ankle joints. This pattern pulls down on your spine, your abdomen, and your lower back and causes chronic tension in your inner thighs and glutes. The result of this thought: every aspect of your coordinated body is compromised.

PRACTICE 11.5 YOUR DYNAMICALLY POISED PELVIS

Your pelvis is movable. So are your legs, arms, head, and whole torso. Enjoy exploring the flow of connection through your whole body, as you allow your pelvis to find its natural balance.

- Pause. Bring awareness to your whole body and the room around you. Breathe. Take a *kinesthetic moment*.
- Bring your attention to your feet.
- Gently begin to shift your weight on your feet, letting these small movements affect your legs and pelvis (and everything else).

- Allow the weight shifts to travel through your whole body.
- Start slowly with small weight shifts, side to side. Then shift your weight forward and back. Let your knees and ankles and all the joints of your feet respond to these movements.
- Begin to allow your pelvis to *initiate* easy weight shifts. You may find your pelvis making circles or figure 8s, with your whole body following the lead of these shifts.
- Enjoy the movability of your pelvis-leg-foot connection. Sense the *reverberation* of these movements as they *sequence* through your whole body.
- Let your "seaweed spine," your head, your buoyant ribs, and your movable arms get in the flow.
- Pause. Note the dynamic balance of your pelvis as it poises over your legs and feet. Expand your awareness to your whole body. Take a *kinesthetic moment*.
- Take a walk around the space. Enjoy the connection and flow in your whole movable body. Practice *inclusive attention*. Pause.
- *Spy back.* What did you notice about your pelvis/leg/foot connection? Were you able to sense the *part within the whole*? How is this experience different from "tuck your pelvis under?"

Your hip joints allow your pelvis, legs, and feet to interact in a weight-supporting, yet dynamically movable relationship. As thought and movement work together, you connect with your whole body: your *body map* unites with the truth of your design. You are "coming home" to yourself.

"Grip the Floor with Your Feet" vs. Your Movable Legs, Ankles, and Feet

Because your feet make direct contact with the ground, they are a source of support and provide valuable sensory information to the rest of your body. If you want to refresh your knowledge of the feet, ankles, and legs, revisit Chapter 7.

- Because your ankles and feet have 20+ bones and 30+ joints, your feet and ankles are highly movable and responsive to changes in balance and weight.
- Your feet and ankles **receive** the support of the floor via *ground reaction force*.

When you "grip the floor," your feet and ankles become rigid and block *GRF*. Your whole body loses its ability to respond quickly and easily to change.

PRACTICE 11.6 YOUR LIVELY LEGS, FEET, AND ANKLES

- Pause. Bring your awareness to your whole body, as you stand and sense your breathing.

- Notice the support of the ground under your feet, sensing the balancing poise of your ankles with your legs and body.
- Begin to explore the movement possibilities at your ankles, shifting your body forward and back, and side to side.
- Explore shifting your weight on your feet in different directions. Allow your ankles and your whole body to respond to these shifts.
- Now begin to shift the weight on your feet in a circular pattern, allowing your body to circle in response to this movement. Your ankle and foot joints continuously respond to these movements.
- Enjoy the movability of your foot, ankle, and whole-body connection.
- Pause. Stand. Take a *kinesthetic moment*. Notice the liveliness of your feet and ankles and their connection to your whole body.
- Take a walk around the space. Enjoy the connected flow of your feet, ankles, legs, and whole body. Practice *inclusive attention*. Pause.
- *Spy back*. What did you notice about the relationship of your whole foot/ankle with your whole body? How was your experience of standing different from "grip the floor with your feet?"

In the Practices above, you experienced the truth of your design through movement. *Spying back* connects your thinking to what you experienced in your body, completing the *body-mind connection*. Once this connection is made, thinking and moving become one. And "the truth will set you free."

Counteracting *Body-Myths*

When you encounter a *body myth*, return your thoughts to your body's true design. Just remembering *the part within the whole* can go a long way toward counteracting these misconceptions.

Myth: "Hold Your Head Up High" or "Stand up Straight" **Think**: My head balances on top of my four balanced curves of my spine, supported by my whole body.

Myth: "Pull Your Shoulders Back"or "Lift Your Chest" **Think**: I can sense the horizontal dimension of my collarbones and shoulder blades, as I allow my chest and upper back to widen. My whole body supports my arm structure.

Myth: "Tuck Your Pelvis/Tail" **Think**: My lower spine lengthens and my tailbone drops toward the floor as my pelvis balances over my legs. My whole body balances around my whole spine.

Myth: "Grip the Floor With your Feet" **Think**: I sense my movable feet and ankles, and my whole body accepts the dynamic support of the floor.

Debunking the Myths: Your Elegantly Unbalanced Joints

> *The human body, being an unstable structure, is constantly in motion, constantly vibrating like a tuning fork around the point of mechanical balance but never fully settling fixedly upon it.*
>
> Irene Dowd, *Taking Root to Fly* [6]

How do you let go of *body myths*? You tune in to your body and listen.

Your body knows it is a coordinated whole, not a collection of parts. Your body knows it is meant to move, rather than rigidly adhering to a fixed position.

The facts of your design, plus your *dynamic thinking*, can undo the harmful *body myths* you encountered above. In the two Practices below, you can explore the "antidote" to *body myths*: a *body-mind* that is poised for movement.

PRACTICE 11.7 **3 PLACES OF POISE**

There are three major joints in your body that interact with each other to connect your whole coordinated body: The A-O joint, the hip joints, and the ankle joints.

We call these "places of poise," because they are delicately movable and yet powerful. Their placement at the top, middle, and bottom of your body gives them a special role to play in your balanced body.

Enjoy exploring the movability and balance available to you through your "elegantly unbalanced joints." [7]

Your A-O Joint

As you play with the movement possibilities of this joint, remember that the center of gravity of your head is forward and upward from the A-O joint. Enjoy the movability of this slight state of imbalance as you explore the poise of your head.

- Pause. Allow the ground to support you in standing. Take a *kinesthetic moment*. Breathe.
- Practice *inclusive attention* as you sense your head balancing at the A-O joint.
- Gently explore the movement possibilities of your elegantly unbalanced head. Play.
- Pause and notice the lively relationship of your head to your whole body.

Your Hip Joints

- Sense the dynamic relationship of your head with the four counterbalancing curves of your spine and your pelvis.
- Allow your whole head and body to balance over your legs at your hip joints.
- Allow your pelvis to move forward and back, side to side, and around, exploring the rolling action of your hip joints.

- Sense the connections from your pelvis up to your head and down to your feet.
- Your arms go along for the ride!
- Pause and notice the liveliness of your hip joints with your whole body.

Your Ankle Joints

- Sense the lively relationship of your head, pelvis, and legs all the way through to your ankles and feet.
- Sense your adjustable ankle joints and their relationship to your lower leg and foot.
- Sense the ground under your feet.
- Begin to delicately shift your weight on your feet forward and back, side to side, and in circles. Your heels and toes adjust to these shifts, but do not lift away from the floor.
- Allow your whole body to respond to these movements in your feet and ankles.
- Pause and notice the lively relationship of your ankles with your whole body.

Connecting 3 Places of Poise: The *Roll-Down*

- Sense the ground under your feet. Breathe.
- As you stand, notice the buoyant connection of your 3 places of poise.
- Your head begins the movement of the *Roll-Down* with a subtle rolling action at your A-O joint in a gentle arc.
- As your head rolls, your neck lengthens in the back and your whole body begins to follow this fluid, arc-like movement.
- Your body follows in a streamlined sequence, connecting the 3 places of poise, until you are upside down, balanced over your legs and feet from your hip joints.
- Pause. Breathe.
- Sense your head–spine–pelvis connection. *Initiate* a rolling action, starting at your pelvis. Your pelvis rolls back and up with your sit bones draping down, and the rest of your body follows in a *sequence*.
- Allow *GRF* to pass through your feet, ankles, and whole leg, supporting the rising action of your torso and head.
- When you come to standing, notice the balance of your whole body, and the lively connection between your 3 places of poise. Pause. Take a *kinesthetic moment*.
- Take a walk around the room. Enjoy the balance and freedom in your whole connected body. Pause.
- *Spy back*. What did you discover about the interaction of your movable ankles, hip joints, and A-O joint? How does this experience differ from your experience of the *body myths*? How can these 3 places of poise serve you as an actor?

When we acknowledge and link these 3 Places of Poise, we have a stronger sense of our body's movability and its built-in connections. Our movement develops qualities of flow and resilience. *Body myths* interfere with the movability, balance, and connection we call **poise**. The 3 Places help us to restore it.

The Ultimate Myth

There is a super *body myth* that is global in its effect on your balanced body. This misconception tops all the others, because it is so widespread in our culture, and because it locks up most of your body, including your breath. Can you guess what it is?

"Pull Your Stomach In" vs. Your Movable Torso

Your stomach is an organ that is part of the digestive process. However, in our culture, we refer to the whole abdominal area as *stomach*. This is a complex area of muscles and organs.

- Your abdominal muscles are arranged in layers. The more superficial muscles are primarily for movement.
- The deeper muscles, closest to your spine, are strong postural muscles, supporting your weight and the balance of your spinal curves.
- Some abdominal muscles begin at your ribs and reach to your pubic bone.

When you "pull your stomach in," you grip in the front of your lower torso, which shortens your muscles, and upsets the balance of weight in your whole body:

- Your back muscles and spine are compressed.
- The movable joints that connect the bones of your torso – spine, ribs, pelvis, and legs – lock into a fixed position.
- Your diaphragm is restricted by the tight muscles surrounding it, and your rib cage and upper spine can no longer move freely in response to your breath.
- Your head no longer delicately balances at the A-O joint, because your whole spine is locked in position, which also affects the movability of your pelvis, legs, feet, shoulders, and arms.
- Your jaw tightens.

You are immobilized!

Consider an alternative: your layers of abdominal muscles are designed to work with the balanced curves of your spine when you sit, stand, and move. The deeper abdominal muscles and the front of your spine provide weight support for your torso. When you are upright, your long abdominal muscles lightly engage, but do not grip.

PRACTICE 11.8 YOUR STRONG, MOVABLE TORSO

In this Practice, think of your stomach as the area between your ribs and pelvis at the front of your body. Some abdominal muscles begin at your ribs and attach to your pubic bone. Others wrap around your sides, connecting your front and back.

These layers of muscles, when lengthened, engage naturally. They work with your back, 3-D spine, ribs, and pelvis to provide upright dynamic balance for your whole 3-D torso.

I investigate: What can I discover about the dynamic relationship between my stomach and my whole body?

- Begin by lying down on the floor in the *balanced resting state*. Pause. Breathe. Take a *kinesthetic moment*.
- Allow your body to rest, and your muscles to lengthen. Trust the support of the floor. Note that your body is 3-D and your stomach is a *part within the whole*.
- Remove the book from under your head. If it is comfortable for you, slide your heels away from your sit bones, until your legs lengthen along the floor.
- Now, laugh – start with saying ha-ha, ha-ha-ha, ha-ha-ha-ha, and continue until laughs begin to rise up in you.
- Let your laughs grow into big, fun belly laughs. Feel your belly jiggle, your spine lengthen, and your stomach muscles let go.
- Allow your body to respond, as your whole body laughs! Take pauses as needed.
- After laughing a minute or two, pause. Breathe. Take a *kinesthetic moment*.
- Allow your legs to lengthen and rest on the floor. Sense your whole back against the floor and the full length, width, and depth of your 3-D torso, including your stomach, ribs, spine, collarbones, and scapula.
- Notice your head, neck, arms, and legs as they rest on the floor.
- Gently slide one heel toward your sit bone until your foot rests on the floor and your knee rises toward the ceiling. Repeat with the other foot and leg.
- Pause. Notice the full length of your 3-D torso – especially your stomach area – and its connections to your neck, head, legs, and arms.
- Gently roll to your side. Use your arms to bring yourself to sitting, then stand. Pause.
- Allow your 3 places of poise to inform your sense of balance. Honor the full length of your 3-D torso and its balance with your pelvis and legs, head, neck, and arms.
- If your abdominal muscles start to grip, invite them to lengthen. Allow your weight to be centered in your spine and deep postural muscles. In this way, your stomach muscles can be lightly engaged. Recognize that your whole 3-D torso is one *part within your whole 3-D body*. Pause.

- Practice a *roll-down* and return to uprightness. Pause.
- Take a walk and enjoy the balance of your 3-D spine, the ease of your whole 3-D torso within your whole *3-D body*. Practice *inclusive attention*. Pause. Take a *kinesthetic moment*.
- *Spy back*. What did you discover about allowing your stomach area to work with your whole 3-D torso? Could you sense your abdominal muscles engage but not grip?

When you experience the balance of your torso with your legs, you can discover the connections between your stomach area and your spine, ribs, and pelvis. These connections can provide support for your whole body, offering greater ease in all your movement.

Counteracting the Ultimate Body Myth

Part within the whole helps clear up the misconceptions that lead to *body myths*.

Myth: "Pull in your stomach" **Think:** I can allow my abdominal muscles to lengthen, widen, and deepen within my whole torso. I can accept the support of my whole *3-D body*.

As actors, we are asked to explore new experiences every time we take a role. We willingly enter the world of the play, however unfamiliar it may be, and step into a character. As you explored the Practices in this chapter, you may have discovered that letting go of *body myths* required you to take a strange new role. Perhaps you felt unsettled as you explored different ways of thinking and moving. Maybe you let go of certain beliefs about yourself and the world around you.

Whatever your experience, be sure that you *PAUSE TO PROCESS body myths*: journal, discuss and play with your discoveries in your daily life.

In the next chapter, you can discover new approaches to integrating all the parts of your body within the whole – providing more support for letting go of *body myths*! You can explore *dynamic thinking* in a whole new way. By directing your thoughts more intentionally, you can bring together all that you have learned about your coordinated *body-mind*.

Key Word: *Body Myth*

Notes

1 John 8:32

2 Crow, Aileen. "The Alexander Technique as a Basic Approach to Theatrical Training," in Rubin, Lucille S. *Movement for the Actor*, New York: Drama Books Specialists, 1980, p. 4.

3 Barstow, Marjorie. *Teacher Training Class. Summer Residential Course in the Alexander Technique.* Lincoln, NE: University of Nebraska, July, 1984.

4 Gelb, Michael. *Body Learning*. New York: Henry Holt and Company, 1994, p. 57.

5 Used with permission.

6 Dowd, Irene, "Visualizing Movement Potential," in *Taking Root to Fly*. New York: Contact Collaborations, 1981, p. 2.

7 Deborah Caplan, "Skeletal Appreciations Inspired by Alexander." The Alexandrian, vol. III, no. 3, Spring/Summer, 1984.

Your Primary Coordination

"Take a gambling chance. When you're ready to learn what you don't know, then you can begin."[1]

Marjorie Barstow

F.M. Alexander developed a unique approach to how we think, move, and function in our daily lives and our specialized activities, such as acting. As a young actor, he discovered that what he thought was an isolated vocal problem, laryngitis, was actually an overall tension pattern that permeated his whole body. Over time, and with patience, he discovered that there is a primary reflex for balance in all of us. He named his discovery the primary control.

Growing up on a horse farm in Australia, Alexander could recognize that when the rider pulls back on the reins, the horse is momentarily stopped. The horse's head, neck, back, and legs become locked in a rigid stance. When the rider releases the reins, the horse's neck frees, and his head begins to release, lengthening his spine, freeing his legs, and allowing him to move again.[2]

As Alexander explored his own vocal issues, he recognized a similar pattern in himself: when he began to speak, his neck tightened, disrupting the natural relationship of his head, spine, and whole body. Over the course of several years, Alexander observed himself in a mirror as he spoke, and he developed a process for awakening and accessing his natural pattern of release and balance. He learned to allow his neck muscles to lengthen, which freed his head to balance on his spine. This gentle change triggered a response throughout his spine, which then allowed his back to lengthen and widen, freeing his legs and arms. He recovered his voice. And he discovered a new way of moving and speaking based on this sense of coordinated wholeness in his body.

This is the truth of our body's design, our birthright. We are born with this built-in response, which activates and connects our whole body when we move. Alexander called the primary control "a master reflex in coordinating the whole psychophysical organism."[3] A whaaaaat, you say? Though the words are old-fashioned, what he is saying is so applicable to our lives in this very moment: we have a built-in response that coordinates our whole *body-mind*.

Over the years, many Alexander teachers have adopted the term *Primary Coordination* (KW) instead of primary control.[4] We prefer *primary coordination*, because it reflects the comprehensive *body-mind* change that occurs when your neck frees, your head balances on your A-O joint, your back lengthens, and your whole body connects in a complete, dynamic relationship.

You are a coordinated whole! When you use your *dynamic thinking* to access your *primary coordination*, old habits and interferences fall away and natural balance is restored. You don't have to control the *PC* or think hard to "make" your body access it, nor do you need to figure out every little habit that is interfering with your *PC*. Instead, your *dynamic thinking* begins the process, and then, your body's built-in coordination takes over. Your body finds its own way, and "the right thing does itself."[5]

Thought and Your Primary Coordination

Throughout this section, we've explored the connection between the way you think and the way you move. You've learned how your thoughts can interfere with your body's natural coordination and how to change your thoughts to reflect the truth about your body's design.

The Practice of recognition, pausing, and choosing another thought, is the process Alexander discovered more than a hundred years ago. He realized that "what you think is what you get." When he found himself in his habitual pattern of tension – tightening his neck and pulling his head back and down – he recognized he had to find a way to change this.

Based on his discoveries, he developed a new approach to disarming the force of habit. He learned to **pause**, which opened a space and gave him time to recognize where he was and what he was sensing. This "open moment" allowed him to make a choice about what could happen next. Over time, he developed a series of *dynamic thoughts* which guided him out of his pattern of tension:

- I wish my neck to be free,
- to allow my head to poise [delicately] forward and up,
- so that my back can lengthen and widen
- and my arms and legs to follow.[6]

This series of thoughts was totally in tune with his body's natural coordination, and his body responded by returning to its perfectly organized support and balance: his *primary coordination*. When Alexander accessed his *PC*, he discovered that he was able to move and speak with energized ease and connection. Marjorie Barstow, a graduate of Alexander's first training for teachers in 1934, called this process the *Sequence of Directional*

Thinking (KW).[7] She noticed that each of these thoughts, when linked together, awaken and enliven our *primary coordination*.

Notice that Alexander's series of thoughts is *dynamic*. They do not lead to a fixed position or holding in any way. The *sequence of directional thinking* is about relationship, connection, and movement. There is no mental image, like "stand up straight," that is then imposed onto your body. Instead, your thoughts work with your *kinesthetic sense*. Alexander learned that there is nothing to do but leave space for something new to emerge. That "something new" is the truth about your body's coordination, which is why these thoughts are so powerful.

Open communication between body and mind is a prerequisite for connecting with *primary coordination*. As we mentioned above, your *kinesthetic sense* is particularly helpful in the process. In the Practice below, awaken your senses and connect your body and mind in preparation for exploring the *sequence of directional thinking*.

PRACTICE 12.1 CONTINUOUS COMMUNICATION: BODY AND MIND

This exploration prepares your *body-mind* to practice the *sequence of directional thinking*. It awakens your *body-mind connection* and all your senses, including your *kinesthetic sense*.

- Stand. Pause. Sense your *3-D body* and breath, see the room around you. Sense the support of the floor. Take a *kinesthetic moment*. Breathe.
- Practice *kinesthetic sensing* (Practice 1.4), raising and lowering each arm, placing your attention on the sensations without analyzing or describing them. Allow your mind to receive information from your *kinesthetic sense*. Pause.
- Sense your head balancing on your A-O joint, supported by your whole spine. Gently explore the sliding, gliding, rolling movement at this joint, by making small movements with your head. Pause.
- *Initiate* a movement from your fingertips, and gently bring your hands up toward your neck. Place your three middle fingers to rest on the sides of your neck, letting your thumbs and pinkies rest where they feel most comfortable.
- Slowly turn your head from side to side, noticing the movement of the neck muscles under your fingers; also sense the movement *kinesthetically*.
- Explore tilting your head in different directions. Sense these movements *kinesthetically*, and notice the sensations of your neck muscles contracting and lengthening under your fingers.
- Move your eyes up toward the ceiling and allow your head to follow your gaze, then move your eyes to look down, following the movement with your head.
- Slowly move your eyes in different directions, allowing your head to follow. Notice the movement under your hands and *kinesthetically*.
- Let your arms come to rest at your sides. Pause.
- Take a *kinesthetic moment*.

- Explore *initiating* more head movements, this time without using your hands on your neck muscles. Notice the effect of these movements on your whole spine. Allow the movements to sequence through your whole spine, torso, arms, and legs.
- Close your eyes and begin to practice "seaweed spine." Enjoy the sensations of shifting your weight and allowing movement waves to flow through your spine. Your head, arms, and legs flow along with this movement.
- After a few moments, pause. Take a *kinesthetic moment*.
- Practice *inclusive attention* as you walk around the space. Pause. Take a *kinesthetic moment*.
- *Spy back*. What did you notice about the way your neck and whole spine responded to moving your head? What was the effect of exploring head–spine–torso movement with your whole body?

This Practice encourages receptivity between your body and mind. With your body, mind, and senses fully awake, you are ready to practice *the sequence of directional thinking*.

PRACTICE 12.2   CONSTRUCTIVE REST: THINKING, SENSING, AND ALLOWING

In this practice, you can explore the *sequence of directional thinking* while lying in *the balanced resting state*. This is another step in developing your *body-mind two-way communication*. It's a dialogue: your thoughts are suggestions, your body responds, and those responses inform your understanding of the way your body works as a whole.

Each part of your body knows its relationship to the whole. You do not need to "make something happen" by physically manipulating your body. Your body responds because your thoughts are in sync with its true design. By practicing non-interference, you allow your body's natural balance to unfold in its own time.

The floor supports your body, so you cannot lose your balance. You are free to experience the re-balancing that occurs when your body responds to your *dynamic thinking*. You can trust that you will create real change through your thinking and your *body-mind connection*.

Enjoy this powerful experience of active non-doing. A light open awareness allows your muscles to lengthen and expand. It is best if your eyes remain open in this Practice, as your eyes offer valuable information about changes as they occur. If you find yourself narrowing your attention or "concentrating hard," you can return to *inclusive attention*.

- Move into the *balanced resting state*. Pause. Breathe. Take a *kinesthetic moment*.
- Notice your *3-D body*, and the continually changing shape of your torso as you breathe.
- Sense the weight of your body against the floor. Allow the floor to support your body and the books to support your head.

- Practice *inclusive attention*. Take a few moments to sense your toes, then move your *kinesthetic awareness* to your feet, moving your attention through your whole body to the top of your head.
- Pause. Notice your breath. Take a *kinesthetic moment*.
- Practice *inclusive attention*, as you bring your attention to your neck. Sense its three dimensions and its cylindrical shape.
- Sensing your whole body, begin a series of *dynamic thoughts*:
    - I wish my neck to be free
    - to allow my head to delicately rotate forward and out,
    - so that my back and whole torso can lengthen and widen,
    - and my arms and legs can follow.
- As your neck frees, you may sense your head releasing out, away from your body, and rotating slightly, releasing pressure from your spine.
- Allow each *part* to find a new relationship *to the whole* as it opens into its full 3-dimensional shape.
- Sense your whole body as you think of your right shoulder moving away from your left shoulder … your left shoulder moving away from your right shoulder … and widening across the upper part of your arms.
- Sense your feet and pelvis supporting your legs. Think of your thighs lengthening, releasing out of your pelvis, and your knees moving forward and away.
- Pause. Take a *kinesthetic moment*.
- Practice *inclusive attention*. Sense your whole body and the space around your body – above you and below your feet, beside you, under and between your legs, in front of you.
- Be aware of your whole body in the space, as you gently roll to your side, use your arms to assist you in bringing yourself to sitting, and then rise to standing. Pause. Take a *kinesthetic moment*.
- Take a walk, noticing the effects of this Practice. Pause.
- *Spy back*. What happened in your body as you offered each *dynamic thought*? What happened as you practiced the *sequence of directional thinking*? How did an awareness of your *primary coordination* affect you as you were lying down, standing, and walking?

This Practice is an experiment in **allowing** something new to emerge. Your thoughts are not demands forcing your body to comply. Instead, they offer gentle guidance – a sort of map, directing you to the treasure hidden beneath the armor of habits.

Though it is quite calming, the *PC* is not a relaxation technique. When your *PC* is actively guiding your movement, your nervous system is calm, and your *body-mind* is in an alert state of readiness, responsive to any stimulus that arises. For you, as an actor, this means that you are truly in the moment, and ready to respond authentically and creatively to the action of the play as it unfolds.

Your Body and Mind: A Continuous Dance

When Alexander developed the *sequence of directional thinking*, he was describing internal sensations and movement pathways that he had experienced many times. He discovered that a specific thought could *initiate* this subtle *sequence* of movements, a "chain reaction," that led his body into an extraordinary coordinated balance.

Alexander learned to trust his *dynamic thinking* and *body-mind communication* to bring about the change he was seeking. If he tried to "make" his body execute the *sequence*, the chain reaction did not occur. He found that he had to **allow** it to happen. His body was returning "home;" it knew the way, and he learned not to interfere with the process.

Learning to access his *primary coordination* completely revolutionized the way Alexander used his body. Through the *sequence of directional thinking*, you, too, can *initiate* a series of inner movement impulses that help you regain your natural poise.

Reading about *primary coordination* is only the beginning. Now is the time to become a movement explorer. You can practice on your own and make your own discoveries. You can find an Alexander Technique teacher to assist you. You can also enjoy exploring this *sequence* through the Practices in this chapter. Experiment!

Below are a few insights that can help you make a *body-mind connection* with the *sequence of directional thinking*:

- "I wish my neck to be free ..." This thought is the first step in releasing excess tension in your neck muscles, and it is the gateway to releasing all other excess tension. In Chapter 8, you learned that excess tension occurs when weight is **held** in a muscle, rather than **moving** through it. Tense muscles are shortening and *over-efforting*; they can't "share the load." "Neck to be free" invites your neck muscles to remember they are *part* of a *whole* – it's OK to allow the muscles to lengthen and share the load.
- "… to allow my head to move forward and up …" This thought encourages a delicate rolling action at the A-O joint. (See Figures 12.1a and 12.1b.) The thought continues to invite movement throughout your neck and begins to take pressure off your spine.
- "… to allow my back to lengthen and widen and deepen …" This thought encourages 3-D movement through your whole spine: up to down, back to front, right to left, and vice versa. It continues the process of releasing excess tension from your entire torso and in your head/spine relationship.
- "… and my arms and legs to follow." With this thought, your collarbones and shoulder blades can release outward. This encourages movement through the rest of your arms – from your shoulder joints to your elbow joints to your wrists, hands, and fingers.This thought also allows your arms to respond to the lengthening and widening of your back.Your pelvis connects and balances with your whole spine, your thighs release out from your hip joints to your knees, and down your lower legs to your ankles and feet in relation to the floor.

- Though this *sequence* sounds like it happens step by step, your body responds by reorganizing and balancing itself very quickly. As Alexander put it: "all together one after the other."[8]

This beautiful example of *dynamic thinking* connects you with your *primary coordination* and informs all your thinking about your movement. When your body is in balance, you are free to act!

The Startle Pattern (KW)

You may be asking, "What does forward and up mean?"

"Forward and up" is the opposite of "back and down," a pattern that occurs when the muscles at the back of your neck tighten. From this pattern of tension, also known as the *Startle Pattern* (KW), "neck to be free" allows your whole head to rise and rotate in an arc-like movement.

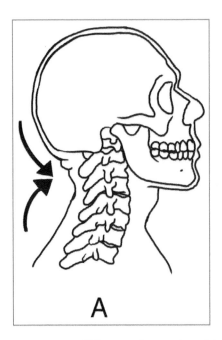 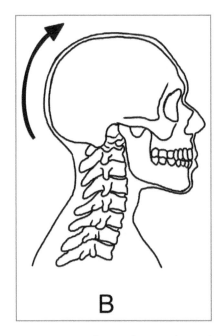

Figure 12.1a When neck muscles tighten, your head is pulled back and down.

Figure 12.1b As neck muscles release, your whole head rotates forward on the A-O joint.

PAUSE TO PROCESS You may want to take a walk, journal, or talk over your discoveries with someone before exploring *PC* and *body myths*.

Primary Coordination and Body Myths

Primary coordination stands in stark contrast to the *body myths* explored in Chapters 10 and 11. *PC* offers a **dynamic** relationship. *Body myths* offer static positions. Worst of all, *body myths* layer a fixed pattern on top of your habitual tension patterns. *PC* is the natural, built-in pattern that is always available underneath our habits of tension. Best of all, with the support of your *dynamic thinking*, you can access *PC*, and old tension patterns simply fall away.

Below is an exploration that offers you the opportunity to return to the *PC* from a *body-myth* posture: "Stand Up Straight."

PRACTICE 12.3 **RELEASING THE MYTH, EMBRACING CHANGE**

Alexander's *sequence of directional thinking* awakened his *primary coordination*, and his whole body responded.

To prepare, awaken your *body-mind connection* by revisiting Practice 12.1: Continuous Communication, above.

With your body, mind, and senses fully awake, you are ready to practice *the sequence of directional thinking* in an everyday situation. Enjoy exploring the way your *dynamic thoughts* invite change, encouraging you to move out of a static holding pattern. You can allow your *PC* to emerge, like a butterfly coming out of a cocoon.

As you practice, remember that there is nothing to do – this is a series of thoughts that guide you toward balance and ease. The changes you experience are a result of your *dynamic thinking*, rather than a goal to be pursued.

I investigate: What can I discover about the contrast between Stand up Straight vs. Primary Coordination?

- Stand. Pause. Take a *kinesthetic moment*. Receive the support of the floor. Breathe.
- Have a walk around the room, practicing *inclusive attention*.
- Pause.
- Give yourself this instruction: Stand up Straight. Move your body into this position. Notice any changes in your breathing, levels of tension, and balance.
- As you practice the directions below, allow your receptive body to embrace the changes that come about as a result of the dialogue between your body and mind.
- Gently bring your attention to the top of your head. Sense the full length of your body, all the way down to your feet on the floor. Expand your attention to all of your three dimensions. Breathe.
- Bring your *inclusive attention* to your neck and its relationship to your whole body. Sense your neck – its full length, width, and depth.
- With a strong sense of the *part within the whole*, allow this gentle thought to arise: "I wish my neck to be free."

- Recognize that this is a *thought*. There is nothing to "do," except allow your body to respond.
- Continue with the sequence of thinking: "To allow my head to poise delicately forward and up, so that my back can lengthen and widen, and my arms and legs follow."
- You can allow Stand Up Straight to fall away as your body responds to this sequence of *dynamic thoughts*. Pause. Breathe.
- Notice the support of the floor under your feet and the dynamic balance of your whole coordinated body.
- If you find yourself stiffening or concentrating hard, release any idea of **getting it right**. Remind yourself that you are designed for movement. The *PC* is not a position.
- Sense your 3 places of poise.
- Let your *primary coordination* be your guide as you take a walk around the room. Practice *inclusive attention*. Pause.
- If you like, continue walking. Give yourself permission to pause and renew your *sequence of directional thinking*, and then explore walking again. Allow the *PC* to guide your movement as you walk.
- Pause. Notice your whole, dynamic, coordinated body. Breathe.
- *Spy back.* What did you discover about inviting your *PC* to emerge from a static pattern of holding? What happened to your breath as your body began to change? How might this process serve you as an actor?

PC fosters a dynamic relationship that is always changing. If you try to "hold onto" the *primary coordination*, you may find yourself in a position just as limiting as Stand Up Straight. Alexander said, we must be willing to "throw it away in order to get it again, for that getting is the important process."[9] If you sense that your body has lost its natural resilience and balance, you always have the option to pause and renew your *directional thinking*. Your *primary coordination* is an "underground stream" that is underpinning all your movement.

Some may be tempted to use the *sequence of directional thinking* as a form of *end-gaining*. Instead, place your attention on the **process**, rather than a predetermined objective. "I don't know what's going to happen," is a helpful point of view.

When you find yourself in a tense holding pattern, simply connect to the *PC*, through *dynamic thinking*, as you did in the Practice above. Holding patterns fall away, your body reorganizes around your spine, and you return to energized balance, "Upright but not stiff, relaxed but not collapsed."[10] You can trust that your body knows the most effective pathway to your *primary coordination*.

Alexander Technique teachers and students have long sought effective ways to access *PC*. A lesson with a qualified teacher's guidance is always helpful. However, Alexander developed his process of awareness, pausing, and *dynamic thinking* through exploration and experimentation. We feel confident that, with practice, you can too!

> "I love this idea of poised movement. When I achieve it, I feel ready for anything, at my best self … This is the way I want my body to feel before I act."
>
> Elizabeth, acting student, FL Atlantic University.[11]

Primary Coordination: The Heart of Your Design for Movement

Primary coordination is at the heart of your movement design, because it unites your whole body, your senses, and your mind. Limiting habits fall away, and you have more choices about how you move. Connecting with your whole self supports your thinking, breathing, and your emotional and physical choices as an actor. You are fully present and ready to respond to any *stimulus*.

As children, our *primary coordination* was always guiding our movement. At age two or three, our heads balanced gently at the A-O joint, supported by the four curves of our spine. Compared to our body weight, our heads were quite heavy. So heavy, in fact, that if our head was out of balance with our spine, we fell down. Watch young children move: you will rarely see them *over-effort*, and their heads are never "back and down."

As an adult, your *primary coordination* may be hidden under habitual tension patterns, but it is still present in your body. We always have access to our *primary coordination*, because it is built into us. It is our birthright.

Even if you are playing a character who has a limp or "stands up straight," the subtle adjustability of the *PC* can support your movement. You can give the impression of stiffness or strain, while still maintaining an inner poise and balance. Through your *primary coordination*, you can move in harmony with your body's true design, avoid injury, and maintain full breath support and vocal ease. It is not necessary to harm yourself in order to act!

Real-life Story: John Discovers the Power of the *PC*

John was worried: he was playing a Greek god in Euripides' tragedy *Orestes*, and he would be walking on stilts! He was an experienced Equity actor, and had performed many classic roles, but this was going to be a challenge. How could he feel stable and strong as Apollo, when he was standing on two sticks?

Fortunately, the theatre had hired a movement coach, who encouraged John to rely on his *primary coordination*. He began by simply walking through the space (without stilts) and practicing *dynamic thinking*. This exploration allowed his legs to become freer and connected to his whole coordinated body.

Then he put on the stilts. As his coach continued to guide him, he began to recognize that his whole body could support this unfamiliar task. With his *PC* at the center of his movement, he could include the stilts as an extension of his legs. He realized that he now had very long legs which connected all the way to his feet and the floor. He incorporated his new legs into his whole body and quickly mastered walking with stilts.

With practice, your *PC* can be at the heart of everything you do, organizing your whole body for dynamic movement and expanding your range of creative choices. *Dynamic thinking* and *body-mind communication* connect you with your *primary coordination*.

PAUSE TO PROCESS before continuing to Section IV. Journal, discuss, and practice!

Key Words: *Primary Coordination, Startle Pattern, Sequence of Directional Thinking*

Notes

1 Conable, Barbara. *Marjorie Barstow: Her Teaching and Training*, 3rd ed. London: Mouritz. 2016, p. 221.
2 Barstow, Marjorie. Teacher Training Class. Summer Residential Course in the Alexander Technique. University of Nebraska. Lincoln, NE. July, 1984.
3 Walker, Elisabeth. *Forward and Away*. King's Lynn, Norfolk: Gavin R. *Walker, 2008*, p. 58.
4 Nicholls, John. *Explaining the Alexander Technique*, AmSat Journal/Spring 2014, Issue no. 5, p. 27.
5 Carrington, Walter and Carrington, Dilys. *An Evolution of the Alexander Technique*. London: Sheildrake Press, 2017, p. 147.
6 Macdonald, Patrick. *The Alexander Technique As I See It*. Brighton: Rahula Books, 1989, p. 47.
7 Barstow. July, 1984.
8 Alexander, F. Mathias. *The Use of the Self*. Centerline Press, 1989, p. 16.
9 As quoted in Fisher, Jean M.O., Ed. *The Philosopher's Stone*. "The Journal of Sir George Trevelyan," by Sir George Trevelyan. London: Mouritz, 1998, p. 94.
10 Attributed to the late, great Tai Chi master, Ben Lo (1927–2018).
11 Quoted from a student journal. Used with permission.

Claiming Your Inner and Outer Space

"Space is a hidden feature of movement and movement is a visible aspect of Space."[1]

Rudolf Laban

The internal space of our body and the external space which surrounds us are filled with potential for connected, creative expression.

You may be unaware of your body's internal space, but you are almost certainly aware of unwanted tension in your body. This tension is created when muscles are chronically tightened, limiting their ability to "take up space." When you fail to claim your internal space, you restrict the natural fluidity of your body and interfere with *sequential* movement.

In Section II, you learned that tense muscles limit the movement in your joints. Excess contraction in your muscles not only interferes with your ability to move, but it creates a barrier between you and the audience. You are literally shrinking inward, withdrawing from the spectators. When this happens onstage, you can end up "pushing," trying to "make something happen" as you perform. When you claim internal space, you can move with ease and allow your performance to unfold moment by moment.

External space is the medium in which movement happens. Space may feel like it's hard to pin down – after all, it's just air! But as actors, we recognize that our use of external space tells the audience about the character's relationship to their world and the people in it. Not only that, our personal perception of space deeply impacts our ability to claim it.

This Section is designed to raise your awareness of and access to your spatial environment, both internal and external. Through the Practices, you can refine and develop your personal relationship to space.

Note

1 Von Laban, Rudolph. *The Language of Movement*, Boston: Plays, Inc. *1974*, p. 4. Used with permission.

Your Inner Space

As you've learned throughout *YBK*, there is so much more to our bodies than the parts we can see. Your *3-D body* includes each internal organ, bone, and even your cells! Each of your muscles has a 3-D shape that shifts and changes as you move. Your internal space expands and contracts according to your thoughts and your responses to the world around you.

Bones don't change their shape. However, as you learned in Chapter 8, your muscles contract and expand. Constant contraction in your muscles limits your internal space, the amount of space at your joint connections, and restricts the free and easy movement of breath. In addition, chronic tension puts strain on your organs. Lack of space in your body stresses you out!

Your perceptions of your body's movability and size are strongly affected by your ability to claim your internal space. In the Practice below, you can explore moving with a sense of your inner space.

PRACTICE 13.1 EXPANDING AND CONTRACTING[1]

Kinesthetic awareness and *inclusive attention* are valuable aids in your exploration of inner space. In this Practice, be aware of sensations as you contract and expand your *3-D body*.

I investigate: What can I learn about my inner space as I move?

- Stand. Bring your awareness to your *3-D body*. Pause. Take a *kinesthetic moment*. Breathe.
- Move to the floor (or a mat) and lie on your back; notice your whole body.
- Move your arms and legs to bring your body into an X-shape.
- Pause and notice your 3-dimensional breath.

- On an exhale, *initiate* movement at your elbows and knees, bringing your legs toward your chest and your elbows toward your knees. Allow this movement to ride on the flow of your breath. Your head remains on the floor (see Figure 13.1).

- Wait for your body's impulse to inhale. As you breathe in, begin to expand. *Initiate* a movement at your fingers and toes, as your muscles release and your arms and legs slowly return to rest in the X-shape.

- Remain here for one complete breath cycle, then repeat the contracting movement on an exhale. Remain in this shape until your body requires breath, then expand as you inhale.

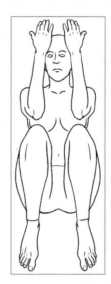

Figure 13.1 Your back lengthens and widens as your elbows and knees fold in toward center.

- Continue exploring as you repeat this *sequence* several times: inhale as your muscles lengthen and expand, exhale as you draw your limbs inward.

- Avoid *over-efforting*; be gentle with yourself as you move and as you rest in the contracted shape. If the rhythm of your breath is ragged or if you stop inhaling as you expand, you may be using more effort than you need. Allow the *sequence* to evolve.

- After several rounds, pause. Take a *kinesthetic moment*.

- Gently roll to your side. After a moment, press your hands into the floor and use your arms to bring yourself up to sitting. Pause for a moment, then come to standing. Pause.

- Take a *kinesthetic moment*. Notice your sense of internal space.

- Practice *inclusive attention* as you take a walk. Enjoy your *kinesthetic awareness* of inner space as you move. Pause.

- *Spy back*. What was your experience of limiting and expanding your physical space? What did you notice about the three dimensions of your body? What did you notice about your inner space as you walked around the room?

When you access your internal space, you free your body and expand your movement vocabulary. By "claiming space" you have more choices about the way you move.

Your Spacious *3-Dimensional Body*

In Chapter 2, you explored your three dimensions through breath and touch. You awakened the counterbalance of front-back, left-right, and top-bottom and connected the six directions into a 360-degree whole. Awareness of your *3-dimensional body* can help you claim your inner space.

Sometimes, a muscle or set of muscles can pull strongly in one direction, leaving its counterbalancing direction "out of the picture." For instance, if your leg muscles are constantly pulling upward, your Big 3 leg joints have less space. Without a downward counterbalance, your feet and legs are lifted away from the support of the ground, and your movement potential is limited.

Your *kinesthetic sense* can help you identify excess tension that is interfering with the interplay of your three dimensions. In the Practice that follows, you can experience the internal space available to you, when your three dimensions are balancing each other in an ever-changing relationship.

PRACTICE 13.2   **THE DIMENSIONAL SCALE – VARIATIONS 1 AND 2 (KP)[2]**

Rudolf Laban developed the *Dimensional Scale* to strengthen the mover's sense of specific spatial pathways. Here, though, you can practice the movements of the *Dimensional Scale* to awaken your **internal** space. We will visit this Key Practice several times in this section, each time with a different focus. Enjoy opening your 360-degree body through this inner space exploration.

I investigate: What can I discover about my counterbalancing dimensions as I move?

Variation 1

This is a simplified version of the scale to awaken your body's connection to the six directions at play in your body's coordination. Avoid thinking of each dimension too narrowly, like a line. Instead, experience each direction as a pathway of movement through your body, ultimately connecting the dimensions into a 360° whole.

- Stand. Pause. Breathe. Take a *kinesthetic moment.* Throughout the Practice, we will refer to this stance as "center." We will pass through "center" or return to "center" throughout.
- Practice *inclusive attention* as you have a walk around the room. Pause.
- With your right arm, reach up toward the ceiling; sense your body extend in the upward direction.
- Lower your arm, pass through center, and reach down to the floor. It's fine to bend your knees. Breathe and sense the downward direction. Return to center.
- Remember that each of these movements opens a dimensional pathway in your body. Avoid defining the direction too narrowly. Your whole *3-D body* is supporting each movement.

- Next, to awaken the horizontal dimension, cross your right foot behind your left foot and reach your right arm across your body with fingers pointing to the left. Avoid *over-efforting*. This is a gentle movement. Do not strain.
- Open your body horizontally by extending your right arm to the right and stepping to the right in an easy lunge. The toes of your right foot can point to the right, while your head and your gaze remain forward.
- After a moment, return to center. Pause.
- Explore your sagittal dimension by stepping back on your right foot as you reach in a backward direction with your right hand, palm facing outward.[3] Gaze remains forward. Enjoy sensing "back."

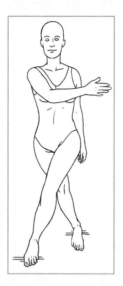

Figure 13.2 Exploring your horizontal dimension.

- After a moment, return to center, and step forward on your right foot in a soft lunge, reaching in a forward direction with your right hand. After a moment, return to center.
- Pause. Notice any changes in your body, particularly the right side, after this exploration.
- Repeat on the left side. Pause. Take a *kinesthetic moment*.
- Have a walk through the room. Give your body, mind, and nervous system a chance to process this exploration. Pause.
- *Spy back*. What did you notice in your first walk? Your second walk? How does an awareness of your dimensionality affect your body, breath, and movement? How does this Practice affect your sense of your inner space?

In Variation 1 you explored each of the six directions, accessing your 3-dimensionality, and filling out the cylindrical shape of your inner body. Even if you can't sense changes, trust that your body has begun to open in subtle ways.

Variation 2 explores the counterbalancing relationships between each of the directions of length, width, and depth. It expands your attention and your *kinesthetic awareness* to include the entire dimension, no matter which direction you are reaching toward.

Variation 2

In Chapter 8 you learned Newton's Third Law of Motion: for every action there is an equal and opposite reaction. As you reach in each direction, use *kinesthetic awareness* to sense that the opposite direction is also at play. Your body's natural *tensegrity* supports both directions simultaneously, as each counterbalances the other.

When we stretch in one direction, there is a pull in the opposite direction, a rippling through the muscles, which stabilizes the movement. We call these *Tensile Forces* (KW); *tensegrity* keeps these forces in balance throughout your body.

Enjoy sensing each dimension **through** your body as the *tensile forces* balance and rebalance your movement.

- Stand. Pause. Breathe. Take a *kinesthetic moment*.
- Reach your right arm up, while still sensing your relationship with your right foot on the floor. Using your *kinesthetic sense*, notice a sense of upward movement through your body **and** downward movement toward the floor.
- Allow weight to move smoothly through your muscles and joints, especially the shoulder joint. Sense the vertical connection, up and down, through your whole body. Breathe.
- Be aware of your vertical dimension as you bring your arm down through center, and continue by reaching downward toward the floor, lengthening your back and dropping your head. It's fine to bend your knees.
- Sense the counterbalance of the upward direction. Recognize that your muscles are moving weight upward even though you are reaching downward. Breathe.
- Rise gently into center and allow your right arm to rest at your side.
- Pause. Sense your vertical dimension.
- Notice any differences in the kinesthetic sensations in your right side compared to your left.
- Continue by crossing your right foot behind and slightly to the left of your left foot, as you reach with your right arm across your body, fingers pointing toward the left.
- Even though you are reaching to the left, sense the counterbalancing direction toward the right side. Avoid *over-efforting*. Breathe.
- Remember that this is not a held position; it is a dynamic relationship. There is directional flow through your body. Breathe and practice *inclusive attention*.
- Step your right foot out to the right, slightly wider than hip width and open your right arm to the right. Your torso remains upright.
- Using your *kinesthetic sense*, feel a sense of movement through your **whole** body to the right, and simultaneously, a counterbalancing direction to the left.
- Breathe, as you notice your spacious horizontal dimension throughout your whole body. Sense the movement through your muscles – this is not a static position.
- Return to center. Allow your arm to rest at your side. Pause. Notice the sensations in your body, including any changes in your right side.
- Continue by stepping back on your right foot and stretching your right arm behind you, palm facing out, pinky toward the floor. Sense the counterbalancing direction toward the front of your body, even though you are reaching back. Breathe.
- Release your arm and let it swing through center as you step forward on your right foot in an easy lunge and reach with your right arm into the forward direction. Sense a counterbalancing release backward through your whole body.
- Return to your starting point. Pause. Notice the interplay of the three dimensions you have explored. You may notice differences in your right and left sides.

- Repeat this process on the left.
- When that is complete, pause. Bring awareness to your whole body and the interplay of all three dimensions simultaneously counterbalancing one another. Sense your 360° body. Breathe.
- Practicing *inclusive attention*, have a walk through the room. Continue to notice your expanded 3-dimensional inner space as you walk. Pause. Take a *kinesthetic moment.*
- *Spy back.* How do these movements and the interplay of the three dimensions affect your sense of your body? What was it like to sense counterbalancing directions in your body? How might this experience serve you as an actor?

When we are upright, there are always subtle internal movements up toward your head, down toward your feet, toward the left and the right, and forward and back. With all three dimensions at play, you claim the cylindrical shape of your body, which allows overly contracted muscles to lengthen, balance, and expand.

Sensing these subtle internal movements (under your skin) may be elusive at first. With practice, this awareness will become second nature, just as you are effortlessly aware of sights and sounds. So, revisit these Key Practices often; you can deepen your "body understanding" each time you explore them.

Developing awareness of the dimensions of your body not only opens your internal space but gives you more movement options. You have 360-degree movement possibilities! In addition, clarifying your three dimensions helps you identify dimensional "confusion." For instance, when we practice the *Dimensional Scale* with the arms in the open horizontal dimension, it is easy to see and feel the shoulders expanding outward side to side.

However, some of us lose the sense of the horizontal shoulder structure, rolling the shoulders forward into the sagittal dimension. When we do this, we limit our internal space and our head is pulled out of balance with our spine. Awareness of your *3-D body* and your *primary coordination* can free you from this contracted position.

Through *kinesthetic awareness* you can expand your range of 3-dimensional movement possibilities. Your movements become simpler, clearer, and more vivid as you honor the directions in your body and in space. Your whole presence is fuller and more dynamic: your *3-D body* has a lively interaction with the 3-dimensional space around you.

> *PAUSE TO PROCESS* Journal or discuss your discoveries before continuing. Take a walk outdoors noticing your inner space.

Primary Coordination and Your Inner Space

Your *primary coordination* opens your inner space because it returns you to your natural coordination. When your body is in balance, excess tension falls away, and you are free to expand in every direction.

As you discovered in the previous section, your whole body claims its natural reflex for uprightness when:

- you wish your neck to be free,
- as your head rotates toward balance,
- to allow your back to lengthen and widen,
- and your legs and arms to follow.[4]

Your body responds to this *sequence of directional thinking*, just as it responds when you are thirsty and reach for a glass of water. Through your *dynamic thinking*, you are actually inviting your *primary coordination* to emerge. You are uncovering what your body already knows.

This process honors the true design of your *3-D body*. You are claiming your inner space, as your muscles lengthen, widen and expand, and you regain your balanced coordination.

Dr. Ted Dimon, author of *Neurodynamics*, says "the sending of messages to muscles is a specific kinesthetic skill that is quite distinct from the use of imagery."[5] He notes that clear kinesthetic thought can be applied when it is most needed, in activity. That is why Alexander Technique is so helpful to actors – your *body-mind connection* can work while you are engaged in something else, even something as absorbing as acting.

With a lively *kinesthetic sense* and *dynamic thinking*, you can reclaim your *primary coordination* and move, supported by your whole coordinated body. You are "Ready for anything, prepared for nothing."[6]

Some Alexander teachers develop simple Practices that create a state of readiness for Alexander's directions. For instance, the *kinesthetic sensing* Practice (1.4) can awaken your *kinesthetic awareness* and your *body-mind connection*.

Below, you will encounter a simple awareness Practice, which connects you to your inner space and can lead you to your *primary coordination*.

PRACTICE 13.3   DISCOVERING INNER SPACE

A portion of this Practice was inspired by an exploration developed by Alexander teacher Mio Morales.[7]

I investigate: What can I discover about the connection between my thinking and my inner space?

- Sit in a chair, with your feet resting comfortably on the floor.
- Pause. Breathe. Take a *kinesthetic moment*.
- Be aware of your whole body, your feet on the floor, your sit bones, and other parts of you that are touching the chair.

- Use your *inclusive attention* to note that you are in a room and there are sights and sounds around you.
- Using your *kinesthetic sense*, scan through your body. If you notice an area of tension, pause and bring your attention to it. Then shift your attention to the area right under or near it. Notice the relative ease there.
- Gently allow your *inclusive attention* to acknowledge the inner space of this area.
- After a few moments, continue your scan, noticing places of tension; then, underneath or near it, a place of relative ease. Give this area *inclusive attention*, as you notice this *part within the whole*.
- After a few moments, repeat the process. Continue in this way a few more times.
- Practice *inclusive attention* as you shift your awareness to your neck. Invite the freedom and space you have discovered in other parts of your body to your neck and follow Alexander's *sequence of directional thinking*.
- Remember, there is nothing to do, only thinking, waiting, and trusting your *primary coordination* to return your whole body to its natural balance.
- Pause and notice your whole self. Rise and stand. Notice your body's balance. You can repeat the *sequence of directional thinking* if needed.
- Allow this thought to arise: I'm going to take a walk around the room. Notice if this thought causes you to restrict your internal space. If so, Pause.
- Practice the *sequence of directional thinking*. Allow your *primary coordination* to guide you as you have a walk around the room. Breathe.
- You can repeat this process of pausing and practicing *directional thinking* as needed. You have an open channel connecting your body and mind: perfect two-way communication.
- Practice *inclusive attention*. You can always renew your *directional thinking* as you move.
- Pause. Take a *kinesthetic moment*.
- *Spy back*. What did you discover about your *PC* as it guided you in this simple activity? How did this Practice affect your inner space? What did you discover about your inner space when you first thought about walking? How can your Practice of pausing and *directional thinking* help you open your inner space in your daily activities?

Your *primary coordination* is always available to you. Your habits may hide it at times, but you always have the option to return to your *PC*, which supports every movement you make. *Body-mind communication* and *dynamic thinking* can return us to our inner space and our body's perfect coordination.

At this point, you've explored your body's design, how it functions, and how you can access its amazing movement potential. Through *inclusive attention*, you've become aware of your body in its surroundings. This is important, because our bodies do not exist in a vacuum. We are always in relationship with the world around us. Our world informs how we use our body.

PRACTICE 13.4 **GET TO KNOW YOUR INNER SPACE – REAL WORLD PRACTICE**

The more you integrate these principles and concepts into your daily life, the more they will be available to you onstage. Below are two applications you might encounter every day.

Hurry Up!

Sometimes it seems that our whole culture is dedicated to speed: "getting there," wherever "there" is. In this Practice, we contrast "getting there" with attention to "**how** I'm getting there." If you are not in a class, practice touching and/or picking up objects in the room you are in, rather than shaking hands.

* Pause. Stand. Notice your 360-degree body. Breathe. Take a *kinesthetic moment*.
* Begin to move about the room; practice *inclusive attention* as you move.
* Notice your inner space as you walk through the room. Notice the others as you pass them.
* Now, with awareness of your inner space, meet others, shake hands, tell them your name. Stay with this intention: make meeting them the most important thing in this moment.
* After 30 seconds of meeting people, begin to walk about the room again.
* Quicken your walk. You are in a hurry.
* Give yourself this task: meet people, shake hands, and tell them your name. Meet as many people as you can in 30 seconds.
* Pause. Take a *kinesthetic moment*. Let the task go. Breathe.
* Return to your normal walk. Notice your 360-degree body, the other people, and the room around you.
* Pause.
* *Spy back*. What was your experience of hurry? What happened to your breath, body, and internal space? How aware were you of the room around you when you were in a hurry? Contrast your two experiences of meeting people.

Variation

* Now, try blending speed and awareness: shake hands with as many people as possible, while *making the meeting* the most important thing. With a little practice you can claim your 360° body and your inner space, even when you are in a hurry. Let your *primary coordination* be your guide!

Space and the Small Screen

In this exploration, you can discover options for claiming inner and outer space, as you use a familiar object.

* Pick up your phone as if you were about to type a text. Pause.

Were you aware of your three dimensions as you moved? What did your head do in relationship to your phone? If your head balanced on top of your spine, and rotated at the A-O joint, great!

For most of us, this may not be what happened.

Here is one pattern that often occurs: our head and shoulders may roll forward (sagittal plane) and contract inward as our arms press into our sides. Our back rounds, and we may even stop breathing! If this or some other pattern of interference occurred, go back and start over. Try the following process. See what you learn!

- Put your phone down, but within reach.
- Pause.
- Look at your phone. Notice if this triggers a pattern of narrowing inward or leaning toward the phone. Check: are you breathing? If not, start over and remember to breathe.
- Pause. Breathe. Take a *kinesthetic moment*.
- Notice your whole body as you see the phone. Remind yourself of your three dimensions.
- Pause and return to awareness of your *PC* if you begin to lose a sense of your *3-dimensional body*.
- Sense your whole spine and the gentle balance of your head at the top of your spine. Breathe.
- Tell yourself you are going to *initiate* a movement from your fingers. Using this initiation and *inclusive attention*, pick up your phone and look at it in your hand, rotating your head at the A-O joint.
- Notice – are you breathing?
- Pause. Recognize that you can renew your *sequence of directional thinking* at any time.
- Maintaining *inclusive attention*, place your awareness on your whole body and the support of your *primary coordination* as you type a message.
- Pause. Put down your phone. Are you breathing?
- Look around the space. Have a walk, noticing your inner space and the interaction of your three dimensions as you move.
- *Spy back*. What did you notice as you followed this simple process? What did you experience as you typed your text? How does awareness of your three dimensions, your *PC*, and *inclusive attention* affect you and the way you move?

When you pause and step back from a *stimulus* – like your cell phone – you open a space to **choose** your response. The pause is your moment of opportunity. Then, by putting your attention on how you are moving, rather than the task, you have power over habitual tension and cluttered movement.

Alexander's process of observing, pausing, and choosing where to put your attention is one of his great discoveries, because it **interrupts** your habit pattern. Then you have options about how you move! Remember, your body is a Rolls Royce, and this process puts **you** in the driver's seat.

This gentle process can be applied to any activity. By placing your attention on your body's *PC* and inner space, you can refine your movement and return to balance. Your perspective broadens, and your relationship to people and the world become richer and fuller. And isn't that the presence we want to have onstage?

As actors, we want to be aware of our body and our relationship to the world around us: we practice *inclusive attention* as we move. Yet, there is one aspect of this relationship that we might overlook. It is a most fundamental relationship, and a powerful movement tool. No matter where we are, it is at play: it is the space we move in. And that is the subject of Chapter 14.

PAUSE TO PROCESS before continuing to Chapter 14. Journal, draw, experiment, discuss, play.

Key Word: *Tensile Forces*

Key Practice: *Dimensional Scale*

Notes

1 There are numerous Practices that begin with the X-shape and move into a smaller more contracted shape. We were inspired by Irmgard Bartenieff, Bonnie Bainbridge Cohen, and Jean Newlove, who influenced our work in this area.
2 Newlove, Jean. *Laban for Actors and Dancers*. London: Nick Hern Books, *1993*. Print. p. 29.
3 This is a departure from Laban's original direction: this movement allows a stronger sensation of the inner dimensions. The original direction is in Practice 15.3.
4 MacDonald, Patrick. *The Alexander Technique As I See It*. Brighton: Rahula Books, *1989*, p. 47.
5 Dimon, Theodore. *Neurodynamics: The Art of Mindfulness in Action*. Berkeley: North Atlantic Books, *2015*, p. 75.
6 Le Foll, Marie-Francoise. "Alexander Class: Guest Artist Series". Teacher Training Weekend. Philadelphia: The Alexander Foundation. April 7, 1992.
7 Morales, Mio. Online Alexander Toolkit. Webinar. May 20, 2018. https://alexanderlearningnetwork.com. Used with permission.

Exploring "Outer Space"

CHAPTER 14

Expansive space is all around us. It surrounds our bodies and the objects that we interact with every day. Space is infinite. Or not.

A lack of space makes it hard for us to move: you can't perform a pirouette in a broom closet. We can restrict our space, not only with walls, but by limiting our perceptions of it. When we do this, we may feel stuck, tense, or even immovable. But when we perceive that we have a lot of space around us, we take a step toward accessing physical freedom and ease of movement.

PRACTICE 14.1   BODY/SPACE RELATIONSHIP

Notice how your body responds to your perception of space and your thinking in this exploration of spatial circumstances.

- Sit in a chair. Pause. Breathe. Take a *kinesthetic moment*.
- Take a kinesthetic journey into your imagination: you are in the middle seat on an airplane or in the back seat of a car. Feel the closeness of the bodies on either side of you.
- Notice the sensations in your body as you sense the lack of space around you. Notice your breathing. Move your body however you feel necessary to accommodate the lack of space. (If you are challenged in imagining this situation – feel free to close your eyes.)
- After exploring for a few minutes, let go of this experience. If your eyes are closed, open them.
- Pause for a moment and note the sensations in your body, as you come back to this moment.
- Now, imagine yourself outdoors, on a beautiful, grassy hilltop, looking out over a lush valley. You are alone, the sun is warm on your shoulders and the breeze soft against your skin. Sense the limitless space around you.

- Notice how your body responds to this wide-open space; allow your body to move any way it desires. Give yourself permission to expand and explore the limitless space around you. If you have closed your eyes, open them.
- After a few moments, bring the exploration to a close, coming back to this moment.
- See the space around you. Note the ways that your body adjusts to this renewed awareness of space. Pause. Breathe. Take a *kinesthetic moment*.
- Have a walk through the room. Practice *inclusive attention*. Pause.
- *Spy back*. What happened to your inner space and your breath when you had limited space? Expansive space? What did you discover about your own 3-dimensionality in relation to your perception of the space around you?

Note how your thinking, your *kinesthetic sense*, and your imagination worked together in this exploration. If we **think** we only have a little space, our body contracts. If we **think** we have a lot of space, our body expands. Our perception of outer space influences our ability to access inner space. When we are onstage, we can consciously claim this interaction, creating a powerful presence.

The explorations that follow are designed to wake up your external spatial sense and make it a partner in your movement life.

PRACTICE 14.2   VISION, IMPULSE, AND OUTER SPACE

Your visual sense can limit or expand your sense of inner and outer space. Note: **peripheral** vision is "side vision:" what your eyes see at the sides when you are look-ing straight ahead.

I investigate: How does my visual field affect my movement?

- Stand. Pause. Breathe. Take a *kinesthetic moment*. Practice *inclusive attention* as you notice the room around you.
- Lie down on the floor on your back and pause to notice your sensations.
- Gently move your eyes to the right and allow your head to follow your eyes. Pause.
- After a moment, allow your eyes to move back to center and your head to follow in response.
- Repeat to the left.
- Close your eyes. Pause.
- Bring your knees up to your chest and bring your elbows toward your knees. Pause.
- With your eyes still closed, allow your head to roll to the right, then your torso, legs and arms follow, until you are resting on your right side, arms and legs rest-ing on the floor. Breathe. Open your eyes. Without moving your eyes or your head, notice what you can see in front of you. After a moment, expand your awareness to include your peripheral vision, allowing your visual field to expand.

- Tune in to your body: as you move your eyes to see more of the room, allow your head to follow your gaze. Allow the rest of your body to respond to these movements.
- Allow your eyes to move toward the left and let your head follow. Allow this movement to *sequence* through your neck, spine, torso, and legs. Allow your head to lead you to rest on your back.
- Breathe. Pause. Take a *kinesthetic moment.*
- Repeat on the other side. Pause.
- Practice this sequence again, once more on each side.

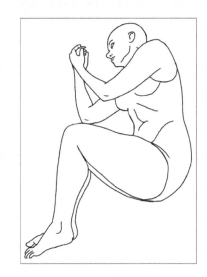

Figure 14.1

- After the last time, pause and rest. Breathe. Take a *kinesthetic moment.*
- Gently roll to one side and press your hands on the floor to sit up. Then move to standing.
- Pause. Notice your visual sense of the room.
- Take a walk around the room. Pause.
- *Spy back.* How did your body respond to changes in your visual awareness? What was it like to sense a movement impulse in your body and follow it? Were there changes in your visual field and *kinesthetic sense* before and after the Practice? What were they?

Our visual perceptions strongly affect our sense of inner and outer space and the sense of connection throughout our bodies. By changing what we see and how we see it, we can limit our sense of space or make space a partner in the way we move.

PRACTICE 14.3 PERCEIVING SPACE

This exploration can alter your perception of space very quickly. Though it contains elements of the earlier Practice, it offers you an opportunity to remain stationary while you develop your spatial awareness and the connection between outer and inner space.

Part I

- Sit or stand. Pause. Breathe. Take a *kinesthetic moment.*
- See the room, the objects around you.

- Place all your attention on a single object, shutting out the other objects.
- Notice what happens in your body – your muscle tension, your breath, as you narrow your vision to this one object.
- After a moment or two, let go of this narrowed focus. Sense your whole body and see the whole room around you. Be particularly aware of your peripheral vision.
- Notice your body – muscle tension, breath, inner space – as you broaden your visual field.
- After a moment or two, look at your object again, while maintaining your sense of the space around you. Allow your eyes to be receptive to the object and the space.
- Continue to observe your body and breath as you walk through the room, seeing the objects, as well as the whole space. Sense your inner and outer space. Practice *inclusive attention*.
- After a few moments, pause. Recognize the interplay between your inner space and the space around you.
- *Spy back*. What did you notice about your body, your three dimensions, and your breath as you changed your spatial and visual awareness? How is your body affected as you become more receptive to the objects and the space?

There is much to be discovered about the relationship between your body, space, and your visual sense whether you are stationary or in motion.

Part II

In this Practice, be gentle with yourself. Concentrating too hard can interfere with breath and movement.

- Stand. Pause. Breathe. Take a *kinesthetic moment*. Notice yourself and the room around you.
- Walk through the room. Notice your breath, eye focus, and any sensations you perceive as you walk.
- Now go outdoors. Notice your sensations and your whole body as you walk.
- After a minute or two, place your visual attention on the space through which you are walking.
- Notice the space between objects, such as between the branches of trees, leaves, cracks in the sidewalk. Notice the changes in the space as people or cars move around.
- As you move about with your visual focus on space, be aware of sensation in your body.
- Be gentle as you explore space and change your visual focus. This is light attention, rather than deep concentration. Think of receiving the space around you.
- Continue your walk with spatial focus for a few minutes.
- Return to the room. Walk the length of the room a couple of times. Notice your breath, eye focus, and any sensations you perceive as you walk.
- Pause. Take a *kinesthetic moment*.

- *Spy back*. How does placing your visual attention on space affect your body? Your breath? How did your second walk through the room differ from the first? Which one felt more comfortable to you? How might awareness of space serve you when you are on stage or in an audition?

Through these Practices, you can recognize that your perception of space is strongly influenced by your field of vision. In addition to visual awareness, your *kinesthetic sense* can support your awareness of your *3-D body* in dynamic relationship with the 3-D space around you.

3-Dimensional Space

Like our bodies, space is 3-dimensional. It surrounds our *3-D body*: our body touches space, and space touches us back. Every time we move, we are making a pathway through space. Our bodies move through space in a variety of ways – curves, straight lines, diagonals, spirals.

As actors, we can claim outer space: our personal space and the infinity of space beyond that. When we acknowledge stage space, and the entirety of the theatre space, our performance can match the size of the space we want to fill.

You can begin by exploring and claiming your personal space: your *Kinesphere*.

Your Kinesphere

> *Contained within the larger environment of the general space, we each have a bubble of personal space that surrounds us. The roots of this word are* kinesis *for movement and* sphaira *for ball or globe. It is literally the sphere in which our movement occurs. It is defined as the space we can access without taking a step to a new place. Our personal reach space, the Kinesphere, stays with us as we travel through the general space.*
>
> Karen Studd and Laura Cox, *Everybody Is a Body*[1]

Kinesphere (KW) is Rudolf Laban's term for our personal movement space. Our *Kinesphere* helps us take ownership of our space onstage. Without speaking a word, we can communicate that we have a space that is ours; we "claim" space, and this "movement bubble" travels with us as we move.

As you explore the Practices below, approach them with a spirit of exploration and discovery. Allow yourself to be surprised by the ways spatial awareness can affect you.

PRACTICE 14.4 **EXPLORING KINESPHERE (KP)**

Activate your *kinesthetic sense* as you explore possibilities for claiming your *3-D space* through this Key Practice. You may enjoy playing music during this exploration.

I investigate: What can I learn about my relationship with the space around me?

- Stand. Pause. Breathe. Take a *kinesthetic moment*.
- Take a walk through the space, noticing your movement, sensations, vision, breath.
- Pause.
- Imagine that you are standing in the center of a bubble. This is your *Kinesphere*. This movement bubble is your 3-dimensional reach-space. Reach for every part of it, while keeping at least one foot on the floor.
- Reach in all directions: up, down, diagonally, back, sideways. Free your legs and torso to support these movements.
- The edges of the bubble are at the extremes of every place you can reach, without moving your feet to a new spot. Explore not only the edges of the bubble, but all the points in between.
- Use your whole body to explore, as you allow different body parts to take the lead: your head, sit bones, elbow, little finger – get creative. The rest of your body can follow the leader.
- Explore high, low, diagonally, and side to side.
- After a few minutes, pause, still maintaining your awareness of your *Kinesphere*.
- Take a walk through the space, taking your *kinesthetic awareness* of your *Kinesphere* with you. Notice your movement, sensations, vision, breath, and your body in the 3-D space.
- If you are in a class, enjoy letting your *Kinesphere* "bounce" off other *Kinespheres*. If you are alone, try "bouncing" your *Kinesphere* off the walls or furniture.
- After a few moments, drop the bouncing, let your *Kinesphere* pass through other people or objects in the room. Be aware of their *Kinespheres* effortlessly intersecting with yours.
- Enlarge your awareness to include your *Kinesphere* within the general space. Sense your body expand within your *Kinesphere* and enjoy the expanse of space beyond it.
- After a few minutes' exploration, pause. Breathe. Notice yourself and the liveliness in your body and its relationship to space. Take a *kinesthetic moment*.
- *Spy back*. What was your experience? What happened in your body when you imagined a "movement bubble" around you? In what ways did your awareness of your *Kinesphere* shift your relationship with space? Did your awareness of space change between your first walk and your last walk? In what ways?

Be gentle with yourself as you develop your awareness of your *Kinesphere*. You are becoming accustomed to a new way of perceiving space and your relationship to it. If you practice this exercise over a few days, your brain and body will begin to absorb (and even celebrate!) this new awareness.

For a boost to your *kinesthetic sense*, return to the *kinesthetic sensing* Practice (1.4) from Chapter 1 or Practice 1.4 Variation in the Appendix. As you practice *kinesthetic sensing*, you bring awareness to the sensation of movement in the muscles, tendons, and joints of your body. In addition, notice that your body is moving through space. Explore your *Kinesphere*. Your arm and your whole body are in an active relationship with the space inside your *Kinesphere*.

Why is an awareness of the *Kinesphere* important? Your *Kinesphere* helps you access 3-dimensional space, your personal movement space within the "infinity of general space." It defines the area **available** for movement. Even if you don't actually gesture into every bit of the *Kinesphere*, the possibility of 360-degree movement enlivens our whole body and our relationship to space as well.

The task of filling infinite space can seem a bit overwhelming, but a personal bubble of space-within-the-space helps us to claim what is "rightfully ours." Our *Kinesphere* is a *part within the whole*. We can own our personal space, while also acknowledging our relationship to the larger space of the stage and the audience.

PAUSE TO PROCESS Journal, discuss, apply what you've discovered.

Key Word: *Kinesphere*

Key Practice: *Exploring Kinesphere*

Note

1 Studd, Karen and Cox, Laura, *Everybody Is a Body*. Indianapolis: Dog Ear Publishing, 2013, p. 107.

Inner and Outer Space

A Movement Partnership

As you discovered in Chapter 14, you can sense the space around you through your *kinesthetic sense*. Although we are unaccustomed to sensing in this way, it is one of the functions of our spatial sense.

Many NBA basketball players have highly developed external *kinesthetic sensing*. They seem to know where everyone is on the court, and where the basket is, even if they are not in their visual field. The most dynamic stage actors have it too. Through *kinesthetic awareness*, they can sense themselves, as well as other actors, the set, and the audience.

You have been practicing *inclusive attention* – using all your senses to notice your whole body and the world around you. Now we refine your attention, as you become more aware of the interaction between your body with space and space with your body.

Your 3-Dimensional Body in 3-Dimensional Space

We experience our bodies most fully when we are aware of our *3-D body* moving within the 360-degree space: not just the *Kinesphere*, but beyond! The explorations below open you to an awareness of both.

PRACTICE 15.1 SPACE WALK

Part I

- Stand in the space. Pause. Sense your *3-D Body in the 3-D Space* (KW) around you. If you like, you can close your eyes.
- Use your *kinesthetic awareness* to sense the space above you – between you and the ceiling; beside you – between you and the walls; and behind and in front of you.

- Open your eyes and have a walk around the room. Notice how sensations change as you get closer to and farther away from walls and objects. After a few moments, pause.
- Continue to sense the space around you.
- Take a walk outdoors. Before you go, tell yourself you are going to use your *kinesthetic awareness* to sense the space around you. This is different than the visual sense of space that you explored in Practice 14.3.
- As you walk, see and sense the space. Sense the space above you, behind you, beside you, in front of you.
- Note that the size and shape of space changes as people and objects get closer to you and farther away. You may notice that your body responds to these changes.
- Take notice of the space gently and with ease. Avoid "concentrating hard". Keep a light *inclusive attention*. Sense yourself within the infinite space as you move through it.
- After 5–10 minutes, return to the room. Pause. Breathe.
- Have a walk around the room. After a minute or two, come to standing.
- As you stand, sense the space above you, behind you, beside you, all around you – even between your legs. Even though you are "standing still," enjoy the interaction of your *3-D body with the 3-D space* and the room around you.
- Pause.
- *Spy back.* How does awareness of your *kinesthetic sense* and the space around you change the experience of a simple walk? How is standing different when you are in dynamic relationship with the *3-D space*? What was your experience of each walk at the beginning, middle, and end of this Practice?

Part II

- Pause, stand in the space. Sense your *3-D body*.
- Take a moment to explore the space around you, your *Kinesphere*, as you did in Practice 14.4. Pause.
- Take a walk through the room, sensing your *Kinesphere* and the general space around you.
- After a few minutes, pause.
- Now take a walk outdoors as you did in Part I above, with this difference:
- Before you take your walk, tell yourself you will use your *kinesthetic awareness* to sense your body, as well as your *Kinesphere*, and the general space around you.
- As you walk, enjoy exploring the relationship between your body, *Kinesphere*, and the general space as you move.
- If you find yourself concentrating too hard or find you are fatigued (remember, this is unexplored territory), pause and sense the general space; you can simply release your awareness of your *Kinesphere*. Continue your walk.
- Play. Imagine that the space is moving through you as you walk. Explore the interaction between your *kinesthetic sense*, your whole *3-D body*, and the 3-D space around you.

- Return to the room and walk through the room with a sense of your *Kinesphere* moving through general space.
- *Spy back*. What differences did you notice in your awareness of space from Part I to Part II? How might this awareness serve you as an actor?

When you are aware of the space around you on stage, your body and mind recognize that there are more movement possibilities available to you. Your body has permission to move in all directions, and you may discover that surprising choices emerge.

> "The ease in movement is something I am discovering. By ease, I mean that feeling of trusting the body to do what it wants to do and recognizing that space is fascinating. There is so much of it to fill and use and the energy that fills it is INTERESTING and UNSTOPPABLE."
>
> Scott, acting student, Florida Atlantic University[1]

PRACTICE 15.2   WAKING YOUR DIMENSIONS

When we act, we want to utilize our whole self within the context of the whole space. Sometimes we can feel flattened out, as if the front part of our body is all there is; or, we can be so focused on our fellow actors that we feel "cut off" from the audience – or worse, they feel cut off from us!

In this exploration, discover all of your dimensions within the 3-D space; awaken them, and let them inform your movement.

Note: in a *kinesthetic moment*, you tune in to your *kinesthetic sense*. Up to this point, *kinesthetic moment* has focused on sensations in your body and relationships within your body. You can also expand your *kinesthetic awareness* to the space around you as well. When you take a *kinesthetic moment*, your *kinesthetic sense* informs you about your inner space, your outer space, and the relationship between them.

You may enjoy playing music to enliven this Practice.

- Stand. Pause. Take a *kinesthetic moment*. Breathe.
- Walk through the room. As you walk, notice that the space around your moving body is ever-changing. Be aware of your sagittal dimension.
- Walk backward for a minute or more.
- Now walk in a horizontal direction, leading with your whole right side. You are facing forward, walking sideways toward the right. After a minute or more, switch to the left.

- Next, walk with awareness of your vertical dimension: up (feel free to lift your arms up above your head to assist with this). Explore down. Stay with each direction for a minute or more.
- Expand your attention to include 360° space and your body in it, as you play with directional movement.
- Sense if any one of the dimensions – vertical, sagittal, or horizontal – seems less available. Move in any way you like to awaken that invisible dimension.
- Let your body tell you how to move to enliven and support an invisible direction. Perhaps you want to stretch or roll or crawl. Maybe you want to slide along the floor. Experiment. There is no right or wrong!
- If you don't sense an invisible dimension, choose a dimension and play!
- Enlarge your awareness to include 3-D space as you move. Sense the relationship between the rounded shape of your *3-D body* and the space around you.
- The three dimensions connect and counterbalance in your body, which is surrounded by space on all sides: explore your *3-D body in the 3-D space*.
- Pause. Walk through the space again.
- Practice *inclusive attention* as you notice any new sensations and awareness of your *3-D body in the 3-D space*. Pause. Take a *kinesthetic moment*.
- *Spy back*. What did you discover? What was your "invisible" direction, if you discovered one? Is it livelier and more accessible after this exploration? In what way? How does this exploration inform your awareness of the relationship of your *3-D body in the 3-D space*?

As you practice, you can discover your comfort zones and your areas of unfamiliarity. They will inform you of dimensions you want to explore further, so you can expand your options when playing a character. There is more to you than your front!

PRACTICE 15.3 **THE DIMENSIONAL SCALE (KP)²**

This Practice follows Rudolf Laban's original form and intention for the *Dimensional Scale*. The variations you practiced in Chapter 13 put emphasis on inner space. Laban developed this Practice (and many others) to clarify pathways in the space around you. Laban sensed that spatial "pulls" could draw our body into these directional pathways: You can sense where you are and sense where you are going. In this way, space becomes a supportive partner of your movement.

You have practiced the *Dimensional Scale* in *Variations 1 and 2*. As you explore the movement sequence this time, follow a slightly different pathway when moving in a backward direction (sagittal dimension): Laban's original direction is to wrap the working arm across your body, hand on the opposite ribs, fingers pointing back. This clarifies your body's relationship to back space and makes a cleaner, clearer pathway in space (Figure 15.1).

I investigate: What can I discover as I move my *3-D body in the 3-D space*?

Part I: 3-D Pathways

- Practice the *Dimensional Scale* (Practice 13.2, Variation 1), using a slightly different focus. This time put your attention on your movements through outer space, rather than your inner dimensionality.
- Pause. Take a *kinesthetic moment*.
- *Spy back*. What is your experience of these movements when you place your attention on space? How does this experience compare with Variations 1 and 2?

Part II: 3-D Body in the 3-D Space

- When you feel ready, employ *inclusive attention* as you practice the scale again. Sense your *3-D body in the 3-D space*. Celebrate the **inner** counterbalancing dimensions of your 360° body within the welcoming 3-D environment of the **outer space**.
- Pause. Stand. Take a *kinesthetic moment*.
- Have a walk around the room. Practice *inclusive attention*. Sense the powerful relationship between your body and the space around you.
- *Spy back*. What did you learn about the relationship between your inner and outer space? How does this Practice affect your sense of yourself and the world around you?

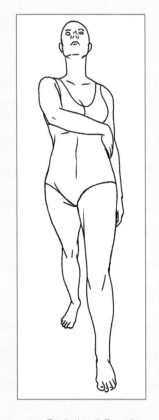

Figure 15.1 Exploring 3-D pathways, *Dimensional Scale*: back space.

Though the Practices you have explored in this section seem simple, they are powerful. These Practices help you develop and refine these important aspects of movement at a fundamental level. Just as musicians practice musical scales, actors can practice movement scales. Then, these basic skills are ready and available when you are rehearsing and performing. You are building your movement vocabulary, so explore these Practices often!

PAUSE TO PROCESS Journal, discuss, play. Discover your *3-D body in the 3-D space*.

In the next Practice, you can explore more ways of developing your inner and outer spatial awareness.

PRACTICE 15.4   **ACTIVATING DIMENSIONAL BALANCE – HURRY**

As we noted in Chapter 13, we live in a "hurry up and get there" culture. Faced with tight schedules and deadlines, we race to the next task with little awareness of the effect on our *body-mind*.

Alexander's process of **observation**, **awareness**, **pausing**, and **choosing** can offer you options for change. Hurry is part of life in our modern world. However, when you lose your sense of wholeness and balance, your 3-dimensionality can help you restore it.

- Stand in the space. Take a *kinesthetic moment*. Breathe.
- Take a walk from one end of the room to the other. Pause. Take a *kinesthetic moment*.
- Now, have a thought, "I have to get there right now!" and hurry to the other end of the room.
- Notice your back as you hurry. Perhaps you can notice that when you move quickly, your back seems to narrow toward the front dimension, "flattening" your body's natural cylindrical shape and lively coordination. When you reach the other end of the room, pause.
- Is your body still in "hurry mode?" What do you notice about your breath and your three dimensions?
- Pause. Breathe. Return to balance.
- Bring attention to your three dimensions. Sense the counterbalance of left and right, top and bottom, back and front.
- Now, walk at your usual pace, bringing particular awareness to the counterbalance of your front and back.
- Think of your whole back counterbalancing the forward motion, providing directional support.
- Your other dimensions are also at play, supporting the balance of your 360° body as you move.
- Play with these connections as you walk. Try walking backward and sensing the counterbalance of your front. Include your sides, top, and bottom.
- Pause. Take a *kinesthetic moment*.
- Now – revisit the thought, "I have to get there right now!" and bring your attention to your *3-D body in the 3-D space*, as you enjoy walking quickly to the other end of the room.
- Sense a strong counterbalancing direction from front to back, and the lively expansion of your whole back body balancing the forward motion as you move through the 3-D space.

- Pause. Take a *kinesthetic moment*.
- If you like, repeat this process a few times. Allow your *inclusive attention* to include all three dimensions and the 3-D space around you.
- Pause. Take a *kinesthetic moment*.
- *Spy back*. What happens in your body when you hurry? To your sense of space? How does this change as you expand your awareness to your *3-D body*, its counterbalancing directions, and the 3-D space?

In this exploration, you are building your ability to track kinesthetic information coming in simultaneously from a variety of sources. In this Practice you were including your *3-D body*, the 3-D space, spatial pathways, and counterbalancing directions all at once. Be gentle with yourself as you practice these new skills. *Fire the Judge. Hire the Witness*.

Three-dimensional awareness invites a sense of expansion even in a stressful situation. You can employ this process to counterbalance any area in your body that feels isolated or overly tense. You give yourself a big gift when you acknowledge and embody your inner and outer 3-dimensionality.

PRACTICE 15.5 CIRCUMSTANCES AND USE OF SPACE

Our relationship to space, both internal and external, changes with our circum-stances. Play the following scene, then *spy back* to note how space affected you in these scenarios.

- Do this improv with a partner.
- Imagine that your partner is an ex-lover, someone who hurt you deeply.
- You are visiting an area for the first time in a year, and you meet each other at an ATM machine by chance. Have a brief encounter, and one of you exit. (You can decide this in advance.)
- *Spy back*. How did each of you utilize space? Did the space between you take on a particular quality? What happened in your body in terms of inner and outer space as the scene progressed?
- Repeat the improv, with these circumstances: imagine that your partner is someone you were close to in high school, but you had lost touch with them.
- *Spy back*.

Inner and outer space support you in communicating circumstances, character and story. Revel in your ability to claim your space!

PRACTICE 15.6   **THE "HOKEY POKEY"**

Before we leave this chapter on your *3-D body in the 3-D space*, have a bit of fun with this old dance. The creators of this song were encouraging dimensional movement, although they probably were not aware of it. Their bodies knew!

Perhaps you are familiar with the "Hokey Pokey". It's a fun way to enliven your coordination and explore your dimensions. You can find the original version of the song from 1953 on YouTube.[3]

- Pause. Stand. Have a walk around the space. Practice *inclusive attention*.
- Awaken your *kinesthetic sense* and your awareness of which dimensions you are activating as you "do the Hokey Pokey." Note the counterbalance of all three dimensions in your body as you move within the 3-D space.
- At the end of the dance, pause. Take a *kinesthetic moment*.
- Have a walk around the space. Practice *inclusive attention*. Pause.
- *Spy back*.

Variation

You can repeat the dance and activate even more dimensions by orienting your body sideways or even backwards to the circle. If you lie down, you can activate your vertical dimension. However, be certain you leave plenty of space around your body, so you don't kick other people or the furniture!

Real-life Practice

The purpose of *YBK* is to expand your movement awareness and develop an array of choices that are effortlessly available to you when you are performing.

As you have worked through the Practices in Part I, you have expanded your body knowledge. We hope you are making discoveries that answer questions like: how does my body work? Can I increase my movement options? How do I access physical freedom and a dynamic presence onstage?

The more you apply the material and your discoveries about them in your everyday life, the more they will be available to you onstage.

- In your daily activities, such as washing dishes or driving, be aware of your *3-D body in the 3-D space*. Practice your visual and *kinesthetic awareness* in these familiar activities. How does this awareness change your perception? Do you find yourself making different choices – less pressure as you handle the dishes or hold the steering wheel? Does your breathing change? How does this awareness affect your movement?

- When exercising – walking, running, practicing yoga, lifting weights – awaken your invisible dimensions and/or sense the 3-D counterbalancing directions in your body. Practice sensing your *3-D body in the 3-D space*.

- In any activity, practice visual and spatial awareness. Note, for instance, how an awareness of the space around your computer – or your body as you work at the computer – can encourage your eyes and your *3-D body* to soften and release.

- You can give your computer (or any object) its own *Kinesphere*, which intersects with your *Kinesphere*. A computer can be a powerful trigger to "flatten" our 3-dimensionality toward it, much like the "Hurry Practice" above. By acknowledging the space and our own *Kinesphere*, we open ourselves up to our *3-D body in the 3-D space*, instead of being "sucked in" to the computer.

- You can include an awareness of your *3-D body in the 3-D space* in any of the Practices in Sections I–III and in your daily life. In this way, you can enliven your self-awareness and your *kinesthetic sensing*.

Recognize that when you tap into the "truth of your body" – in this case, 3-dimensional awareness – good things happen! Though it may feel like magic, you are simply honoring your *body-mind connection* and respecting your body's natural coordination.

Real-life Story: Jack Discovers the Power of His *3-D Body in the 3-D Space*

In the final assignment in Alexander Technique class, students are invited to apply all they have learned to a role in which they would never be cast. Jack, who is a Leading Man type, chose to explore completely new territory: "I Don't Know How to Love Him" from *Jesus Christ Superstar*, sung by Mary Magdalene. As Jack wrote:

"Mary is reflective and deep. She is trying her best to figure herself out, which is what this song is all about.

My process began with what this song meant to me, and where I would like to perform it. A small concrete prayer room was ideal, because it was intimate and featured a prayer rug attached to a wall. I discovered I was utterly helpless and in need of guidance.

While I am not particularly religious, I was baring my heart to this unmovable stone and prayer rug, hoping someone, the universe, God, anyone at all would hear my cry. I was able to use my whole body freely and expressively. My back alone communicated my message to the audience while I sang, or rather pleaded, with this immovable stone.

I had to exist in a world that was completely three-dimensional: my audience behind and beside me, my objective in front of me, and the feelings and sounds on all sides. I found a moment in the music that moved me to stand and turn from the wall, addressing my audience in full.

It all felt so right, to let the creative energy flow through my body without any obstruction. At that moment I knew this artistic journey was complete, and I knew I could call on this experience whenever I might need it."[4]

Through your *kinesthetic sense*, your *3-D body* receives the information it needs to make the most of your dynamic relationship with your inner and outer space. *Body-mind* constant two-way *communication* can be a deliberate choice that puts you in charge of how you move. This has wonderful benefits: your breath, muscles, bones, joints, senses – all work in harmony for support and ease, leaving you free to act!

> Key Word: *3-D Body in the 3-D Space*

Notes

1 Quoted from a student journal. Used with permission.
2 Newlove, Jean. *Laban for Actors and Dancers*. New York: Routledge, *1993*. p. 29.
3 The performers who originally recorded the "Hokey Pokey" are Ray Anthony and His Orchestra with vocals by Jo Ann Greer and the Skyliners. https://youtube.com/watch?v=Q_XN6HUTZ7E.
4 From a student journal. Used with permission.

Pathway to Presence

Putting It All Together

To have presence, you must be present in your Body.

Joan Schirle Dell' Arte International[1]

Every aspect of movement and acting work begins with you, your whole self: *body-mind*, breath, movement, and sound. You are your own artistic instrument.

As you have learned in the previous chapters, your body is designed for a wide array of movement possibilities. When your finely tuned body and mind are in sync with one another, you are ready to respond to each moment in performance. Whether you are moving dynamically through space or embracing stillness, you can make detailed choices for a broad range of creative expression.

One of the assignments in our movement classes is called The Great Performance Project. We pose a question, "How do you recognize a great performer?" The students are asked to select an actor whom they consider "great," choose three criteria for excellence, and apply them to a selected performance by this artist.

Our students say a great performer:

- invites the audience to "come along for the ride"
- is someone "being" not "performing"
- is totally committed, immersed, immediate (in the moment, in each moment)
- makes strong choices and reveals emotional range
- has a sense of rhythm and timing
- dares to reveal their whole self, be vulnerable, and share their vulnerability with an audience.

These performance qualities invite the audience into the character's emotional journey and the story of the play. As one student noted, "acting is allowing yourself to be human, with the whole world watching."[3]

As we watch these fine performers, we experience a sense of keen anticipation as we wait for their next move or response. The excitement and pleasure of watching them arises in not knowing what they will do next. We know that whatever they do will be done with spontaneity, yet totally in keeping with the arc of the character they have created and the given circumstances of the play. Their commitment is so complete, their instrument so well trained and highly responsive, that we cannot take our eyes from them. We become fascinated, as we attempt to "figure out" this compelling character. We are watching the artistry of great actors and their amazing ability to shape a variety of human experiences for the viewers' delight.

As an actor, you can learn an enormous amount about presence from watching the work of great performers. The goal is not to imitate, but to be inspired to discover your own unique abilities.

> "Step into another person's shoes and allow them to live through your body."
> Colby, acting student, Rider University[2]

Trust yourself: you can awaken your creative impulses, your ability to be fully alive in each moment, and risk exploring new territory. Become alert, aware, and awake!

In the first four Sections of *YBK*, we have introduced you to what your body knows: the truth about your body's actual design. And the truth is you are designed for movement, not postural holding. And this is also true: postural holding patterns block your creative impulse. But with the knowledge and experience of your design, you build a foundation: an open, receptive instrument, which supports your deepest creative instincts.

In this section, we revisit and deepen key concepts and movement explorations: *kinesthetic awareness*, breath support, *initiation* and *sequencing*, and your *3-D body in the 3-D space*. Each time you return to these foundations for movement, you deepen your *body-mind connection* with them. You are developing pathways that lead to a strong and compelling onstage presence.

Notes

1 Schirle, Joan. "The Actor's Network of Stimuli: Playing Fully, Playing with Ease," International Congress for the Alexander Technique, Plenary Speaker, Loyola University, Chicago. August 2018.
2 From a student journal. Used with permission.
3 From a student journal. Used with permission.

CHAPTER 16

Connecting Body, Mind, Breath, and Space

As an actor, you learn to develop a character and map their journey through the play. The ground floor of your work as a performer is connecting with your whole self, based on the foundational movement principles of your body's design. This *body-mind connection* provides a three-tiered "safety net" for your work: creating from the "truth" of your body's design, the dynamic power of your breath, and your relationship with the space around you.

These tools will enhance the quality of your personal warm-up and provide the focused energy necessary for you to be responsive to the text, the director, and the other actors.

PRACTICE 16.1 WARMING UP – MAKING CONNECTIONS

This exploration reconnects you with yourself in a "new-old way." Returning to these simple explorations of body, breath, and space can be new every time you experience them. As you practice, allow them to enhance your sensitivity to yourself and your surroundings.

Following the *spy back* at the end of this Practice, you can take this experience of breath, body, and space directly into Practice 16.2.

Part I: Connecting Movement and Breath

This exploration revisits Practice 13.1 (Expanding and Contracting) with a different focus: sensing diagonals in your body and in space.

- Lie down on the floor. Pause. Take a *kinesthetic moment*.
- Move into the *balanced resting state*.
- Take a few moments to receive the support of the floor and allow your breathing patterns to calm and deepen. Ride your exhale to completion, pause, and allow the inhale to happen spontaneously.

- When you are ready, begin to allow small body movements to ride on the flow of your breath. Perhaps your head will gently roll from side to side, or your arms, legs, and whole torso may subtly move.
- Taking your time, gradually allow your breath to guide you back to the *balanced resting state*.
- Pause. Take a *kinesthetic moment*.
- Remove the book from under your head.
- Allow your hands and feet to lead the way, as you release your arms and legs into the shape of an X.
- Notice that your X forms two diagonals, one from your right hand to your left foot, and one from your left hand to your right foot. Sense these diagonal connections through your whole body.
- On an exhale, allow your elbows and knees to move toward each other, and toward your center, as you did in Practice 13.1.
- Continue breathing. On your next exhale allow your hands and feet to guide your return to the full X-shape. As you move, notice the diagonal connections and the diagonal movement pathways, from your center out to the edges of your fingertips and toes.
- Repeat this sequence several times. Pause.
- Rest in the X-shape, sensing the diagonal connections in your body.
- Pause. Take a *kinesthetic moment*.

Part II: Breath, Body, and Space

- From your resting place in the X-shape, exhale as you bring your elbows and knees toward center.
- Rest for a moment, then allow your head to gently roll to one side, letting your spine and whole body follow.
- After a moment, press your hands into the floor to sit up. Then come to standing. Allow your movement to "ride on the flow of your breath."
- Stand. Pause. Take a *kinesthetic moment*.
- Sense your feet on the floor and the support of the floor. Sense this support moving up through your whole body.
- Sense the lively connection from your head through your spine, and into your arms and legs.
- Breathe.
- Move through your joints, beginning with your hands, as you did in Practice 4.1. Savor the fluid movement of each joint before moving to the next.
- Breathe as you play with joint movement – include everything! – throughout your whole body, ending with your feet.
- Pause. Breathe.
- Become aware of standing in the center of your 3-dimensional *Kinesphere*.
- Explore your *Kinesphere*. Riding on the flow of your breath, allow your arms and legs to lead your whole body into movement.

- You can *initiate* movement from anywhere in your body as you continue exploring your *Kinesphere*. You are in a dance with breath, body, and space! Pause.
- Breathe. Sense your body in your *Kinesphere* within the *3-dimensional space* of the room.
- Take a walk through the space, recognizing the vibrant connection of your body, breath, and *3-D space*.
- Pause and notice your dynamic presence. Take a *kinesthetic moment*.
- *Spy back*. How does an awareness of breath, body, and space affect your movement? What new sensations or connections did you discover in this Practice?

Through these explorations, you may notice that you are becoming more comfortable in your body. You can sense your breathing. Perhaps your mind is calmer, your body more energized, and you are more receptive to incoming information. Take this lively sense of presence into the next Practice, as you allow your body, mind, breath, and space to support you in front of an audience.

> As you go through your day, you may sometimes feel out of balance or disconnected. You can return to ease by gently asking three questions: how 3-dimensional am I? How is my breathing? How am I sensing my *3-D body within the 3-D space*?

PRACTICE 16.2   ENTERING AND EXITING

The explorations above offer you an experience of all you have explored and discovered about your body's design as you prepare for performance. When you are onstage, your *body-mind* knowledge is there to support you.

In the Practice below, experience your whole self as you explore these simple, familiar actions: enter the space, pause, and exit. Recognize that your purpose is not to entertain, but to be fully present in front of a friendly audience. Approach this exploration with non-judgment, and a spirit of curiosity.

I investigate: What can I learn as I stand in front of an audience, sensing myself and the space around me? What do I notice as I simply stand, offer, and receive?

Part I: Enter, Pause, Exit

If you are in a class, every actor should experience Part I, before going on to Part II. In Part I, actors can enter in groups of five or six.

- Take a moment to sense your whole self, your connection with the floor, your breath, and the space around you.
- Walk into the space and face the viewers.
- Pause.

- Allow your connection to your body, mind, breath, and space to support you. Allow yourself to be receptive to the connections between yourself, the space, and the viewers.
- When you sense the moment is complete, exit.

Part II: Enter, Pause, Gesture, Exit

Now, each person enters the space one at a time.

- Take a moment to sense your whole self, your connection with the floor, your breath, and the space around you.
- Walk into the center of the space and face the viewers.
- Pause.
- Create a whole-body gesture – a 3-dimensional movement – that expresses your sense of yourself in this moment. Pause.
- Exit.

Part III: Words

Each actor enters one at a time.

- Take a moment to sense your whole self, your connection with the floor, your breath, and the space around you.
- Walk into the center of the space and face the viewers.
- Pause.
- Say a sentence that reveals how you are feeling in this moment. Pause.
- Exit.
- *Spy back.* What did you discover about yourself and your connections with your body, mind, breath, and space in these three simple actions? What thoughts or emotions arose for you when you were standing in front of the audience? What did you discover about your relationship to the audience? What was the experience of allowing yourself "to be seen?"

Because of this stripped-away simplicity of these actions, you have the opportunity to sense basic moments of interference and moments of connection. Without judgment! Just curiosity.

And you are not alone! You are developing a presence based on deep knowledge. When you connect with your body, mind, breath, and space, you create a powerful sense of yourself, and you have the confidence to be present in the moment.

Recognize that you are enough, you are more than enough! You are standing on a firm foundation, and you have the power to be fully present in motion or in stillness.

PAUSE TO PROCESS Journal, discuss, play with these simple concepts.

Practicing Presence

Each of us is gifted with a unique presence in the world, both in our everyday life, and through the artistic choices we make. Your personal connection with body, mind, breath, and space is completely distinctive. And it is these connections that provide the foundation for your one-of-a-kind presence onstage.

This chapter brings together all you have learned in *YBK*. Through the Key Practices below, you can discover how your whole coordinated *body-mind* can support you in every moment – on and off the stage.

PRACTICE 17.1   MAKING CONNECTIONS THROUGH SUSPENSION AND SUPPORT (KP)

This exploration, a variation on a Practice from Betsy Polatin's book *The Actor's Secret*,[1] awakens your *body-mind connection* and your *primary coordination*. It gives you the opportunity to sense your whole self: the suspension of your weight throughout your body, and simultaneous support from the floor upward.

Part I

- Stand. Pause. Take a *kinesthetic moment*.
- Bring your attention to the top of your spine (at your A-O joint).
- Allow:

  your neck to be free

  your head to free forward and up (slight rotation of your head)

  your back to lengthen and widen

  your shoulders to widen out of your back, your elbows to free away from your shoulders, and your wrists and hands to free away from your elbows.

  your ribs to move easily with your breath, along with your sternum and spine

your knees to release away from your pelvis, and your ankles to release
   away from your knees
your feet to lengthen on the floor.
- Notice the dynamic buoyancy of your whole body.
- Sense the support of the ground through your feet.
- Allow your ankles, knees, and hip joints to be open to receive the support.
- Allow the support from the ground to come up through your legs, spine, torso, arms, and head.
- Sense the dynamic relationship of your whole *3-D body in the 3-D space*.
- Pause. Breathe. Take a *kinesthetic moment*. See and sense the room around you.
- Take a walk around the space, practicing *inclusive attention*. Pause.

Part II

This exploration follows Part I. Toward the end you are going to share a bit of text. Choose one of these lines to share: "Let's jump ahead," "I look up to her," "Take the first step." Or use a sentence of your own.

- Remember the line that you have chosen. When you meet someone, come to standing, take a moment to sense your whole self, your sense of *suspension and support*. Take in the other person and share your line. The other person receives the line, then shares their line, while you become the receiver.
- When your interaction is complete, continue to move around the room.
- Practice this several times, maintaining your sense of *suspension and support*. Notice your whole *3-D body in the 3-D space* as you walk, pause, speak.
- When the Practice is complete, pause. Take a *kinesthetic moment*.
- *Spy back*. What did you discover about *suspension and support*? How do they contribute to your sense of presence? Were there moments in the Practice when you felt like you lost your sense of wholeness? When? What did you do to regain it?
      Part II: What was the experience of sharing your line with another person? What was your experience of being the listener?

This Practice allows us to experience another *friendly fact*: our bodies are simultaneously suspended from the top down and supported from the ground up. You can sense a "two-way street" of suspension and support throughout your body. Our weight falls toward the ground through the effects of gravity, and *GRF* engages our muscles and bones to support our weight all the way up to the top of our heads.

In his groundbreaking book, *Neurodynamics*, Alexander Technique teacher and educator Dr. Ted Dimon explains,

> *We support from the ground up because we have to apply force to the ground to come up off the ground ... The body must also be organized from the top down, because it cannot maintain lengthened and efficient support against gravity unless the head leads and the spine lengthens. So, the structure is supported from the ground up but organized from the top down.*[2]

Remember that your *primary coordination* is your natural state. Tension and "holding patterns" are interferences with your body's natural balance. Your *PC* returns you to alert readiness; it is the "underground stream" connecting your *body-mind* and supporting your dynamic presence.

Below, you can build on the skills and body-knowledge you have learned so far, as you explore another pathway to presence: the *5 Cues*.

The *5 Cues*

The *5 Cues* (KP) are a series of *dynamic thoughts* designed to connect and enliven your whole body. Each cue focuses on awakening your coordinated body from the ground up and building awareness of your whole self.

The *5 cues* connect the elements of the *body-mind* vocabulary you have been building in all of Part I. With your *body-mind connection* as a foundation, the *5 cues* unite the *friendly facts* of your body's design, *tensegrity*, *ground reaction force*, and *primary coordination*. This one dynamic movement sequence is a progression that leads you to ease, power, and grace onstage.

The *5 cues* are:

- *Grounding*
- *Centering*
- Expanding
- *Poising*
- Flying.

The *5 cues* offer you connection throughout your whole body and to the world around you. They clarify your relationship to yourself, to the supportive ground, and the 3-D space. They work with your natural balance, unite your whole body, and activate your *PC*. Because they lead to dynamic presence, our students find that the *5 cues* are a great prep for the moment before they enter.

In the Practices that follow, you can explore each of the *5 cues* and the *dynamic thinking* that activates them. As preparation for your exploration, take a "movement pause:" return to the simplicity of your relationship with the space around you.

PRACTICE 17.2   **THE POWER OF SPACE**

This Practice reminds you that your *3-D body* moves *in the 3-D space*. This is a foundation for activating the *5 cues*.

I investigate: What can I learn about being receptive to myself, others, and the *3-D space*?

- Pause. Stand. Breathe. Take a *kinesthetic moment*.
- Remind yourself that your *3-D body* moves *in the 3-D space*.
- As you stand, accepting the support of the floor, sense your breathing and your whole self, with no expectations.
- Allow your eyes to be soft and receptive as you notice the room around you.
- Begin to walk, continuing to see with soft and receptive eyes.
- Sense yourself and receive your surroundings as you walk in various pathways: forward, backward, sideways, circles, spirals, diagonals.
- Pause often, and simply allow your awareness to include yourself, the space, and other people if you are in a group setting.
- Pause. Breathe. Take a *kinesthetic moment*.
- *Spy back*. What did you discover about receptivity and awareness of space? How might this Practice affect your onstage presence?

This Practice offers you simplicity – reconnecting with body, breath, and space – your foundation for presence. This is the starting place for building a performance. Take this sense of presence with you as you explore the *5 cues*.

PRACTICE 17.3   **EXPLORING THE 5 *CUES***

Dive into the *5 cues* with a spirit of curiosity and discovery. This Practice has five different explorations; some of them you have experienced in other chapters. *PAUSE TO PROCESS* any time you tire or feel like you have had enough information for now!

Cue #1: Grounding

Grounding activates a **lively** relationship between your feet and the floor. Some people think that pulling their weight downward and pressing their feet into the floor will ground them. However, as you learned in Chapter 8, if you honor your body's design and the natural force of *GRF*, you discover that *grounding* is a source of dynamic support.

When you are grounded, *GRF* gives your body a boost upward. Think of the difference between a rubber ball bouncing off the floor vs. dropping a bean bag.[3] Explore your dynamic connection to the ground, as *GRF* and your body's natural *tensegrity* offer you a sense of your whole supported self.

Before you begin this exploration, you may want to review the section on *GRF* and *grounding* in Chapter 8, especially the "weight triangle: 50/30/20" in Practice 8.3.

I investigate: What can I discover about my relationship to the ground?

- Pause. Stand. Breathe. Take a *kinesthetic moment*.
- Sense the support of the floor underneath your feet.
- Lightly shift your weight from foot to foot, sensing any changes in each foot as it alternately leaves and touches the ground.
- Bring your awareness to your lively, springy arch as it responds to these movements.
- Notice the response of your whole body to these movements.
- Shift your weight toward the front of your feet, then toward the back, assisted by the rolling action of your ankle joints. Now shift your weight from side to side on your feet.
- Pause.
- Play with moving your weight in circles inside the triangle of your foot.
- Give yourself this *dynamic thought*: I can sense a "two-way street" that lengthens my foot forward toward my toes and backward toward my heels.
- Your ankles, knees, and hip joints are balancing and rebalancing as they go along for the ride.
- Expand your awareness to include your whole body and the space around you. Pause.
- Now let your feet really meet the floor, and let the floor meet your feet. Notice how support from the floor rises through your whole body.
- You can allow your weight to balance on your feet: 50/30/20.
- Take a walk. Experience the connection of your springy foot with the ground and the buoyant release as your foot leaves the ground. Pause.
- Sense your connection to the ground and the support through your whole body.
- Move any way you want through the space, noticing the connection and the springiness of your feet, legs, and whole body: skip, run, jump, play!
- Pause. Take a *kinesthetic moment*. Sense the support of the floor through your feet, ankles, and whole body.
- *Spy back*. What did you learn about balance, support and your connection to the floor? Is the floor friendly? How does this Practice affect your sense of *grounding*? What do you know now that you didn't know before this Practice?

Your whole body has a flexible and powerful relationship with the ground when you "stand on your own two feet."

Cue #2: Centering (KW)

Continuing the journey from the ground upward.

I investigate: How can I *center* myself?

Part I: Explore Your Center of Gravity

- Pause. Stand. Breathe. Take a *kinesthetic moment*.
- Sense your *3-D body surrounded by the 3-D space*.
- Bring your attention to the full length of your body from the top of your head down to your feet.
- Locate your *center* of gravity: place a thumb on your belly button and let your fingers spread on your stomach, pinky draping down toward your pubic bone.
- Place the **back** of your other hand on your sacrum. Your two hands are one behind the other. You are cradling the geographic *center* of your body.
- Your *center* of gravity allows you to balance easily on one leg and then shift your weight to the other leg. Allow your *center* to guide you as you move.
- Allow your hip, knee, and ankle joints to respond to these weight shifts.
- Move your legs further apart and shift the weight of your pelvis to the right side, releasing at your hip, knee, and ankle joints on the right, while your left leg lengthens. Then reverse the movement to the left.
- Enjoy the sensation of moving your *center* of gravity from side to side. Pause.
- With your hands still cradling your *center*, take a walk, noticing the sensations of movement under your hands.
- After a few moments, take your hands away as you continue to walk. Practice *inclusive attention*. Allow your sense of *center* to be the guide for your whole *3-D body* as you walk through the *3-D space*. Pause.
- Take a *kinesthetic moment*.

Part II: The Hub of a Wheel

Your *center* can be compared to the *center* of a wheel, the hub, with spokes radiating in all directions.[4]

I investigate: Where is my *center* and how does it affect me when I move?

- Stand with your arms and legs extended out from your *center* of gravity into the shape of an X.
- Shift your weight onto your left leg, allowing your whole body to rotate around your *center*. Your right foot leaves the floor, and your whole body tilts as you extend out of *center*. Breathe.
- Enjoy the experience of the counterbalancing forces within your *3-D body* as you move *in the 3-D space*. Your body's *tensegrity* supports you as you move.

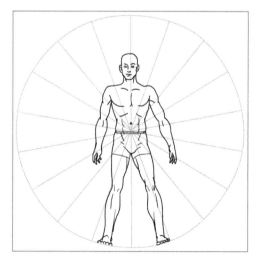

Figure 17.1 Your *center* radiates support through your whole *3-D body*.

- Bring your weight back onto both legs.
- Repeat on the other side.
- Play with tilting your whole body from left to right. Be aware of the space around you – the "X" helps you access your sense of moving through space. If you continue this movement in one direction, you could do a cartwheel!
- Trust your *center*, which creates a natural balance for your body and your movements in space.
- Lower your arms, bring your legs to balance underneath your pelvis. Notice how your *center* of gravity is still influencing your balance and coordination in space and the lively relationship of your feet with the floor.
- Have a walk through the space, noticing your lively relationship with the floor and the way your *center* influences your movement. Pause.
- Take a *kinesthetic moment*.
- *Spy back*. How does this Practice affect your understanding of *center*? How do *grounding* and *centering* work together when you are moving? When you are still?

Grounding and *centering* provide a sense of energy and stability in movement and in stillness.

Cue #3: Expanding

Explore the expansive qualities of your whole spine, 3-D torso, and whole body.

If you need a refresher of "seaweed spine," you can revisit Practice 11.2.

I investigate: What can I learn about the expansive relationship of my 3-D torso with the rest of my *3-D body*?

- Stand. Pause. Take a *kinesthetic moment*.
- Notice the subtle shape changes in your torso as you inhale and exhale.
- Practice "seaweed spine," exploring the movement potential of all four spinal curves: turning, spiraling, rippling, rolling.
- Practice small movements, as your 24 vertebrae, sacrum, and coccyx engage in a subtle, vibrant dance.
- Notice how your ribs and pelvis become part of this dance.
- Sense the counterbalancing directions (*tensegrity*) of each dimension as you move.
- Sense these movements rippling outward, connecting your whole 3-D torso with your whole *3-D body*.
- Notice that *grounding* and *centering* support these expansive movements.
- Pause. Take a *kinesthetic moment*.
- Have a walk through the space, allowing *grounding*, *centering*, and *expanding* to be at play with each other as you move. Pause.
- *Spy back*. What do you notice about the expansive connection of your 3-D spine and torso with your whole body?

With the support of *grounding*, *centering*, and *expanding*, you are ready to explore *poising* and *flying*.

Cue #4: *Poising* (KW)

By *poising*, you can sense the buoyant relationship of your whole head with your whole body. If you would like a refresher about the A-O joint, revisit Chapter 5.

I investigate: What can I discover about the connection of my whole body with the *poise* of my head?

- Pause. Breathe. Take a *kinesthetic moment*.
- *Ground* and *center* yourself. Sense the expansiveness of your whole *3-D body*.
- Bring your attention to your whole head and its relationship to your spine and whole body.
- Explore the *poising* balance of your head with your whole body by delicately nodding "yes."
- Notice the rolling, sliding, and gliding action of your A-O joint.
- With small movements, explore all the directions that your head can move from its dynamic balance at the top joint, supported by your whole spine.
- Sense the *reverberation* of these movements in your whole body, such as your back lengthening and widening. Notice a sense of *suspension and support*.
- Pause. Take a *kinesthetic moment*.
- Notice your *grounding*, *centering*, *expanding*, *poising* body and the space around you.
- *Spy back.* What do you notice about the relationship of your feet to your head? How does the *poise* of your head affect your whole body?

The lively *poising* of your head influences the freedom and ease of your whole body. This dynamic relationship is supported by *grounding*, *centering* and *suspending*.

Cue #5: Flying

Explore the lightness and ease of your arm movement, supported by your whole body in lively partnership with the ground.

Note: you may find that when the first four cues are activated in your body, your arms simply "want" to release out of your back and up into space. Should this sensation arise, just go with it!

I investigate: Do I have wings?

- Pause. Breathe. Take a *kinesthetic moment*.
- *Ground* yourself. *Center*. Sense the *expansion* of your whole torso and your head *poising* at your A-O joint.
- Sense your buoyant arm structure, including your collarbones and shoulder blades.
- Invite a widening direction through your collarbones in the front and your shoulder blades in the back.

- Your arms lengthen out of this powerful source of support all the way to your fingertips.
- Your arms are supported by your whole body.
- Take a moment to *ground, center, expand,* and *poise,* which frees your arms to "fly" up, out and slightly forward in space. Think of yourself as a bird spreading its wings.
- Sense the connection through your whole body from the ground up, with your whole back supporting your arms all the way to your fingertips.
- Sensing your whole body, and the support of the ground, allow your fingertips to lead your arms down to rest at your sides.
- Pause. Take a *kinesthetic moment.*
- *Spy back.* What do you notice now about your arms and their relationship to your whole back, and your whole coordinated body?

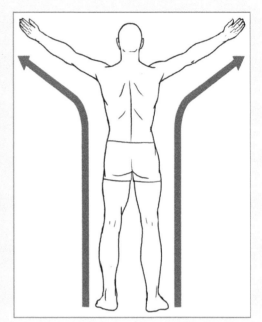

Figure 17.2 Your arms can fly – up and out – supported by your back.

When you practice the *5 cues*, each *part* is activated *within the whole.* No part of you is left out. All parts participate in your dynamic movement.

PRACTICE 17.4   A SEQUENCE OF DYNAMIC THINKING – THE 5 CUES

Now that your body knows the *5 cues* sequence from the inside out, you can activate them with your *dynamic thinking.* Each cue leads you to the next one, and they build on each other. Together, they unite your mind and body in a coordinated whole. Review Practice 16.2, Parts I and III before you begin.

- Pause. Stand. Take a *kinesthetic moment.*
- Sensing your whole body, practice *dynamic thinking* to activate each cue in order, from the ground up.
- *GROUNDING*: accept the dynamic support of the ground and GRF, which leads to
- *CENTERING*: sensing your *center* radiating energy and stability to your whole body, which leads to

- EXPANDING: allowing your whole 3-D torso to expand and connect with your whole body, which leads to
- *POISING*: sensing the dynamic balance of your head with your whole body, which leads to
- FLYING: allowing your arms to release up and out and slightly forward on a diagonal, emerging from your whole back, and supported from the ground up.
- Pause.
- When you are ready, allow your arms to come back to your side. Take a *kinesthetic moment*.
- Have a walk around the space. A sense of buoyancy and wholeness is supported by your *dynamic thinking* and the *5 Cues*. Pause.
- You are ready to Enter. Return to Practice 16.2, Parts I and III. Before your entrance, practice the *5 cues*. Remember: think, and your body will respond.
- When you practice Part III of Practice 16.2, use a line from a play or monologue that has strong meaning for you.
- Pause.
- *Spy back*. What did you experience when you activated the *5 cues*? What did you experience when the *5 cues* became the foundation for Entering, Speaking, and Exiting?

You may notice that when the *5 cues* work together, you have a strong sense of support from the ground up, and a simultaneous suspension from the top down. The *5 cues* actually activate your *primary coordination*, giving you a sense of *suspension and support*.

The *5 cues* connect and energize you from head to toe, front to back, and fingertip to fingertip. Your whole body is alive and awake. They support you as you access the *PC*. When you activate the *5 cues*, your whole self is awake and in motion, ready to act!

> *PAUSE TO PROCESS* You have reached the end of Part I! Your body and mind are in continuous two-way communication. You are intimately acquainted with your joints "where movement happens." You have the freedom to accept the support of your breath, expand into *3-D space*, and access your *primary coordination*.
>
> Pause. Give yourself a pat on the back. Celebrate all you know. Journal, revisit Practices, process with a friend, practice *constructive rest*. Write, draw, and discuss the ways that your Part I discoveries can support you as an actor and as a human being. Take this body-knowledge into your daily activities.

Now that you know your whole instrument, you are ready to play. And Play is the subject of Parts II and III. In Part II, your finely tuned, responsive instrument – your *body-mind* – will support you as you explore the Elements of Expression. You can discover more choices and more ways to reveal your character in performance.

Key Words: *Centering, Poising*

Key Practices: *Suspension and Support, 5 Cues*

Notes

1 Polatin, Betsy. *The Actor's Secret. Berkeley:* North Atlantic Books, 2016. Print. p. 54. Used with permission.
2 Dimon, Theodore. *Neurodynamics*, Berkeley: North Atlantic Books, 2016. p. 16.
3 Carol Boggs, personal communication, August 26, 2018.
4 Dowd, Irene. *Taking Root to Fly,* New York, Contact Collaborations, 1981, p. 10.

Elements of Expression

PART II   ELEMENTS OF EXPRESSION

Introduction to Part II

As you discovered in Part I, you are a coordinated whole. You create from your *body-mind* instrument, and you move more easily when you are in tune with its inherent design. You also learned that your relationship with your body and the world around you determine how you move. Through your explorations of body, mind, breath, and space, you discovered movement habits that were not serving you. You now have a choice about how you move. You are ready to play!

Part II: Elements of Expression builds on what you learned in Part I. From your open and receptive instrument, you are free to explore your most authentic impulses, your physical imagination, and the elements that create every movement you make. These "movement basics" are the ingredients that, when you put them together, make a delicious savory, sweet, and spicy performance. They move you beyond your everyday choices into extra-ordinary expression.

Each of us has our "go to" gestures, body use, and spatial relationships, but these familiar choices may not be the best ones to create a role. Through the Elements of Expression, you can explore character and environment and emotions that may be unfamiliar to you but are essential to the world of the play. These explorations provide a safe and effective way to move beyond your comfort zone.

There's an expression we sometimes use when we feel our acting is disconnected from the character and text: I felt like I was in my head. "Getting out of our heads" is the reason exploration is vital to creating character movement. Your brain creates conditioned responses: years of habit influence the considered decisions of the intellect, because it is responding to **your** relationship to the world.

You can see how this might be a problem. Let's say that you are an outgoing, friendly person, playing the reclusive Laura Wingfield in Tennessee Williams' *The Glass Menagerie*. If you make a mental decision about Laura's movement, you might say – "I'm going to move timidly because this character is timid" – and then manipulate your body to fit your conception of what a timid person looks like.

However, when you cultivate the Elements of Expression, they become part of your movement vocabulary. Your conditioned intellect begins to recognize new possibilities, and your whole being becomes more receptive to a broad range of physical expression. Your body, mind, and being are communicating!

As you prepare a role, begin by exploring a wide variety of movement. Through this process, you will find that the best choices simply emerge, from the inside out. Your body, mind, and imagination are free to create from all the factors that contribute to the character's physical life and your unique expression of them.

Your body knows, because you are a coordinated whole. Enjoy your explorations as you dive into these vital, freeing Elements of Expression.

Authenticity and Commitment

In Section V, you read about the "Great Performance Project," in which our students write about the qualities they observe in great actors. Their observations led them to use words like, "totally immersed" and "dares to reveal their whole self." A great performance appears spontaneous and "real," because the performer commits to the character and the action of the play, and then, responds authentically to each moment as it unfolds.

Every actor, from the beginner to the most experienced professional, relies on their expressive instrument – body and voice – to share the internal life of their character with an audience. When your instrument is open and free, you liberate your imaginative *body-mind*, and you can express your most genuine creative impulses. Like the great performers, you can develop a committed, compelling performance from your whole, authentic self.

In this section, you can discover another basic movement foundation, *Authentic Impulse* (KW). When you trust your authentic self, you can connect with your deepest, most original impulses. You give your creative *body-mind* permission to play and explore, opening the door to expressive movement.

You will find that you can be "totally immersed" and "reveal your whole self," when you are supported by the simple, yet powerful principles in the chapters that follow:

* *Authentic Impulse*
* *Kinesthetic Body/Life Body*
* *The Four Brothers: A Feeling of Ease, Form, Wholeness, and Beauty*

When you are grounded in these elements of expression, you can discover a whole new world of specific, surprising, inspired creative choices, choices that grow out of your own experience. You can connect with your deepest *authentic impulses*, and they will support you in every imaginative endeavor.

Creative Commitment

Each time we pause and take a *kinesthetic moment*, we give ourselves a chance to wake up our senses and our *body-mind connection*. When we pause, we are making a commitment to our creative growth as actors.

Michael Chekhov's acting technique emphasizes the importance of pausing. He felt that each time we enter a rehearsal or begin a performance, we must make a commitment to our creative selves: "… develop a feeling that you are a creative person, that you are capable of creating anything."[1]

When we act, we step out of our everyday lives and into an artistic world of creativity and imagination. Chekhov felt that it was essential to acknowledge and commit to this creative state.

PRACTICE VI.1   CROSSING THE THRESHOLD (KP)[2]

Crossing the threshold is a core Practice in the Michael Chekhov work. In this Key Practice, you are invited to pause and take a moment to commit to your creative work and yourself as an artist. This is a powerful exploration in a group setting, yet it is also creates a strong sense of commitment when practiced by an individual.

Begin with a commitment: I allow my creative imagination to serve me in this Practice.

- The group stands in a circle. Pause. Take a *kinesthetic moment*.
- Sense the ground under your feet. "Breathe in your natural rhythm with a feeling of ease. As you breathe, imagine that you are breathing in a sensation of openness which flows through your body. On the exhalation imagine you are opening the space around you."[3]
- See the others in the circle. Recognize them as your fellow artists.
- Imagine a golden line on the floor in front of the feet of the artists in the circle. The line makes a complete circle. The group is standing outside the circle.
- Imagine that outside the circle is your everyday world with all your concerns and responsibilities and relationships.
- Imagine that inside the circle is your artistic world of imagination and creativity.
- When you feel ready, step across the threshold into the circle. You are committing to leave your ordinary world and enter the extraordinary world of creative imagination.
- Wait until the entire group is inside the circle. Look around and see your fellow artists. Accept the support of the floor.
- Take a walk around the room, sensing yourself, the space around you, and your fellow artists.
- Pause. Take a *kinesthetic moment*. You are ready to dive into your artistic work!

This Practice connects your body, mind, and imagination, because you are affirming yourself as an artist. You are making a commitment to be present and available to your creative work. It is a strong beginning for every rehearsal, performance, or class.

When the rehearsal, class, or performance is over, you can return to the circle, and step out of it and into your everyday life. Trust that your creative work will be available – waiting for you – the next time you *cross the threshold*.

Key Word: *Authentic Impulse*

Key Practice: *Crossing the Threshold*

Notes

1 Chekhov, Michael. Transcribed by Deirdre Hurst du Prey. *Lessons for Teachers*. Ottawa: Dovehouse Editions. p. 31.
2 While we have practiced *Crossing the Threshold* in many settings, we acknowledge the influence of our teachers in the Chekhov Technique for their guidance over the years – in particular, Mark Monday and Joanna Merlin.
3 Joanna Merlin. Personal correspondence. April 13, 2019. Used with permission.

Authentic Impulse

Listening Within

One of our tasks as actors is to discover the difference between "conditioned response" and *authentic impulse*. Conditioned response takes us down a well-established pathway, one that feels safe and familiar to us, but it may not have a lot in common with the character's behavior. *Authentic impulse* is the "road less traveled," to quote Robert Frost's famous poem.[1] *Authentic impulses* arise from our deeper human nature, beyond our own personality choices.

Our conditioned responses guide us well in our daily lives: we have to consider the consequences before we yell at our boss, even if they are being completely unreasonable! As children, we learned to share, instead of keeping all the candy for ourselves; we learned not to pull away when great Aunt Tilly leaned in to kiss us – no matter how terrifying her moustache was.

Your conditioned brain is designed to keep you safe – and therefore, offers the limited, well-tested choices that have served you in the past. Onstage, though, it might be infinitely more interesting if we do run away from Aunt Tilly: think of the hilarious chase scene that might follow!

How do we access our *authentic impulses*? First, we can access freedom of movement through our bodies, as you discovered in Part I. We can also commit to a different set of values beyond what we have considered to be safe or "acceptable" social norms. Instead, we can embrace a "new normal."

- We recognize that our "internal support system" aids us when we are acting:
  our body-mind intelligence
  our sense of wholeness
  our imagination.
- We teach ourselves (our conditioned brain) that within our creative environment:
  authenticity can be safe,
  empowering,
  fun!

- We commit to:
      nurturing and
      finding delight in our
      unique, authentic responses
      in each moment.

In Part I, Know Your Instrument, you began to recognize and release harmful *body-mind* movement patterns. You may have found yourself in new territory, making "new choices." You allowed your *authentic impulses* to guide you. Authenticity can support you in every moment onstage.

You may be asking, "How do I recognize an *authentic impulse*?"

- It feels effortless – I'm not "trying to make it happen."
- It spontaneously arises without thinking about it.
- My body easily follows the impulse.

Through your work in *Your Body Knows* you have cleared away the misunderstandings and misuse of your body and its design. Your whole self has become a channel for authentic expression. A strong, underlying stream of unique inner impulses can now become the foundation for your character choices. You are free to respond to each moment of the play, and your performance becomes more truthful, spontaneous, and filled with a sense of energized ease.

Beginning: Tuning into *Authentic Impulse*

When we were babies, we learned to move by experimenting: we rolled from side to side, we reached out with our fingers and toes, we learned to sit, crawl, and eventually stand and walk. Amazing accomplishments!

As babies, we playfully took time to connect with, and explore the movement pathways in our bodies and in the space around us. We were preparing our bodies and minds to respond to our world by testing things out, improvising, and seeing what worked and what didn't: we fell down and got up many times. This process was awakened by our curiosity and cultivated by our courage as we explored the unknown.

The core of all movement work is *authentic impulse*. We may not know what's inside us until we take the time to listen. Accessing your authentic response is a rewarding and freeing process. Allow yourself to approach each moment without judgment. We can remember and reawaken these qualities of courage, commitment, and play that we had as children.

> Note: warm up your body and breath and awaken your *kinesthetic sense* before you begin any of the Practices in Part II. In Appendix I, you can find a list of warm-ups – most of which you encountered in Part I.

PRACTICE 18.1   FOLLOWING AN IMPULSE

This exploration can help you develop your sensitivity to *authentic impulse* vs. conditioned response.[2]

In the Practice below, you can discover the many subtle movement possibilities that lie just below the surface of your outer body. Your body knows! Be patient, take the time to allow movements to surface naturally, and then disappear as other movements take their place. Follow the lead of your inner impulse.

This Practice requires a partner who acts as an observer of your movement. Your eyes will be closed, so your observer also provides gentle guidance, to direct you away from walls, furniture, other people, etc. As much as possible, the observer keeps their distance from the mover (6–8 feet), placing their body between the mover and an object when necessary.

When necessary, an observer can use a gentle touch to encourage the mover to go in another direction. Non-interference and non-judgment are the order of the day. To avoid injury to themselves or someone else, movers should open their eyes if they are going to move through space suddenly or quickly, as your observer may not be able to keep up with you.

In the sharing period, movers speak first, then observers share their experience of witnessing the mover's journey. Commenting on the movement ("That was great!") is not appropriate; it is most helpful to the mover if observers share only what they saw ("Toward the end, your movements became very small and soft").

In addition, it is best to have a facilitator who has an overall view of the movers. They can assist the observers in creating a safe environment for everyone.

(Note: for a solo Practice, go to Appendix I.)

I investigate: Can I get out of my own way and allow myself to follow my deepest movement impulses?

- It is helpful to read through all the directions below before beginning this exploration.
- As the mover, you can lie down on the floor with your eyes closed. Allow the back surfaces of your body to connect with the floor.
- Take some time to breathe and listen to the rhythmic movement of your breath.
- Your observer stands 8–10 feet away if possible. The observer's task is to provide a "safe space" physically, mentally, and emotionally for you, the mover.
- If there is a person leading the exploration, they can offer a cue to begin and assist the observers. If not, the observer can be the timekeeper. Fifteen minutes is a good time frame for this exploration.
- When the cue to begin is given to the mover, they can continue to lie on the floor, turning their attention to any small movements taking place in their body.
- If you are the mover, perhaps your head is delicately shifting, or maybe you feel some movements of release in your back.

- As you continue to notice your breathing, you may begin to feel small movement impulses. They may appear in your feet or hands, or perhaps in your torso, arms, or legs.
- If the impulse is strong enough, you may find it begins to move through your body. Allow the impulses to guide you into movement.
- You may sense that your body wants to change shape. You can recognize the inner impulse that initiates any spontaneous movement.
- You may find you want to change your relationship with the floor; follow these impulses.
- You may begin to recognize when the movement happens naturally and when you are "making" it happen.
- At times you may rest in stillness.
- No judgement is necessary as you allow movement to travel through you in various pathways, or as you pause and then resume, following your *authentic impulse*.
- At 14 minutes, the leader or observer advises the mover(s) to begin to bring their exploration to a close.
- Complete your exploration. Pause. Rest. Observers continue to give movers space and open attention.
- After a minute or two, sit up, and your witness can join you. Sit back to back on the floor. Sense your partner's breathing.
- Then after a minute or two, turn around and share your experience, with the mover speaking first.
- After each person has shared their experience, change roles.
- *Spy back.* Were you aware of trying to get it right? Rushing? Excess tension? How did you cope with these interferences? Was it scary to wait for an impulse? In what way? Did you want to "make something happen?" If you allowed creative impulse to guide you, what did you discover?

Learning to wait, listen, and allow is at the core of discovering your *authentic impulses*. Perhaps this Practice was challenging for you. You are not alone. This exploration takes time and gentle attention to your self and the process. Approach without judgment.

Revisit this Practice often. The rewards are great: allowing ourselves to move from our *authentic impulses* rescues us from our habitual responses. It's like letting down the walls that have imprisoned our creative possibilities.

Cause and Effect: Our Habits on Parade

In Chapters 10 and 11, you explored *stimulus* and *response* in a series of Practices: Three Thoughts/Three Bodies. You discovered how simple, everyday thoughts – a *stimulus* – caused you to respond in a particular way.

When we are onstage, we experience a host of powerful internal and external *stimuli*. The strong *stimulus* of an audience can trigger habitual fears and old patterns. Many of us find we want to retreat into the safety of our habits, such as "trying to make something happen." These knee-jerk responses simply add a layer of excess tension. They limit our choice palette and cut us off from our creativity.

One of the most freeing things you can do for yourself as a mover, an actor, and a human being is to recognize and release habitual movement patterns. We can learn to welcome another possibility, an authentic *response.*

When you are in a performance situation, it helps to know your habitual *responses* and what *stimulates* them. Here are some habitual *responses* to *stimulus* our students have experienced in the presence of an audience:

- The need to please
- The need to do it right
- The need to entertain
- The need to anticipate/fill the gap quickly
- The need to "do:" overload and over-endow the material
- The need to "make something happen" by using excess tension

Our students have recognized that these *response* patterns can be an attempt to mask fear and control audience reaction. Every performer has experienced one or more of these responses at some point. However, there is good news: with awareness and a strong movement foundation, you can make another choice!

Here are some alternative approaches:

- Pausing, and allowing yourself time to open to the *stimulus* and let it "cook."
- Letting go of the fear of looking foolish: taking a risk.
- Remaining open to the "give and take" between you, the other performers, and the audience.
- Allowing your senses to inform you (sight, hearing, *kinesthetic awareness*) as a powerful support for making creative choices.
- Allowing your breath to support you as you move through each moment.

In the first list, perhaps you saw some of your own habitual *responses* to an audience. The second list offers new possibilities, a "way out" of habits that can limit your creativity and hide your authentic self.

In the next Practice, you can explore some of the alternative approaches offered above. You can discover deeper layers of your *kinesthetic awareness* and *authentic impulse*, as you encounter the *stimulus* of an audience.

PRACTICE 18.2   VARIATION: ENTERING AND EXITING

In Practice 16.2, you connected to your body and the space around you, as you practiced being present before an audience. Now, explore this Practice again, giving attention to your *authentic impulses*, and remaining open to the "alternative approaches" mentioned above.

When you recognize your habitual *response*, pause, breathe and wait for a deeper impulse to arise. Trust yourself. You are all you need. *Authentic impulse* provides you with powerful support in rehearsal and in performance.

I investigate: What happens when I allow *authentic impulse* to support me in front of an audience?

- Stand. Pause. Breathe. Take a *kinesthetic moment*.
- *Cross the threshold.*
- Revisit Practice 16.2, Entering and Exiting, with attention to *authentic impulse*, habitual response, and alternative approaches.
- *Spy back.* What did you discover about your habitual responses to an audience? your authentic responses? What are you learning about recognizing your habitual response and accessing *authentic impulse*?

The core of *authentic impulse* is to learn to listen to your body, to connect with an inner personal and physical impulse which wants to be expressed in movement or in stillness. And you can begin here and now: you can pause, connect with yourself, and develop the ability to "listen within."

All movement begins from the inside: from your breath, the beating of your heart, the balancing and rebalancing of your muscles and joints. Your *authentic impulse initiates* a movement that can *sequence* through your body and being. Trust these impulses. Your movement will become more spontaneous, connected, and whole, and your artistic choices can emerge from that "alive" place inside you.

Real-life Story: Bri Allows Her Body to Think for Itself
In movement class, Bri discovered the joys of allowing her body to "lead the way." This is an excerpt from her journal:

One of the biggest movement discoveries that I've made during my time here: In order to silence my mind and be in the present moment, I have to allow my body to think for itself. Or rather, I have to trust that my body knows what it's doing better than my mind does. And when I do that, I'm able to act on impulses that my mind wouldn't let surface before.

Now, I'm much, much better about letting my body do the thinking and allowing my mind to take the backseat for just a little bit. And, when I allow my body to think and my mind to cease interfering, there is so much more movement available to me. I roll and flip and slide and kick and flail and stretch and contract without my mind telling me to. My **body** tells me to do it, and that's an experience that I have been working on for so long – and I'm so, so happy that I've finally found that relationship with my body.[3]

Notes

1 Frost, Robert, "The Road Not Taken," *Mountain Interval*. New York: Henry Holt and Co. 1916. Print, p. 9.
2 Mary Starks Whitehouse's work in *authentic movement* inspired us to develop this Practice in recognizing *authentic impulse*. You can read about Ms. Whitehouse and her work online at this website: www.authenticmovementcommunity.org.
3 From a student journal. Used with permission.

Your Body Leads The Way

We express our inner life through our body. We may have spent much of our lives hiding our emotions and desires. But as an actor playing a character, it's vital that we share them in an artistic, yet authentic, way. Our expressive *body-mind* tells an audience what's going on **inside** our character. We want the messages to be clear, clean, uncluttered, and yet strong enough to communicate to the back row. We must translate our inner experience into an outer expression.

By getting to know your instrument and your *authentic impulses*, you have developed a more easeful and responsive body. You can navigate between the subtlest emotion or outrageous physical silliness, as you trust your *body-mind* to lead the way.

Now, you can experience even more directed, strong, spontaneous movement through your imaginative exploration of two whole-body concepts: *Kinesthetic Imagination* (KW) and *Life-body* (KW).

Your Kinesthetic Imagination

Jean Houston, author of *The Possible Human*, coined the term *kinesthetic body* to describe sensing movement with our *kinesthetic imagination*. Dr. Houston defined kinesthetic body as "the body of your muscular imagination." She developed a process of imagining the *kinesthetic* sensations of a movement, then following it/repeating it with our physical body. *Kinesthetic imagination* can enliven our simplest movements and become an essential support for complex ones.[1]

In their book, *Spaces of Creation*, authors Suzan Zeder and Jim Hancock offer this advice when exploring movement with your *kinesthetic imagination*: "… the key is trust. Skepticism and doubt are self-induced blockades to the full exercise of our capacity to imagine."[2] If you find yourself doubting that you can sense an "invisible" movement, *Fire the Judge* and *Hire the*

Witness! Discover how your *kinesthetic sense* can pave the way to clarity and ease in your movement.

PRACTICE 19.1 DISCOVERING YOUR KINESTHETIC IMAGINATION

In the exploration below, you can explore your *kinesthetic imagination*: discover how imagined sensations influence your physical body when you move. This Practice is different than visualizing a movement – you are sensing the movement through your *kinesthetic imagination*.

In this exploration, we refer to your "real" body – your physical body – and your *kinesthetic body*, sensing with your *kinesthetic imagination*.

This Practice was inspired by Jean Houston's kinesthetic body explorations in *The Possible Human*. She suggests that you allow yourself to experience the sensations of your imagined movements "as vividly as possible."[3] Awaken your *kinesthetic sense* and let your brain take a back seat: allow your *kinesthetic imagination* to lead the way.

I investigate: How does sensing movement with my *kinesthetic imagination* affect the movement of my real body?

Part I

You may remember the *kinesthetic sensing* Practice (1.4) from Chapter 1. Here we build on that simple exploration. As you imagine the movement kinesthetically, practice *inclusive attention*. Avoid "disappearing" into your imagination: include your whole *3-D body within the 3-D space*!

- Pause. Stand. Take a *kinesthetic moment*. Breathe.
- Notice your arms resting at your sides, supported by your whole body.
- Place your attention on sensation as you turn your palm to face the side of your leg and gently raise your right arm by bringing your hand and arm forward and then overhead (Figure. 19.1).

As you lower your arm, notice all the sensations in your whole body as you move.

- Pause. Breathe. Repeat the movement with your real right arm.
- Pause.
- Now let your real right arm rest at your side. Use your *kinesthetic imagination* as you raise your *kinesthetic arm*, experiencing the *kinesthetic sensations* "as vividly as possible."

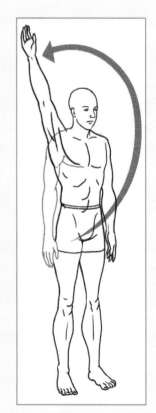

Figure. 19.1

- Lower your *kinesthetic arm*.
- Pause. Breathe. Repeat the movement with your *kinesthetic arm*.
- Pause.
- Now raise your real arm – still placing your attention on sensation – and lower it.
- Raise your *kinesthetic arm*, then raise your real arm to join it.
- Lower your *kinesthetic arm*, then your real arm. Pause.
- Repeat this process: raise your *kinesthetic arm*, then your real arm, then lower your *kinesthetic arm* followed by your real arm. Pause. Breathe.
- Take a *kinesthetic moment*. Notice any differences between your right and left arms.
- Repeat with your left arm. Remember to practice *inclusive attention* as you do this. Pause.
- Now, explore raising your *kinesthetic arm* and physical arm together. Do this on both sides. Pause.
- Taking your time, try other movements with your *kinesthetic arm* followed by your real arm. It is important to allow both the *kinesthetic arm* and the real arm to make complete movements. (No shortcuts.)
- Practice moving your *kinesthetic arm* and your physical arm together and separately.
- Pause. Have a walk around the room, practicing *kinesthetic awareness*. Pause.
- *Spy back*. What was your experience of sensing movement with your *kinesthetic imagination*?

Part II

You can, of course, explore any movement at all with your *kinesthetic imagination*. Below are some suggestions for challenging and expanding your *kinesthetic imagination*. Have fun. Play. Explore new possibilities.

- Pause. Stand. Take a *kinesthetic moment*. Breathe.
- Step forward with your kinesthetic body. Pause. Breathe.
- Step back with your kinesthetic body. Pause. Breathe.
- Repeat this movement with your real body. Pause. Breathe.
- Repeat the movement with your kinesthetic body, then with your real body. Pause. Breathe.
- Now step forward with your kinesthetic body. Follow this movement with your real body: sense your real body stepping into your kinesthetic body.
- Step back – first with your kinesthetic body then step into your kinesthetic body with your real body.
- Play with various combinations of real body/kinesthetic body – sometimes allowing your kinesthetic body to step first, sometimes your real body.
- Experiment: allow your kinesthetic body to step back as your real body steps forward, then step again to rejoin them.
- Branch out: try repeating the Practice by stepping in different directions or explore other movements, such as jumping or lunging. Sense the movement with your

kinesthetic imagination, then follow the movement with your physical body and vice versa. Pause.

- Take a *kinesthetic moment*.
- Have a walk around the space. Note the sensations in your body. Pause.
- *Spy back*. What was the experience of moving using your *kinesthetic imagination*? Did you notice differences when you allowed your real body to follow the pathway made by your kinesthetic body? What were they?

Playing with your *kinesthetic imagination* can take you out of your "movement box." Any movement you can imagine kinesthetically can then be repeated physically: walking, dancing, stage combat, speaking. It heightens your *kinesthetic sense* and makes it more available in your everyday activities and onstage.

Jean Houston notes that, when you practice movements with your *kinesthetic imagination*, be certain you rehearse the entire movement – beginning, middle, and end.[4] You can understand that you might have a physical "disconnect," if you imagined the sensations of ice skating with ease, but did not imagine the sensations of stopping!

As you explore on your own, experiment: sometimes you may find it is more helpful to begin with real body, and sometimes with *kinesthetic imagination*. You decide what works best in each situation. Your kinesthetic body knows, and it can lead your real body into "not just improvement but, equally important, an attitude of greater confidence and courage."[5]

The Little Intellect

In *How to Use this Book*, we noted that trying to analyze what we are doing, *as* we are doing it, can be at cross-purposes to our creative work. Now, as we wade bravely into the river of our creative imagination, we can find our logical mind wanting to take charge of the process. After all, we've come this far without the "foolishness" of the *kinesthetic imagination*!

As actors, we must exercise our imaginations, just as we exercise our bodies. We are in a world of make-believe when we are onstage. We want our imaginations, bodies, and logical minds to work in harmony – not fight each other!

Michael Chekhov, the great acting teacher, recognized that our analytical brain could stifle our imagination when we are rehearsing or performing. He had a name for the part of your brain that wants to control and comment on your creative explorations. He called it the *Little Intellect* (KW).[6]

The *little intellect* can interfere with our creative process by judging and commenting as we explore and play. It can distract us with comments like, "What is this for?" or "Oh, that really worked, how can I keep that?" and even, "You are so awkward. Everybody's looking at you."

Chekhov developed *spy back* to put the *little intellect* in its proper place. Through *spy back*, your intellect plays a productive (non-interfering) role in your creative process. Its role is to understand, and then put into words, what you have already discovered through your experience.

When we practice *kinesthetic imagination* and *life-body*, we are bypassing our habits and conditioning; we can allow our body to lead us into creative, easeful, dynamic movement. If you find your *little intellect* wanting to judge or criticize, take a moment to breathe and recommit to the process. Because … your body really does know.

Life-Body: The Energy Within

Lenard Petit, master teacher of the Michael Chekhov Acting Technique, uses the term *life-body* to describe the sense of movement and energy that is always flowing within us.[7] *Life-body* is the vital force that is always present in our living body. It is an inner energy – the energetic force that moves us, as we translate our *Inner Experience to Outer Expression* (KW) – an expression that can be seen and felt by an audience.[8]

Have you ever had a moment onstage when you felt "scattered," like you couldn't control your energy? Maybe you felt like you were "bouncing off the walls," because you felt nervous – or fearful. This energetic state is not useful to an actor, because the audience receives messages that are fragmented and, possibly, disconnected from the action that is happening onstage.

Life-body is one way out of this frenetic activity. Even if the script calls for frantic action, *life-body* can organize your energy, so you can play the moment with clarity and purpose.

Life-body is slightly different than your *kinesthetic imagination*. When we imagine the sensation of a movement, we are connecting with our body intelligence, how to accomplish a movement. *Life-body* is a no less real experience of the flow of energy within our body, which includes our emotional energy, our passions, the life-force that drives us to act. *Kinesthetic imagination* is focused on the sensation and organization of our physical movements. *Life-body* is a bit broader, as it includes both physical sensation and personal energy moving within and beyond our body.

Both *kinesthetic imagination* and *life-body* help us to do three things:

1. Recognize that we have the imaginative power to ease and energize our movement.
2. Have a sense of our whole, well-organized body – without fear – when we are preparing to move and when we are moving.
3. Put our attention on action – what we are doing – not on ourselves. It is practically impossible to be self-conscious when we are experiencing action through our *kinesthetic imagination* and/or *life-body*.

Kinesthetic imagination helps us simplify complex movement or find our way out of an interfering habit. *Life-body* provides a supportive sense of energetic flow, even beyond our body, whether we are standing still, moving, or performing. Your balanced and available body-instrument is your foundation for *kinesthetic imagination* and *life-body*.

Most important, don't get hung up on the terms. Play with *kinesthetic imagination* and *life-body and* treat them as useful "helpers" to support your movement life. Many of our students use the terms interchangeably. Let them serve your body, mind, and imagination.

PRACTICE 19.2 DISCOVERING YOUR LIFE-BODY

(Thank you to Lenard Petit, whose *life-body* exercises inspired this exploration.)[9]

Your personal connection with your body's inherent design is the foundation for your work with *kinesthetic imagination/life-body*.

Warm up your *body-mind* and *kinesthetic sense* before you begin this Practice.

"You must *believe* that it is possible to do this with your imagination, then it becomes a fact" Lenard Petit.[10]

Part I: Energetic Warm-up

- Stand. Pause. Breathe. Take a *kinesthetic moment*.
- Begin by raising your real right arm out to the side to point at an object across the room from you. Practice *kinesthetic sensing* as you do this. Have an awareness of your whole body supporting this action. Practice *inclusive attention*.
- Lower your arm, continuing to be aware of your whole body. Pause.
- Repeat this action. Pause.
- Now imagine that inside your real arm is another arm made of energy. It has the same shape as your arm. Use your *kinesthetic imagination* to sense your energy arm.
- With your real arm at your side, lift your energy arm to point at the object. Allow your real arm to follow the energy arm. Breathe.
- Lower your energy arm, then allow your real arm to follow. Pause.
- Repeat on the left side. Pause.

Part II: Energetic Flow

- With an awareness of your *life-body* moving with your real body, raise your right arm to shoulder height and point to the right.
- Have a sense of your energy flowing through your whole body into your arm and hand and reaching into the space just beyond your hand.
- Now sense your energy reaching all the way to the wall to your right, then beyond the wall into the outdoors.
- Let this energetic stream continue all the way around the Earth, until it comes in the opposite wall of the room.

- Raise your left arm, pointing to the left, and receive the energy through your pointing finger and into your left arm, so there is a continuous stream from your right arm, around the Earth and back into your whole body. Pause.
- Lower your real arm and *life-body* arm to your side.
- Pause. Take a *kinesthetic moment.*
- Repeat with your left arm. Remember that the continuous flow of energy is moving through your whole body.
- Lower your real arm and *life-body* arm to your side.
- Pause. Take a *kinesthetic moment.*
- Activate your *life-body* to awaken the *5 cues*: *grounding, centering,* expanding, *poising,* flying, and allow your real body to follow.
- Bring your arms down to your sides and pause.
- Have a walk around the room, practicing *inclusive attention.* Pause.
- *Spy back.* How does *life-body* affect your sense of yourself and your movement possibilities? What is your experience of directing your energy beyond your body? How does that energize your sphere of attention and your relationship with the space around you?

Our *life-body* helps us direct our energy and our movement. It fills your body and streams into the space around you. It leads you into a sense of connection throughout your body and aids you in translating your *inner experience* into a clear and focused *outer expression.*

As you play with *life-body,* it becomes easier and easier to access – it simply becomes a part of your process. Your movement becomes more easeful and your actions more focused, because your body is merely following the pathway made by your perfectly authentic *life-body.*

In the chapters that follow, you will have the opportunity to explore your *kinesthetic imagination* and *life-body* further. Let your *kinesthetic imagination* guide you into movement that is purposeful, easeful, and authentic. You can rely on these valuable tools to lead the way.

PAUSE TO PROCESS Discuss or journal about your experience and play with kinesthetic body/*life-body* in your daily life.

Key Words: *Kinesthetic Imagination, Life-body, Little Intellect, Inner Experience to Outer Expression*

Notes

1 Houston, Jean. *The Possible Human*. New York: Jeremy P. Tarcher/Penguin. 2nd edition, 1982, p. 9.

2 Zeder, Suzan with Hancock, Jim. *Spaces of Creation*. Portsmouth: Heinemann, 2005. p.106.

3 Houston, p. 20.

4 Houston, p. 21.

5 Houston, p. 20.

6 Petit, Lenard. *The Michael Chekhov Handbook*. New York: Routledge, 2010, p.31.

7 Petit, p. 32.

8 Chekhov, Michael. *To the Actor: On the Technique of Acting*. New York: Routledge, 2002, p. 26.

9 Petit, Lenard. *The Michael Chekhov Handbook*. New York: Routledge, 2010. pp. 33–35. Used with permission.

10 Petit, p. 34.

The Four Brothers

The great acting teacher, Michael Chekhov, recognized that there are certain guiding principles that govern our movement and our acting – in fact, these traits are present in all great works of art. These elements aren't just labels imposed by Chekhov – rules to be obeyed. Instead, when we allow them to, these principles – which Chekhov dubbed *The Four Brothers* (KW) – simply emerge as we make our creative choices.[1]

The four brothers are:

- A *feeling of Ease*
- A *feeling of Form*
- A *feeling of Beauty*
- A *feeling of Wholeness*.

It's significant that Chekhov describes each of the *brothers* as a **feeling**. His language suggests that we can sense them in our body. Each one can be an inherent part of every movement, and we experience them – rather than impose them – within our moving bodies. Our attention to the *four brothers* supports our movement, as well as our acting, and our work becomes fuller and more satisfying for us and for the audience.

The Four Brothers: A Feeling of Ease, Form, Beauty, and Wholeness

Throughout Part I, you learned the true facts of your body's design. You **are** designed for movement. You discovered that your body is receptive to your *dynamic thoughts* and your mind is receptive to your expressive body. Your *body-mind* offers inspired possibilities for action, speech, and vivid gestures: artistic support for the character's whole journey through the play.

The four brothers support and enlarge the movement journey you have taken so far. They invite you to dig deeply into your creative gold mine, discover its treasures, and then translate your *inner experience to an outer expression*.

Michael Chekhov said, "There are no purely physical exercises in our method … This process makes the physical body more and more sensitive in its ability to receive our inner impulses and convey them expressively to the audience."[2] *The four brothers* expand our definition of movement – what it can be, and what it can express.

A Feeling of Ease

When do you feel at ease? Relaxing on the beach or listening to favorite music? Maybe walking outdoors on a pretty day fills you with a *feeling of ease*.

Where do you observe ease around you? A cat leaping gracefully into a chair? A young child skipping?

Pause. What images arise from your imagination when you think of "ease?" For many, images that inspire "moments of ease" also create an emotional response of happiness or joy. Perhaps you sense your body expand, and your breathing ease and deepen.

With an inner expansiveness in our bodies, we are more responsive to whatever is happening in the moment. Our body feels softer, yet our *life-body* is energized and "ready for anything." Our whole being is open, alive, and available to the action of the play.

Hard vs. Soft

In Part I, you discovered how tight, hard muscles interfere with your ability to move. Michael Chekhov believed that nothing can happen in a hard body. An inner *feeling of ease* is essential to our ability to respond to the action onstage.

You also discovered in Part I that your thoughts influence your movement. Your *dynamic thinking* can lead you into a *feeling of ease*. Try this:

- Take a moment to pause. Notice the support of the floor or the chair, if you are sitting. Give yourself the *dynamic thought*: I wish to experience a *feeling of ease*. Allow yourself to wait without expectation. Notice what happens to your body and breath. From this place of ease, take a walk around the room. Speak a few words. Continue to renew your *dynamic thinking*: I wish to experience a *feeling of ease*.

What did you notice about your movement when you changed your thinking? Recognize that the *feeling* (sensation) *of ease* arises from within you, when you allow it to happen.

Please note that a *feeling of ease* should not be confused with relaxation or a lack of energy. When our bodies are at ease, we experience a sense of connection and 3-dimensionality in our movements. A fine actor, like Benedict Cumberbatch, seems to ride on an "inner flow" of energized ease, even in moments of strong physical action, such as fencing.[3]

In the Practice below, note how exercises you experienced in Part I can help you access a sense of energized ease.

Warm-up: Easy Does It

Begin with a *dynamic thought*: I wish to move with a *feeling of ease*.

Practice the *dimensional scale*. Place your attention on *ease* and enjoy a sense of connection and flow throughout your body as you move. When you have completed the Practice, pause. Breathe. Take a *kinesthetic moment*.

Now, activate the *5 cues*. Have a walk around the space. Pause. Take a *kinesthetic moment*.

These warm-ups inspire a *feeling of ease*. Now that your body is awake and your mind is calm, you are ready to continue exploring ease in the following Practice.

PRACTICE 20.1 **STEPPING INTO EASE**

Set up one or more chairs around the periphery of the room before beginning this exploration.

I investigate: How do I experience ease?

- Stand. Pause. Take a *kinesthetic moment*. Breathe.
- Sense the inner movements of your breathing; notice the coming and going of your breath as you inhale and exhale.
- Allow your body to breathe itself.
- Notice small movement changes in your body as you breathe. You may notice subtle shifts of weight, changes in the balancing of your joints, muscular adjustments.
- Allow these sequential movements to pass through you with ease.
- Allow this *dynamic thought* to be your guide: "I wish to experience a *feeling of ease*."
- With this *feeling of ease*, allow your whole body to melt toward the floor.
- When you reach the floor, lie on your back and allow your whole body to rest with the floor's support.
- Pause. Breathe.
- Sense your *life-body* and allow it to lead you back to standing.
- Walk through space as you allow ease to move through your hip joints, knee joints, ankles, and feet. Each movement flows from one joint to the other as you walk.
- After a few moments, turn to the right with a *feeling of ease*. Then turn to the left. Then turn in any direction with a *feeling of ease*.
- Return to walking around the room. After a few moments move with ease to a chair and stand with your back to it. Pause. Breathe.
- Allow your *life-body* to lead the way as you move from standing to sitting.
- Pause. Breathe. Rest, and allow yourself to sense the connection between your body, the chair, and the floor under your feet.
- Allow your *life-body* to guide you back to standing. Take a walk.

- Move to another chair and sit. Rest. Then stand.
- Continue to explore these simple actions with a sense of ease: walking, sitting, standing.
- Pause often and notice the ongoing sense of *ease* within your body, even when you are sitting and standing still.
- *Spy back*. How does a *feeling of ease* change the way you do these simple activities? How might a *feeling of ease* influence other activities? Your movement onstage?

The four brothers rely on our trust. By trusting that ease is a quality **within** our movement, we can let go of unneeded effort and tension. Our whole coordinated body can move with a sense of connection, balance, and flow – freeing us to respond authentically to each moment. As Lenard Petit says, "Your very first choice is to soften. Then something can happen."[4]

In the Practice above you explored the ways that a *feeling of ease* influences and supports simple, familiar movement. Now, you are ready for the next step. Enjoy the delightful pleasure of interacting with another person – with ease.

PRACTICE 20.2 PERSON TO PERSON[5]

Two or more people can enjoy this exploration. Be sure your body is warmed up before you begin.

- Pause. Sense your *3-D body*, breath, and the space around you.
- Have a thought, "I wish to move with a *feeling of ease*."
- Allow the *feeling of ease* to energize your whole body as you begin to walk around the room.
- See and sense the space in the room as you move through it.
- See the other people in the room. Notice the ever-changing space between people as they move.
- With a *feeling of ease*, begin to make eye contact with others as you pass them.
- As you meet the next person, link elbows with them and circle each other. Be aware of your inner and outer space as you do this.
- Then part from each other. Sense a *feeling of ease* as you do this.
- Repeat this action (with different partners, if possible) several times.
- When you meet the next person, add a simple activity – speak their name as you circle with them. And they can speak yours. Maintain a *feeling of ease*.
- Allow this joining, circling, speaking, and parting to be supported by the *feeling of ease*.

- Repeat this Practice with other partners. Notice the space around you, breathe, and allow the *feeling of ease* to influence your connection with the other person.
- After a few minutes, begin to walk around the space again with a *feeling of ease*. Make eye contact with others.
- As you meet the next person, maintain a *feeling of ease* as you greet them any way you like.
- Continue to greet others as you meet them.
- After a few minutes, walk around the room again with a *feeling of ease*. Pause.
- Take a *kinesthetic moment*.
- *Spy back*. What did you notice about moving with a *feeling of ease*? How does a sense of space influence your *feeling of ease*? What did you experience as you interacted with others with a *feeling of ease*?

This exploration is a useful reminder of what often happens in an acting scene: we meet someone, we interact with them, and we leave. Through this simple Practice, you cultivate ease and spontaneity in your relationship with another person. You are developing a valuable skill, applicable in all of your artistic work.

You don't have to work for a *feeling of ease*; in fact, that's the opposite of ease! Instead, you can allow movement to pass through you in a connected, playful way. Your character may be depressed or heavy with care, but as the actor, you can portray these qualities with artistic ease.

You can cultivate a *feeling of ease* in your movement, as you go through your day. Ask yourself: are the choices I'm making taking me toward ease or away from ease? By doing this, you can build your trust in this *brother*, and then it will be available to you when you are performing.

A Feeling of Form

Your body has a form – a unique shape – and your movements do too. Chekhov emphasized that every movement has a *feeling of form* – a beginning, a middle, and an end. Form begins inside us, as an impulse, and then moves into an *outer expression* that can be seen by our audience.

This may seem like it's stating the obvious, but many of us forget form when we are in the heat of performance. An actor may begin a gesture and then let their arm hang in mid-air, as if they forgot it was there. Or, possibly, they make the gesture in space, and then drop their arm like a stone, as if the first part of the gesture was so tiring, they had no energy to return their arm to their side.

When our acting has a *feeling of form*, we have a sense of each movement as a specific moment in time and a pathway in space. Every movement – from crossing the room to waving good-bye to a good friend – has an arc: it has a distinct beginning, it goes somewhere, and it comes to a satisfying moment of completion. It is not a process that is controlled intellectually, it emerges from an inner *feeling of form*.

Your *authentic impulse* aids you in finding a distinct beginning to a movement; your ability to follow that impulse, and bring it to a completion, gives a gesture or movement its form. Bring your awareness of form to the simple warm-up below.

Warm-up: Shape and Form

Each part of this warm-up has a beginning, middle, and end. Activate your awareness of *a feeling of form* as you practice.

Begin with a dynamic thought: I wish to move with a *feeling of form*.

Practice the *Dimensional Scale* with a *feeling of form*. Sense the beginning, middle, and end within each movement. Notice the pathways you make in space and the changing shape of your body as you move. When you have completed the Practice, pause. Breathe. Take a *kinesthetic moment*.

Now, activate the *5 cues*. Have a walk around the space. Pause.

PRACTICE 20.3   SENSING THE FEELING OF FORM

This exploration revisits Practice 1.3, Parts I and II. Throw an imaginary ball with a partner, with your attention on sensing the *feeling of form* as you move.

As you practice, remember that the *feeling of form* is **within** the action of throwing and catching – this is a process of discovery, not a set of rules to be imposed on your movements.

I investigate: How can a *feeling of form* support my movement?

- Pause. Stand. Breathe. Take a *kinesthetic moment*.
- Begin with a thought: I wish to experience a *feeling of form* as I move.
- Allow your *life-body* to lead your movement as you throw an imaginary ball.
- As you practice, place your attention on the **process** of moving with a *feeling of form*: beginning, middle, and end.
- Enjoy the pathways you are making in space and sense the changing shape of your body. Breathe.
- You can change the ways you throw the ball – hard or soft, overhand, underhand, behind your back.
- After several minutes, pause. Take a *kinesthetic moment*.
- Have a walk around the space with a *feeling of form*. Pause.

- *Spy back*. How does a *feeling of form* influence your movement? Could you sense the *feeling of form* within the movements? Could you sense the changing shape of your body? What was that like?

By sensing a *feeling of form*, you can experience more clarity in your movement. Your body knows the pathway of every movement from beginning to end.

The *feeling of form* lives in you: every breath you take has a beginning, middle, and end. There is something very satisfying about beginning something, experiencing it, and completing it. This applies not only to movement, but to speaking a line, rehearsing a scene, and performing a play. Living within the *feeling of form* can bring clarity and a sense of immediacy to your work.

PRACTICE 20.4 A FEELING OF FORM: MEETING AND SPEAKING

In this exploration, you will meet another person and say a simple line. Place your attention on the **process** of moving and speaking – with a *feeling of form*.

Be prepared to speak the opening line of a monologue or a line from a play. If you don't have one, here's a suggestion: "I remember that day we went to the beach."

If you are in a group, divide into Group A and Group B. Group A will speak first, and Group B will receive. Helpful hint: Group B should wear something, like a wristband, to distinguish them from Group A. Remember to warm up before you begin.

I investigate: How does *a feeling of form* influence me when I'm speaking with another person?

- Pause. Stand. Breathe. Take a *kinesthetic moment*.
- Begin with a thought: "I wish to experience a *feeling of form* as I move and speak."
- Begin to walk around the space with a *feeling of form*.
- Be aware of the other people in the room. See each person as you pass them.
- Notice the changing shape of the space, as people move.
- Practice a *feeling of form* as you make eye contact with the next Group B person you meet. Pause, take them in, and share your line. Bring this moment to completion and move on.
- Maintain the *feeling of form* as you move around the space again.
- Repeat this action with others. Be aware of your actions happening within your *Kinesphere* and the larger space of the room.
- Continue in this way several more times. Pause.
- Repeat the Practice with Group B as speakers and Group A as receivers. Pause.

- Walk around the room with a *feeling of form*. Pause. Take a *kinesthetic moment*.
- *Spy back.* As you interacted with others, what was your experience of a *feeling of form*? How might a *feeling of form* serve you as an actor?

When you develop your awareness of a *feeling of form*, you can begin to notice it and cultivate it in your creative process. For instance, each time we Pause, *cross the threshold*, or take a *kinesthetic moment* we can acknowledge a *feeling of form*: we are taking a moment to **begin** or **complete** each Practice or part of a Practice.

> *PAUSE TO PROCESS* before continuing to the other two *brothers*. Journal about and discuss your discoveries. In what ways might you cultivate a *feeling of form* and a *feeling of ease* in your everyday life?

A Feeling of Beauty

All true creations of art are beautiful, because they are an expression of our humanity. When Chekhov spoke of beauty in our work, he was not describing the way we look: cultural preferences of perfect bodies and facial features. Instead, he was referring to a sense of our humanness, and the beauty of allowing that to be revealed in an artistic way.

Lenard Petit refers to this *brother* as **authenticity**.[6] Each part of our world – people, objects, etc. – is unique. Our uniqueness makes us – and everything around us – beautiful. We recognize and honor authenticity in ourselves, others, and the world around us. Beauty supports a stronger sense of presence, because we are allowing ourselves to be seen.

PRACTICE 20.5 **A FEELING OF BEAUTY**

In this exploration, you will begin with an appreciation of your own body, sensing the fluid quality of your weight as you gently move.

To prepare your body, mind, and imagination, fill a plastic bag half full of water and close it tightly. Holding it in both hands, explore the sensations of shifting the water – sloshing it – from side to side and forward and back. In the warm-up below, you can enjoy sensing your weight fluidly moving in your body, just as the water moved in the plastic bag.[7]

Divide into Group A and Group B. Each person places a small object in the room. Though this Practice is designed for a group, you can adapt it if you are working solo.

I investigate: How does a *feeling of beauty* affect my relationships with others and the world around me?

Warm-up: Sensing Your Moving Body

Recognize the unique and beautiful qualities that are inherent in these movements.

- Lie on the floor in the *balanced resting state*. Pause.
- Give yourself a thought: I wish to move with a *feeling of beauty*.
- Begin to sense the weight of your body as if it were liquid. Let the liquid weight slosh toward your right side – allowing your body to roll toward the right, then let it slosh toward the left, rolling to follow the flow as you "slosh" from side to side.
- Slosh onto your back. Imagine a wave flowing down toward your feet, and then sloshing up toward your head in a gentle rocking motion. You can allow your feet to leave the floor, bringing your knees toward your chest as you explore.
- After a few minutes, allow the flow of weight to roll you toward your feet and up toward your head. Roll forward and back, until you come to a seated position. Pause.
- Notice the room around you. Sense your *3-D body in the 3-D space*.
- Move any way you like as you continue to slosh your weight in any direction you choose.
- Your arms can participate in the sloshing. Explore your whole *3-D body in the 3-D space*, making large and small movements.
- Allow this exploration to bring you to standing. Pause. See and sense the room around you.

Part I: Making Contact

- Take a *kinesthetic moment*.
- Begin to walk around the space. See the entire room and the space, including the space between the objects. Notice the shapes and the colors in the room.
- Sense the floor under your feet and feel its support as you walk.
- Look around the room, see an object – it doesn't have to be your object – and move to it. Notice its colors, shape, textures. Pick it up and experience its qualities with your hands. Recognize its uniqueness.
- Bring your exploration to completion. Pause.
- Group A, put your object down; Group B, keep your object. Everyone, return to walking around the room.

Part II: Giving and Receiving

- Make a commitment to approach this Practice simply and authentically.
- With an awareness of yourself and the space, notice the other people in the room.
- Be aware of the changing space between you and the others as you move through the room.
- Notice each person's unique qualities and their miraculous bodies.

- Group B, notice if a person is carrying an object in one of their hands. Find a person without an object, and make this offering: "Here, this is for you." Give them your object. Group A, receive the object.
- When you are ready, part from each other. Partner A keeps the object.
- Continue walking through the room, seeing the others in the room. Group B are now the receivers, and Group A are the givers.
- Repeat the giving and receiving process with a different person. When B has received the object, part from each other, and return to walking around the room.
- Continue this process of giving, receiving, and parting for several more cycles.
- When this process feels complete, put down all the objects. Continue walking around the space.
- Have a sense of giving and receiving as you pass each person. Receive the space and sense the space receiving you, as you move through it.
- After a few moments, pause. Take a *kinesthetic moment*.
- *Spy back*. What did you discover about a *feeling of beauty* in these simple actions? How might a *feeling of beauty* serve you as an actor?

The *feeling of beauty* is a movement principle that supports your *authentic impulses*, and allows you to make deeper connections with your expressive self, and the expressive qualities in others.

A Feeling of the Whole

Ease, Form, and Beauty unite to create a *Feeling of the Whole*. The fourth *brother* provides the essential throughline for all of your character's unique choices and actions within the play. With a *feeling of the whole*, you can reveal and sustain the total arc of your character's journey for the audience. In actual practice, each moment of the play can reflect this *feeling of the whole*.

PRACTICE 20.6   A FEELING OF WHOLENESS

This exploration is designed for work in a group or with a partner. Allow a *feeling of the whole* to inform your movements and your awareness.

Warm-up

- Pause. Stand. Breathe. Take a *kinesthetic moment*.
- Take a moment to sense your body within your *Kinesphere*. Without moving through the room, begin to explore your *Kinesphere* with small and large movements.
- After several minutes. Pause. Breathe.

- With an awareness of your whole body and your whole *Kinesphere*, begin to walk around the room.
- Sense others' *Kinespheres* and your own as you move. Enjoy "bouncing" your *Kinesphere* off others' *Kinespheres*.
- After a few minutes, return to walking around the room, and allow your *Kinesphere* to gently pass through others' *Kinespheres* as you walk. Pause.
- Take a *kinesthetic moment*.

Connecting

- Resume walking around the room with a sense of yourself, the others, and the changing space as the moving bodies shape and reshape it.
- Make eye contact with the next person you meet. Pause and notice the space between you. Share a moment of connection, commitment, and safety before you make physical contact.
- Gently reach toward each other, as you allow some part of your skin come into contact with their skin; a hand, a finger, an arm. Let your senses take in the feeling of contact with another person.
- Begin to move gently in a variety of ways, allowing your point(s) of contact to change as needed: fingertip to fingertip, back to back, etc. Enjoy the pleasure of sharing your unique self with your partner's unique self.
- Sense a *wholeness* in each movement, in your connection to your partner, the space around you, and the "dance" you are creating together. Don't try to make something happen: just acknowledge and allow *a feeling of the whole* to guide you as you move.
- After a couple of minutes, without speaking, the two of you can complete your duet. After acknowledging the moment of authentic connection, you can depart from each other.
- Continue to move around the space and notice yourself and the other people in it.
- Pause. Take a *kinesthetic moment*.
- Meet with your partner and *spy back*.
- *Spy back* with the whole group. How did *a feeling of the whole* inform your movement? What was your experience of *wholeness* in relation to your partner and the room around you? Did you notice an emotional response to *wholeness*?

A feeling of the whole creates continuity in your movement, as well as in your relationship with others and your environment.

> *PAUSE TO PROCESS* Practice *the four brothers* in your daily activities and in your interactions with others. Notice how each *brother* is always present, even if you are focusing on one of them. A gentle awareness of *ease*, *form*, *beauty* and *wholeness* can transform even the most mundane task into a satisfying and enjoyable experience.

Practicing *The Four Brothers*

The four brothers invite you to put your full attention on the present moment: self-consciousness falls away, and you experience a sense of readiness for each moment as it unfolds. They awaken your creativity, stir your imagination, and support a readiness for artistic expression.

You can enjoy practicing all *four brothers* in the explorations below.

PRACTICE 20.7 **MORE GIVING AND RECEIVING**

Ball games are a classic warm-up in the Chekhov work: they engage and energize your *body-mind*, while you practice *the four brothers* and interact with others. We recommend using a Koosh ball at first, as it is easier to catch.

In this exploration, allow *the four brothers* to inform your movements as you practice giving and receiving. Throw with a *feeling of ease*, use your *whole* body, recognize a clear form in each movement – beginning, middle, and end. Throw the ball underhanded – and aim for the receiver's heart.

Appreciate the beauty in your movement and your interactions with others. *Fire the Judge, Hire the Witness*: you can learn much when you drop the ball – continue to practice *the four brothers*, as you retrieve the ball and return to the circle.

- Stand. Pause. Breathe. Take a *kinesthetic moment*.
- Give yourself this thought: I wish to throw the ball with a *feeling of ease*, *form*, *beauty*, and *wholeness*.
- Follow the steps for Practice 1.3 with this difference: throw a Koosh ball with a partner or in a large circle with your classmates.
- Each time you throw the ball, make a connection with the person you are throwing to. The interaction is complete when the receiver catches the ball and meets your eyes, giving both of you a clear beginning, middle, and end.
- After several minutes, pause. Take a *kinesthetic moment*.
- *Spy back*. What did you learn about *the four brothers* in this simple – possibly challenging – interaction?

Through this exploration, you build *body-mind communication*, sensing yourself while your attention is on an activity. As you practice with a partner or the group, you can develop your ability to respond spontaneously to a *stimulus*, while allowing *the four brothers* to support and inform your movement.

In the next Practice, you can trust *the four brothers*, *life-body*, and *authentic impulse* to be your guides in a simple improvisation.

PRACTICE 20.8 **THE FOUR BROTHERS IN ACTION**[8]

This exploration is designed for two or more people. Place a bench or two chairs side by side in the space. If you are in a class, this Practice can take place in front of an audience. The ball game (or another practice of your choosing) can be your warm-up.

Trust *the four brothers* and your *authentic impulses*. Avoid "planning ahead." Allow yourself to respond spontaneously to whatever arises.

I investigate: What can I discover about myself and the world around me when I trust the *four brothers*?

- Before you enter the space, pause. Breathe. Take a *kinesthetic moment*.
- Person #1: Enter, cross to the chair, and sit. Breathe.
- Person #2: Enter, cross to the chair, take a moment to sense your breath cycle, and sit.
- Person #1: Allow the second person's presence to change you in some way and let this stimulate an impulse to rise and exit.
- Person #2: Another person will enter and sit beside you. Allow this person's presence to change you in some way, rise and exit.
- Continue in this way until all participants have had the chance to take both roles. Pause.
- *Spy back*. What did you discover about yourself and your impulses in these simple actions? Were you able to allow *the four brothers* to guide you? Why or why not? What did you discover as an audience member observing these interactions?

What have you learned from exploring *the four brothers?* How do they inform or support you as you move? How do *the four brothers* affect your expressiveness?

Chekhov's work opens deep and poetic access to the soul of the actor. When we allow ourselves to be truly authentic, we commit to using our whole self in the creation of vibrant characters.

For further exploration: you can find more Practices in Appendix I.

PAUSE TO PROCESS

Key Word: *The Four Brothers*

Notes

1 Chekhov, Michael. *To the Actor.* New York: Routledge, 2002. p. 13.

234 ELEMENTS OF EXPRESSION

2 Chekhov, Michael. *On The Technique of Acting*. New York: Harper Perennial, 1991, p. 43.

3 You can view Benedict Cumberbatch in "Hamlet Fencing Scene 2015" on YouTube. www.you tube.com/watch?v=5R7PJy2MHpg.

4 Petit, Lenard, FAU master class, Boca Raton: Florida Atlantic University. January 9, 2017.

5 Portions of this Practice were inspired by experiences in Fernando Calzadilla's Rasaboxes work-shops at the Miami Theatre Center, 2013–2016. Used with permission.

6 Petit, Lenard. *The Michael Chekhov Handbook*. New York: Routledge, 2010, p. 27.

7 *Sloshing* and *rocking* are terms used in Integrated Movement Studies (IMS), which combines the work of Rudolf Laban and Irmgard Bartenieff. IMS was co-founded by Peggy Hackney and Janice Meaden. You can read more about IMS at their website, www.imsmovement.com.

8 We were introduced to this Practice in a class with Cathy Albers at the Great Lakes Michael Chek-hov Consortium. Used with permission.

Foundations

Like the other movement pioneers, Rudolf Laban was intensely curious about our body's design, and its effect on our movement choices. He observed and studied how people move: factory workers, office workers, dancers, actors, musicians, and people in the street. His system and theories of movement are far-ranging and complex. In this Section we offer you a practical taste of one small part of Laban's vast contribution: the elements of movement.

Through his observations, Laban discovered that each of our movements share certain fundamental qualities. He observed that every movement is made up of four elements: Time, Space, Weight, and Flow. In his book, *The Mastery of Movement*, he describes these "motion factors:"

> It is a mechanical fact that the weight of the body, or any of its parts, can be lifted and carried into a certain direction of space, and that this process takes a certain amount of time … The same mechanical conditions can also be observed in any counter-pull which regulates the flow of movement.[1]

Every movement you make has a direction in Space, it occurs at a certain speed (Time), and it has a sense of Weight. In addition, every movement can be fluid or restricted (Flow) – or anything in between. Laban realized that each person has a unique relationship with these elements of movement, which he referred to as *Efforts* (KW). The *Efforts* reflect our inner attitude – emotional, psychological, and physical – toward the world.

Each of them offers a broad range of expression within it that can be explored along a *Continuum* (KW): from the subtle to the extreme. Laban recognized that at one end of the *continuum* are fighting/resisting qualities, and at the opposite end are indulging/yielding qualities: "We can observe people yield to the accidental forces of weight, space and time, as well as to the natural flow of movement … or … they fight against one or more of these factors by actively resisting them."[2]

THE *EFFORTS*

Your full range of expression exists between the two extremes of the *Effort continuum*.

Indulging/Yielding Qualities   Fighting/Resisting Qualities

TIME

Sustained/Lingering————————————————————Quick/Sudden

WEIGHT

Light/Limp————————————————————Strong/Heavy

SPACE

Indirect/Flexible————————————————————Direct/Focused

FLOW

Free/Unrestrained———————————————— Bound/Restrained

Through the *Efforts*, you can truly step into another person's shoes.[4]

Laban developed a language of movement based on these elements, and he emphasized that we can make a conscious choice about how we use them. His writings and teachings have had a profound impact on the way movement is perceived and explored in the world of acting and dance.

Through the *Efforts*, you can discover ways of moving that may not have occurred to you. As Laban said, we can become "conscious of our choice, and can investigate why we so choose."[3] Through the *Efforts*, you can step out of your everyday experience and discover a character's movement from the inside out.

Key Words: *Efforts, Continuum*

Notes

1 Laban, Rudolf, *The Mastery of Movement*, 4th ed. Alton: Dance Books, Ltd., p. 20.
2 Laban, p. 20.
3 Laban, p. 20.
4 Laban, pp. 73–74.

Space

Space[*] is a lively partner in our movement, because we are in a constant – highly visible – relationship with it. Offstage, the way we relate to space reveals our personal approach to life and the world around us. Onstage, our relationship with space informs the audience about our character and their role in the action of the play.

Laban observed that our **attention** to Space is a factor in our movement choices. If we are very focused, we know where we want to go, and we move in the most efficient way to get there. Our movements are Direct, following the shortest distance between two points. If our attention is unfocused, then our movements are more flexible or Indirect. Our destination is not clearly defined, and our movements may wander, following spirals or arcs.[1]

Space *Effort* reflects our intentions. When our intention is on a specific goal, our attention is narrow, focused. Our movements are Direct, suggesting certainty and decisiveness. Indirect movements reflect an emphasis on each moment of the journey rather than the destination. A person who is Indirect might seem curious or uncertain. In her book, *Laban for Actors and Dancers*, Jean Newlove refers to Direct Space *Effort* as "economical, restricted" and Indirect Space *Effort* as looking "around the spatial garden."[2]

Discover how attention to Space can affect your movement in the scenario below:

Sense your personal space, your *Kinesphere*.

Imagine that someone is blowing bubbles, and one floats into your *Kinesphere*. With your index finger leading the way, you reach out and pop it. Each time a bubble floats into your *Kinesphere*, you can explore Direct movements by focusing on the bubble and popping it. Use any part of your body. Pause.

---

* The word *space* has many meanings for us, as movers. In this chapter, Space with a capital "S" refers to Laban's *Effort*, our attitude toward space. When a small "s" is used, we are referring to space itself, general space.

Now change your intention: enjoy the many bubbles floating through your *Kinesphere*. Let them touch you as your stretch your arms out and play among these lovely transparent spheres. Allow your movements to become Indirect as your attention expands to your whole *Kinesphere*. Your movements may cause bubbles to pop, but in an indirect, unintentional way. Pause.

One or many. That is our choice in Space *Effort*: single-minded focus on a specific point or multi-focused attention within "the spatial garden."

Consider Ebenezer Scrooge, the protagonist in *A Christmas Carol*. He is a character who experiences deep transformation in the course of the play. In the early scenes, Scrooge is all business, a man of few words, Direct and to the point. He trudges through the streets of London on Christmas Eve, focused on only one goal: making money. He does not see or participate in the joyful, teeming life around him.

After his transformation, Scrooge is motivated by giving, rather than taking. His movements become Indirect, as he is continually delighted by the sights, sounds, and people around him – and his intention to take part in all of it.[3]

Like Scrooge, when your intentions change, your relationship to space shifts, and your movements change. You can explore this *body-mind connection* in the Practice below.

PRACTICE 21.1 RELATIONSHIP – SPACE

In this exploration you can discover how a shift in attitude can change your Space *Effort*. As with all the Practices in *YBK*, warm up before you begin. For warm-up suggestions, visit the first page of Appendix I.

Before you begin, place ten smallish objects around the room – anything from a book, to a pen, to a sock will do. You will need a bag or box into which you can place these objects. This Practice works best if you have a partner who can place the objects around the room again after you complete the first scenario.

I investigate: What can I discover about the relationship between my attitude, my goal, and my relationship to Space?

- Stand. Pause. Breathe. Take a *kinesthetic moment*.
- Have a walk around the room, noticing the space around you as you walk.
- Play as you move through space, exploring the ways you can alter your attention to Space. You can move in straight lines, circles, spirals, and everything in between. Practice *inclusive attention*.
- Pause. Take a *kinesthetic moment*. Notice the space around you.
- Allow the imagined circumstances below to influence your relationship to Space as you move through the room to place the objects in your bag:
  You have just ended a long-term toxic relationship. Though your ex-lover has moved out, evidence of their presence is all about you. You are determined to rid yourself of any reminders of them and set yourself free once and for all.

Gather these objects and put them in your bag.

When you have finished gathering, exit the room to discard the bag. Good riddance!

* Release the imagined circumstances. Re-enter the room.
* Pause. Breathe. Take a *kinesthetic moment*.
* You or your partner can place the objects around the room again.
* Allow a new set of circumstances to influence your relationship to Space:

Your much-loved teacher has passed away, and their family has allowed you to take some remembrances from their classroom. A couple of friends have asked you to get a memento for them as well. Explore the classroom and discover significant objects as you choose the ones to remember your teacher by.

When you've collected the objects, take them with you as you exit the classroom for the last time.

* Release the imagined circumstances. Re-enter the room.
* Pause. Breathe.
* You or your partner can place the objects around the room again.
* Allow another set of circumstances to influence your relationship to Space:

You are at an outdoor market. You have plans to meet someone soon, so you aren't looking for anything to buy. Enjoy taking in the sights, smells, people, and the interesting items for sale. Pause.

Release the imagined circumstances. Have a walk around the space, practicing *inclusive attention*. Pause.

* Take a *kinesthetic moment*.
* *Spy back*. Describe your attitude toward Space in each scenario. How did your intention influence your use of Space? When were you most Direct? Indirect?

Our attitude and our needs determine our use of Space *Effort*. Our movements may cut through space or embrace it, expand into it or retreat from it. When our attention is intensely focused, we may respond to space in a single-minded, controlling way. As our intentions become more Indirect, we may regard space as a partner, or even a friend, and bask in the relationship.

In the next Practice, you can explore the entire Space *continuum*, from Direct to Indirect.

PRACTICE 21.2   EXPLORING THE SPACE CONTINUUM

As you explore the Space *Effort continuum*, you can say a line or a phrase and discover how speaking is affected by your movement. Two options are "Let's move ahead," or "I look up to her." You can also choose a few lines from a scene or monologue.

Warm up before beginning this Practice: suggested warm-ups are on the first page of Appendix I.

I investigate: What can I discover about my relationship to space, as I gradually move along the *continuum* between Direct and Indirect?

* Stand. Pause. Breathe. Take a *kinesthetic moment*.
* Take a moment to connect to your sense of *suspension and support*. Expand your awareness to include your whole body and your place within the room.
* Take a walk around the room. Practice *inclusive attention*.
* Play with single-focused and multi-focused attention to space. Enjoy the Direct and Indirect movements that arise as you change your relationship to Space.
* Pause.
* Pick a point across the room and point Directly to it. Then walk Directly to the point you chose.
* When you arrive at your point, turn, pick another point, and repeat the process.
* Continue in this way, pointing and moving Directly.
* Occasionally speak your line as you move from point to point. Think of allowing the line to "come out of this body."
* Let your need to reach your point become stronger with each cross, as your movements become more and more Direct. From time to time speak your line.
* When you have reached extreme Directness, and you feel you are at the end of the *continuum*, begin to move back toward the middle of the *continuum* where you began. Shift your attitude toward reaching your point. Gradually soften the movement as you point to your goal.
* When you reach the middle of the Space *Effort continuum*, continue your shift of intention. Let your focus become more inclusive, as it becomes less import-ant to you to reach your goal.
* Each time you point and walk, allow your movements to become more Indirect.
* Occasionally, speak your phrase. See what it's like for your line(s) to "come out of this body."
* You can move through the room any way you wish, gradually letting go of single focus, and let go of pointing to your goal. Forget about moving to a point and expand your attention. Wander.
* Continue to breathe and occasionally speak your phrase.
* Once you have reached the Indirect end of the *Effort*, begin to return to the middle of the *continuum*. Enjoy each specific moment as you explore every part of the progression.
* Speak your line at various moments. If you choose, you can return to pointing before you move. Take your time as you complete this process.
* When you feel you have reached the center of the *continuum*, move any way you like, exploring your relationship to Space.
* Pause. Breathe. Let go of the Practice.
* Take a *kinesthetic moment*. Pause.
* *Spy back*. What did you discover about your relationship to the Space *Effort con-tinuum*? What areas of the *continuum* felt most comfortable to you? Uncomfort-able? What is your experience of Space *Effort* in your daily activities?

Every time you move, you displace space, making a pathway through it. As you may have noticed in the Practices above, your spatial pathways become a reflection of Space *Effort*. A flexible intention results in more expansive movements and spiraling or curved spatial pathways. A Direct intention inspires narrower movements and straight pathways in space. Laban pointed out that spatial pathways can be curved or angled, linear or wavy, and everything in between.[4]

Knowledge is power. Knowing your spatial preferences gives you the power to choose how you move. You can have a specific relationship to Space whether you are moving or standing still.

> *PAUSE TO PROCESS* Journal or discuss your discoveries. Notice your relationship to Space *Effort* as you move through your day.

PRACTICE 21.3 CROSSINGS – SPACE

In the Practice below, you can refine your relationship to the Space *Effort continuum* even more. Feel free to move any way you like as you cross the room, including jumping, scooting, crawling, or slithering.

Warm up before beginning this Practice: suggested warm-ups are on the first page of Appendix I.

I investigate: What can I discover by moving Directly and Indirectly?

Part I: Solo

- Stand. Pause. Take a *kinesthetic moment*. Breathe.
- Have a walk around the space, practicing *inclusive attention*. Pause.
- Bring your attention to your *Kinesphere*. Explore Direct and Indirect movements within your *Kinesphere*.
- Pause.
- Move to one end of the room, facing the opposite end. Pause. Take a *kinesthetic moment*.
- Cross to the other end of the room.
- Pause. Turn around and face the other end.
- Pick a point at the other end of the room.
- Notice if your body "prepares" to cross. If so, Pause. Bring your attention to your *3-D body within the 3-D space* and return to balance.
- Think of moving in a focused, Direct path to your point.
- Now, sense your *3-D body* as you cross Directly to your point.
- When you reach the other side, turn around. Pause.
- Think of moving in the "spatial garden."
- Sense your *3-D body* as you enjoy your Indirect journey through the room.
- At some point, you will reach the other side of the room. When you do, pause.

- Think of crossing the room again, gradually moving through the entire Space *continuum* from Indirect to extremely Direct. Now cross the room. Allow your inner impulses to guide you. Breathe.
- Turn around and pause to allow your inner impulse to guide you into Directness.
- Begin a cross back to the other side, moving through the entire Space *continuum* from Direct to Indirect. Breathe as you move.
- Pause. Take a *kinesthetic moment*. Release the Practice.
- Take a walk through the room. Practice *inclusive attention*. Pause.
- *Spy back*. What were your sensations as you explored the Space *continuum*? What did you notice about your breath? Were there parts of the *continuum* that seemed familiar? Unfamiliar? What were they?

Part II: Duet

If you have a partner, you can play with the "dance" between Direct and Indirect. Before you begin the Practice, choose which partner will begin with Directness, and which will begin with Indirectness.

In this exploration, you can be inspired by your partner, as you move through the entire *continuum*.

- Stand. Pause. Breathe. Take a *kinesthetic moment*.
- Take a walk through the room. Practice *inclusive attention*. Become aware of the others in the room.
- Move to one end of the room, facing your partner at the other end of the room. Pause.
- Become aware of your *Kinesphere*, and begin exploring it with Direct or Indirect movements, whichever you have chosen. Pause.
- When you and your partner are ready, begin to move toward one another – one of you moving Directly and the other, Indirectly. Be aware of your *3-D body* as you move.
- Meet in the middle of the room and enjoy a few moments of interaction, moving in a little "dance" at the two ends of the *continuum*.
- After a few minutes' exploration, begin to "exchange" Space *Effort*. The Direct partner will gradually become Indirect, and the Indirect partner will gradually become more Direct. Your *life-body* can guide your movements.
- At some point, move away from your partner and continue in your new *Effort* to the other end of the room.
- When you reach the other end of the room, turn around. Pause. Return to balance. Take a *kinesthetic moment*.
- Take a walk around the room, enjoying your new awareness of Space *Effort* as you move.
- Pause. Take a *kinesthetic moment*.
- *Spy back*. Meet with your partner and share your experience. If you are in a class, meet with the whole group as well.

Not only does our relationship to Space *Effort* affect how we move, but Direct or Indirect movements can evoke feelings or remind us of specific circumstances. You may have discovered that certain emotions or feelings arose as you moved from one end of the Space *continuum* to the other. What sorts of circumstances come to mind as you moved in a highly focused, Direct way? When you moved Indirectly, with multi-focus?

Exploring the *Efforts* is like a creative "workout," preparing you for the challenge of the "playing field" in performance. Of course, Space is only one of the *Efforts*. In the next chapter, you can discover how the Time *continuum* affects your movement.

At the end of this Section, you will have the opportunity to combine the *Efforts*, which is not only fun, but can lead you to discover a character's movement from the inside out.

Space Answers the Question

"How do I focus my attention, as I relate to the space around me?"

The two ends of the *continuum* are:

DIRECT: aiming, pinpointing, straightforward, focused on a single path, certain, decisive.

INDIRECT: flexible, devious, curious, generous, indecisive, wandering.

PAUSE TO PROCESS Journal, discuss, practice. Notice your relationship with Space *Effort* in your daily activities.

Notes

1 Laban, Rudolf. *The Mastery of Movement*. Alton, UK: Dance Books Ltd., 2011, p. 69.
2 Newlove, Jean. *Laban for Actors and Dancers*. New York: Routledge, 2010, p. 53. Print.
3 The film version of *Scrooge*, the musical by Leslie Bricusse, has the added ingredient of choreography in it, making it particularly easy to spot Space *Effort*. You can find numerous clips from the movie on YouTube. A particularly good example of the contrast between Direct and Indirect use of Space is "Father Christmas" and "I Hate People" in the early part of the movie and "Thank You Very Much/Father Christmas" near the end.
4 Laban, p. 129.

Time

Everyone has a personal relationship with Time,* ranging from: "I have all the time I need," to "I'll never have enough time!" When we move, we measure time in two ways: tempo (from fast to slow) and duration (from short to long).

Laban observed that our personal relationship with Time exists on a *continuum*, ranging from quickness (urgency in time, wanting to be first person to arrive at the wedding) to sustainment (lingering in time, savoring each moment of a wonderful first wedding anniversary dinner). Our preferences toward Time influence how we express ourselves and how we move in the world.

Certain adjectives can describe a person's attitude at each end of the Time *continuum*. A person who is focused on Quickness might be considered a "go-getter," highly efficient, and someone who "always gets the job done on time." A person who lingers and indulges in Time might be seen as leisurely, unhurried, or calm.

We have the ability to move easily along the Time *continuum*: to move from zipping along in Time one moment and prolonging Time in the next moment. In the Practice below, you can explore both Quick and Sustained relationship to Time.

PRACTICE 22.1   RELATIONSHIP – TIME

Consider the differences in Time *Effort* in a simple action, like walking. Remember to warm up before you begin this exploration.

- Pause. Breathe. Take a *kinesthetic moment*.
- Allow yourself to respond to each of the imaginary circumstances below.

---

* The word *time* has many meanings for us, as movers. In this chapter, Time with a capital "T" refers to Laban's *Effort*, our attitude toward time. When a small "t" is used, we are referring to time itself, the hours and minutes of our days.

- You are returning from a wonderful evening with a friend, whom you have not seen in a long time. It is a beautiful summer night, and after you say good-bye to them, you take a leisurely stroll home in your familiar neighborhood. You remember all of the wonderful times you have shared with your friend over the years.
- Pause. Breathe. Return to balance.
- You are returning home by subway in New York City late at night. As you exit the station, you remember that you forgot to turn the oven off before you left. You race home, and discover that all is well, and you quickly turn the oven off.
- Pause.
- *Spy back.* How do your movements reflect your relationship to Time in each scenario? What did you notice about your breathing in each scenario?

Each day we effortlessly shift from one relationship with Time to another, naturally moving between Quickness and Sustainment depending on the situation.

PRACTICE 22.2   EXPLORING THE TIME CONTINUUM

Time is concerned with our sense of urgency or quickness, or our choice to savor each moment as it occurs. An idea may come to us "suddenly," or we may "gradually" realize that we need to make a telephone call to an old friend.

In the Practice below, you can explore attitudes that affect your relationship with Time.

- Pause. Stand. Take a *kinesthetic moment*.
- Have a walk around the room. Practice *inclusive attention*.
- As you walk, notice your connection with the floor, and take your time to move your body in various pathways through the space: forward and back, side to side, diagonals, in circles, and spirals.
- Enjoy the differences between each pathway. Now begin to move more quickly through each one.
- Play with the full range of the Time *continuum* from quickness to sustainment. Your explorations may take you from short, fast movements to prolonged, slow movements.
- Pause. Take a *kinesthetic moment*. Breathe.
- Imagine that it is summertime, and you are strolling through a beautiful garden at night, savoring each moment as it occurs.
- Take your time to pay attention to the uniqueness of each flower, and the full moon above you.
- Enjoy the beauty of the moon's reflection on the flowers, and delicious fragrances of each one.

- Reach the very end of the *continuum*, where your movements are as leisurely and prolonged as possible.
- Pause. Experience a moment of *inclusive attention*, as you appreciate the beauty of the evening, and your surroundings.
- Pause. Breathe. Take a *kinesthetic moment*.
- Begin to simply walk through the room again, enjoying your connection with the floor, and the sustained, easeful quality of your movement.
- As you continue to walk through the garden, you sense a presence behind you. You gradually become fearful, as you notice that when you pause, they pause.
- You begin to feel a sense of danger. An inner urgency arises in you, but you keep walking slowly.
- The person continues to follow you, and you begin to walk a little bit faster. They also walk faster.
- You begin to walk even faster, and then you break out into a run, leave the garden, and go out into the street, where you find your best friend, who has been looking for you. The person behind you has disappeared. You are safe!
- Release the imagined circumstances. Pause. Take a *kinesthetic moment*.
- Walk around the room. Enjoy your connection with the floor, noticing your relationship with Time as you move. Pause.
- *Spy back*. When you played with the Time *continuum*, what did you discover? What was your favorite part of the *continuum*? What was your experience of Time in the scenarios? How did your relationship to Time change in each of the scenarios?

In our daily lives, we are in a continuously changing relationship to Time. As you explore the Time *continuum* you can discover your "everyday" relationship/attitude toward Time. Then, you can give yourself permission to step out of your "comfort zone" and broaden your movement vocabulary.

Be aware of your breath and tension level as you explore. *Kinesthetic sense* and *inclusive attention* are your friends. They can alert you to *over-efforting*. Keep this awareness in mind as you explore the Time *continuum* in the explorations below.

PRACTICE 22.3   CROSSINGS – TIME

In this Practice, your movement choices can become increasingly nuanced as you explore the entire range of the Time *continuum*.

I investigate: What can I discover as I explore my relationship to Time?

Part I: Solo

- Stand. Pause. Take a *kinesthetic moment*. Breathe.
- Have a walk around the room, practicing *inclusive attention*.
- As you walk, notice your connection to the floor, and your relationship to Time as you move through the room.

- Move to one end of the room and face the opposite end. Pause. Take a *kinesthetic moment*.
- Walk to the other end of the space.
- Pause. Turn around and face the other end.
- Think of crossing again. Notice if your body "prepares" to cross. If so, Pause. Bring your attention to your *3-D body in the 3-D space* and return to balance.
- Now, enjoy the movement of your coordinated body, as you cross the space. When you reach the other side, turn around.
- Pause to allow your inner impulse to guide you into an expansive relationship with Time.
- Now cross the space again, luxuriating in Time, taking all the time you need to sense and savor the sensations in your body, in every movement, and every moment. Pause.
- Turn around. Breathe.
- Allow your inner impulse to guide you into a sense of urgency. Sensing your whole *3-D body*, move back to the other side as Quickly as possible.
- Pause. Breathe. Turn and face the other end of the room.
- Cross the room, exploring the entire Time *continuum*. Begin with slower, Sustaining movements, which increasingly become Quicker as you reach the other side. Pause.
- Turn around and return to the other side, moving from Quickness to Sustainment.
- Pause. Take a *kinesthetic moment*.
- Take a walk around the space. Practice *inclusive attention*.
- *Spy back*. What were your sensations as you explored the Time *continuum*? What did you notice about your breath? What parts of the *continuum* seemed familiar? Unfamiliar?

Part II: Duet

If you have a partner, you can play with the "dance" between Quickness and Sustainment. Before you begin the Practice, choose which partner will begin with Sustainment, and which will begin with Quickness.

- Stand. Pause. Breathe. Take a *kinesthetic moment*.
- Take a walk around the space. Practice *inclusive attention*. Become aware of others in the space.
- Move to one end of the room, facing your partner at the other end of the room. Pause.
- Begin to explore your *Kinesphere* with small movements, from your end of the Time *continuum*. Think of your *Kinesphere* as a playground. Have fun with Quick movements or Sustained movements, depending on which end of the *continuum* you have chosen to explore first.
- When you and your partner are ready, begin to move toward one another – each of you exploring your end of the Time *Effort continuum*.

- Meet in the middle of the room and enjoy a few moments of interaction, moving in a little "dance" joining the two ends of the *continuum*.
- After a few moments, begin to "exchange" the Time *Effort*. The "Quick partner" will gradually become Sustained, and the "Sustained partner" will gradually become Quick.
- At some point, move away from your partner and continue in your new *Effort* to the other end of the room.
- When you reach the other end of the room, turn around. Pause. Return to balance. Take a *kinesthetic moment*.
- Take a walk around the room, enjoying your new awareness of Time *Effort* as you move.
- Pause. Take a *kinesthetic moment*.
- *Spy back*. Meet with your partner and share your experience. If you are in a class, meet with the whole group as well.

"Time flies when you're having fun!" This old saying, and many other statements about time, reveal a wide range of possible attitudes toward our use of the hours in our day. As you explore the Time *continuum*, you can discover your personal relationship with Time.

What are your Time habits? Always rushing? Slow and deliberate? By exploring Time, you can begin to expand your personal range of choices, and you may discover exciting new approaches to how a character may express their relationship to Time.

Time Answers the Question

"What is my relationship to the passing seconds, minutes, and hours of my life?"

The two ends of the *continuum* are:

QUICK/SUDDEN: staccato, speedy, energetic, prompt, rapid, abrupt, quick-witted

SUSTAINED/SLOW: smooth, persistent, lingering, long-winded, leisurely, deliberate.

PAUSE TO PROCESS Journal, discuss, practice. Notice your relationship with Time *Effort* in your daily activities.

Weight

All day, every day, our movements reflect our changing relationship with weight – not as pounds on a scale, but in our shifting attitudes toward how we activate movement. Laban emphasized that Weight[*] *Effort* refers to the amount of power or strength we require when we move. Our actions can be Light or Strong (and everything in between).

Our personal attitude toward Weight arises from our preferences – the way we see the world and our place in it. A simple movement, like a handshake, can reveal the way we relate to others and to ourselves. One person might choose a tight grip (Strong Weight *Effort*), while another responds with a gentler grip (Light Weight *Effort*). How might each person see their world – or the person they are meeting?

We can discover much about someone from their relationship with Weight. On the Stronger end of the *continuum*, a person might be considered powerful, vigorous, or earthy. A person with Lighter preferences might be seen as whimsical, soft, or delicate.

Of course, nobody "lives" at one end of the *continuum* all the time. We are always responding to circumstances. When we are happy, we may say, "I feel lighter than air!" We might sense our feet barely touching the ground as we move. On the other hand, if we are angry, we may stomp out of the room or slam our fist into the table.

As we go through our day, we constantly adjust our Weight *Effort*: we may be pushing a piano in one moment and a baby carriage in the next. We shift effortlessly from Strength

---

[*] The word *weight* has many meanings for us, as movers. In this chapter, Weight with a capital "W" refers to Laban's *Effort*, our attitude toward weight. When a small "w" is used, we are referring to weight itself, the force of gravity and/or pounds on a scale.

to Lightness and back again. In the Practice below, you can explore Weight *Effort* as you respond to changing circumstances.

PRACTICE 23.1   RELATIONSHIP – WEIGHT

Consider the difference in Weight *Effort* in a simple action.

- Stand. Pause. Breathe. Take a *kinesthetic moment*.
- Allow yourself to respond to each of the imaginary circumstances below.
- You are on the roof of a house with raging floodwaters all around. You see someone in a rowboat at the end of the street. Wave to attract their attention. You can use sound as well.
- Pause. Breathe. Let go of the imagined circumstances. Return to balance.
- You are waiting in the checkout line at the grocery store. In the shopping cart in front of you is a cute baby who looks at you solemnly. You wave. Feel free to use words or sounds.
- Pause.
- *Spy back*. How does each situation affect the Weight of your movements? What was the difference in the sounds you made in each scenario?

Each situation inspired a certain Weight *Effort* in your movement, and you easily shifted from one to the other. We swing between Strong and Light movements hundreds of times a day without thinking about it.

If you like, repeat this Practice and see what it's like to choose a different Weight response to the imagined circumstances. Experiment with the opposite choice: if you were Strong in the first scenario, can you discover a movement that is Lighter?

Sensing Your Weight

Laban said, "The variety of human character is derived from the multitude of possible attitudes towards the motion factors."[1] As an actor, you want access to the whole Weight *continuum*, because your character's attitude toward Weight could demand it.

Sensing your weight offers you vital information about your approach to Weight *Effort* and refines your ability to move between Strength and Lightness. In previous chapters, you have practiced sensing your weight:

- Constructive Rest 1: you allowed your weight to release into the floor.
- Practice 8.1: you sensed weight moving through your joints and body as you raised and lowered an arm and discovered weight in your legs.
- Practice 8.3: you accepted the support of the ground, sensed your weight on your feet and throughout your body.

In Constructive Rest 1, you practiced giving your weight to the floor. Laban saw this surrender to Gravity as a Passive aspect of Weight *Effort*.

When we take an Active approach to Weight *Effort*, we move with intention. However, if we are tired or drunk, our response to Weight becomes more Passive, and our body might become floppy or sink heavily into a collapse. As we activate Weight, we move along a *continuum* between Light and Strong. If we surrender our weight to Gravity, we move between Limp and Heavy.[2]

Weight sensing helps you discern the differences between Active and Passive, Strong and Light. You can be grounded and standing in readiness or momentarily surrender your weight before actively pushing off the ground to leap into the air.

Actors take an Active approach to Weight *Effort*, because they move! In the practices below, you can discover your own attitude toward activating your weight, as you explore the Weight *Effort* continuum from Strong to Light and back again.

PRACTICE 23.2 **EXPLORING THE WEIGHT CONTINUUM**

As we noted above, Weight *Effort* focuses on the amount of force used to move, rather than pounds recorded on a scale. The two are certainly related, but a very thin person can still move with Strength!

Below, discover how your intention influences your relationship with Weight *Effort*.

- Pause. Stand. Take a *kinesthetic moment*. Breathe.
- Walk around the room. Practice *inclusive attention*.
- As you walk, notice your connection to the floor, and the amount of strength you use to move your body through space. Pause.
- Allow these imagined circumstances to affect your attitude toward Weight *Effort*: you are your younger self, living in your parents' house, and you have been partying late – past curfew. You must walk down a very long hall and past their bedroom, where they are sleeping, to get to your room.
- As you approach the open door of their bedroom, allow your movements to become lighter and lighter. Keep breathing!
- Reach the very end of the *continuum*, where your movements are as light as you can possibly make them – Perhaps your arms float up toward the ceiling in response to the "lightening" of your movement.
- Once you are past their bedroom, you can gradually move along the Weight *continuum*, back to your usual attitude toward the Weight *Effort*. You gratefully reach your bedroom undetected.
- Release the imagined circumstances. Pause.
- Take a *kinesthetic moment*.
- Walk around the room again, enjoying your connection to the floor, and the strength you use to move your body through space.
- Now, allow these imagined circumstances to affect your attitude toward Weight *Effort*: You have just heard that your best friend's fiancé has dumped them, weeks before their wedding. You decide you must speak to your friend.

- As you walk to their house, you become more and more determined to tell off their fiancé. Your movements become stronger and stronger as you contemplate putting this loser in their place.
- Now, begin to think about what a jerk this person has always been, and realize that your friend is probably way better off without them. Your movements begin to lose some of their strong determination, as you contemplate a different mission: to comfort your friend.
- Move back along the Weight *continuum*, sensing the Weight *Effort* appropriate to your new attitude, and your new mission. Pause.
- Release the imagined circumstances. Take a *kinesthetic moment*.
- Have a walk around the room, practicing *inclusive attention*. Notice your relationship to the Weight *Effort* as you move.
- Pause.
- *Spy back*. How did your relationship to Weight *Effort* change in each scenario? What did you discover about your "everyday" relationship/attitude toward Weight? Were you ever outside your comfort zone in this Practice? If so, when?

As your attitudes toward the world around you change, so does your relationship to each of the *Efforts*. Begin to pay attention to "where you live" on the Weight *continuum*, and notice when a *stimulus* causes you to make another choice!

For some of us, Strength can be accompanied by unwanted tension, and Lightness can cause us to lift our weight up and pull away from the support of the floor. As you refine your ability to access the Weight *Effort* and sense your weight, remember to include the valuable lessons you learned in Part I: *Suspension and Support*, *Primary Coordination*, *Three Places of Poise*, *grounding*, *centering*, *reverberation*, and the wholeness of your *body-mind*.

These practical lessons remind you to practice all the *Efforts* with a sense of balance and ease in your *3-D body*. Allow *the four brothers* to support you. If you find yourself *over-efforting*, pause, and reconnect through the *5 cues* or *the sequence of directional thinking*. In this way, you can support the *Efforts* while working safely, in tune with your body's perfect design.

PRACTICE 23.3 **CROSSINGS – WEIGHT**

In the exploration below, you can become even more nuanced in your ability to embody each part of the Weight *continuum*. As you cross the room, feel free to move any way you like, including jumping, scooting, crawling, or slithering.

I investigate: What can I discover about my movement choices as I explore the Weight *continuum*?

Part I: Solo

- Stand. Pause. Take a *kinesthetic moment*. Breathe.
- Have a walk around the space, practicing *inclusive attention*.

- As you walk, bring your awareness to the Weight *Effort*. Notice your connection to the floor, and the amount of strength you use as you move your body through space.
- Move to one end of the room, facing the opposite end. Pause. Take a *kinesthetic moment*.
- Cross to the other end of the space.
- Pause. Turn around and face the other end.
- Think of crossing again. Notice if your body "prepares" to cross. If so, Pause. Bring your attention to your *3-D body in the 3-D space* and return to balance.
- Now, taking the time to enjoy the movement of your whole coordinated *body-mind*, cross the space. When you reach the other side, turn around. Pause.
- Explore the Light end of the Weight *continuum* by beginning a gentle bounce, allowing your heels to come off the floor. *Reverberate*.
- Perhaps your arms float up toward the ceiling. After a few moments, pause and return to balance.
- Maintaining this Light approach to Weight, cross the room. Pause.
- Turn and face the other end.
- Begin to bounce again, releasing at your Big 3 leg joints. Your heels remain connected to the floor. Sense your Strong connection to the ground with each bounce. Remember, there is buoyancy even in Strength: *Reverberate*. Pause.
- Maintaining this Strong approach to Weight, cross the room. Pause.
- Turn and face the other end.
- Cross the room again, gradually moving through the entire Weight *continuum* from Lightness to extreme Strength by the time you reach the other side. Pause.
- Turn around and cross back to the other side, moving from Strength to Lightness.
- Pause. Take a *kinesthetic moment*.
- Take a walk around the space, enjoying your relationship with Weight as you move. Practice *inclusive attention*.
- *Spy back*. What were your sensations as you explored the Weight *continuum*? What did you notice about your breath? Were there parts of the *continuum* that seemed familiar? Unfamiliar? What were they?

Part II: Duet

If you have a partner, you can play with the "dance" between Strong and Light. Before you begin the Practice, choose which partner will begin with Lightness, and which will begin with Strength.

- Stand. Pause. Breathe. Take a *kinesthetic moment*.
- Take a walk around the space. Practice *inclusive attention*. Become aware of the others in the space.
- Move to one end of the room, facing your partner at the other end of the room. Pause.
- Begin a small weight shift from side to side, playing with the Strength or Lightness of these movements, depending on which end of the *continuum* you have chosen to explore first.

- After a few moments, pause. Take a *kinesthetic moment*.
- When you and your partner are ready, begin to move toward one another, any way you like – each of you moving with Strength or Lightness.
- Meet in the middle of the room and enjoy a few moments of interaction, moving in a "dance" at the two ends of the *continuum*.
- After a few moments, begin to "exchange" Weight *Effort*. The "Light partner" will gradually become Strong, and the "Strong partner" will gradually become Light.
- At some point, move away from your partner and continue in your new *Effort* to the other end of the room.
- When you reach the other end of the room, turn around. Pause. Return to balance. Take a *kinesthetic moment*.
- Take a walk around the room, enjoying your new awareness of Weight *Effort* as you move.
- Pause.
- *Spy back*. Meet with your partner and share your experience. If you are in a class, meet with the whole group as well.

As you explore your personal relationship with Weight, play! Playing with the *Efforts* is key to expanding your movement vocabulary. Play is also helpful in making each part of the *continuum* more accessible to you. Playing in the entire Weight *continuum* allows you to develop movement for a variety of characters, from the most determined to the most delicate. And, equally important, you can embody your character in each moment, as their attitudes toward Weight *Effort* shift throughout the play.

> Weight Answers the Question
>
> "With what amount of force do I meet the challenges of life?"
>
> The two ends of the *continuum* are:
>
> STRONG/HEAVY: powerful, sturdy, impactful, weighty, collapsed
>
> LIGHT/LIMP: airy, delicate, wilting, gentle, soft

> *PAUSE TO PROCESS* Journal, discuss, practice. Notice your relationship with Weight *Effort* in your daily activities.

Notes

1 Laban, Rudolf. *The Mastery of Movement*. Alton, Hampshire, UK: Dance Books, 2011. p. 20.

2 Hackney, Peggy. *Making Connections: Total Body Connectivity Through Bartenieff Fundamentals*. New York: Routledge, 2002, p. 220.

Flow

Whether we are moving or stand still, we experience ease or restraint in our bodies. Laban referred to this ease or resistance to movement as Flow. Flow can run freely, like water, or it can be restrained, as if there were a barrier resisting the flow. Flow offers foundational support to all the other *Efforts*.

Flow exists on a *continuum* that ranges from Free Flow to Bound Flow. In Free Flow, the movement is ongoing, streaming, unrestricted: we might say, "Go with the flow!" or "Just go with it!"* With Bound Flow, the movement is restricted, held back: we warn, "Be careful!" or "Watch out!"

Pause for a moment and notice the Flow of your breath as it easily moves in and out of your body. After a few cycles of breath, try a few simple movements, "riding on the Flow of your breath." Now hold your breath. Make those same movements. Pause and return to comfortable breathing. What do you notice about the connection between Flow, movement, and breath?

In our lives, there is a constant play between these two ends of the spectrum of Flow. The undercurrent of Flow creates dynamic continuity within your body, which enlivens your outer movement. By exploring the *continuum* between Free and Bound, you can discover a new range of possibilities for building character movement.

PRACTICE 24.1   EXPERIENCING FLOW

The activities below invite a sense of freedom or a sense of restraint. Enjoy exploring both ends of the Flow *continuum*. Warm up before you begin.

---

* The words *flow* and *free* have many meanings for us, as movers. In this chapter, *Flow* with a capital "F" refers to the *Effort*, your attitude toward Flow, while a small "f" refers to a sense of movement and connection throughout your body. *Free* with a capital "F" refers to the yielding end of the Flow *Effort*. When a small "f" is used, we are referring to an expansive, unrestricted sensation in your body.

Free Flow Activities

#1 This Practice is best if you have a real swimming pool or a pile of pillows, a large bed, or gym mats to jump into.

* Pause and notice the free flow of your breath. Take a *kinesthetic moment.*
* Imagine you are running down a grassy hill and jumping into a swimming pool.
* Go!
* Pause. Release the imagined circumstances and have a walk around the room.

#2 It's helpful to have a partner to play this scene with you.

* Pause and notice the free Flow of your breath. Take a *kinesthetic moment.*
* Imagine you are going up the walk to your friend's house to tell them they've won a big award.
* Go!
* Pause. Release the imagined circumstances and have a walk around the room. Switch roles with your partner.

#3 This Practice requires a visit to your local playground or park.

* Enjoy a sense of freedom as you swing on the swings, jump onto the spinning merry-go-round, or slide down the slide.

Bound Flow Activities

#1 For this Practice, your partner can walk beside you to ensure your safety.

* Pause and notice the Flow of your breath. Take a *kinesthetic moment.*
* Take a walk with your eyes closed.
* Pause. Open your eyes. Take a *kinesthetic moment.* Switch roles.

#2 Pause and notice the Flow of your breath. Take a *kinesthetic moment.*

* Imagine you are crossing a stream on stepping stones that are set somewhat far apart.
* After several minutes' exploration, pause. Release the imagined circumstances and have a walk around the room.

#3 It's helpful to have a partner to play this scene with you.

* Pause and notice the Flow of your breath. Take a *kinesthetic moment.*
* Imagine you are going up the walk to your friend's house to tell them that their car, which you borrowed, has been stolen from your driveway.

- Play the scene.
- Pause. Release the imagined circumstances and have a walk around the room. Switch roles.
- *Spy back*. What did you discover about your relationship to Flow? How do different circumstances affect your relationship to Flow?

Through the next Practice, you can discover your own preferences on the Flow *continuum*. By exploring the entire range of Flow, you can broaden your comfort zone and give yourself a creative present: an expanded range of expression through movement in space.

PRACTICE 24.2   EXPLORING BOUND AND FREE FLOW

Explore the Flow *continuum* as you experience Bound and Free movement. Warm up before beginning.

I investigate: What is the experience of Flow in my body and in space?

- Stand. Pause. Breathe. Take a *kinesthetic moment*.
- Take a moment to connect to your sense of suspension and support. Expand your awareness to include your whole body and your place within the room.
- Take a walk around the room. Practice *inclusive attention*.
- Begin to sense a light breeze blowing at your back. As you walk sense the breeze becoming a little more noticeable; allow it to lessen the effort of walking, as you experience a sense of buoyancy.
- Increase the wind a little more. Let its Flow assist the sense of freedom in your walk.
- Continue increasing the breeze at your back bit by bit, allowing your movement to Flow more and more freely. Savor each stage of exploration along the Flow *continuum*.
- When you have reached the extreme end of Free Flow, begin to lessen the breeze at your back. Move back along the *continuum* toward center, until the air is calm again, and you are again walking around the room.
- Now begin to feel the breeze blowing against your face and the front of your body.
- Allow the light pressure to slightly restrict your forward motion. (It should not be so strong that it blows you backwards!)
- As you continue to sense a stronger breeze, and the wind impeding your forward motion, allow your movement to become more and more contained until you reach a point of intensely Bound Flow. Be sure that you continue to breathe.
- Sense the wind begin to lessen and move back along the Flow *continuum* until you return to a sense of balance between Bound and Free.

- Pause. Take a *kinesthetic moment*.
- Take a walk around the space, exploring Bound and Free Flow, moving any way you like. Pause.
- *Spy back.* How does Flow affect your movement? Were you able to breathe throughout the Practice? If not, were there moments when you held your breath? Where is your comfort zone in the Flow *continuum*?

The joy of exploring the specificity of each of the core *Efforts* – Space, Time, Weight, and Flow – can expand your creative movement vocabulary. In the next Practice, you will have the opportunity to deepen your investigation of the *continuum* from Free to Bound Flow, both individually and with a partner. Enjoy discovering the wonderful possibilities inherent in each one.

PRACTICE 24.3   CROSSINGS

In the explorations below, you can explore the possibility of becoming more nuanced in your ability to move through the Flow *continuum*.

This movement element is always present; you are simply developing your awareness and refining your ability to access it.

I investigate: What can I learn about my relationship to Bound and Free Flow?

Part I: Solo

- Stand. Pause. Take a *kinesthetic moment*. Breathe.
- Have a walk around the space, practicing *inclusive attention*.
- As you walk, bring your awareness to the Flow factor of your movement. Notice your connection to the floor and to the Flow of your movement as you explore the space of the room.
- Move to one end of the room, facing the opposite end. Pause. Take a *kinesthetic moment*.
- Cross to the other end of the space.
- Pause. Turn around to face the other end.
- Think of crossing again. Notice if your body "prepares" to cross. If so, Pause. Bring your attention to your *3-D body in the 3-D space* and return to balance.
- Allow your inner impulse to guide you into a restrained sense of Flow.
- Taking the time to enjoy the movement of your coordinated body, move across the space while "reining in" the Flow.
- Turn around. Pause. Allow your inner impulse to guide you into Free Flow.
- Move across the space with an unrestrained sense of Flow.
- Turn around. Pause. Breathe. Return to an attitude of resistance to Flow.

- Now, cross back to the other side, allowing your inner impulse to guide you through the entire *continuum* from Bound to Free Flow.
- When you reach the other side, turn around. Pause. Breathe. Return to an attitude of freedom.
- Cross to the other side, moving along the entire *continuum* from Free to Bound Flow.
- Pause. Take a *kinesthetic moment*.
- Take a walk around the space. Practice *inclusive attention*.
- *Spy back*. What were your sensations as you explored the Flow *continuum*? What did you notice about your breath? Were there parts of the continuum that seemed familiar? Unfamiliar? What were they?

Part II: Duet

If you have a partner, you can play with the "dance" between Bound and Free. Before you begin the Practice, choose which partner will begin with Free Flow, and which partner will begin with Bound Flow.

- Stand. Pause. Breathe. Take a *kinesthetic moment*.
- Take a walk around the space. Practice *inclusive attention*. Become aware of the others in the space.
- Move to one end of the room, facing your partner at the other end of the room. Pause.
- Allow your whole body to move, playing with Free or Bound Flow, depending on which end of the *continuum* you have chosen to explore first. Pause.
- When you and your partner are ready, begin to move toward one another – each of you exploring your end of the Flow *Effort continuum*.
- Meet in the middle of the room and enjoy a few moments of interaction, creating a little "dance" together from the two ends of the *continuum*.
- After a few moments, gradually begin to "exchange" the Flow *Effort*. The "Free Flow" partner will gradually become Bound, and the "Bound Flow" partner will gradually become Free.
- At some point, move away from your partner, and continue in your new *Effort* to the other end of the room.
- When you reach the other end of the room, turn around. Pause. Return to balance.
- Take a walk around the room, enjoying your new awareness of the Flow *Effort* as you move.
- Pause. Take a *kinesthetic moment*.
- *Spy back*. Meet with your partner and share your experience. If you are in a class, meet with the whole group as well.

Flow, or the lack of it, is our response to the ongoing stream of events in our lives. Our view of the world and how we see other people affects the way we enter and move through that stream. Via Laban's work, we can learn to recognize and enliven our daily relationship with Flow. And we can also discover that, like the other Efforts, the Flow *continuum* supports our artistic choices.

In Chapters 21–24, you have explored each *Effort* individually, so you could discover the broad expanse of move-

> Flow Answers the Question
>
> "What is my relationship to the unending stream of life events?"
>
> The two ends of the *continuum* are:
>
> BOUND/RESTRICTED: uptight, unyielding, restrained, fearful, cautious
>
> FREE/UNRESTRAINED: uninhibited, wild-child, fearless, spontaneous, liberated, unbound

ment that is inherent in each of them. Yet, all of them are always present, in every move you make. Become curious about the movement possibilities offered by the *Efforts*: you are creating fertile ground for authentic character movement.

In the next chapter, you will have the opportunity to play with these foundations of movement in combination.

PAUSE TO PROCESS Journal, discuss, practice. Notice your relationship with Flow *Effort* in your daily activities.

Exploring the *Efforts*

CHAPTER 25

Though Space, Time, Weight, and Flow are present in every movement, most people are unaware of them. They don't care or need to know that they are moving Quickly, Lightly, Directly, in Free Flow, as they climb a flight of stairs. However, the *Efforts* are self-revelatory; they expose the mover's personality and state of mind to the world. Others can see that a person is strong, dedicated, flighty, hot-tempered, weak, or easy-going based, primarily, on the way the *Efforts* appear in their movements and their speech.

As a performer, you want to know the *Efforts*, because they are the material you have to work with. Costume and set designers rely on the elements of design to support them in shaping the play's environment and the characters' appearance. Actors can rely on the elements of movement to inform them as they develop their characters' physical presence.

In the Practices below you can play with combining the *Efforts*.[1] Discover the fun of allowing movement, and perhaps a character, to emerge as you explore.

PRACTICE 25.1 TAKING A BOW

Allow the indulging/yielding or fighting/resisting qualities of the *Efforts* to inform your movement as you enter, bow, and exit. You can choose: Strong/Light, Quick/Sustained, Direct/Indirect, Bound/Free. Other descriptors: Heavy/Soft, Sudden/Slow, Linear/Flexible, Restrained/Unrestrained.

Though this Practice is set up for group work, with a little imagination you can explore it solo. It is important *not* to plan, but to let the *Effort* quality be your guide.

I investigate: How can the *Efforts* inform my choices as I move?

- Before you enter each time: Pause. Breathe. Take a *kinesthetic moment*. Activate the *5 cues*.

Round 1: One Effort at a Time

- Each person takes a turn to enter the space, allowing an *Effort* quality to guide their movement. They move to the center of the space and take a bow using a different *Effort* quality, then exit, using a third *Effort* quality. For example, enter with Strength, bow Indirectly, and exit Freely.
- After each person has completed their exploration, *Spy back*. How did the *Effort* quality influence your choices? Were you surprised by what you did or what you observed in others? If so, how?

Round 2: Two Efforts at a Time

A tip: Continue breathing as the *Efforts* are called out. Practice *inclusive attention*.

- Draw two *Effort* qualities out of a hat. Enter with those *Efforts*. When you reach center, someone in the class calls out two more *Effort* qualities for your bow, then after you bow, they give you two more *Effort* qualities for your exit.
- *Spy back*. What was the experience of allowing two *Effort* qualities to inform your movement? How did your choices differ from your "everyday" movement? What surprised you about you did or what you saw?

Round 3: Four Efforts at a Time

- Begin a simple activity, such as sweeping the floor. Someone in the class calls out one *Effort* quality, and you continue sweeping with that quality. After a minute or two, they call out a second *Effort* quality. Continue sweeping and add the second *Effort* quality.
- Continue in this way with a third and a fourth *Effort* quality.
- Allow a sound or words to come out as you work.
- Finish the job. Speak a line or make a sound and exit the space – still embodying your four *Effort* qualities. (If you like, before you exit, you can also shift to the four opposite *Effort* qualities, speak a line or make a sound, then exit.)
- *Spy back*. What was the character or situation that emerged from the four *Effort* qualities? How were they different from your usual choices?

When you combine the *Efforts* and play with shifting them along the *continuum*, you may be surprised by the physical choices that arise. For instance, you may have discovered that your bow became a unique personal statement. Perhaps you discovered your inner diva!

In the next Practice, you can explore the *Efforts* in relationship to a character.

PRACTICE 25.2   **DISCOVERING WHERE A CHARACTER "LIVES"**

When you rely on the *Efforts* to inform you, you will find that clear and specific movement choices begin to arise. Your character will tell you their relationship toward Time, Space, Weight, and Flow.

In this exploration, you will need memorized text for a character you're exploring. It can be lines from a monologue, scene, or play. You also need to know the character's world and their given circumstances. This is an advanced Practice, and it is best to have a facilitator reading the instructions (or tape them).

Warm up before you begin this exploration.

- Stand. Pause. Take a *kinesthetic moment.* Breathe.
- Begin to move around the space. Allow the four *Effort continuums* to inform your movement: Space, Time, Flow, Weight.
- Pause.
- Begin to walk through the space, moving Directly from point to point.
- See what it's like to speak a character line or two from this attitude toward Space. Continue walking and become more Direct. Breathe. Speak a line.
- Continue this process until you feel you have reached the extreme end of the Direct *Effort* quality.
- Begin to move back toward the center of the Space *continuum.* Try a line or two out of this body.
- Begin to move more Indirectly through Space. At various intervals, speak your line, allowing your movement to inform you.
- Continue this process until you feel you have reached the extreme end of the Indirect *Effort* quality. Then begin to move back toward the center of the *continuum.*
- As you walk more Directly, continue to speak your line. Discover where, on the *continuum*, this character is most "at home."
- When you have discovered the character's preferred relationship to Space, spend a few moments exploring the *Effort* and its effect on spoken text.
- As you speak text, you can also explore different movements, like picking up an object, pausing, crossing your arms, waving, etc. Remember that the text and the movement grow out of the relationship with the Space *Effort.*
- After a few moments, return to your usual relationship with Space, letting go of the character choices. Pause.
- Now, repeat this Practice with each *Effort continuum*, beginning with Time. When the character makes their choice in the Time *continuum*, take a few moments to explore it fully. Speak some text.
- Now "add in" the choice that you made in the Space *continuum.*
- Continue moving about the room and speaking a line or two, allowing the *Effort* qualities of Time and Space to interact.

- Allow each of the *Effort* qualities to change as needed as the character discovers how to "live" in the interaction of the two *continuums*. After exploring this relationship, move back along the *continuums* to center.
- Pause. Let go of the character choices.
- Have a walk around the space, returning to your usual relationship with the *Efforts*. Pause.

If you are feeling like you have "had enough," *PAUSE TO PROCESS*, and return to this Practice another day. Go to the *spy back*.

- Continue following this process as you explore Weight and Flow, one at the time. Allow the character to discover where they "live" on each *continuum*, then add the other *Efforts* one at a time.
- Your lines will be very helpful in this process of discovery. Use them only a sentence or two at the time – discover differences in the line and the way you say it – as you move along the *continuum*.
- You may notice that the *Effort* qualities shift as the lines change. Allow this to happen. Your character has a "home" relationship to Time, Space, Flow, and Weight, but this can change moment to moment.
- When you have completed the process, having joined all four *Efforts*, you can release the *Effort* qualities. Or, if you like, you can take a minute to share text with a partner as you experience your character's new physical presence. Then release the character choices.
- Continue moving for a few moments as you return to yourself. Pause.
- Take a walk around the room as yourself. Pause. Take a *kinesthetic moment*.
- *Spy back*. What was the experience of allowing a character to "choose" where they live on the *Effort continuum*? What, if any, were the challenges of allowing your body to choose, rather than your brain? Were there any surprises? If so, what were they?

In our culture, making a choice is a considered decision, weighed in our minds, based on the information available to us. We aren't accustomed to allowing our *body-mind* to connect with the inner life of the character and allowing that process to inform our choices. This Practice offers a different way of creating character movement, and it allows your whole *body-mind* to participate.

You may have found this Practice challenging, overwhelming, and uncomfortable. That can be part of the creative process. Visit this Practice often. You can make new discoveries each time. You will find that it gets easier and more fun. Best of all, if you approach it without preconceived ideas, you can discover that movement choices simply arise. The choices "show up" because you and your character are connected through movement and the world of the play.

As you explored the *Efforts*, you discovered where you are most comfortable on each *continuum*. Your character has a place where they "live" on the *continuum* as well. You don't have to manufacture believable character movement. The *Efforts* can "tell" you where the character lives, where they are coming from. You can learn to rely on your deep *body-mind* knowledge that is connected to your imagination, the source of your creativity.

Real-life Story: Sean Discovers Vershinin Through the *Efforts*

While working on Vershinin in Chekhov's *Three Sisters* in a scene study class, Sean first approached the character from an intellectual standpoint, which trapped him in preconceived ideas about a Russian military officer in 1905.

"While working on the scene and my character development, there was something 'stiff' about Vershinin that my professor and I felt needed to be released. So I simply started exploring this idea of 'space' and changing up my Laban *Efforts* from 'heavy' to 'light' and 'bound' to 'free' and 'direct' to 'indirect' and 'fast' to 'slow' and BOOM. It was as if Vershinin himself were speaking to me through my body saying, 'Yes, I am a military man who is a trapped by the stiff structure of Russian society, but look at all these other things I am! I am a hopeless romantic, funny, and desperately in love with Masha!' I slowly began to discover through approaching the text 'body first,' that there was a whole mountain of gold that was waiting to be discovered.

Vershinin became ... pliable in his movement, but more importantly, he became the exact opposite of what I initially thought he had to be. By throwing away all preconceived notions and playing ... I discovered a new world that lives in Vershinin ... And more than that, when I let go and play and approach from body first, the gold is resurrected.

I've also found that thinking 'horizontally' rather than 'vertically' has helped shape who Vershinin is to me, rather than a preconceived thought of who he has to be. [The importance of] spatial awareness is acute and may just be the key to my continued explorations in my movement training.

All in all, allowing myself to simply play in reckless abandonment and using the four elements of movement has done wonders for my ability to tackle period characters. I've learned to ... play with no fear, no judgement, it's okay to fail, body first, and soften to allow your body to be flexible in your approach to any text that may be given to you."[2]

More Practices with the *Efforts* are available in Appendix I.

PAUSE TO PROCESS Journal, discuss, practice. Notice your relationship with the *Efforts* in your daily activities.

Notes

1 Laban developed a complex movement system based on combining the *Effort*s. Though the Action Drives and other combinations are beyond the scope of *YBK*, you may want to investigate them. There are numerous books that explore his system, including *The Laban Workbook for Actors* by Katya Bloom, et al.

2 From a student journal. Used with permission.

Your Responsive Body, Mind, and Imagination

New. "New" feeds our creativity. Each time we begin work on a role, we can approach it with a spirit of discovery – we can explore character traits and feelings and movement we've never experienced before. This is not new for the sake of new: this is discovery based on knowledge. Through your work in *YBK*, you have built a strong physical foundation, you have a connection between your body and mind – you can allow your imagination to soar.

Your body always has a relationship to whatever is going on in your life, whether you are seated in a chair reading a book, walking on a crowded street, or performing onstage. Your responsive *body-mind* is so versatile that you can be yourself, an actor, and you can be a character, simultaneously. It's a miracle, isn't it, that we can imagine ourselves in a set of circumstances, night after night, and bring a character to life in front of an audience? Astonishing!

Your responsive *body-mind's* versatility and intelligence is a valuable resource in your process of creating a character. The movement pioneers discovered that you can find a "way in" to the character through movement. Their work puts your body-mind-imagination in constant, easy communication, and frees you from forcing your body to carry out pre-determined character choices. Instead, you can discover your character's physical life from the inside out.

In this Section, *Your Responsive Body, Mind, and Imagination*, you can explore the power of your body-mind-imagination through:

- Qualities of Movement
- Shape
- Character Space
- Connecting with Text and Imagery.

Like the movement pioneers, you can discover that your body's imagination is so strong, it can lead you into new creative territory. The connection of your body-mind-imagination can guide you to the artistic world that lives inside you, a world that is anything but ordinary.

Qualities of Movement

Each of us approaches life and the world from our own unique perspective, as do the characters we create. Our *inner experience* of ourselves creates the foundation for our *outward expression*. Michael Chekhov recognized that movement frees our inner impulses and transforms them into a physical expression that can be seen and heard by an audience. Movement liberates the creative possibilities that live within us.

In this chapter, we introduce you to Chekhov's movement qualities – foundational ways of moving that can inspire your character's physical life and emotional expression. The four *Qualities of Movement* (KW) are:[1]

- Molding
- Flowing
- Flying
- Radiating.

They awaken your imagination, enhance your creative potential, and each one inspires a unique and specific way of moving. But more than that, they actively connect the character's *inner experience* with *outward expression*.

Chekhov recognized that your terrific trio – body, mind, and imagination – leads you into a creative realm that transcends our analytical brain. The four *qualities of movement* create a process of discovery: you can allow your *body-mind* to choose **how** your character moves at any moment. Enjoy mining your creative treasures as you explore Molding, Flowing, Flying, and Radiating.

Molding

When you are Molding, you are shaping the space around you. It's important that you allow your inner impulse to *initiate* and guide your movement; you are not just imitating an outward appearance.

As you move through space, imagine you are moving through a resistant but pliable substance such as mud or clay. Your movement is continuous and strong, without excess tension.

PRACTICE 26.1 MOLDING

Molding is connected to Earth. The strength of your movements rise from your connection with the ground. Allow the dense yet pliable quality of the natural element of Earth to inform your movement.

Warm up before you begin.

I investigate: What is my inner response to Molding?

- Stand. Pause. Take a *kinesthetic moment*. Breathe.
- Allow your inner impulse and *life-body* to be your guide as you *cross the threshold*.
- Pause. Allow the images below to awaken your inner impulses.
- Imagine that the space around you is thick, like wet clay or mud. Allow your *life-body* to guide you as you slowly Mold the "clay" that surrounds you. You can *initiate* the movement from anywhere in your body: your head and spine, your hands or feet, your pelvis, etc.
- Allow the resistance of the clay/mud to inform your movement pathways and patterns.
- Begin to carve your way through the space, enjoying the continuous Molding movements you are making with your whole body.
- You can Mold with any part of your body and move in any direction: up, down, forward, back, side to side. Breathe.
- After Molding for a few minutes, pause. Take a *kinesthetic moment*. Breathe.
- *Spy back*. What did you discover about moving in this way? Were these movements familiar? Uncomfortable? Did they awaken an emotional response? In what way?

Chekhov noticed that each of the four qualities awaken an inner response. Perhaps you experienced a sense of determination or purpose as you explored Molding. Each of the *qualities of movement* can evoke a response without forcing something to happen. You can enjoy the experiences that arise and build on them as you practice.

Flowing

Chekhov's concept of Flow is different from Laban's. This quality of movement refers to the sense of freedom that you might experience when riding the current of a river. In fact, Chekhov connected Flow to the element of Water. Flow supports and guides your movement – it can change direction at any moment, taking you with it. You can lightly skim through the water, ride the rhythm of the ebb and flow of the waves, or flow along with a stream.

When you Flow, your movements are clearly defined, yet pass freely through your whole body. Warm up before beginning this Practice.

PRACTICE 26.2 **FLOWING**

I investigate: What is my *inner response* to Flowing?

- Pause. Stand. Take a *kinesthetic moment*. Breathe.
- Allow your inner impulse, *life-body*, to be your guide as you *cross the threshold*.
- Pause. Allow the images below to awaken your inner impulse:

Imagine that you are surrounded by Flowing water. Allow the current to carry you, as you freely move through the space.

- You can move wherever the current takes you. One movement leads easily to another. Allow the tempo and direction of the Flow to change as the impulse arises.
- You can travel in any direction in space, and allow Flow to change the shape of your body, as you explore your relationship to the changing current.
- Pause. Take a *kinesthetic moment*. Breathe.
- *Spy back*. What did you discover about moving in this way? Were these movements familiar? Uncomfortable? Did they awaken an emotional response? In what way?

As you explored Flowing, perhaps you experienced an inner response of freedom or "going with the flow." Characters and situations may come to mind as you explore Flowing. Enjoy discovering how the *outer expression* can influence an inner response.

> *PAUSE TO PROCESS* if you need a break before continuing to explore the other two *qualities of movement*.

Flying

Flying is connected to the element of air. When you Fly, you move through the air, in a clear direction, with lightness and ease. Your inner impulse guides you; you are not blown along by the wind, although you can glide and change direction as you choose. You can enjoy changes in tempo and the strength of your movements.

Warm up before beginning this Practice.

I investigate: What is my inner response to Flying?

- Stand. Pause Take a *kinesthetic moment*. Breathe.
- Allow your inner impulse, *life-body*, to be your guide as you *cross the threshold*.
- Take a moment to give yourself permission: allow the images below to awaken your inner impulse.
- Imagine that your bones become hollow, and filled with air. The air outside your body is light yet supportive.
- Allow your arms to spread out of your back, as you Fly through the space. Follow your inner impulses as you move through the air – up and down and around. Travel with ease and lightness.
- You can also pause, and sense the inner quality of Flying, as you simply feel the air moving around you. Allow this inner quality to guide you into movement again.
- Pause. Take a *kinesthetic moment*. Breathe.
- *Spy back*. What did you discover about moving in this way? Were these movements familiar? Uncomfortable? Did they awaken an emotional response? In what way?

As you explored Flying perhaps you experienced an inner response of anticipation, joy, or excitement. The *outer expression* leads to the *inner experience* and vice versa.

Radiating

Radiating is connected to the element of Fire, which can be burning slowly within you, or sending energy out into the space around you. You are in connection with your *life-body*, and it sends rays of light into the air, out beyond the physical boundaries of your body.

Radiating opens your *3-D body* to the 3-D space around you. It becomes the underpinning for all your movements and ignites your inner presence.

Warm up before beginning this Practice.

I investigate: What is my inner response to Radiating?

- Pause. Stand. Take a *kinesthetic moment*. Breathe.
- Your inner impulse, *life-body*, can be your guide as you *cross the threshold*.

- Pause. Let the images below to awaken your inner impulse.
- Allow your body to be filled with light. Send the light streaming out from your heart into in all directions.
- Move through the room as though you are filled with light, guided by an inner "glow," Radiating from center outward into the whole space.
- Allow rays of light to emerge from your fingertips, your elbows, your knees, your feet as you continue to move. Allow these powerful internal rays to guide you as you move through the room.
- Radiate toward others and receive from them.
- Pause. Take a *kinesthetic moment*. Breathe.
- *Spy back*. What did you discover about moving in this way? Were these movements familiar? Uncomfortable? Did they awaken an emotional response? In what way?

As you explored Radiating, perhaps you discovered an inner response of compassion, happiness, or a desire to light up the world around you. When we Radiate, we offer our performance as a gift to the audience.

Each of these *four Qualities* (Molding, Flowing, Flying, Radiating) are powerful tools which create a strong sense of the inner life of your character. They support the physical, mental, and emotional life of your character from the inside out, as you can discover in the Practice below.

PRACTICE 26.5 MOVEMENT QUALITIES AND TEXT

In this exploration, you can discover your character's movement preferences and inner motivation by practicing text with the *qualities of movement*. You will need to know the play and the given circumstances for your character. Select memorized text, preferably a monologue, for this exploration.

Warm up before beginning this Practice.

I investigate: How can the *qualities of movement* inform me about my character and text?

- Stand. Pause. Take a *kinesthetic moment*. Breathe.
- Take a walk through the room, sensing your movement and the space around you. Pause.
- *Cross the threshold*.
- Working from inner impulse, begin moving around the room in the quality of Flow.
- Speak your monologue as you move in Flow. Allow the movement to affect text, and vice versa.

- When you complete the monologue, release the quality of Flow. Return to walking around the room. Sense your movement and the space around you.
- Repeat this process with each of the other movement qualities, Molding, Flying, Radiating, one at the time.
- When you have completed exploring each of the qualities, release the quality, and return to walking through the room. Pause
- Now, give yourself permission to move with **any** of the four *movement qualities* as you speak your monologue. Working from impulse – discover which quality wants to be expressed through each moment of text. In other words, don't think about your movement, let your body lead the way. Take your time! Have fun!
- Pause. Take a *kinesthetic moment*. Have a walk around the space.
- Now, present your monologue to a partner or the class (or an imaginary audience if you are working solo). Allow the discoveries you made in the Practice to be alive in you and inform your work. Follow your *authentic impulses*: there is no right or wrong. Pause.
- *Spy back*. What *qualities of movement* inspired you as you spoke your monologue? Which *qualities of movement* were most familiar? Least familiar? Were there any surprises or discoveries?

This Practice allows you to make connections between movement, character, and text. Guided by your inner impulses, you can allow the *qualities of movement* to inform each moment of the monologue or play as it unfolds. Your *inner experience* becomes a specific *outer response*.

Each of the qualities awakens you to an unending stream of artistic possibilities, guided by your imagination, your movement through space, and the deep body knowledge you have gained. The *qualities of movement* provide specificity in the creation of your character and they enliven your physical presence onstage.

PAUSE TO PROCESS Journal, discuss, practice, and explore.

Key Word: *Qualities of Movement*

Note

1 Chekhov, Michael. *To the Actor on the Technique of Acting*. New York: Routledge, 2002. pp. 7–13.

Shape

In Part I, you developed a deeper understanding of your body's design for movement, a foundation for balance, ease, and clarity. Your open and available instrument supports your explorations of new movement possibilities, like the *qualities of movement*. You are discovering that your creative *body-mind* is your artistic palette and an endless source of creative expression.

In this chapter, you can explore more about your expressive *body-mind* through *shaping*, an amazing tool for creating your character's unique *3-D body in the 3-D space*.

Shaping (KW) is creating sculptural forms with your body in space. *Shapes* are not predetermined, held positions. Instead, *shape* begins with a desire to express a word, a creative statement, a relationship. Your expressive inner impulse begins a *shape*, and then guides you into movement. *Shape* is a pathway from *inner experience to outer expression*.

Because it begins with an inner impulse, shaping creates a connection through your whole *3-D body-mind*, whether you are moving or still. Your *body-mind* is wide awake and ready to respond to every moment.

Shaping:

- Creates dynamic sculptural forms in space – in stillness or in movement.
- Is a partnership between your whole *3-D body-mind* and the *3-D space*.
- Can be initiated anywhere and go anywhere in your body.
- Can be limited to small, precise choices, expand into large, spacious choices, or a mix of both.
- Is an *outer expression* of an *inner experience*.

Shaping creates a readiness in your body for playing a broad spectrum of characters, allowing each character to be unique. Through *shaping*, you can discover your character's movement from the inside out.

Shape in Stillness and Movement

Shape teaches us how to be alive in our bodies: *3-D body in a 3-D space*. It also invites us to explore unfamiliar territory; movement arises that we might never discover otherwise. When we warm up the connections throughout our *body-mind*, anything is possible.

Shape arises from your inner impulses (beginning), it moves through you (middle), and takes form (end). You can change *shapes* easily as your inner impulses dictate. When you create a *shape*, you aren't stiff like a statue. Instead, *shaping* energizes the movement pathways in your body.

Even in stillness, *shape* is active from the inside out. Your *life-body* keeps it alive within you. This *inner experience* is the rocket fuel that propels our *outer expression*. In the Practice below, you can discover your body's responsiveness and pliability through your dynamic *shape*.

PRACTICE 27.1 **INTRODUCTION TO SHAPING**

Let your inner impulse guide you as you warm up and make connections in your body through *shape*-making. Each time you form a *shape*, allow the *feeling of form* to guide you: beginning, middle, and end. Each *shape* can be a starting place for another *shape* to begin.

Note that the word *shape* refers to forming a 3-D sculpture in the *3-D space*, supported by your *life-body*. When we use the word *shaping*, we are referring to continuously changing 3-D movement, with an awareness of your *3-D body* as you move *in the 3-D space*.

Part I: Exploring *Shaping*

- Pause. Stand. Take a *kinesthetic moment*. Breathe.
- Activate the *5 cues* to create a sense of "readiness" in your whole body. Pause.
- Tune in to your *life-body* as your inner guide to moving through the following exploration.
- Notice your hands. Begin to open and close your hands with ease.
- Sense the *shaping* of your hands as you make a slight fist and then open and spread your fingers.
- Continue to move your fingers and hands and allow the movement to spread through your wrists, elbows, shoulder joints, shoulder blades, and collarbones. Notice the changing *shape* of your arm structure as you move.
- Continue *shaping* as you move your arms through space; forward and back, up and down, side to side. Your arms have a *shape* and they are also *shaping* the space around you.
- Allow your arms to continue *shaping* in any way you choose. Let these movements *sequence* through your whole body in response.
- Pause. Stand. Take a *kinesthetic moment*. Breathe.

- Notice your feet. Begin to roll through one foot, lifting your heel and allowing the movement to travel all the way to your toes. Notice that your whole leg will respond, creating a new *shape*, all the way through your ankle, knee, and hip joints. Now, reverse, returning your heel to the floor. Repeat on the other side.
- Allow your feet and legs to continue *shaping* as you choose, and let these movements *sequence* through your whole body in response.
- Pause. Breathe. Take a *kinesthetic moment*.
- *Spy back*. What did you discover about the relationship between *sequencing* and *shaping*? Were you able to sense a 3-D quality in your body as you were *shaping*? In what way?

Part II: Body Leads and *Shape*

- Begin to create different body *shapes* based on specific *body leads*. *Initiate* a movement at your elbow and let this movement guide your whole body into a *shape*.
- Sustain the *shape* for a moment, and then allow a new *lead* to create a new *shape*.
- You can begin the *shape* from anywhere in your body (your thumbs, your elbows, your ribs, etc.). As you move from *body lead* to *body lead*, begin to fluidly change *shape* according to each new *initiation*.
- As your *body leads* change, you can begin continuous *shaping*. Notice how your *3-D body* connects these movements within the 3-D space.
- After *shaping* for several minutes, pause. Breathe. Take a walk through the space, noticing sensation and connection within your whole body.
- Pause. Take a *kinesthetic moment*. Breathe.
- *Spy back*. What was your experience of continuously changing and following the *body leads*? When you paused at the end of the exploration, what did you notice in your whole body?

Part III: Creating *Shapes* – Movement in Stillness

Remember the dynamic qualities of *shaping* and bring them to this Practice of creating *shapes*.

- Stand. Pause. Take a *kinesthetic moment*. Breathe.
- Listen for an inner impulse to guide you into a *shape* that connects your whole body, and then follow the impulse as you form the *shape*. Pause. Though you are in a state of stillness, notice the dynamic quality of your *shape*.
- After a moment, release your *shape* and return to standing. Pause. Take a *kinesthetic moment*.
- Repeat a few more times. Pause.
- Now, take eight counts to gradually allow yourself to move into a *shape* that connects your whole body.

- Pause. Breathe.
- From this *shape*, take eight counts to move into another *shape*, noticing the journey of change through your body from one *shape* to another (*sequencing*).
- Continue this Practice by changing *shape* every four counts, then every two counts, and then move through a series of *shapes* of one count each.
- Pause. Release the *shape*. Notice sensation in your whole body as you simply stand in the space.
- Walk through the space, still sensing the wide range of movement possibility that can surface at any moment.
- *Spy back*. What is it like to experience movement in stillness? What was your experience of time and *shaping*? How can *shape* and *shaping* serve you as an actor?

With this Practice, you have explored options for moving your *3-D body within the 3-D space*. You have allowed your inner impulse to guide you into new and surprising possibilities. You've allowed fluid movement to *sequence* through your body, and you've created *shapes* that are alive from the inside out.

In the next Practice, you can use this *body-mind* knowledge for self-expression.

PRACTICE 27.2 SHAPE AND IDENTITY

This exploration allows you to express yourself personally and artistically through *shape*. Each *shape* you make is unique and emerges from you as a personal statement. You are bringing your *inner experience* of yourself and your body into the realm of creative *outer expression*.

Remember a *feeling of form* – beginning, middle, and end – as you create each *shape*. *The four brothers* will support you in this exploration.

Although this Practice is designed for a group, you can adapt it if you are working solo or with a partner. Warm up before you begin.

- The group stands in a circle. Everyone pauses, breathes, and takes a *kinesthetic moment*, practicing *inclusive attention*.
- Allow your *life-body* to guide you through the actions that follow.
- *Cross the threshold*.
- Going around the circle, each person steps forward one at a time, says their name, steps back, and pauses. Allow your movement to ride on the flow of your breath.
- Everyone pauses, breathes, and takes a *kinesthetic moment*.
- Next, each person steps forward, one at a time, creating a full-body shape as a personal expression of Self. Take your time and allow your *shape* to emerge from your inner impulse. Radiate. Then, pause, release the *shape*, and step back into the circle.

- When everyone has completed their *shape*, pause. Breathe. Take a *kinesthetic moment*.
- Finally, each person (the mover) allows their inner impulse to guide them, as they step forward again, repeating their full-body *shape*. Pause. Release the *shape* and step back.
- Then, everyone (including the mover) steps forward together, allowing inner impulse to guide them, as they echo the mover's whole-body expression.
- Everyone releases the *shape* and steps back together.
- Continue around the circle until the whole group has repeated each person's *shape*.
- Pause. Breathe. Take a *kinesthetic moment*.
- As a group, everyone allows their *life-body* to guide them as they step forward, simultaneously repeating their personal *shape*. Everyone pauses.
- Sense yourself within the whole circle. Guided by your *life-body*, everyone releases their *shape*, and simultaneously takes a step back.
- Pause. Breathe. Sense your connection with the whole group. Take a *kinesthetic moment*.
- Have a walk through the room, sensing your own expressive *shape* alive within you. Notice the *shapes* of others as you move.
- *Spy back*. What did you experience each time you expressed your Self through movement in the group? What did you discover about yourself, when creating your own *shape*? What did you learn when you echoed another person's *shape*?

Through this Practice, you have experienced firsthand how *shape* can be a reflection of a whole person: yourself. You allowed *shaping* to guide and support your *3-D body* when you moved through *3-D space*. You have also experienced "stepping into another person's shoes," as you assumed others' *shapes*. This is a significant step in discovering a character's physical identity: you experienced new *shaping* possibilities, as well as another person's whole-body expression of themselves.

Now, your wide-awake 3-D body-mind-imagination can lead you into new *shapes* as you explore a character's relationship to their world.

PAUSE TO PROCESS Journal and/or discuss *shaping*. Explore and observe *shaping* in others and in your daily life.

Discovering Character Body through Shape

Each character you play has a distinct way of "seeing" and "being" in their world. Just as you made a *shape* that expressed you in the Practice above, you can explore how a character chooses a *shape* from the inside out.

Allowing your character to play with *shape* is a way to bypass any preconceived ideas about how a character moves. Although an audience may never actually *see* these *shapes*, they can inform all your movement through the lively guidance of your *life-body*. *Shaping* is a process that allows your character to come alive through authentic, unique 3-D movement.

In the Practice below, you can explore a full-body expression of your character's identity.

PRACTICE 27.3 CHARACTER AND SHAPE

This exploration is similar to the *Shape* and Identity Practice above, with this difference: instead of *shaping* from your personal experience, you will be practicing *shape* as a character that you are currently exploring. It is helpful to have some of the character's dialogue memorized, although it is not necessary.

Since you have already explored a similar Practice, the instructions below are less detailed, so look back at Practice 27.2 if you need to refresh your memory. Although this exploration is designed for a group, with a little imagination, you can adapt it for working solo or with a partner.

Your *life-body* can be your guide each time you move into *shape*. Your movement rides on the flow of your breath. Warm up before you begin.

- Stand. Pause. Take a *kinesthetic moment*. Breathe.
- *Cross the threshold*.
- Take a moment to connect with your character's world and their relationship with it.
- Each time you step into the circle, do so as your character.
- The first time you step into the circle, simply say your (character's) name. Step back.
- Second time – allow your inner impulse to guide your (character's) body into a *shape* that is a full-body expression of themselves. Radiate. Release the *shape* and step back.
- Third time – everyone steps into the circle simultaneously and moves into their character *shape*.
- After a few moments, release the *shape* and step back. Pause. Continue to sense your character *shape* within you.
- Allow your *shape* to remain alive within you, as you begin to move about the room as your character. Greet others or speak a line. Allow gestures to emerge.
- *Shape* remains alive in your *life-body*. Your expression of *shape* may change as you interact with others.
- Enjoy getting to know your character's *3-D body*. Feel free to pause and renew your *shaping* at any time, then return to interacting with others.
- After a few minutes, pause. Return to the circle and release your *shape*. Look around the circle and see the others.
- Step back across the *threshold*.

- Have a walk around the room as yourself, seeing and greeting others. Pause. Take a *kinesthetic moment*.
- *Spy back*. What did you discover about your character's *shape*? How does *shape* influence your character's movement? Were you affected by others' *shape*s? In what way? How might this work serve you as an actor?

The given circumstances of your life determine how you move in your world. This is true of your character as well, and your imagination allows you to "live" in their world and discover their *shape*. When you have internalized your character's s*hape*, it lives in your *life-body*, guiding not only your movement, but influencing all your artistic choices.

Shaping brings your body alive as you respond to the world around you. It can lead you to deeper connections with text as well as character. In the Practice below, enjoy exploring your inner responses to text and the power of your full-body expression of words and images.

PRACTICE 27.4 **SHAPING ENERGIZES TEXT**

In a way, actors are interpreters for the audience. There is so much we want the audience to understand as they journey through the play with our character. Our whole self – body, mind, and imagination – supports us in every aspect of our performance, including our interpretation of the playwright's words.

In this exploration, give yourself permission to follow your *authentic impulse* as you explore a whole-body response to text.

Part I: Words

Make a list of adjectives that produce a response in your body when you say them. For instance: *joyful, shameful, murderous, peaceful*. In our classes, we write the word on slips of paper, and the speaker draws them out one at the time.

This Practice is best with two or more people. One person is the speaker, while the other(s) are the mover(s). If you are in a group, divide into Group 1 and Group 2. Warm up before you begin.

- Stand. Pause. Breathe. Take a *kinesthetic moment*.
- *Cross the threshold*.
- Begin to move about the room, noticing your *3-D body in the 3-D space*.
- Notice the others around you as you move.
- The speaker calls out a word.
- Following *authentic impulse*, each mover responds to the word by assuming a *shape*. Once you have created your *shape*, allow a lively sense of connection throughout your body. Radiate.

- The speaker can invite Group 1 to release their *shape* and view the Group 2 *shapes*, and then return to their *shapes* while Group 2 views.
- The speaker can invite the movers to resume walking through the room.
- Repeat the Practice five or six times. Pause.
- Have a walk around the room. Pause. Take a *kinesthetic moment*.
- *Spy back*. What was your experience of allowing your whole *body-mind* to respond to a word? Was this exploration outside your comfort zone? If so, in what way? Was your *little intellect* active as you approached this Practice? If so, how?

Part II: Monologue

In this exploration, work with a memorized monologue. Choose a phrase from the beginning of the monologue, one from the middle, and from the end. Each phrase represents a distinct moment in the character's "progression" through the monologue.

You can – for the purpose of the exercise – change the phrase into your own words. For instance, in Olga's opening monologue from Anton Chekhov's *Three Sisters*, she speaks of her father's funeral a year ago and her desire to return to Moscow. You might choose to express her journey through the monologue with these three phrases: "It's been a year since Father died." "I love Moscow in the spring." "I want to go home so much."

- Pause. Stand. Breathe. Take a *kinesthetic moment*.
- *Cross the threshold*.
- Speak your first phrase aloud, then follow your *authentic impulse* as your body responds and moves into a *shape*. Take all the time you need for this process.
- Once you have moved into a specific *shape*, take a moment to sense your *3-D body in the 3-D space*. Radiate.
- When you feel ready, release the *shape* and return to standing. Pause.
- Repeat this process with your second and third phrases. Pause.
- Now, explore moving into your first *shape*; from there, move into your second *shape*, and then, move from there, on to the third. Take all the time you need to allow the movements to *initiate* and *sequence*. You can allow your *life-body* to lead the way.
- Return to standing. Pause.
- Now, repeat this process of moving from *shape* to *shape* as you speak your entire monologue. Allow the text, the timing of your movement, and your *authentic impulses* to guide you.
- When the text and *shaping* are complete, Radiate for a moment.
- Return to standing. Pause.
- Now, perform your monologue. Give yourself permission to move and speak as your *authentic impulses* arise.

Though you are no longer physically *shaping*, you can trust that the movements that you've explored are alive in your *life-body* and guiding your physical presence. Pause.

- *Spy back.* What did you learn about the text, your body, your mind, and your imagination through this Practice? Did anything change for you as you performed the monologue? How might this work serve you as an actor?

Shaping is a key to specific physical expression of your character. Change your *shape*, and you change the internal landscape of your character and their response to the world around them. Through *shape*, you can explore their entire journey through the play: relationships with other characters, text, environment, space, action. Your inner connection to *shape* gives your character 3-dimensional life onstage.

> *PAUSE TO PROCESS* Journal, discuss, practice. Observe how *shape* influences your daily life and your work in class and rehearsal.

Key Word: *Shaping*

Spatial Tools

Through the Practices in *YBK*, you have already discovered some useful spatial tools, such as *Kinesphere*, *3-D space*, and spatial pathways. The way you use space deeply affects the way you see the world and the way others see you.

You may have an expansive view of the world, and "take up a lot of space." Others may see this use of space as friendly or outgoing. Alternatively, if we encroach on others' space, we can cause resentment or dislike.

Onstage, the way you use space conveys a wealth of information to an audience. In this chapter, you have the opportunity to polish and refine your spatial skills, as you explore tools that help you discover how your character relates to space. When you are specific in the ways you use space, your character has more vitality and definition, and you strengthen your stage presence. The audience sees a clearly defined character responding to the action of the play moment by moment.

Near-, Mid-, and Far-Reach Space

Day in and day out, we change our relationship to space as we change activities. It doesn't take a genius to recognize that throwing a ball requires much more space than tying your shoe! Onstage, changing your relationship with space frees your inner impulses and informs your movement choices.

Rudolf Laban observed people using personal space, and described three primary spatial relationships: *Near-reach*, *Mid-reach*, and *Far-reach Space* (KW).[1] In *near-reach space*, we carry out activities like brushing our teeth. Most of our daily activities, like eating and typing, occur in *mid-reach space*. Outdoor activities, like playing tennis, require *far-reach space*, which can even extend beyond our body, like "reaching for the stars."

Our perception of the world also affects which spatial relationship we "live in" at any given moment. Superman's relationship to space is quite different than Clark Kent's.

Exploring space can offer you powerful information about your character and their relationship to the world.

PRACTICE 28.1   DISCOVERING NEAR-, MID-, AND FAR-REACH SPACE

In this exploration, discover how your use of space affects your sense of yourself and your response to the people around you.

This exercise is best practiced in a group, but with imagination can be adapted for one or two people.

I investigate: How does my use of space affect my relationship with myself and the world around me?

Part I: Spatial Relationships

- Stand. Pause. Take a *kinesthetic moment*. Breathe.
- Sense yourself within your *kinesphere* and spend a few minutes exploring it with all the parts of your body. Pause.
- Now, imagine that your personal space has contracted, and you only have space that extends two inches from your body. Explore the space two inches from your body – above your head, behind your back, around your legs. This is *near-reach space*.
- Allow any part of your body to lead this exploration.
- After a few minutes, begin to move around the room in *near-reach space*. Notice how moving in *near-reach space* affects the length of your stride as you walk.
- When you meet another person, discover what it's like to shake hands with them in *near-reach space*.
- Do continue to breathe!
- Explore other activities in *near-reach space*, like sitting, or picking something up off the floor.
- After a few minutes' exploration, pause. Breathe. Return to your usual relationship with space, and take a walk around the room.
- Pause.
- Now, imagine that your personal space is about 18 inches from your body. Explore this *mid-reach space* all around your body. Allow any part of your body to lead this exploration.
- After a few minutes' exploration, begin to move around the room in *mid-reach space*.
- Discover what it's like to shake hands with another person in *mid-reach space*. Breathe.
- Explore other activities in *mid-reach space*. Move an object from one place to another. Imagine some props, as you water plants, do dishes, or blow bubbles. Play.
- After a few minutes' exploration, pause. Breathe. Return to your personal relationship with space as you walk around the room.

- Pause.
- Now, imagine that your personal space has expanded to your full *kinesphere*. Explore this *far-reach space* all around you. Allow any part of your body to lead this exploration.
- After a few minutes' exploration, begin to move around the room in *far-reach space*.
- Discover what it's like to shake hands with another person in *far-reach space*. Breathe.
- Explore other activities in *far-reach space*. Throw a ball, wave to a friend. Play.
- After a few minutes' exploration, pause. Breathe. Return to your personal use of space as you walk around the room.
- Pause.
- *Spy back.* What did you discover about your relationship to space? Did different personalities emerge from your use of space? How did your changing relationship to space influence your interactions with others?

Part II: Space Informs the Moment

Before beginning this Practice, decide whether you will work in *near-*, *mid-*, or *far-reach space*. As the improv unfolds, you can shift your use of space to suit each moment.

You can work with a partner or with a group. One group are the Receivers and the other, the Givers. As you play your scene, trust the *feeling of form*, as you create a clear beginning, middle, and end.

- Pause. Stand. Take a *kinesthetic moment*. Breathe.
- *Cross the threshold*.
- As you explore this Practice, cultivate an awareness of your *3-D body in the 3-D space*, regardless of whether you are in *near-*, *mid-*, or *far-reach space*.
- Have a walk around the room in your chosen use of space. Note if a personality begins to emerge. You can cultivate this character throughout the Practice. Pause.
- Receivers, position yourself somewhere in the room. Begin an activity – typing, painting, hoeing a garden, exercising – maintaining your chosen relationship to space. Continue until you are interrupted by a Giver.
- Givers, imagine that you have an object you want to give to a Receiver. Maintaining your chosen relationship to space, offer them your object, saying, "Here, I got this for you."
- Improv a short scene, allowing your relationship to space to change as needed. When the scene comes to completion, pause.
- Take a walk around the room, returning to your personal relationship to space. Pause.
- Givers and Receivers switch roles, and choose a different relationship to space. Repeat the Practice in this new role. Pause.

- *Spy back* with your partner, then with the group. How does your relationship with space change your relationship with the world around you? How did your relationship with space impact your improv? How and why did your relationship with space change during the improv?

Part III: Space Informs Text and Character

In this exploration, you will need a well-memorized monologue with a clear understanding of the character's given circumstances. If you have a partner, each partner can perform their monologue, with the other partner as audience, before beginning the Practice.

Enjoy exploring *near-*, *mid-*, and *far-reach space* as you allow your relationship to space to influence text.

- Pause. Stand. Take a *kinesthetic moment*. Breathe.
- *Cross the threshold.* Pause.
- Sense yourself in *near-reach space*. Have a walk around the room in *near-reach space*. Pause.
- Play your entire monologue in *near-reach space*.
- Pause. Release *near-reach space*. Have a walk through the room simply noticing your *3-D body in the 3-D space*.
- Pause. Repeat the above process, moving in *mid-reach space*, then in *far-reach space*.
- When you have explored your monologue through all three spatial relationships, have a walk around the room, noticing your *3-D body in the 3-D space*. Pause.
- Now, perform the monologue for your partner, allowing your body to choose your spatial relationship moment to moment. Before you begin, give yourself the thought: "I can move in *near-reach*, *mid-reach*, or *far-reach space* as I explore (*name of character's*) relationship to the world around them."
- Pause. Take a *kinesthetic moment*. Have a walk around the room. Switch roles with your partner.
- *Spy back.* What did you discover about your character's relationship to space in this monologue? Were there surprises? What were the differences between the monologue at the beginning of the Practice and the end?

As actors, understanding our relationship to space can support our authenticity as a character. If we try to **show** an audience that a character is shy, for instance, we may create an external picture – our preconceived idea of an introvert.

However, when you really understand a character and your relationship to the world, you can let go of preconceived ideas. You know that the character is responding to internal and external events, and your body will relate to space based on those circumstances. By trusting your inner impulse, your spatial relationships can change moment to moment. Your performance can be both specific and authentic.

Actor Kinesphere/Character Kinesphere

You may be asking: how can I maintain the integrity of a character in *near-reach space*, while including an audience? It's a fair question. It would be very difficult to include the audience if your spatial awareness stopped just two inches from your body.

However, you know that you are an actor on the stage, not the character. By using your *kinesthetic sense* and your *life-body*, you can maintain your personal sense of space while simultaneously playing the character's spatial choices.

Your personal *Kinesphere* is a constant; it is your personal reach-space, and that is unchanging. Even if the character doesn't **use** all the space in your *Kinesphere*, the space is **available**. Through your *kinesthetic sense*, and *body-mind communication*, you can maintain an awareness of your actor *Kinesphere* and your character *Kinesphere* simultaneously.

PRACTICE 28.2   **ACTOR KINESPHERE AND CHARACTER KINESPHERE**

Approach this Practice with curiosity.

I investigate: What can I discover about the relationship between my actor *Kinesphere* and my character *Kinesphere*?

- Pause. Stand. Take a *kinesthetic moment*. Breathe.
- Take a few minutes to explore your entire *Kinesphere*. Allow different parts of your body to lead this exploration. Play.
- Pause. Take a *kinesthetic moment*. Breathe.
- Activate the *5 cues*. Have a walk around the room. Pause.
- Speak this line: "I don't think I should be here."
- Repeat the line in *near-reach space*. Feel free to explore *near-reach space* as you speak the line.
- Move through the room in *near-reach space* – speaking your line to others whom you meet.
- Pause.
- Sense your whole *Kinesphere*, sense its spaciousness and *3-dimensionality*. Remind yourself that your whole *Kinesphere* is available to you, even if you don't use it.
- Repeat the exploration with an awareness of your whole actor *Kinesphere*, while your character remains in *near-reach space*. Pause.
- Repeat the Practice again, exploring other spatial relationships – *near-*, *mid-*, and *far-reach* – in the character *kinesphere*, while maintaining a sense of your actor *Kinesphere*. Play.

- If you like, add one or more of these lines: "Maybe I made a mistake." "Let's go home." "I want to know."
- Pause. Have a walk around the space, as you return to your accustomed relationship with space.
- Pause. Take a *kinesthetic moment*.
- *Spy back*. What did you discover as you played with actor and character *Kinesphere*? What were your challenges? How did you address them?

You may already have a natural awareness of your whole *Kinesphere* when you perform, regardless of your character's relationship to space. However, for many of us, this is a learned skill – allowing our performance to fill space, regardless of the character's relationship to the world around them. If you found this Practice challenging, explore it again tomorrow. You may find that your body-mind-imagination has integrated these helpful concepts, and character *Kinesphere*/actor *Kinesphere* are easier to access.

The way you use space can inform every aspect of your physical life, so ask yourself: how do I use space on a daily basis? What are the factors in my life that determine my spatial relationships? When you know your personal preferences, you can avoid imposing them on your character. Then you are free to enter your character's spatial world. Revisit these Practices often, and let your body-mind-imagination lead you to your character's unique relationship to space.

PAUSE TO PROCESS Enjoy your new awareness of spatial tools. Notice them in your daily life, in rehearsal, and onstage. Share your discoveries with a friend, classmate, or in your journal.

Key Words: *Near-reach Space, Mid-reach Space, Far-reach Space*

Note

1   Laban, Rudolf. *The Mastery of Movement*. 4th Ed. Alton: Dance Books, 2011. p. 35.

Text and Your Responsive *Body-Mind*

Anything you do
Let it come from you.
Then it will be new.

Stephen Sondheim, *Sunday in the Park with George*[1]

As actors, we know that expressing text and imagery is so much more than understanding the meaning of the words and saying them clearly. We recognize, of course, that our whole *body-mind* supports our diction and vocal production. But, more than that, our relationship to the words we are saying evokes a whole *body-mind* response.

When we speak our lines, we want the text, even heightened language like Shakespeare, to seem as if we are speaking our own words. Yet we may not know how to make the text alive and immediate for ourselves and our audience. The Practices in this chapter are designed to help you bridge the gap between an intellectual understanding of text and **owning** the text.

In the Practice below, you can discover the freedom of speaking text while you explore 3-D spatial pathways with your whole *3-D body*.

PRACTICE 29.1 DIMENSIONAL SCALE AND TEXT

This exploration has a simple premise: Your Body Knows so much about the text you are speaking, and it wants to respond. This Practice frees your inner impulses. Approach with a spirit of discovery.

You will need a well-memorized monologue and a clear understanding of the character's given circumstances for this exploration. It is fun and informative to practice with a partner – one person observing the entire Practice and acting as an audience for the monologue. If you are working with a partner, perform your monologue for them, as a benchmark, before beginning the Practice.

I investigate: How can my *3-D body in the 3-D space* open me to new possibilities?

- Pause. Stand. Take a *kinesthetic moment*. Breathe.
- Practice the *Dimensional Scale* once as a warm-up. Remind yourself: I can allow *the four brothers* to guide my movement as I practice. Pause.
- Practice the *Dimensional Scale* while speaking your monologue. Do not try to coordinate the words with the movements. Instead, allow the words to ride on your movements and the flow of your breath.
- You may find that inflections and meanings change – allow these new expressions as they occur. You may also discover that your movements are influenced by the text: different *Efforts* and *qualities of movement* may arise.
- Continue repeating the scale until the monologue ends. Pause. Take a *kinesthetic moment*.
- Now perform your monologue without the *Dimensional Scale*. Before you begin give yourself the thought: I am a *3-D actor in a 3-D space*.
- As impulses arise, allow your body and voice to follow them. These may be surprising – just go with them and see what you discover. Remind yourself that this is a rehearsal, not a performance – approach with a spirit of curiosity. Pause.
- Take a *kinesthetic moment*. Have a walk around the space. Pause.
- *Spy back*. How does your *3-D body* support your acting? How was your monologue different after practicing it with the *Dimensional Scale*? Did this Practice help you to "own" the text? In what way(s)?

Fall in love with your *3-D body* and explore text with the scale often. This Practice can refresh text that you have been performing for a long time, or help you work through a scene, or even a moment, that is eluding you. Through this exploration, your deepest impulses are free and available to guide your performance.

Imagery

When the playwright's words are poetic or the text has strong imagery, we can appreciate the beautiful language. Sometimes, though, we may find ourselves *over-efforting* as we try to "make" the audience understand the meaning or emotional content. Your *body-mind* knows how to bring the language alive and how to express it with your whole self.

Remember: your body has a relationship to everything that happens – and it will express that relationship as long as you don't interfere. Some actors refer to this process of connecting with text as "getting it in my body." You can further develop this phrase by saying, "I'm getting it in my *body-mind*."

In the next Practice, you can explore your *authentic impulses* as you connect body, text, and imagery.

PRACTICE 29.2 EXPLORING IMAGES AND YOUR INNER RESPONSE

In this exploration, you will need a memorized monologue or poem with strong imagery and/or poetic language. One of Agnes's speeches from the Epilogue in Tony Kushner's *A Bright Room Called Day* would serve. Tom Wingfield's opening or closing monologue from *The Glass Menagerie* is also useful. This Practice can be helpful when working with Shakespeare, Chekhov, or even the lyrics of a song.

To provide a benchmark, speak the text, as if performing it, before you begin the Practice. If possible, do this with a partner.

The purpose of this exploration is to embrace text with your whole body – to let your body fully express your relationship with each image.[2]

Before you begin, go through the monologue/poem and write down the images, each one on a separate piece of paper. It's fine to work with only a portion of the monologue – like eight to ten images – for this first time. If, for instance, you were working with Tennessee Williams' *The Glass Menagerie*, you might break down a few of the images in Tom's monologue at the end of Scene 7 this way:

"I pass the *lighted window of a shop* where *perfume* is sold. The *window is filled* with *pieces of colored glass, tiny transparent bottles* in *delicate colors*, like *bits of a shattered rainbow*."[3]

You would write each image (in bold in the example above) on a separate piece of paper.

When you have warmed up, enjoy moving in response to each of your images.

- Stand. Pause. Take a *kinesthetic moment*. Breathe.
- *Cross the threshold.*
- Both partners can do this first part of the Practice on their own.
- Spread the papers with the written images around you on the floor and lie down with one of them in your hand.
- After pausing for a moment, read the image on your slip of paper, then put it aside – away from the others.
- Say the word or phrase aloud several times – listen to your body's *authentic impulses* as you respond to the image.
- As the impulse arises, begin to "move the image." This is not mime – instead, it is an inner impulse that arises from the text and becomes an *outer response*. You may find yourself standing, *shaping*, rolling, spiraling – allow your body to lead the way.
- Notice your impulses when speaking the words; each time you say it may be different – quickly, slowly, loudly, softly – explore the image physically and vocally.

- After a time, develop a whole-body movement that expresses the phrase – it may be big and sweeping, or small and contained. You may stand, sit, move through space, or anything in between. Whatever you choose, note the support of your whole body, and breath, even if the movement is small. Your movement will have a beginning, middle, and end – and a clear pathway through space.
- Speak the words as you enjoy the expressiveness of your *3-D body in the 3-D space*. After practicing your movement a few times, pause. Release the image. Return to lying on the floor.
- When you are ready, pick up the next image and repeat the process. You do not need to explore the images in order.
- Continue this process until you have worked through each image.
- Now put the images in order and connect your gestures to each other in a movement sequence. Feel free to refer to your written images if you forget what comes next.
- When you have completed this process, you will have connected all the images through a series of movements. Speak the images in order as you move through your sequence. Pause.
- Now, stand. You are going to perform your whole monologue. The images remain alive in your *life-body*; allow them to inform your performance of the monologue. Follow your *authentic impulses* as new choices arise. Remember this is a rehearsal, so do not censor your impulses.
- Pause. If you are working with a partner, switch roles.
- *Spy back*. What was your experience of exploring the images with your whole body? Were you surprised at your response? What happened when you performed your monologue at the end of the Practice? Were you making new choices? What were they? What was the experience of witnessing your partner's monologue?

Your body has a relationship with the text: when you give yourself permission to explore text physically, new and unexpected choices arise. Your physical life becomes more authentic and expressive, and it actually requires less energy to perform, because your *body-mind* and imagination are in sync.

Throughout Part II, you have explored Elements of Expression and connected them with your body-mind-imagination. With a wealth of creative movement knowledge to support you, you can explore fearlessly, and transform your character's desires and dreams into visible action for an audience.

"Educated exploration" is key to opening the pathway between *inner experience* and *outer expression*. You can trust your body to lead you into your character's physical life, so explore confidently. The transformative Practices in Elements of Expression will support you as you approach rehearsal and performance in Part III.

PAUSE TO PROCESS Journal, discuss, explore!

Notes

1 "Move On" from SUNDAY IN THE PARK WITH GEORGE. Words and Music by Stephen Sondheim (c) 1984 RILTING MUSIC, INC. All Rights Administered by WC MUSIC CORP. All Rights Reserved Used by Permission Reprinted by Permission of Hal Leonard LLC.

2 Kristen Linklater and the late Cicely Berry, both pioneers in teaching and coaching voice and text, have long advocated exploring the connection between body and text. Their work inspired this Practice.

3 Williams, Tennessee. *The Glass Menagerie.* Copyright © 1945, renewed 1973 The University of the South. Reprinted by permission of Georges Borchardt, Inc. for the Estate of Tennessee Williams.

Creative Practice

Introduction to Part III

Every exploration in *Your Body Knows* is a creative practice: your creative juices flow when you discover new ways of moving. Perhaps you've surprised yourself by the choices you've made as you've explored the Practices in Parts I and II. You've discovered an important fact about movement work: a free body frees your mind and imagination too!

You have the knowledge you need to explore movement choices in a monologue, a scene, or a whole play. You have truly expanded your movement vocabulary. You make educated choices, and you know how to let your *body-mind* discover a character's physical life and their relationship to the world around them.

We might have titled Part III: **Expanded** Creative Practice. Here, you can build on your creative discoveries from Parts I and II, as you work with other actors to develop a performance for an audience. You can expand your focus: move beyond opening your body and unleashing your creative powers to shaping your performance and interacting with others. Your physical choices are informed – and enhanced – by the creativity of the playwright, the ensemble, even the audience.

Movement supports you as you develop your character and tell the story the playwright has written. Through movement, you can:

- Prepare your body and mind for rehearsal and performance.
- Explore your relationship with other actors and the audience.
- Create character.
- Discover the power of spatial relationships in telling the story.
- Deepen your connection to given circumstances.
- Include your audience while sustaining a clear relationship to an ensemble.

As you explore Part III, you can learn to trust yourself and the process of developing a character for performance. You have experience and knowledge. You have so much to draw on, and your creativity never runs out. It is always there for you. Your discoveries are alive in your *life-body*, a never-ending source of support in every moment.

In a way, Part III: Creative Practice, is about the *part within the whole*, the *part* you play within the *whole* story, the *whole* ensemble, the *whole* production, and the *whole* audience experience.

Whole-body Warm-up

CHAPTER 30

Staccato-Legato

Michael Chekhov designed *Staccato-Legato* (KP) as a whole-body warm-up that wakes you up from the inside out. This Practice follows a specific form that creates a powerful ease of connection within your whole *body-mind* as you move. It is a foundational Practice in the Chekhov Technique, and it is a perfect warm-up for rehearsal or performance.

This single, powerful warm-up unites many movement elements you've explored in *YBK*:

*   *3-D Body in a 3-D space*
*   *Grounding, centering,* and transfer of weight
*   *The four brothers*
*   *Life-body*
*   The *elements of movement*: Time, Space, Weight, and Flow
*   Translating an *inner response to outer expression*
*   Directional pathways in space
*   *Inclusive attention.*

How can one Practice do all of that? Through the genius of Michael Chekhov! *Staccato-legato* is simple, "stripped down," yet it combines these movement basics and allows them to shine forth. In fact, it is because the Practice is simple that these elements can merge in such a rich and cohesive form.

Through the Practices in *YBK*, you have explored each of the movement foundations in the list above. Your *body-mind* knowledge will support you as you practice *staccato-legato*.

> Multi-Tracking (KW)
>
> As you combine the movement foundations that come together in *staccato-legato*, you rely on a skill that you use every day, but may not have a name for: *multi-tracking*.[1] Not to be confused with *multi-tasking*, which is doing two activities at once, *multi-tracking* is the awareness of mental, sensory, and physical information

as we carry out our daily activities. Throughout *YBK*, you've been practicing *inclusive attention*; now *multi-tracking* invites you to expand this skill.

In modern life, we are constantly tracking the numerous details of our inner and outer world. Just think how many "tracks" are required when you drive a car: you are monitoring the pressure of your foot on the accelerator or brake, your hands on the wheel, the space between the cars, the shape of the road, speed, horns honking. At the same time, you are listening to directions on your GPS and following them!

Our brains are wired for *multi-tracking*: with practice, these detailed information tracks unite in a single cohesive experience called "driving a car." It is a single task that requires multiple systems – physical, mental, and sensory – to complete. Yet, as you are driving, the tracks effortlessly merge into one experience. Almost every activity we do requires *multi-tracking* to one degree or another.

Perhaps you looked at the list of movement foundations that we practice in *staccato-legato* and wondered: how can I possibly do all of that at once? The answer is *multi-tracking*. Recognize that these foundational elements are built into you, into movement itself. Through your awareness, you can sense yourself, the space around you, and your pathways in space as you move. *Multi-tracking* allows you to practice – and master – these supportive movement foundations

Basic Concepts

Legato and *staccato* describe the way you move in the Practice. These terms, often applied to music, also relate to elements of movement you learned in Section VII. When you practice in *legato*, your movements are sustained and flowing; *staccato* movements are light and quick.

Take a moment to practice *legato* and *staccato*. You can allow your *life-body* to precede your physical body.

- For *staccato*: imagine a fly on your left forearm – with a light, quick movement of your right hand and arm, brush it away. Repeat on the other side.
- For *legato*: in a sustained and flowing movement, practice smoothing the fabric of your real or imagined shirtsleeve over your lower arm. Repeat on both sides.
- Practice other movements in *staccato* or *legato*. Connect your breath to these qualities as you move. Notice the feelings, and even circumstances, that are called to mind as you move in these ways.

In *staccato-legato*, each movement has a distinct Form and moves in a clear direction: right, left, up, down, forward, or back. Each movement in a direction begins with a slight movement in the opposite direction. For instance, if you are moving forward, you allow your arms to initiate a slight backward movement, before you lunge. This Form gives the movement a place to come **from** and provides energy as you move into the directional pathway.

When you practice *staccato-legato* with *inclusive attention*, you can release unwanted tension. You can also *initiate* the process of guiding movement from *within*, instead of mechanically imitating an external form. *Staccato-legato* invites you to connect your whole *body-mind* from the ground up, all the way through to the crown of your head and the tips of your fingers.

You can experience a liveliness, even a sense of joy, as you move in distinct and clear pathways in space. Enjoy "putting it all together" in this foundational whole *body-mind* Practice.

PRACTICE 30.1 STACCATO-LEGATO[2]

This Practice can be experienced individually or in a circle with a group.

Remember that Form begins from **within** ; it emerges into the outer movement that can be seen. You will move in the six directions, extending both arms (a different movement than in the *Dimensional Scale*).

As you explore *staccato-legato* this first time, keep it simple. Rather than *multi-tracking* all the movement elements, simply allow your *life-body* to guide you, as you awaken your *3-D body within the 3-D space*.

Each movement begins with an inhale, and you exhale as your arms and fingers extend into space. Breath matches the *staccato* or *legato* qualities of each movement.

I investigate: What is my experience as I allow my *life-body* to guide my movement in a simple Form?

- Stand. Pause. Breathe. Take a *kinesthetic moment.*
- Take a moment to bring your awareness to your *3-D body in the 3-D space*. Sense the connection between your feet and the ground.
- Activate the *5 cues*. Breathe.
- Return your arms to your sides. Pause. This is your starting place.
- Begin the form in *staccato*. Allow your *life-body* to lead these movements.
- *Right*. Inhale. On the exhale, allow your *life-body* to lead from center, turning to the right as your arms move back slightly, then extend to the right, palms down, as you lunge. Hands and fingers extend in a strong *staccato* movement on a quick exhale. Now follow this movement with your physical body (Figures 30.2 and 30.3).

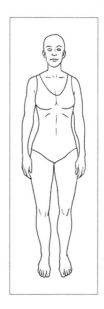

Figure 30.1 The starting place.

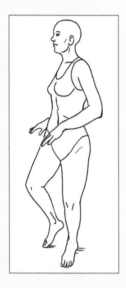

Figure 30.2 Your arms draw back as you prepare to lunge.

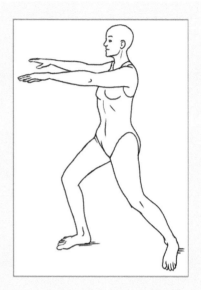

Figure 30.3 Lunge to the right in a whole-body movement.

- Be at ease, as you allow your arms to release forward and out from your back. Your back is long and wide, and your feet are grounded. *Radiate*.
- Return to the starting place.
- *Left*: Take a dynamic pause before allowing your *life-body* to repeat the Form to the left – with light, quick movements – and then follow with your physical body. *Radiate*. Return to the starting place.
- Pause. Breathe.
- *Up*: In a light, quick, whole-body movement, your *life-body* leads as you inhale and slightly release your Big 3 leg joints, then exhale and lengthen as your fingertips lead your arms upward from center, allowing your legs to separate slightly. Your feet remain grounded. As your arms reach their full length, your fingertips extend and expand, you exhale and look up (Figure 30.4).
- Follow this *life-body* movement with your physical body. *Radiate*.
- Return to the starting place. Take a dynamic pause.

Figure 30.4 Sense your connection to the floor as you extend upward.

- *Down*: Allow your *life-body* to lead, as you inhale and lift your hands and forearms slightly away from the floor, then in a light, quick movement exhale and extend your arms downward and slightly in front of you. Your fingertips extend diagonally toward the floor as you exhale. Your legs bend slightly at your Big 3 leg joints. Repeat with your physical body. *Radiate* (Figures 30.5 and 30.6).

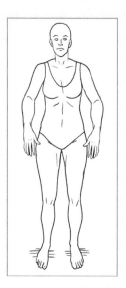

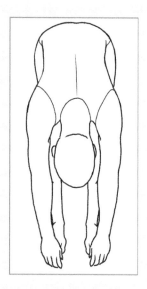

Figure 30.5 Your arms and hands ease away from the floor as you prepare to direct your movement downward.

Figure 30.6 Release your Big 3 leg joints as you move downward.

- Return to the starting place. Take a dynamic pause.
- *Forward*: Let your *life-body* lead this whole-body gesture. As you inhale, draw your arms back slightly, then exhale and lunge quickly forward from center; extend your arms in front of you and exhale. Gaze forward, your back long and wide, with your left leg lengthened behind you, and both feet grounded. Follow with your physical body. *Radiate* (Figure 30.7).
- Return to the starting place. Pause. Breathe.
- *Back*: Your *life-body* leads: inhale as you bring your arms slightly forward, then exhale as you quickly step into a backward lunge from center as your arms reach backward on a diagonal and

Figure 30.7 Lunge forward in a whole-body gesture.

you exhale. Allow your front leg to lengthen. Both feet are grounded. Look up as your body slants in a backward direction. Follow with your physical body. *Radiate* (Figure 30.8).

- Return to the starting place.
- Pause. Breathe.

Allow your *life-body* to be your guide:

- Repeat the form in *staccato*. Pause.
- Repeat the entire form in *legato*, using sustained, flowing movements. Pause.
- Repeat the form in *staccato*. Pause. Take a *kinesthetic moment*.
- Practice *inclusive attention* as you have a walk around the space. Pause.
- *Spy back*. What did you notice about your body and mind as you practiced? Were you able to sense your whole *3-D body in the 3-D space*? What was your experience of your body and mind before the Practice? After the Practice?

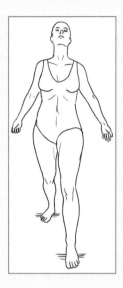

Figure 30.8 Lunge backward, sensing your *3-D body in the 3-D space*.

Staccato-legato connects your whole *3-D body*, and strengthens your awareness of the *3-D space* around you. When you practice with a group, this movement sequence can create a strong sense of ensemble among the actors, both in class and onstage. Practice it daily, and notice how it energizes, connects, and focuses your body and mind.

You can, of course, vary the Practice, by exploring *legato* first. The exploration above is strongly energizing. Its opposite – two *legato*, followed by one *staccato*, then another *legato* – is more calming.

We often practice *staccato-legato* with actors in an ensemble before rehearsal and performance. We have great respect for this Practice, and we hope you will too. If you bring your whole *kinesthetic awareness* to it, *staccato-legato* provides a sense of calm, powerful presence and readiness for your creative work. It connects you with your body and the space around you. You can rely on its support as you approach the creative Practices in the chapters that follow.

Key Word: *Multi-tracking*

Key Practice: *Staccato-Legato*

Notes

1 *Multi-tracking* is a term developed by Jean Houston, PhD. Her Practices for enhancing your multi-tracking abilities are fun and enlivening. Houston, Jean. *The Possible Human*. New York: Jeremy P. Tarcher/Putnam. pp. 74–77. Print.

2 *Staccato-legato* was first developed by Michael Chekhov during his teaching residency at Dartington Hall in England (1936–1939). Zinder, David. *Body Voice Imagination*. New York: Routledge, 2002, p. 46. Print.

Movement, Character, and Relationships

Putting Principles and Skills Into Practice!

In this chapter, you can draw on all you have learned in Parts I and II, as you explore a specific character and their relationships through movement. The Practices invite you to discover your character's physical presence and embody their movement journey throughout the play. You can make surprising and energizing discoveries by exploring intangible qualities like emotion and relationships through movement.

The explorations below can serve any acting technique, from Stanislavski to Chekhov to Meisner. They can free your imagination and unleash rich creative choices that serve your performance.

Personal Preparation

Preparing for rehearsal is all about "doing your homework," both mental and physical. You must know the outer circumstances of your character's life, in order to activate your *inner impulses*. Before beginning any of the Practices in this section, become very familiar with the play, the character's relationships, major character facts, their hopes, and desires.

Warming up wakes up your *body-mind* connections, freeing you to act on impulse. *Staccato-legato* is the perfect warm-up for any of the explorations below.

PRACTICE 31.1 PROCESS: DEVELOPING CHARACTER CHOICES

For this Practice, do your homework on the play and your character. Memorize at least a few lines. Whether you are working on a monologue, a scene, or a play, choose lines from the beginning, middle, and end. This will help you in discovering your character's arc in the play. If you know all your lines, all the better!

You are familiar with these Practices, as you explored them in Sections VII and VIII. Think of this as character *Movement Homework* (KP), the explorations that lead you to dynamic, specific character choices. *Movement homework* awakens artistic creation.

Over a week or two, explore your character's relationship to their inner and outer world through space, *shaping*, the *elements of movement*, and the *qualities of movement*. *Life-body*, *authentic impulse*, and *the four brothers*, as well as your body-knowledge from Part I, will support you in these Practices.

- Before you begin each day's exploration, warm up with *staccato-legato* or another Practice for connecting your body and mind.

Revisit *Elements of movement*

- Over a couple of days – explore your character's relationship to the *elements of movement*: Space, Time, Weight, and Flow. Explore each element along the entire *continuum*. Then revisit Practice 25.2 to discover where your character "lives."
- *PAUSE TO PROCESS* before continuing the next exploration. Take some time to learn how your discoveries inform your work in rehearsal.

Revisit *Qualities of movement*

- Over a couple of days, become reacquainted with the *qualities of movement*: Molding, Flowing, Flying, Radiating. Then revisit Practice 26.5.
- *PAUSE TO PROCESS*. Rest and absorb! Play with your discoveries in rehearsal and the influence of the *elements of movement* and the *qualities of movement* on each other.

Revisit *Near-*, *mid-*, and *far-reach space*

- Discover your character's relationship with space: *near-*, *mid-*, and *far-reach*. Revisit Practice 28.1, Parts I and III.
- *PAUSE TO PROCESS*. Play. Discover the interaction between *elements of movement*, *qualities of movement*, and spatial choices. Explore your discoveries in rehearsal.

Revisit *Shaping*

- Explore *shaping*: Revisit Practices 27.2 and 27.3, Part II.
- *PAUSE TO PROCESS*. Take time to explore your *shaping* choices in rehearsal. Then discover how *shaping* interacts with the other choices you have made.

Spy back

- It may be useful to *spy back* on your own after each exploration. You can also talk over your discoveries with your scene partner, if you have one. Journaling your *spy back* can also help strengthen your *body-mind connection*, especially if you are working alone.

Each of these Practices can influence your choices at different times – sometimes *flowing* may be your primary guide, and in the next moment, *near-reach space* and *quickness* may take over. Since your body knows, you can trust that the right choice will arise as you need it, and the other choices will support it. All of these choices are alive in your *life-body*.

Through the explorations above you can discover your character's range of movement as they journey through the play. When you do your *movement homework*, you can bring strong choices – mental, emotional, and physical – into rehearsal and performance. You build a foundation, which supports you as you respond to the unfolding action of the play.

Movement and My Character's World

When you are performing a monologue, you don't have a set to establish the character's environment, so you want to be very clear about the physical aspects of their world. In the previous Practices, you've done your *movement homework*, based on the character's given circumstances. You have discovered your character's relationship to their world and how it affects their movement.

You've explored a general sense of your character's world, but what are the specifics? You have a relationship in space with every object, person, or place that you mention in your monologue, and that relationship strongly influences the way you move and use the space around you.

In the Practice below, you can discover your personal spatial relationships, as you describe a familiar location.

PRACTICE 31.2 **SPACE STORIES**

This exploration is intended for two or more people. If you are working solo, imagine your partner and film yourself while you talk.

Part I

- For this Practice, stand or sit, as if you were delivering a monologue for an audition.
- Pause. Stand (or sit). Breathe. Take a *kinesthetic moment*.
- Think about your room in your home or in the home you grew up in. Tell your partner about your room, describe it in detail. Pause.

- Switch roles.
- Now, each of you can give feedback about what you observed when your partner spoke. Were you with them in their room? How did their movement affect what you knew about their room? How did each person feel about their room?
- Next, talk about the street that your home is on (or was on). Describe it, and an activity you do (or did) on your street – or describe your neighbors or businesses on your street. Pause.
- Switch roles.
- Take turns giving feedback. How did your partner's movement change as they talked about their street? Did they change the way they used space? Spatially, where was the street as your partner described it? Off to the side? Behind them? Did they seem to be standing on the street as they talked about it or was it far away?
- Now give your partner directions to get to your current home. Start with the country, state, and city; then add the street, and describe landmarks that will help them find it. Pause.
- Switch roles.
- Both partners: without thinking about it, point to your house in the direction that you are imagining it (in relationship to where you are now).
- Give feedback to your partner. What did you see as your partner talked? When they pointed to their house, was it where you thought it was when they were speaking?
- *Spy back*. Share your experience of how your movement changed as you spoke about your room, your street, and gave directions. How might this work influence you as an actor?

This Practice can be expanded: you can make a connection to a character's home, or any place or person that is important to a character's relationship to their world. Through this specific work, your gestural life and use of space is supported and your "movement palette" expands.

Part II

Every time your character speaks about a place or an experience, that place or that experience is located **somewhere** in relationship to where they are now. The distance, the size of the place, the importance of the experience will affect the way you move, gesture, and use space.

If you are speaking of several places, each location and what it looks like must be clear to you: mind, body, and space. Then, as you move, you are in a specific relationship with the places and events. If it is clear for you, then it will be clear for the audience.

For instance, in the opening monologue in *Three Sisters*, Olga talks about the cemetery where her father was buried, about waking up in her room, about seeing birch trees, and about Moscow in spring. She would have a strong sense of where those places are, in relationship to where she is standing as she speaks. Some may be low (perhaps the cemetery is in a valley), some may be high (the birch trees). The performer playing Olga can let the image guide them.

It isn't necessary to physically indicate where these places are in performance. When you sense where they are, and practice placing them in space, they become a reality for you, just like your room in your house.

For this exploration, you will need a memorized monologue which mentions persons, places, objects, or events. You can work with a partner or solo. If you are working solo, make a commitment to be as verbal and detailed as you were in Part I above. You may want to film yourself.

Warm up before you begin.

I investigate: How does my specific relationship to people, places, and things affect my movement?

- Pause. Stand. Take a *kinesthetic moment*. Breathe.
- Perform your monologue. Pause.
- Sit or stand and take several minutes to remind yourself of the people, places, things, and events in your monologue. Develop an image of what each looks like – describe it aloud as you did your room in the Practice above.
- Now, perform the monologue. Each time you mention a person, place, or thing, whether it is near or far, point toward it. Don't think about it, just point. You are placing it in space, near or far, in relationship to yourself. For now, don't be too literal about where you should place it for the best performance, just choose a specific place. You can adjust it later.
- Pause. Take a *kinesthetic moment*. Have a walk around the space.
- Pause. Activate the *5 cues*.
- Now, perform the monologue, as you might in the play or an audition. Allow your *body-mind* to respond to the personal and spatial relationships you've developed. Trust that if it is clear for you, then it will be clear for the audience. You don't have to "show" them. Be at ease in your body. Pause.
- *Spy back*. What was your experience of pointing to clarify spatial and personal relationships? How does this Practice shift your awareness of the events and places in your character's world? What was the difference between the first and second times you performed your monologue? If you are working with a partner, hear their feedback, then switch roles.

When you have a strong spatial and personal relationship to places and events in your character's world, they come alive for you, and your body and gestural life will show it. The audience can see in your eyes that you are connected to the images and the words you are saying, and they willingly go with you on your character's journey.

PAUSE TO PROCESS Journal, discuss, practice. Become aware of your spatial relationship to the places, people, and objects in your world – even when they are not physically present.

As you have discovered, you can connect physically with any aspect of a play, including words, images, and feelings. In the exploration below, you can go a step further: exploring your character's journey.

Movement Monologue

Every character ends a monologue, scene, or play in a different frame of mind than at the beginning. They experience a journey, and their emotions and relationships shift as they travel into new territory. Our work as actors is to embody those changes.

A *Movement Monologue* (KP) is an exploration that can help you discover and refine your character's physical and emotional life. It is a one- to two-minute physical expression of a character's arc, their inner journey, in a monologue, scene, or play.

The purpose of a *movement monologue* is twofold: to connect to movement impulses without the constraints of text, and to embody the character's journey.

Through movement, you can freely express what is spoken and unspoken in the text, including a character's emotions and desires. This work deeply informs the words you speak, your characterization, and your physical life in rehearsal and performance.

In a *movement monologue* you:

- Turn on your terrific trio: *body-mind-imagination*.
- Create a movement story with a beginning, middle, and end.
- Tell the story through the movement principles and elements you discovered in Parts I and II.
- Use your whole body to express the character's journey/transformation in the monologue, scene or play.

A *movement monologue* is not a literal picture of the things the character does in the play/scene, such as drinking, sitting, shaking hands, etc. The monologue may incorporate literal movement, but each literal or symbolic gesture (such as hands in prayer) acts as a catalyst for further exploration.

You can trust your body to make choices. Follow your deepest impulses and invite your intellect to take in information. Impulse happens without thought and feels effortless. Give in to the process, explore fully, and you will be rewarded with surprising, imaginative, creative choices. After exploring freely, your intellect can participate, as you choose how to shape your *movement monologue*.

Your whole body is your expressive instrument, and everything you have learned in Parts I and II of *YBK* supports your exploration.

PRACTICE 31.3   MOVING YOUR CHARACTER'S JOURNEY

For this Practice, you need a memorized monologue that you know well.

Develop a *movement monologue*, which expresses some aspect of your character's inner journey. Set a goal of using three or four movement elements that you have studied, such as *3-D space, shape*, the *Efforts*, and *qualities of movement*. You do not speak your lines during a *movement monologue*, although sound or words may emerge spontaneously.

At the end of each day's work on your *movement monologue*, you can take time to perform the text, allowing your movement work to live in your *life-body* as you speak.

Avoid choreographing a dance. Dance is wonderfully expressive, but it follows a specific form. It has rules and particular ways of moving. The well-known shapes and spatial pathways may actually interfere with your *authentic impulses*. Experiment. If you find yourself choosing dance forms, expand, enlarge, and develop them. Use movement tools and your impulses to take you some-where new.

If you feel stuck, try going to extremes, using the movement tools you have learned, or try the opposite of whatever you are doing. Explore fully, before you choose and shape your *movement monologue*.

There are as many ways to develop a *movement monologue* as there are people. Below is one tried-and-true approach. There are other approaches in Appendix I.

Give yourself several sessions to develop your *movement monologue*.

Part I

- Warm up before you begin to work.
- Perform your monologue.
- Choose three lines, one that expresses the beginning of your character's arc, one from the middle, and one from the end of your character's journey. Or, you can write your own phrases that express three key moments or three key char-acter desires at the beginning, middle, and end of your monologue.
- Lie down, sit, or stand. Close your eyes. Repeat the first line to yourself several times. Let it resonate in your body.
- Follow your impulse to form a whole-body *shape* or movement in response to this line. Give yourself time to explore fully, pausing often to absorb your experi-ence. You can repeat this process several times. Pause.
- Now, repeat the process with your second line, and then your third line. If you like, develop a specific *shape* or a movement sequence for each line. Pause.

- Expand your exploration, experimenting with your three lines and allowing movement to arise. Pause.
- Perform your monologue again. The movement and shapes live in your *life-body*. Enjoy allowing them to inform your performance. Pause.
- *Spy back*. What have you discovered about the different shapes and/or movement responses each line evokes in your body? What emotions arise? How do these movements express your character's journey? What do you know about your character's inner journey now that you didn't know before?

> *PAUSE TO PROCESS* Return to this Practice at another time. Journal or share with others, as you give your terrific trio a chance to process the experience.

Part II

- Warm up. Activate the *5 cues*.
- Perform your monologue.
- Return to the work you did in Part I, and take a few minutes to explore, refine, and develop your choices. Pause.
- Begin to explore the movement that will express the rest of the story: the journey that happens **between** the shapes/movements you chose for each line in Part I. Give yourself permission to explore a variety of movement choices – the entire range of large and small, molding and flying, direct and indirect, and more – every opposite you can think of.
- Explore what happens for your character between each of those three lines. You can use the entire space of the room. Invite your body to express your character's transformation. Experiment.
- At any time, you can pause and *spy back*. If you feel like going on, continue until you have begun to shape your choices into a repeatable *movement monologue*.
- Before you conclude this rehearsal, pause. Then perform your monologue as if for an audience. Though you will not physically express your movement monologue, allow your discoveries to inform your choices as you perform.
- *Spy back*. How does this movement exploration influence you as you perform your monologue? How did your performance change from the beginning to the end of the Practice?

PAUSE TO PROCESS before continuing to Part III.

Part III

- Warm up.
- Perform your monologue allowing your movement choices from your previous rehearsal to live in your *life-body*. Pause.

- Revisit the choices you made in your last rehearsal. Continue to explore, discover, tweak, and shape until you have developed a one- to two-minute *movement monologue*.
- You can add sound or words for emphasis or to express emotional content or qualities. Sound should arise spontaneously. It is not the focus, but a supportive element, enhancing your movement. Pause.
- As you hone your movement choices, simplify. Discover the continuous thread of your character's journey that guides you to express each moment cleanly and clearly. Pause.
- When you are ready, perform your *movement monologue*. Pause.
- Now, perform your monologue. As you speak the text, allow your *movement monologue* to live in your *life-body* and inform your choices. Pause.
- *Spy back*. What discoveries did you make? What was your experience of performing your monologue before and after your *movement monologue*?

Movement monologue is a process that supports your work in rehearsal and performance by deepening your connection to your character and grounding their journey in your body. Then, when you return to performing the text, you can sense a directed stream underlying your movement that guides you from moment to moment. Your choices are interesting and rich, yet always focused around the character's overall story.

When your whole body is engaged in exploration of text, imagery, and emotional content, these elements become grounded in your movement, and connect you to a wider array of physical choices. You get to be completely creative and explore without the constraints of period, style, or language. Discover, discover, discover!

Scene Preparation

Two creative imaginations are better than one! When creating a scene, two actors can explore their world together by adapting the Practices above. Each of you can explore your *movement homework*, bringing your discoveries into rehearsal with your partner.

REVISIT PRACTICE 31.1

Variation for Scene work: You can have fun playing through your scene together, exploring each *Effort* one at a time. We would recommend no set, other than a couple of chairs.

For instance, you can play through the scene, exploring the Space *continuum*. Each partner can pick a starting place on the *continuum* and explore Direct and Indirect as you play the scene. Practice in a large, open rehearsal space, and allow yourself to explore the extremes of the *continuum* and everything in between. You can choose any of the other *Efforts* as well. Afterward, *spy back*.

You can also devise a similar exploration with the *qualities of movement*. How do contrasting movement *qualities* affect conflicts in the scene?

REVISIT PRACTICE 31.2

The two of you can share Space Stories, adapting the Practice for your scene. Each actor can share their character's relationship to the setting, the landscape, the room the characters are in, what lies beyond that room, or any other aspect of their physical world.

REVISIT PRACTICE 31.3

Before exploring *movement monologue* for scene work, you want to be very familiar with your own character's arc in the scene.

With your partner, create a *Movement Duologue* (KP) – a *movement monologue* for two! – for the scene. One way our students create a *duologue* is to develop individual *movement monologues* for the scene. Then they unite them into a single *movement duologue*, adapting them as necessary to explore the tensions and desires of the characters as they interact in the scene.

You can find other suggestions in Appendix I or discover your own method of creating a *movement duologue*.

Our students find that performing their *movement duologue*, then playing through the scene immediately following, inspires clear, creative choices. When they create a *movement duologue*, they know much more about the arc of the scene and each moment that supports that arc.

> *PAUSE TO PROCESS* Journal and discuss your discoveries with your partner or classmates.

Developing Character Relationships

As you saw in the Practice above, movement can provide a base for exploring character and scene structure. But what about exploring relationships between characters? Through movement, actors can explore what is unsaid, and they can connect with themselves and each other. In scenes that require physical contact, movement provides the support actors need to connect safely and comfortably.

This is a general Practice for working with space, physical contact, and relationships for two actors in a scene. Before you begin, memorize the scene, and do your *movement homework*, as in Practice 31.1. Warm up before you begin.

A note about working with a partner: when touch is involved, especially if the partners do not know each other well, take a moment to stand face-to-face. Then take hands and pause, sharing a moment of connection, commitment, and safety before moving into the exploration below.

Part I: Making a Connection

- Pause. Breathe. Take a *kinesthetic moment*.
- Stand back to back with your partner. Sense their back against yours. Gradually become aware of their breathing.
- Allow the contact between your backs to soften. Sense the mutual support.
- After several moments, gradually separate and walk away from each other. You may be able to maintain the memory of your partner's back, even though you are not touching them.
- Turn and face each other, sensing your back and your partner's back.
- Move toward each other, still sensing your back. Pause, allowing a comfortable space between you. Continue to sense your back, your partner's back, and the 3-D space around you.
- If you like, make contact with your partner, taking their hand, or some other gesture of connection. Breathe. Take a *kinesthetic moment*.
- When this gesture is complete, release the contact. Thank your partner.
- Pause. Breathe. Take a *kinesthetic moment*.
- Run your scene.
- *Spy back.* What did you discover about your characters' personal connection?

Becoming comfortable with physical contact can be an important aspect of actor/ character relationships. Simple connections like the ones in this Practice can be a powerful first step in developing your comfort level with your partner. Part I can be repeated, allowing the actors to move toward a more intimate connection, if needed.

In Part II, discover how space can provide valuable information about character relationships.

Part II: The Dynamic Space Between Characters

In Chapter 28, you explored your personal relationship with *near-*, *mid-*, and *far-reach space*. This spatial awareness can also apply to the distance between you and another person. Each space can express the connection – or disconnection – between the characters. The *far* space: creating distance between the characters. The *mid* space: creating an ordinary range of space between the characters, as in daily conversation. The *near* space: creating intimacy or strong conflict between the characters.

Because you are standing in one place in this Practice, the space between you and your partner becomes a strong influence in the scene. Enjoy exploring the impact of dynamic space.

I investigate: How do spatial relationships affect our characters' journey in a scene?

- Pause. Breathe. Take a *kinesthetic moment*.
- Stand on the opposite side of the room from your partner. Explore the whole scene while standing opposite each other in *far* space. Pause.
- Breathe. Take a *kinesthetic moment*.
- Move to stand about five feet away from your partner. Explore the whole scene while standing opposite each other in *mid* space. Pause.
- Breathe. Take a *kinesthetic moment*.
- Move about a foot away from your partner. Explore the whole scene while standing opposite each other in *near* space. Pause.
- Breathe. Take a *kinesthetic moment*.
- Now, move, as you play the whole scene again. You are not using your blocking but exploring the dynamic space between you and your partner. Allow your impulses to guide your choices between *near, mid,* and *far space*. Pause.
- Breathe. Take a *kinesthetic moment*.
- *Spy back* with your partner. What did you discover?

When you return to your blocking and play the scene again, notice how this Practice affects the scene, and allow adjustments as needed.

Our students have discovered that this exploration creates a powerful, yet simple, connection between themselves and their partner. The structure of stillness deeply informs their spatial choices; their impulses become crystal clear. Then, when they rehearse the scene with movement, the perfect spatial choice – *near, mid,* or *far* – arises in each moment.

Movement and Desire

Every character has unique personal needs, and they want other characters to meet these needs. Very often, though, their desires are unspoken – part of the subtext of the play. Yet, they can deeply influence the way the character moves and uses space.

Others' desires also have an influence on our relationships and our movement. The Practice below allows you to explore your character's needs – and their responses to others' needs – through simple movements.

ACTION IMPULSES

In this exploration, a few simple physical actions allow you to explore your character's inner life and their responses to others:

* Stepping forward
* Stepping back
* Turning away
* Turning your back
* Pausing.

These are actions we often use in our daily lives. Sometimes we're responding, sometimes we're trying to get something, sometimes we're protecting, or even lying. You can explore these five actions in your scene, allowing your *authentic impulses* to support your choices in each moment.

These simple actions free you from having to manufacture blocking choices. This is a Practice in simple *stimulus* and *response*. You can discover your inner impulse and follow it in one of the five actions.

You and your partner will need a memorized scene. This Practice is most effective when you are very familiar with the given circumstances, and you have been rehearsing the scene for a while.

I investigate: How do my character's inner responses inform my actions?

* Warm up.
* Standing about 10 feet apart, play the scene without words, using only the five actions. Take your time and allow each impulse to arise. Pause.
* Breathe. Take a *kinesthetic moment*.
* Repeat the Practice with dialogue. You may find that different choices arise. Pause.
* Breathe. Take a *kinesthetic moment*.
* Rehearse the scene with blocking, allowing new choices to arise as needed. The five actions become inner impulses that guide you through the scene.
* When the scene is complete, pause. Breathe. Take a *kinesthetic moment*.
* *Spy back.* Share your discoveries with your partner.

Even though there are a limited number of actions in this Practice, you can discover ease and freedom in their simplicity and directness. Your choice palette is uncluttered, and you make specific responses, because these basic movements are clear and well defined. The five actions provide your *body-mind* with a distinct path from *inner experience* to *outer response*.

Though these five actions may seem static to the casual observer, perhaps you discovered that there was a lot going on under the surface. You were experiencing the character's subtext, via your inner impulses. Through this work, you can gain clarity about each moment – not just intellectually, but with your being. Then you are free to move, ready to play: you've clarified your personal impulses, and you are also in tune – resonating – with your scene partner.

Creative play can yield amazing, unexpected discoveries, especially when you share your process with other artists. Experiment. Surprise yourself. Discover the unique possibilities waiting for you, as you explore your character, relationships, and environment through movement.

> *PAUSE TO PROCESS* Discuss and journal about your discoveries.

> Key Practices: *Movement Homework, Movement Monologue, Movement Duologue*

Performing for an Audience CHAPTER 32

My Space, Your Space, Their Space

As actors, we perform with an ensemble in front of an audience. At any given moment, we must be aware of ourselves, the other actors, and the people who are observing us perform. We play each moment as truthfully as we can, without becoming self-conscious, presentational, or so focused on the onstage action that we exclude our audience. It is a true balancing act, and we are perfectly equipped for it.

For generations, actors have developed skills that can support this *multi-tracking* juggling act, a set of guidelines that, once you know them, become a part of your acting technique. These tried and true communication tools can guide you to informed choices about how you use stage space and position your body. Some are tools you've already encountered in *YBK*, like *Kinesphere*. Others you may have picked up from acting in plays or from acting class.

Every actor should know these simple staging principles. Here are the areas to consider:

- Your location on the stage
- Your *Body Position* (KW)
- The focus of the action
- Your relationship to space, the set, and the other actors
- The messages that your body and your use of space are conveying to the audience.

As you've discovered, your body is a strong communicator. In addition, your use of stage space and your physical relationship with other actors convey a wealth of information to the audience. This is basic movement knowledge, and once you absorb these useful tools, they will support your acting, your fellow actors, and the production – cleanly, clearly, and specifically.

Know Where You Are Onstage

Do you know why staging the play is called "blocking"? Because, back in the day, the director – or before directors, producers – divided the space on a proscenium stage into "blocks." You may be familiar with the diagram below, which indicates the nine *Stage Areas* (KW). The three *Stage Planes* (KW) are: upstage, center, and downstage.

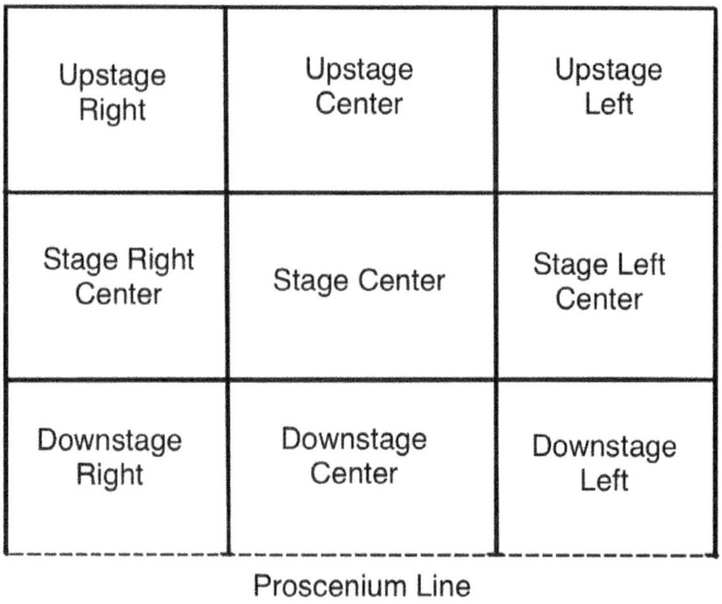

Upstage Right	Upstage Center	Upstage Left
Stage Right Center	Stage Center	Stage Left Center
Downstage Right	Downstage Center	Downstage Left

Proscenium Line

Figure 32.1 Each block represents a *stage area*. Each horizontal row of blocks forms a *stage plane*.

This diagram is a little misleading, because it tends to make us think that we are walking to a spot on the stage floor, and our feet mark our place on the stage. Instead, think of each block as floor **plus** the 3-D space. You are standing on the floor within that space, and you can fill it with your whole *3-D body* and your *Kinesphere* too!

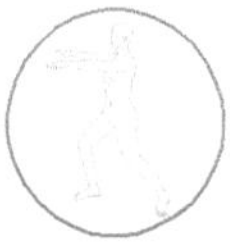

PRACTICE 32.1   **PLAYING WITH STAGE SPACE**

In this exploration, you can become more specific about your position and use of space on the stage. If possible, work with a partner or group. You can spend time onstage, exploring spatial relationships. You can also observe from the audience and discover how stage positions affect audience perceptions of the action.

- Go to a proscenium stage, or designate stage space and audience space in a large room. Spend time in each of the nine stage blocks. Speak some lines in each one. Learn what it is like to occupy that area of the stage. Awareness of where you are on the stage helps you make more informed spatial choices.
- If you can work with a partner, or if you are in a class, spend time in the audience watching others as they explore the different stage positions. Does one position on the stage draw your eye more than another?

- If two people are on the stage, one left center, and the other down right, who is in the stronger position? Try out different compositions with other actors.
- Experiment with a few lines, while playing in different planes with a fellow actor. One of you can remain stationary, and the other can move to different areas/planes. When an actor changes their position on the stage, and says the same line, does it change your perception as an audience member? Does it change the story? In what way?
- Practice entering from different positions on the stage. Decide before you enter where your entrance is going to end. Play with different spatial pathways for your entrance, such as UR to C or CL to DC.
  Enter with *a feeling of form*: your entrance has a beginning, a middle, and an end. Watch others enter; notice which entrances have the strongest dramatic effect. Why?
- Next, play with exiting.
- *Spy back.* What did you discover about *stage areas*, space, and relationships with other actors? How might this work serve you as an actor?

Though every stage is not a proscenium stage, it's always helpful to sense your physical relationship to other actors – in any stage configuration. Be aware of when you are on the same plane, above another actor, beside them, or below them. With this simple awareness, you can avoid upstaging another actor, or being upstaged yourself! You can make knowledgeable choices that support you and your fellow actors!

Your Body Position

You may already be familiar with these terms: ¼ right, profile left, full front, full back. These are terms that describe *body positions*, i.e., which direction you are facing, on the proscenium stage.

Your *body position* communicates important information to the audience. Are you open and sincere, are you trying to hide something, are you outgoing or shy? Your *body position* helps you tell the story!

The *positions* are a communication tool between actor and director, but they are so much more than that. Your *body position* in relationship to the audience and other actors can support your dialogue and your subtext simultaneously. However, if you don't know how to use these tools, you may end up telling the wrong story!

As you explore these communication tools, keep in mind that they are not static! The word *position* is a bit problematic for actors, because, as you have discovered throughout *YBK*, your body is dynamic! Also, the terms don't address "everything in between" the eight positions. It's best if you think of the *body positions* as guidelines that describe your *3-D body in its 3-D* relationship with *space*, the other actors, and the audience.

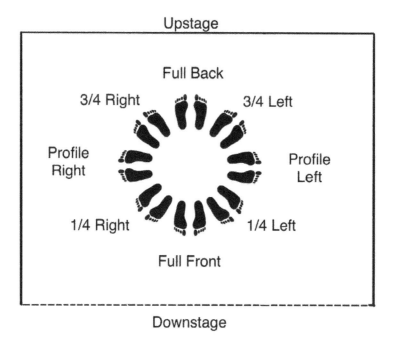

Figure 32.2 *Body positions* carry strong messages for the audience.

PRACTICE 32.2 **BODY POSITIONS, SPACE, AND STORYTELLING**

This exploration is designed for at least three people, two onstage or in the area of the classroom designated as the stage, and one as audience. It is very structured; only one person changes position at a time. It allows the viewer to see and actors to experience the impact of different *body positions* in a simple interaction.

Part I: Body Messages

- Actors A and B go onstage. Actor C – or the class – is the audience.
- Standing about 6–8 feet apart, both actors face full front. What's going on? What's the story/relationship of these two people, from the audience perspective? What do the actors experience? How do they perceive their relationship?
- How does the story change if both actors look to their right? What if the stage right actor then looks to their left?
- Now, both actors remain in the same place on stage, and Actor C instructs one actor to change their *body position*, such as "Turn to profile L." How does this change the story? What's the audience perspective? The actor's

experience? Continue to play with three to four more changes, changing the *body position* of one actor at a time.

- Change roles. Repeat until everyone has been an actor and an audience member.
- *Spy back*. What did you discover about the impact of simple changes in *body position*? Were you surprised by the stories that arose in your imagination? Why or why not?

Part II: Add a Line, Exploring Spatial Relationships

Actor A is the speaker, Actor B is the listener, Actor C, or members of the class, observe and offer changes in *body position*. Change roles as needed.

- Using a simple line, "I'll do whatever you want," explore how the story (and the line delivery) changes as the actors take different *body position*s. Actor C gives one change in *body position* to one actor at a time. Share impressions – actors and audience – each time you create a new composition.
- Now, add distance into the staging. What happens if the actors' *body position*s stay the same, but the distance between them changes?
- You can add a chair for sitting (or even standing on). You can invite an actor to kneel or sit on the floor. How does the actors' height (level) or activity change the story for the actors? For the audience?
- Now, allow the listener to respond to the speaker's line. The listener can change *body position* or distance as they feel the impulse in response to the line. They may make a large movement, crossing to the speaker, or a small one, like turning their head. See what you can learn from making a clear and specific choice.
- This Practice can be intense. Pause, breathe, and have a walk around the room.
- *Spy back*. How does changing *body position* and distance between the actors change the quality, and even the content, of a simple interaction?

Your character's journey in the play is told through your body, space, and relationships. Your *body position*, your height (sitting, standing, lying down), and the distance between you and other actors can clarify each moment.

Part III: No Words Scenework

Exploring *body positions* and distance between you and another actor offers insights into your scene and also, character relationships. Wait a day or two after you explore Parts I and II before continuing with Part III.

Place any furniture that you will need for playing your scene.

- Warm up before you begin.
- Enjoy playing a two-person scene that you know very well. Play the scene without words, allowing your *body position* and the distance between you and your

partner to express each moment. Allow your impulses to guide you. Take your time.

- *Spy back* with your partner. Pause.
- Repeat one or two more times. You may want to experiment with other "rules," such as moving only as much as needed or, the opposite, expanding each movement to enlarge your expression of the moment.
- Now play the scene through with dialogue. You may find that new impulses move you to unexpected relationships with your scene partner. Allow the blocking to change as needed to accommodate your new discoveries.
- *Spy back* with your partner.

(Note: it can be fun and informative to ask someone to watch your scene without words and tell you what they think is going on in the scene. This is especially effective if they do not know what scene you are doing!)

Through these explorations, you can experience the power of your body in space. Whether you are in a two-person scene or in a crowd, this knowledge leads you to simple, direct choices that support the story and your character's journey.

As you work with these tools, you can allow them to inform your physical and spatial choices in your scene work. *Body position* and blocking guide your *authentic impulses* and support even the subtlest changes in relationship.

Spatial Circles

As you know, your *kinesthetic sense* supports both physical and spatial awareness. When you sense your *Kinesphere*, you claim your personal space and enlarge your presence onstage. With your *3-D body in the 3-D space*, you are free to act – all 360° of you.

Your *Kinesphere* can also guide your spatial relationships with others. Your use of space tells the audience about your character's relationships and how your character is responding to the action of the play. For instance, what might you be communicating to an audience when your *Kinesphere* intersects with another character's *Kinesphere*, especially for a prolonged period of time?

In Chapter 14, you played with bouncing your *Kinesphere* off other actors' *Kinespheres*. You claimed your space, while respecting their space. When characters' *Kinespheres* intersect, something intense and strong is happening between them – often a moment of intimacy or anger. Our students refer to these moments as "kiss or fight." These events have special significance in the story, and we learn to use them sparingly and savor them when they occur.

PRACTICE 32.3 **KISS OR FIGHT**

This Practice supports specific spatial choices.

You will need a partner and a memorized scene, or you can work with an open scene – you can find one at the end of Appendix I.

It is fine to work on a scene that has already been blocked. This exploration is most effective if there is at least one other person who can act as your audience/ observer.

I investigate: How do specific spatial choices support my acting in scene work?

- Warm up. Pause.
- Play through your scene with your scene partner, with your audience observing. Improvise blocking if the scene has not already been blocked. Pause.
- Now, rehearse your scene (without audience), allowing the blocking to change as you explore a variety of spatial relationships through *body position*s and *stage areas*.
- Limit the number of times the two characters' *Kinesphere*s intersect to a maximum of two.
- When the scene is blocked, pause. Have a walk around the space.
- Play through the scene with the new blocking with your audience observing. Pause.
- *Spy back* with your partner and your audience. What were the differences between the first and second times you played the scene? Were there new dis- coveries about the character's actions, relationships, and their arcs in the scene? What were they? How might this Practice serve you as an actor?

In this Practice, you can discover the power of specific spatial choices. Relationships and action become clearer moment to moment. Your *Kinesphere* supports your awareness and use of space in rehearsal and performance.

PAUSE TO PROCESS Journal, discuss, investigate spatial choices.

Beyond Your *Kinesphere*

Have you ever watched a scene between two or more actors, where it seemed that they were so involved with each other, that the audience was simply left out in the cold? To the observer, it can seem like the actors' *Kinespheres* have collapsed on the downstage side! They may be *radiating*, but only toward each other. They have lost their sense of the whole space.

For many, this problem may simply be an oversight. As actors, we spend hours of rehearsal discovering our relationships with the other characters and our responses to their actions. They are our primary focus. Then, onstage, we may find it challenging to share our performance with the audience, especially in moments of high conflict. Actors must be intentional about enlarging their focus, because they have another relationship to develop – with the audience.

You can begin to include the audience by recognizing your *Kinesphere* as a *part within the whole*. Any time you are onstage, you can sense your personal space, others' personal space, and the general space that surrounds everyone onstage. You can even imagine the stage space as a very large *Kinesphere* that contains your *Kinesphere* and the *Kinespheres* of all the other actors as well – all are *parts within the whole* stage space.[1] That's step one.

Step two expands your *kinesthetic imagination* even farther. You can imagine another *Kinesphere* surrounding the audience: actors have *Kinespheres*, the stage has a *Kinesphere*, and the audience also has a *Kinesphere*.

Finally, in step three, you can sense an even larger *Kinesphere*! This one includes all the smaller *Kinespheres*: the actors, the stage space, and the audience space. In this spatial image, actors and audience claim their own space, while sharing an all-inclusive theatre space!

PRACTICE 32.4   **SHARING AND CLAIMING SPACE**

If you don't have access to a stage, you can work outdoors, and designate a stage space and an audience space.

- Go onstage with a scene partner. Stand at least 6 feet away from each other. Take a *kinesthetic moment*.
- Sense your *Kinesphere*. Next, sense your partner's *Kinesphere* and your own *Kinesphere*. Speak a few lines to them.
- Now, sense a larger *Kinesphere* that includes the whole stage space. Continue to be aware of your own and your partner's *Kinespheres* within the whole stage space. Pause.
- Explore this new awareness. Move around the stage. Sense the support of these *Kinespheres*. Pause.
- With an awareness of the smaller *Kinespheres* within the larger *Kinesphere* of the stage space, run a few lines with your partner. Pause.
- Next, sense a *Kinesphere* that surrounds the audience. Sense that the audience has their space, and you and your partner have your space. Pause.
- Move around and exchange a few lines again, continuing to sense both shared space and personal space. Pause.
- Finally, sense the larger *Kinesphere* that surrounds all the other *Kinespheres*. Actors and audience are connected, and they each have their personal space as well. Pause.

- With a gentle awareness of shared space and personal space, play through your scene with your scene partner. Trust that you have activated your spatial awareness – avoid placing too much attention or effort on maintaining it. Pause.
- *Spy back*. What did you and your partner discover about shared space and personal space? What did you discover about your relationship with the audience?

Awareness of personal and shared space creates a dialogue with your brilliant body-mind-imagination. These spatial images can become second nature, subtly supporting you whenever you perform. Your body knows the size of the space you want to fill, and the amount of energy that is needed to expand your performance to the last row of the audience. The audience responds to your strong onstage presence, and audience and actors are joined in a mutual journey.

The Focus of the Action

You are so powerful onstage – you can switch the audience's attention on and off, just by what you are looking at, the way you turn your body, or where you stand. You have the power to focus the audience's attention on the action of the story.

Much of a director's job is to stage the play in such a way that the audience's attention is focused at the right place at the right time. Focus helps the audience follow the story. Some directors are very hands on, place every actor on the stage, and tell them where to move. Even in this case, you will make more specific spatial choices and you will be a better storyteller, if you understand the space you are filling onstage and your relationship to the entire company.

Giving and Taking Focus

What does it mean when we say, "steal focus" or "give focus?" No one wants to act with a scene stealer or someone who upstages them. Very often, it is ignorance on the part of the offending actor – they simply don't know what they are doing. We don't want you to be that actor. Learn to give and take focus with a few simple choices.

Ways you can take focus:

- Open *body position*
- Movement – a cross or a gesture can draw the audience's attention
- Separate from or stand in front of a crowd
- Choose a strong stage position
- Stand upstage of the person you are speaking to.

Taking focus is a good thing – unless you are not the focus of the action! Then it becomes stealing focus!

Real-life Story: Karen's Discovery

Karen was a professional actor performing in a comedy. She was onstage as two actors played a scene downstage of her, and they were getting a lot of laughs. One night, she noticed they didn't get their laugh on a particular line. She didn't think much of it, until she noticed the same thing the next night. She couldn't hear anything different in what they were doing, but the audience definitely wasn't laughing.

Curious, Karen began to investigate what might be happening onstage to steal their laugh. She was embarrassed to discover that it was her! She was putting her down-stage hand in her pocket on the punchline, and this was enough to direct the audience's attention away from the focus of the action. After that, Karen made sure that she put her hand in her pocket on the laugh, not the punchline.

Ways to give focus:

- Cultivate an alert, dynamic stillness in your body. Practice active listening.
- *Body position* – turn your body toward the focus of the action.
- In carrying on a dialogue, stand in the same plane or downstage of the speaker.
- Look in the direction of the action (eye focus).

Remember, the director isn't onstage. Actors are. Whether we are playing a lead or an extra, directing the audience's attention is part of our job as a member of an ensemble. As actors, we want to educate ourselves about focus, so we can give it when needed, and take it when it's our turn.

Real-life Story: Benedick Shares and Gives Focus

One of our students was struggling in rehearsal, playing his first lead role, Benedick in Shakespeare's *Much Ado About Nothing*. He knew his lines and blocking, his soliloquies were wonderful, and he seemed to be perfectly cast as the man's man who falls in love for the first time. But he lacked strength in the scenes when others were onstage with him, and particularly in the scenes with Beatrice. We saw that he was very supportive of the other actors, but he didn't seem to accept their support when he was the focus in a scene.

One day in rehearsal, he and Beatrice were exploring their verbal sparring match in Act I, scene 1. They were asked to face each other and press into each other's hands. When it was Benedick's line, he could add pressure and push into Beatrice's hands; she could resist the pressure and try not to back up. She could do the same with her lines. The actors made a commitment to control the amount of force they were using, to avoid injury to themselves and their fellow actors.

The entire company was onstage, and for the purposes of the exercise, the women reinforced Beatrice by standing on her side and cheering her on, and the men did the same for Benedick. It was a raucous time, with much clapping and cheering.

Then when they played through the scene afterward, Benedick had become a much stronger adversary for Beatrice. He played to win, and he had no trouble taking focus when it was his turn. An added benefit was, that when he fell in love with Beatrice, there was a distinct contrast in his behavior. The audience could tell he was a changed man.

How did Benedick take focus? Remember: your *body position* can help you be seen, give focus to your fellow actors, and help them give focus to you. Before the exercise, Benedick was playing in profile or ¾ much of the time – his attention was only focused on Beatrice in their scenes together. He seemed unaware of personal and shared space, and his *Kinesphere* had shrunk to *near-reach space*.

After the exercise, he played in profile less, and when he delivered a "zinger" to Beatrice, he sometimes opened to full front, or even slightly turned his back to her, while he looked for the support of his friends. He had a palpable sense of owning his space and sensing the larger *Kinespheres* of the whole space. His presence said, "I belong here. I'm in charge!"

The entire company, including Beatrice, responded to Benedick's expanded awareness. The actors who were listening to their "merry war" were also clearer about their role in focusing attention. The scenes were lively and specific, and most important for the audience, established the comic, yet caustic, tone of Benedick and Beatrice's relationship.

Continue exploring spatial tools by practicing them and by watching others use them in rehearsal and performance. You will become skilled at seeing when actors use these tools effectively, and when they are unaware of the space around them. With the power of spatial knowledge, you can become more specific and more intentional in your choices. You can **know** the story you are projecting to the audience and **play** within the big picture.

Key Words: *Body Position, Stage Area, Stage Plane*

Note

1 Our use of *Kinesphere* in this context expands Laban's original definition. Our students find this image of multiple *Kinespheres* supports them as they develop their spatial skills.

Movement and Space

CHAPTER 33

Creating the World of the Play

Throughout *YBK*, we have focused on your individual movement and the way it supports you as a creative artist. In this chapter, our focus broadens, as you work with an ensemble in preparation for production. The power of movement can bring actors together as a group of committed artists.

When the whole company is attuned to each other, they can confidently enter the world of the play together, with the director as their guide. Movement builds ensemble, and it unites the company by grounding the play's conflicts and circumstances in their bodies.

Before exploring the world of the play through movement, actors must have a common understanding of that world and their relationship to it. Table work offers the cast an opportunity to read the play together and begin their investigation of character, relationships, themes, and given circumstances. In this way, there is a shared vision among the company. Individual actor research cannot replace this important step.

The company is then ready to leave the table and explore the world of the play through movement. The play moves off the page and comes to life in the bodies of the actors as they physically engage in the given circumstances. A director or a movement coach can develop creative Practices that support the actors as they explore the environment and relationships that shape the characters' lives.

As actors discover the world of the play together, they develop a deeper level of connection with each other and the production as a whole. They value creating the world of the play; they know who lives there, and their place in it. As the ensemble works together, everyone learns to honor the contributions of each person, the ensemble as a whole, and their mutual dedication to bringing the landscape of the play to vibrant life.

The movement principles and elements in *YBK* provide a strong foundation for actors' work as they rehearse a production. In this chapter, we share some movement Practices we have used in support of the rehearsal process. We have chosen two plays as illustrations: *Three Sisters* by Anton Chekhov, and *The Laramie Project* by The Tectonic Theater

Project. Meade has been the movement coach on two productions of *Laramie*, and we had the great pleasure of working together, Jana directing and Meade coaching movement, on a production of *Three Sisters*.

Although produced a century apart, *Three Sisters* (1900) and *Laramie* (2000) have some major theatrical aspects in common:

1. They were each written for an ensemble: a group of actors who have been working together for a significant amount of time. Chekhov wrote his play for the actors who formed The Moscow Art Theatre, under the direction of Konstantin Stanislavski. The Tectonic Theater Project is a collective of actors and writers who wrote *The Laramie Project* from selected interviews with the townspeople and outsiders. The whole group created a work of documentary theater together under the guidance of Moises Kaufman and Leigh Fondakowski.
2. Each play focuses on the theme of change: changing times, changing relationships, changing world and social events. Each play takes place in a small, isolated town, seemingly safe and ordinary. In each play, a social/political shift occurs that changes the status quo of the town and the characters.
3. Each play is about personal challenge: the effect of significant events on the world view of the people involved, and how they – individually and collectively – meet that challenge. In *Three Sisters*, change comes gradually over the course of four Acts. In *The Laramie Project*, the change occurs abruptly and violently.

As you've discovered throughout *YBK*, your *authentic impulses* guide your movement, as your character responds to the events of the play. These events have a context – social structure, setting, history, relationships – all influence each character's movement. When you are alive in your body and you know your relationship to your character's world, your impulses simply arise, and they are spot on.

Actors become an ensemble as they explore the setting and social structure of the play together. Each character responds differently, of course, but everyone participates in establishing a common understanding of the environment and given circumstances. All the actors are responding to the same world.

Creating Ensemble

Movement provides groundwork that serves the production as a whole. These explorations offer support in four major ways:

Warming Up With Intention

Individual warm-ups wake up actors' bodies and connect the group.

- Warm-ups designed for the individual actor within the group setting.
- Warm-ups designed to unite the whole group as a committed, cohesive working ensemble of actors.

Entering the World of the Play

The group explores given circumstances: time period, location, opposing forces.

- Exploring the landscape, environment, and *atmosphere* of the play.
- Exploring the relationships among the whole group of characters within the play.
- Developing individual and group relationships within the given circumstances and events of the play.
- Exploring significant moments in the play.

Relationships

Establishing the intimate groups in the play: duets, trios, quartets.

- Breaking down the various relationships between the characters into smaller groups, such as family, profession, or class.
- Exploring subtext.
- Exploring the specific connections within each group.

Transformation

Embodying personal and social changes.

- As events unfold, social status, relationships, settings, and circumstances change for groups and individuals.

Through exploration and discovery, movement prepares you and the whole ensemble to bring the play to life.

Warming up With Intention

Specific personal warm-ups create a well-tuned instrument, offering you a readiness for "play." Your personal warm-up is the foundation that connects you with yourself and heightens your responsiveness to the other actors. Your enlivened body is ready to connect with the ensemble as you bring the play to "life" together.

Though the work is individual, when actors warm up together, they have a common experience and a common goal. Each exploration cultivates a finely tuned, engaged company of actors, preparing them to enter the world of the play together.

How do you warm up with intention? You focus your attention with a purpose, such as: "To prepare my body and mind for rehearsal/performance" or "To be present within the ensemble."

You can enjoy warming up. Find pleasure in sensation. Play. You can focus your attention on your experience, and at the same time, recognize that each person is also experiencing their body opening, their breath deepening. Warming up is a time to focus on freeing your body and quieting your mind within the whole ensemble.

It is so tempting to skip this important step. Be vigilant! Be wise! Warm up, with intention.

PRACTICE 33.1 INDIVIDUAL AND GROUP WARM-UPS

Individual Warm-ups

Warm-ups open creative space. You are waking and calming your responsive *body-mind* as you prepare for rehearsal or performance.

The Practices are for the whole group unless otherwise stated. We recommend warming up with the ensemble while standing in a circle.

These Practices from previous chapters provide a thorough warm-up. It isn't necessary to use all of them. Choose a few to awaken your *kinesthetic sense*, your responsive *body-mind*, and connect you to the 3-D space.

- Moving Through Your Joints (Practice 4.1)
- A Movement Duet – Joints and Breath (Practice 4.2)
- Movement Can Begin Anywhere and Go Anywhere (Practice 9.3)
- The *Roll-Down* (Practice 7. 5)
- Introduction to *Shaping* (Practice 27.1)
- The *Dimensional Scale* (Practice 15.3)
- Exploring *Kinesphere* (Practice 14.4)

Group Warm-ups

- *Staccato-Legato* (Practice 30.1)
- *Crossing the Threshold* (Practice VI.1)
- Person to Person (Practice 20.2)

As you warm up, notice your expanding *kinesthetic awareness*, your *3-D body in the 3-D space*, the calmness of your mind, and your connection to the group. Warming up also prepares you for the nervous energy that can come with performance. You are well rehearsed in opening your body and quieting your mind. Should stage jitters arise, your intentional warm-up can produce the familiar sense of calm and balance that you have practiced many times.

Building Ensemble: Entering the World of the Play

Every actor has a body; every character has a body. The character's body, just like the actor's body, developed in response to their world. The details of the characters' story are rooted in geographic location, time, social and family structure, relationships, and political factors – all contribute to the rich tapestry of the characters' lives.

Movement allows you to experience these forces in your body, mind, and imagination: you and your fellow actors can share a deeply rooted connection to the world of the play.

PRACTICE 33.2   **PERSONAL CONNECTIONS**

As people, we act out of our personal relationship to the world around us. In this Practice, that's what you are doing – expressing yourself, your unique identity – and acknowledging the identity of others.

- Warm up.
- Revisit Introduction to Shaping, Part II (Practice 27.1), allowing each member of the ensemble to express themselves through *shape* in the group.
- When everyone has shared their *shape* in the circle, begin to move about the space. Your *shape* is alive in your *life-body*.
- When you meet someone, pause.
- Greet the other person by sharing your *shape*, then releasing it. Remain receptive as the other person greets you with their *shape*.
- When the second person releases their *shape*, both pause, breathe, and share a *kinesthetic moment*.
- Return to moving about the space and repeat with other members of the group.
- At the end of the exploration, return to the circle.
- Pause. Breathe. Take a *kinesthetic moment*.
- *Spy back*. What did you experience when you shared your essence/*shape* with another person? And what did you experience when they shared their *shape* with you?

This Practice helps you get to know your fellow actors better. Bypassing words, each person interacts through self-expression, and everyone begins to establish relationships with each other. In a way, each person steps into their fellow actors' shoes – or body! – as they experience another's *shape*. This Practice also provides the groundwork for the ensemble to explore character *shaping* and relationships in later rehearsals.

After warming up and getting acquainted, the company can begin to explore the specific world of the play. These Practices can connect the actors with themselves, each other, and the given circumstances. The play itself provides the foundation and the inspiration for the explorations.

The Laramie Project

The Laramie Project is a series of monologues and short scenes performed on a bare stage, with functional furniture (chairs and tables when necessary). Following Matthew Shepard's murder in Laramie, WY, The Tectonic Theater Project conducted hundreds of interviews (1998–2000) with the people of the town, and the text of the play is taken verbatim from these conversations.

Laramie, Wyoming, is small: population 26,687. The surrounding landscape includes the vast plains and the open sky, with the mountains in the background. The open stage offers a sense of the immense space of the West, and also reflects the "live and let live" attitude of the community of Laramie.

The bare stage and the verbatim text create a straightforward, "stripped away" quality in the artistic elements. The characters, the people of Laramie, are there to "tell the truth" as they see it. In rehearsal and performance, the actors were supported by their knowledge of the movement foundations you have been exploring in *YBK*. With open and available bodies, they developed a very simple, authentic acting style.

Below are three explorations, examples of work developed for the company of *The Laramie Project*. These Practices focus on building ensemble, exploring the landscape and relationships, and the changes that shape the characters' common experience.

PRACTICE 33.3 DEFINING THE LANDSCAPE

The exploration below was designed to give the actors an experience of the landscape and *atmosphere* of the town of Laramie, Wyoming. (Michael Chekhov used the term *Atmosphere* (KW) to describe the characters' physical, psychological, and emotional environment.[1])

Because the play is set on an open stage, with only a few chairs and tables, defining the space is especially important in this play. Each actor is encouraged to sense the vastness of the landscape and their place within it.

The Practice asks the question: what is the character's relationship with their environment, and what effect does it have on their lives? The actors themselves assist each other in defining the scope of the landscape.

Before beginning the Practice, the company warms up their *3-D bodies in the 3-D space*, as suggested in Practice 33.1.

- The group stands in a circle. Pause, breathe, take a *kinesthetic moment*.
- Everyone *crosses the threshold*.
- Divide into groups of four. Person 1 stands in the middle as their character, and the other three people group beside and behind them, leaving enough space

between them to suggest a large, open landscape. Person 2 is behind, persons 3 and 4 are on either side.

- Person 1 stands in the center of their *Kinesphere*, experiencing the sky above them and the ground below.
- Person 2 stands at ease, conscious that their presence defines the mountains in the background. Person 1 senses the mountains behind and the open prairie in front.
- Persons 3 and 4 define the forest. Person 1 experiences the forest and the entire 3-dimensional landscape.
- After a few moments, Persons 2, 3, and 4 step away, and Person 1 experiences the full magnitude of the 360-degree landscape while standing alone. Pause.
- Within the groups, each person takes a turn in the center.
- At the end of this exploration, each person walks through the space, sensing themselves in relation to the huge landscape, while seeing each person as they pass by.
- Return to the group circle. Pause. Breathe. Take a *kinesthetic moment*.
- *Spy back*. Discuss the effect of the landscape on the individual residents of Laramie, and on the events of the play.

Because their bodies are open and responsive, the actors are ready to connect with the landscape and allow it to affect them. It influences the way they move (different than moving in a crowded city). In a rehearsal, you can talk about it, but until you **experience** it, you can't play from that deeply grounded knowledge.

The beauty and serenity of the natural surroundings in Laramie heighten the impact of the violent events in the play. The vast landscape contrasts with the daily lives of the people in this small Western town and transforms the events into a universal story of life and death.

These universal themes are not playable actions, of course. But as an actor, you can experience the play's environment and dwell in the landscape. You can become aware of its power and develop a resonance with it. Your relationship with the environment can then inform all of your actions – spatial, physical, and emotional.

A strong internal and physical sense of setting supports you, as you explore character and relationships with the ensemble.

PRACTICE 33.4 CHARACTER, SHAPE, AND RELATIONSHIPS

Movement and space offer valuable insights into character relationships. You can use the Practices below to deepen your knowledge of your character's identity and the place they occupy within the community.

As you warm up, you may want to revisit Practice 33.2, Personal Connections.

Part I: Character Identity

- Revisit Practice 27.2 and share the essence of your character through *shape*. Note: this is your character shape at the **beginning** of the play.

Part II: Meeting and Greeting (Practice 33.2)

This exploration provides a simple moment of connection between characters.

- Stand. Pause. Breathe. Take a *kinesthetic moment*.
- Move through the room, meeting and greeting with your character *shape* as you did in Practice 33.2.
- At some point, begin to let go of your character *shape*, and simply sense the essence of your character from within, meeting and greeting others by saying hello.
- Return to the group circle. Release your character and their inner *shape*. Stand. Pause. Breathe. Take a *kinesthetic moment*.
- *Spy back*. Share your experiences of this Practice with the whole group. What happened when you released your character *shape* and said hello to the others?

Part III: Meeting and Greeting in Later Scenes

This exploration can act as a lead-in for a run-through of the latter part of the play after the murder.

- After warming up, the group gathers in a circle as their characters.
- Pause. Breathe. Take a *kinesthetic moment*.
- Take a moment to see the others in the community and make eye contact.
- Walk through the space, pause as you meet someone, share a moment of silence.
- Repeat with other members of the community.
- When the Practice feels complete, everyone returns to the circle, sharing a final moment of silence.

The Practices above can serve almost any play. They allow each actor to discover and express their character's inner state through *shape*/gesture. The explorations can also focus on establishing relationships between characters at the beginning of the play, and any changes occurring later in the play.

The explorations below focus on the relationships between the people of Laramie during the events of the play.

PRACTICE 33.5   **ESTABLISHING RELATIONSHIP AND GROUPS**

The company warms up, *crosses the threshold*, and takes a pause before beginning. In this Practice, actors explore their character's physical and personal relationship within the community.

Actors can use the entire stage space, as they explore where their character fits in relationship to the others in the town.

Possible choices for each person in creating this arrangement:

Spatial Relationships – exploring the *near*, *mid*, *far* distance between characters.
Body positions – facing someone directly, turning on a diagonal, or turning your back to another character.
Locations on Stage – gravitating toward center stage, skirting the edges, or anywhere in between.

The Community of Laramie

I investigate: What is my character's place within the Laramie community?

- The entire group stands around the edge of the rehearsal space or the stage.
- Each character chooses a place to stand onstage, one at a time.
- Characters choose their place in relationship to the others, allowing the whole community picture to gradually evolve.
- The actors onstage make adjustments to reflect their relationship, as each character finds their place in the community.
- When the community feels complete, everyone pauses, breathes and takes a *kinesthetic moment*.
- Have a walk around the space, seeing the others as you move.
- Gather in a circle for *spy back*. What did you learn about your character's place in the community?

The Community of Laramie: Specific Relationships

- The Practice above can be expanded to allow the group to arrange themselves in relationship to a specific character. This allows the characters to discover more subtle relationships with each other.

One vivid grouping might be to have someone stand in for Matthew Shepard. The group can arrange themselves around him in their relationship to him at the beginning of the play.

The Community of Laramie: Final Portrait

- Late in the rehearsal process, in a similar Practice, the townspeople pose for a Final Portrait, a black and white moment in time, as they are at the end of the play. The characters stand much closer together, as if in front of a camera.

This exploration calls for more subtle physical choices, as the characters adjust to the tragedy and their new place in the town.

The Practices above rely on all you have learned in *YBK*. Though these explorations do not require much time in rehearsal, they reap great rewards for individual actors and the ensemble. Open, available actors take these Practices to heart, and their commitment yields a wealth of benefits: spatial awareness, specific relationships, and authentic, truthful responses to the action of the play.

Three Sisters

Chekhov wrote *Three Sisters* for the ensemble of actors of the Moscow Art Theatre. Chekhov's ability to create the specific world of the play, and to paint in-depth and poetic portraits of the characters who inhabit that world, is his unique gift to the development of contemporary theatre.

Establishing the World of the Play

The setting of the play is a provincial town in Russia around 1900. The location is boring and lonely for the educated, upper-class characters in the play: no theater, symphony, museums, or social season in this small, dreary town in rural Russia. The main characters have little in common with the people of this town, whom they experience as vulgar and ill-bred.

The three central characters are the daughters of General Prozorov; they have enjoyed a certain stature in the community as long as their father was alive. Since his death a year ago, the young women have pinned their hopes on their brother Andre to pursue a professorship and rescue them from the provincial life. For the Prozorovs and for the officers stationed in this town, life revolves around the enjoyment of each other's company, the educated and refined minority in this community. Faraway Moscow is the dream of a happier life situation for the sisters.

The play takes place over two years. It begins in spring – a season of hope, new life – then moves to midwinter, a year and a half later. The third act takes place the following

In a period play like *Three Sisters*, actors may be wearing period costumes which call for a particular way of moving. But the deep humanity of the characters – their needs, choices, and actions – are relevant today and can be felt by everyone.

An actor can get caught up being perfectly in period and find that they lose their connection to the physical and emotional underpinning of the play. While we do not address period movement in *YBK*, we would like to offer one important observation: never imitate the outward movements of the period without learning why the people move the way they do. What is the inner world of the character and the sensibility of the times that influence the manners of the characters? All movement grows out of human need. Find that need, and period movement will come to life in your body.

summer, and the final act is in autumn.

Although *Three Sisters* was written over a hundred years ago, the themes explored in the play – love, loss, family, changing times – are universal. The characters are also universal in their desire for understanding, acceptance, freedom, and love.

The following explorations offer examples of movement work and its power to support the rehearsal process. The Practices provide a foundation for the actors' creative journey: they build a cohesive ensemble and inspire commitment to the artistic vision of the production. Below, you can discover how the Practices you encountered in *The Laramie Project* can be modified to suit the specific given circumstances of *Three Sisters*.

PRACTICE 33.6   ACT I – A CELEBRATION

In contrast with the bare, open stage space and minimal furniture in *The Laramie Project*, Act I in *Three Sisters* takes place in the well-furnished drawing room of the family home in a provincial town in Russia in 1900.

And yet, there is a distinct quality of spaciousness in the environment. It is noontime on a warm sunny day in May, and the windows of the house are wide open; light is streaming into the room. The weather is "glorious," and everyone has gathered to celebrate Irina's 20th birthday.

Part I: Act I – The Environment

The year-long period of mourning their father's death is over. Irina, the youngest sister, is wearing a white dress, instead of her usual black mourning clothes. Today is her birthday, and officers from her father's regiment are arriving to celebrate with the sisters. Everyone is feeling hopeful about the future, and grateful for the warm sunshine.

The Practice below supports the actors' experience of the *atmosphere* in the opening act of the play.

- The cast assembles in a circle, warms up, and *crosses the threshold*.
- The actors take a walk around the room. After a few moments, they find a space in the room where they can lie on the floor.
- Each actor closes their eyes, pauses, and breathes. After a moment, they move into a fetal position, lying on their side. They are hibernating – protecting themselves from the cold and dark of winter.
- In their own time, each actor connects with their character and the given circumstances: the sun, the warmth, the windows open wide. They allow their body to respond.
- Gradually, each character moves from the floor to standing, drinking in the *atmosphere* of warmth and celebration.
- Once standing, each character opens their eyes and pauses, seeing the others and the space around them.

- The characters begin to move through the room, as they greet other people. For many characters, joyous meetings and interactions occur, between one person and another, and even in groups. Other characters may be more reserved.
- The director or movement coach brings the Practice to completion. The actors are ready for Part II of this Practice.

Part II: Act I – Relationships

This exploration is similar to Practice 33.4, in which the residents of Laramie formed spatial relationships on the stage. In this scene, however, the emphasis is not on the loosely linked relationships of the Wyoming townspeople, but a closely knit group of friends and family in a familiar household setting. The environment/*atmosphere* established in Part I of the Practice supports this scenario.

In preparation for Part II of this Practice, actors were asked to bring a small object or write a card that they would like to give Irina for her birthday. The exception was Vershinin, who simply greeted Irina and wished her a happy birthday.

For this Practice, let go of any idea of being on a proscenium stage; there is no audience, and you can take your place anywhere in the room.

- After completing Part I, Irina sits in a chair, center stage. Everyone pauses.
- Each actor enters one at a time. They greet Irina and offer her their gift, then choose a place to stand nearby, based on their personal relationship with her. (See Practice 33.4, *The Laramie Project*.) As each character is added, there are continual changes in spatial relationships (*near*, *mid*, *far*) and *body positions*.
- The characters may also greet one another, as they find their places in the group.
- When the composition of the group is complete, everyone Pauses. They see and acknowledge each other and their honored friend.
- All breathe and take a *kinesthetic moment*.

Now the cast can bring their experience into a run-through of Act I. Afterward, the company can *spy back*.

As the play unfolds, the happiness and hope of Act I gives way to more serious concerns, and the environment and relationships also shift. In Act IV, the characters face the chill of autumn and their rapidly changing world.

PRACTICE 33.7 ACT IV – THE LONG GOOD-BYE

The core actions in Act IV focus on saying farewell. The regiment of soldiers is leaving town: a sense of loss prevails. The loss itself cannot be played, but must serve as the undercurrent for each character's actions. The exploration below illuminates the theme of change, letting go, and saying good-bye.

The company warms up before beginning this Practice. The director or movement coach is guiding the actors in this exploration.

- The whole company stands in a circle, warms up, and *crosses the threshold*, stepping into their character.
- Each character takes a moment to see and receive the others, remembering their history with each of them.
- When ready, each person begins to walk through the space, seeing and receiving as they pass each other. Pause.
- Each person takes a moment to reflect on the character who is most important to them in the play and turns to face them. (Their important character may be facing someone else.)
- They walk toward their important character, pausing when they are a few feet away. (This may take some adjustment, as one person's important character may be walking toward someone else.)
- They pause and see their important person.
- If they choose, they can move closer to this person and touch them. Pause.
- The director or coach invites each person to step back, turn, and walk away.
- Then the coach directs them to turn and see and/or reach for their important person one more time.
- Pause. Gradually, everyone returns to the circle. See the others in the circle.
- Closure options:
  - *Spy back or*
  - Run Act IV, then *spy back*.

This Practice allows the ensemble to "own the loss," rather than playing it. Their experience then informs their choices as they play the action of Act IV.

In our production, this Practice came at a point when the actors were off book, and we had run each of the four acts in recent rehearsals. When the actors ran Act IV after this exploration, a deep sense of loss permeated the act. The actors' work was so strong that, after we talked about their experience, we did not work any more that night. We went home, so that their bodies, minds, and imaginations could continue to process the experience.

"Saying good-bye" is a core action in Act IV. In this exploration, the actors played this action as a personal objective, which heightened their physical and emotional connection to it. The simple and specific structure of the Practice supported their exploration, as they each encountered the loneliness and distance, the things unsaid, the desires unfulfilled. These deeply felt discoveries built dynamic actions and relationships, which the actors could call upon and renew each night of performance.

Creating Your Own Explorations

Each time you approach a play, you can develop explorations that serve yourself, the ensemble, and the production as a whole. Directors, movement coaches, or actors can invent creative explorations that inspire individuals and connect the ensemble.

Below are some key elements to consider as you create your own Practices:

1. Explore landscape/environment/*atmosphere* of the play or specific scenes.
2. Explore the relationships, including subtext, between characters and groups.
3. Explore the core action of a scene, such as saying good-bye in Act IV of *Three Sisters*.

Tips for developing explorations:

1. Discover the movement elements that can support a simple exploration of the action, relationship, or environment. For example, focusing on Space: exploring degrees of distance and closeness between characters can reveal the level of intimacy in their relationship.
2. Trust the body of knowledge you have acquired through the journey of *YBK* and trust the awakening of your own creative instincts to guide you to the right structure for each exploration.
3. Always: Be simple. Go deep. Strip away what is not needed.

The world of any play can be explored and integrated through creative movement Practices. This work takes you to the heart of the action of the play: as an actor, you can embody the given circumstances, the character relationships, and deepen your connection with each member of the ensemble.

These explorations awaken the actors' imaginations and strengthen the action of the play. Given circumstances, actions, and character relationships are alive in the actors and "happening for the first time," each night of rehearsal and performance.

You can discover more Practices for exploring the world of the play in Appendix I.

Key Word: *Atmosphere*

Note

1 Chekhov, Michael. *To The Actor*. New York: Routledge, 2007. pp. 47–50.

Conclusion

Throughout *YBK*, you have taken a journey toward creating a powerful, authentic perform-ance presence on stage. You have learned that "you are designed for movement." Your *dynamic thinking* has partnered with the *friendly facts* of your anatomy to support and enliven your creative movement choices.

You have encountered the movement pioneers – Alexander, Laban, Chekhov, and others – and explored their work from the inside out, with your body, mind, and imagination. You have journeyed into unexplored movement territory and opened up many new possibilities.

In this last section, you have discovered how to use creative movement to embody your character within the world of the play. Through your curiosity and your willingness to explore, movement concepts have come alive in your body. You have discovered how to bring the play to life for yourself, and for the audience.

Your *body-mind* knowledge will support you now and in the future. If you are working out at the gym, you can remember that no movement happens in isolation and allow weight to sequence through your muscles. If you are practicing stage combat, you can notice the *shapes* you are making and allow body, breath, and space to guide your movement. In rehearsal and performance, you can recognize and follow your inner impulses as they lead you to authentic outer expression.

Like acting, movement study is an ongoing process. You can find inspiration by revisiting the Practices in *YBK* and exploring additional Practices in Appendix I. Through Appendix II, you can delve more deeply into the work of the movement pioneers and discover other resources for continuing your movement studies.

Remember: the movement principles you have learned are alive in your creative *body-mind*, and they support all the juicy art you make. We hope that your movement work continues to serve your acting goals and support you in becoming the actor you want to be. We wish you all good things as you continue your acting journey.

Real-life Story: The Value of Creative Play

As a student actor, Jorge was frustrated: he felt he was a serious actor. And he did not enjoy what he thought of as "games" in his classes; he craved serious study to support his passion for great acting.

Then he was cast in one of the silliest plays ever written – *A Flea in Her Ear*.

Playing two roles – a drunken porter, Poche, and the respectable Victor Chandebise – Jorge found that his ideas about serious acting were getting him nowhere.

He began to play some of the "games" from movement class. Surprise! "Play" led him to creative, yet authentic choices for embodying two distinct characters. They broadened his movement palette. He even discovered that, through the *Efforts*, he could explore the specificity and timing demanded by farce.

Jorge found that creative play is serious study. He became committed to curiosity and confidently explored his movement options in every role he played.

Key Words and Key Practices

Centering (Ch. 17) – the sensation of balance that originates in the area midway between your head and feet and the support that radiates from it; the center of gravity in your body

Continuum (Sec. VII Intro) - the range of movement available within each of Laban's Efforts: Space, Time, Weight, and Flow

Dynamic Thinking (Sec. III Intro) – thoughts that gently activate ease of movement; dynamic thoughts are receptive to your *kinesthetic sense* and grounded in the facts of your body and how it moves

Efforts (Sec. VII Intro) – Rudolf Laban's term for your relationship to the four elements of movement: Space, Time, Weight, and Flow

End-gaining (Ch. 10) – putting results ahead of process; disregarding how you are moving in favor of reaching a predetermined goal

The Four Brothers (Ch. 20) – Michael Chekhov's guiding principles that provide continuity for everything we do as actors; the Four Brothers are a foundation for our movement and our acting: a Feeling of Ease, a Feeling of Form, a Feeling of Beauty, a Feeling of the Whole

Friendly Facts (Sec. II Intro) – the truth of your body's design, which supports dynamic movement; body-facts

Ground Reaction Force (GRF) (Ch. 8) – the upward force exerted by the ground on your body, equal to the weight your body exerts on the ground; GRF causes your muscles to activate, spreading ground support upward and outward throughout your body

Grounding (Ch. 8) – the dynamic relationship between your feet and the ground; accepting support of the ground throughout your whole body

Inclusive Attention (Ch. 1) – awareness of your whole *3-D body* and the world around you; inclusive attention draws information from all your senses, including your kinesthetic sense

Initiation (Ch. 9) – the specific place in your body where a movement begins

Inner Experience to Outer Expression (Ch. 19) – Michael Chekhov's term for translating an actor's intellectual and emotional response into actions that can be seen and felt by an audience

Kinesphere (Ch. 14) – your sphere of movement, your personal 3-D reach space

Kinesthetic Awareness (Ch. 1) – light, gentle attention to movement sensations throughout your body, as well as an awareness of your body in space

Kinesthetic Imagination (Ch. 19) – sensing a movement in your body before you actually do it; allowing imagined *kinesthetic sensations* to organize your movement

Kinesthetic Sense (Ch. 1) – our spatial and muscular sense; the sensation of movement in the muscles; muscle memory; the awareness of the relationship of your body to itself and the space around it

Life-body (Ch. 19) – the vital sense of movement and energy that is always flowing within our living body; the energetic force that moves us: life-force

Little Intellect (Ch. 19) – Michael Chekhov's term for the analytical part of our brain that judges and comments on our creative explorations

Multi-tracking (Ch. 30) – our ability to notice and combine multiple threads of information as we execute a task. Onstage this might include *kinesthetic awareness*, ensemble, blocking, and sensory information such as lighting, sound, and audience response

Near-reach, Mid-reach, Far-reach Space (Ch.28) – Rudolf Laban's definition of our personal relationship with space, within the *Kinesphere* and beyond. Our use of space connects us and defines our unique relationships with people and the world around us

Over-efforting (Ch. 8) – using more muscle force than we need when we are moving or standing in stillness; over-efforting occurs when we interfere with the flow of movement through our muscles, bones, and joints

Part Within the Whole (Ch. 4) – every part of your anatomy has its function within the whole of your body. No part moves in isolation, and when we move a specific part of our body, we broaden our attention to include its connection to the whole. Your *primary coordination* is a guide for each *part within the whole*

Phrasing (Ch. 9) – allowing every movement to have a beginning (initiation), middle (sequencing), and end (natural conclusion)

Poising (Ch. 17) – sensing the dynamic balance of your head with your whole body

Primary Coordination (Ch. 12) – the naturally balanced relationship of your head and spine to your whole body; our dynamically organized support and balance

Qualities of Movement (Ch. 26) – Developed by Michael Chekhov, the *Qualities of Movement* are foundational ways of moving: *molding, flowing, flying, radiating*

Response (Ch. 10) – a movement we make in reaction to a *stimulus*

Reverberation (Ch. 8) – the sharing of effort from muscle to muscle, as movement *sequences* through your body. "Give and take" between muscles, bones, and tendons as they support or yield to a movement

Sequence of Directional Thinking (Ch. 12) – a series of *dynamic thoughts* which guide us out of a pattern of tension, and return us to our *primary coordination*

Sequencing (Ch. 9) – once a movement begins, the pathway it follows through your body

Shaping (Ch. 27) – creating 3-D sculptural forms with your body in space, in movement or in stillness

Spy back (Introduction) – a moment to look back on an exploration and describe your experience

Stage areas (Ch. 32) – divisions indicating parts of the stage – there are nine stage areas, known as blocks. The blocks farthest away from the audience are: up left, up center, up right. The blocks in the middle are: center right, center, center left. The blocks closest to the audience are: down left, down center, down right

Stage plane (Ch. 32) – each horizontal row of blocks (the areas – up, center, down) on a stage

Startle Pattern (Ch. 12) – a pattern of tension that occurs when the muscles at the back of your neck tighten. The startle pattern is a whole-body *response* to stress or danger. When this pattern becomes chronic, it causes an imbalance throughout your whole body, interfering with your *primary coordination*

Stimulus (Ch. 10) – an internal thought or external event that provokes a *response*

Tensegrity (Ch. 8) – In your body, the bones provide a structure that both stretches and stabilizes the muscles. The tension of your tendons and muscles maintains the integrity of the bony structure, and therefore, no movement happens in isolation

Tensile Forces (Ch. 13) – The balance of muscles, tendons, and bones that stabilize and energize our movements; opposition. Tensile forces are always balancing and rebalancing our bodies within the force of gravity

Key Practices (Listed Alphabetically)

5 Cues (Ch. 17) – a series of dynamic thoughts designed to connect and enliven your whole body. Each cue focuses on awakening your coordinated body from the ground up and building awareness of your whole self. The 5 Cues are: *grounding*, *centering*, expanding, *poising*, flying

Balanced Resting State (Ch. 3) – lying down with your head supported by books, the soles of your feet on the floor, your knees toward the ceiling, and your whole back and upper arms supported by the floor. The *balanced resting state* provides restful support for your spine and whole body

Constructive Rest (Restful Break #1) – lying down in the *balanced resting state* and bringing awareness to your coordinated *body-mind*. Constructive rest offers a restful pause to "reset" your *body-mind*. Your body receives constructive thoughts designed to release habitual tension patterns, and your mind listens to the *kinesthetic* messages your body is offering

Crossing the Threshold (Sec. VI Intro) – a core practice in the Michael Chekhov Technique in which you are invited to pause and take a moment to commit to your creative work and yourself as an artist. Often practiced at the beginning of a rehearsal, actors step across an imaginary line into their character and the world of the play

Dimensional Scale (Ch. 13) – moving in the vertical, horizontal, and sagittal directions to awaken your *3-D body* and strengthen your sense of *3-D space*. Developed by movement pioneer Rudolf Laban

Exploring Kinesphere (Ch. 14) – an activation of your *kinesthetic sense* as you explore possibilities for claiming your 3-D space within your "movement bubble"

Kinesthetic Moment (Ch. 1) – a moment of stillness, a pause, placing light attention on the *kinesthetic* sensations of your *3-D body in the 3-D space*. Your mind is quiet, as it receives *kinesthetic* sensation – without trying to describe it. *Kinesthetic moment* is usually practiced in a movement exploration – at the beginning, to prepare your *body-mind*, or at the end, to allow you to take in the experience

Kinesthetic Sensing (Ch. 1) – placing your attention on sensation – without trying to analyze or describe it. You are strengthening *kinesthetic* communication from your body to your mind

Movement Duologue (Ch. 31) – a *movement monologue* for two, expressing the characters' arcs and the arc of a scene

Movement Homework (Ch. 31) – the foundational explorations, such as *the qualities of movement* and the *Efforts*, that lead you to dynamic, specific character choices

Movement Monologue (Ch. 31) – a one- to two-minute physical expression of a character's arc, their inner journey, in a monologue, scene, or play

Moving Through Your Joints (Ch. 4) – taking a "movement tour" of the multiple possibilities for unique joint action throughout your body; sensing the joint connections between your bones

Roll-Down (Ch. 7) – A whole-body movement sequence that connects all your joints as you roll your head forward with your torso following, then return your body to upright balance

Staccato-Legato (Ch. 30) – a dynamic whole-body practice developed by Michael Chekhov, which explores tempo, six directions, and your *3-D body in 3-D space*

Suspension and Support (Ch. 17) – a whole-body practice developed by Betsy Polatin: sensing our body's ability to suspend and support simultaneously

Appendix I
Practices for Further Exploration

We encourage you to revisit the Practices throughout *YBK*. You will find that each time you visit them, you can discover something new. As Michael Chekhov said, "Repetition is the growing power."[1]

Some of those Practices are particularly helpful as warm-ups, and we've listed them below. After the warm-ups are other explorations that provide additional investigations into the elements and principles you have explored in *YBK*.

Warming Up

Warm-ups are essential to an actor's *mind–body* connection. Warm-up Practices awaken your *kinesthetic sense*, calm your *body-mind*, free and enliven your whole body, and connect with your *primary coordination*.

Below are suggested Practices for warming up. You can choose which ones work best for you. You can create your own warm-up sequence from those listed, or from other Practices that awaken, calm, and center you. When practiced in a group, these warm-ups can also create a sense of ensemble.

The Practices in Chapters 2 and 3 are useful as warm-ups.

The explorations in Chapter 11 free your body from unnecessary tension and connect your whole body through your *3 Places of Poise* (Practice 11.7).

Key Practices for warming up:

Practice 1.4 *Kinesthetic Sensing*
Practice 4.1 *Moving Through Your Joints*
Practices 13.2 and 15.3 *The Dimensional Scale*
Practice 17.4 *The 5 Cues* is an effective way to connect with your *primary coordination*.

Practice VI.1 *Crossing the Threshold*
Practice 30.1 *Staccato-Legato*

The Practices below are arranged by chapter, and you can explore them as you are ready. They provide further support for your explorations into your creative *body-mind-imagination*. Let your curiosity and your needs be your guide.

Section I: *Kinesthetic Sensing, 3-Dimensional Body, Breath*

As you become more familiar with your senses, your body, and your breath, you can move on to more complex explorations. Enjoy developing your *kinesthetic sense*, your *3-D body*, and *inclusive attention*.

REVISIT PRACTICE 1.3

Though you are developing some important movement awareness in this Practice, don't forget to play! This Practice is different than the ball games in Chapter 20. As you play, place your attention on all the aspects of your *kinesthetic sense*, such as relationship, effort, and sensation.

Part I: Solo

* Follow the steps for Practice 1.3, Part I with this difference: use a real ball (hint: a Koosh ball or bean bag is easier to catch).
* *Spy back*. What did you notice about the amount of effort you used as you threw the ball and caught it? How did you respond, body and mind, when you failed – or almost failed – to catch the ball? What did you notice about your breath? How does this information serve you as an actor?

Through this Practice you can expand your awareness of your body and breath, while your primary focus is the activity. This prepares you to be more aware of your physical presence when you are performing.

Part II: Partners

* Repeat Part I above, with a partner.

Practicing with a partner allows you to respond spontaneously to an activity, while maintaining *kinesthetic awareness*, of course! These skills are most helpful to you onstage.

Revisit this Practice often as you work your way through *YBK*.

REVIST PRACTICE 1.4 VARIATION   KINESTHETIC SENSING

Remind yourself: when you are practicing *kinesthetic sensing*, the analytical part of your brain "takes a back seat." Your mind receives sensation, without analyzing or describing it. *Spy back* offers the chance to put words to your physical experience.

In this exploration, you can experience the sensation of movement in your muscles, tendons, and joints in a more complex action: walking.

- Stand. Pause. Take a *kinesthetic moment*.
- Have a walk around the room, as you practice *kinesthetic sensing* and *inclusive attention*.
- Allow your analytical brain to become receptive to the *kinesthetic sensations* of walking.
- After several minutes, pause. Breathe. Take a *kinesthetic moment*.
- *Spy back*.

PRACTICE 2.4   GETTING TO KNOW YOUR 3-D BODY

- You can become more aware of your *3-D body* by paying attention to any activity in daily life, such as brushing your teeth, driving, or washing dishes. Your *kinesthetic sense* and *inclusive attention* can guide you. What happens if you sense your back when you are brushing your teeth? How about when you are washing dishes?
- Spend time looking in the mirror – at something other than the front of you. Not in a critical way, but just turn to the side and become more familiar with that part of you. Look at your back – all the way from the back of your head to your heels. After several minutes, close your eyes and sense each of your dimensions and the balance available when all three are equally at play in your body.
- Move your *3-D body* any way you like. Play. Diagonals and spirals connect your three dimensions. With *kinesthetic sensing* as your guide, discover the interplay between them. Pause. Take a *kinesthetic moment*.
  Now, with your *3-D body* wide awake from practicing 3-D movement, try speaking a few lines, a poem, or singing. Maintain your inclusive awareness of your *3-D body* as you speak.
- *Spy back*. What is your experience of your *3-D body* in these activities?

REVISIT PRACTICE 3.2   **VARIATION: 3-D BREATH – SITTING/STANDING/IN MOTION**

In the variations below, remember to practice *inclusive attention* while exploring your 3-D breath. These practices should be explored over several days, not all at once. Warm up before you begin.

- Repeat Practice 3.2 while seated, then while standing. Each time you explore the Practice, focus on each dimension separately. Then you can connect them: experience all three dimensions at once – the cylindrical shape of your moving torso – as your whole body breathes.
- You can also experience each individual dimension of your 3-D breath in simple activities: type, sing scales, practice vocal exercises, or walk.
- Next, explore the interplay of your three dimensions as you practice these activities.
- Pause. Take a *kinesthetic moment.*
- *Spy back.*

Section II: You Are Designed for Movement

Before beginning any of the explorations in Section II, warm up by moving through your joints or one of the Practices in the Warm-up section above.

Individual Practice: Section II

REVISIT PRACTICE 5.3   **VARIATION: EXPERIENCING THE FULL LENGTH OF YOUR SPINE, PART II**

In Practice 5.3, you walked with the back of your hand on your sacrum and your other hand on the back of the fat part of your head, sensing your whole spine within your whole body (Figure 5.8). Now, you can repeat this Practice, and carry this sense of your whole spine into sitting.

This exploration is most effective when you have a working knowledge of your Big 3 leg joints, so you may want to wait till you have read Chapter 7 to explore this Practice.

- After walking and sensing your whole spine, stand a few inches in front of a chair. Release your Big 3 leg joints, allowing your thighs to release from your pelvis, the backs of your knees to come forward, and your ankle joints to release in response.
- Maintain a sense of your whole spine – hands remain on your head and sacrum – as your body lowers in space.

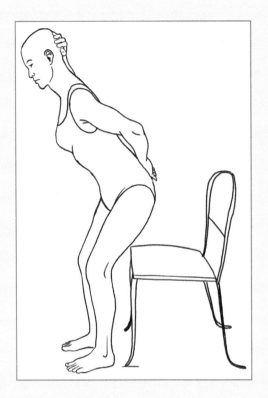

Figure A.1

- Notice that you maintain the integrity of your whole spine as your sit bones meet the chair.
- Pause. Remove your hands and let them rest at your sides or on your lap. Enjoy the sense of your whole balanced body as you sit. Take a *kinesthetic moment.*
- Continuing to sense the full length of your spine, come to standing.
- Practice walking as you sense the full length of your spine. When needed, you can pause and replace your hands at the top and bottom of your spine as a reminder.
- Return to the chair and, without using your hands as reminders, sense the full length of your spine as you sit.
- *Spy back.* How does sensing your whole spine affect your movement? What did you discover about your body's natural balance when sitting?

PRACTICE 7.6   **THE TWIST**

The Twist was a popular dance from the 1960s. Perhaps you've seen it.

In this dance, you can explore a wealth of twisting action throughout your body, activating your joints and all their connections. It's a good idea to warm up your leg joints – examples in Chapter 7 – and your whole body before beginning this Practice.

Before you begin, watch the video of Chubby Checker, the singer who made *The Twist* famous, on YouTube, and note all the ways he uses twisting action in his joints in this fun video: www.youtube.com/watch?v=pHGXwQeUk7M. You can also watch vintage videos clips of other people doing *The Twist*. You will want to play music for this Practice!

Notice that *The Twist* originates from your pelvis, your center of gravity. Be sure that you don't isolate your legs but allow them to be supported by your whole body.

Part I

- Pause. Breathe. Take a *kinesthetic moment*.
- Now try *The Twist*!
- If you like, you can begin by standing on one leg and twisting the other leg, to get a sense of the rolling action at your hip joint. Then switch sides.
- Gradually begin the full-body motion of the dance. Bring awareness to the 3-D spiraling movements in all your joints. Most of all, have fun using your expressive body!
- After you dance, pause. Take a *kinesthetic moment*.
- Practice *inclusive attention* as you have a walk around the space.
- *Spy back*. In what ways does your knowledge of joint action impact these movements? What do you notice about your whole body when you allow your joints to work together?

Part II: Variation

After you have read and experienced *initiation and sequencing* in Chapter 9, you can repeat this Practice, playing with different *initiations* while twisting. This can be especially fun when standing on one leg and twisting the other leg. Try *initiating* your leg twist from your heel, your knee, or your hip joint. Note how differently each choice then *sequences* through your leg and then through your whole body!

This is another Practice that will "grow" as you learn more about your coordinated body. Revisit often!

PRACTICE 9.4 **ARM JOINT SEQUENCE**

We discovered this Practice in a workshop with Alexander/Laban teacher Melody Schaper (used with permission).

Enjoy *sequencing* through the joints in your whole arm structure. This exploration has a lot of detail – you may wish to have someone guide you by reading the instructions for you, or you can record them.

- Stand. Pause. Breathe. Take a *kinesthetic moment*.
- Have a walk around the room, noticing sensation.
- Lie on your back with your knees up and your feet resting on the floor. Allow your arms to stretch out on the floor, palms up, on either side. Extend your arms directly out from the shoulder joint, not lower or higher. (An interesting kinesthetic experiment is to sense this, then look to see if your arms are actually lined up with your shoulder joints. This will give you an idea if your *body map* and your awareness match up with each other.)

Sensing Your Arm Structure

- Begin by closing your eyes and use your *kinesthetic awareness* to sense each part of your arm structure on your right side.
  Sense each part in a *sequence*, one part at the time, from your fingertips, through your fingers, hand, wrist, lower arm, upper arm, all the way through your collarbone and shoulder blade.
  Then reverse: Sense each *part within the whole* in a *sequence* from your collarbone/shoulder blade to your fingertips.
- Repeat with your left arm.

Sequencing Through Your Arm Structure

Allow your whole body to support your movement, as you explore this *sequencing* Practice.

- Returning your attention to your right side, with both arms still on the floor, *initiate* a movement of your fingertips and thumb, moving them gently toward the left side of your body.
- Let each part of your finger follow the tip. Then allow your hand to follow your fingers. Arms are still on the floor at this point. Breathe as you move.
- Next, your wrist follows your hand, followed by your lower arm. As you move through your elbow joint, your upper arm remains on the floor. Fingertips are still leading the way toward the left side of your body. Breathe.
- Next, your upper arm follows your lower arm, and your shoulder blade and collarbone follow. Breathe.

- Your right fingertips and arm are reaching to the left. Breathe.
- Now reverse: breathe and allow each joint to roll and glide as you "unfold." *Initiate* an opening from your collarbone and shoulder blade. Your shoulder blade comes to rest on the floor, followed by your upper arm, lower arm, wrist, hand, fingers.
- Your entire connected hand/arm/shoulder blade is outstretched on the floor.
- Pause. Rest. Breathe. Take a *kinesthetic moment*. Repeat on the other side.

Practicing the Flow of Movement

- Practice this *initiation* and *sequencing* exploration several times. Place your attention on sensing movement, and allowing movement to flow through your whole body, not just your arm. (This flow includes your breath!)
- You can try this sequence at different speeds as well; continue to keep the *sequence* clear and the movement flowing – avoid unnecessary tension for the sake of going "fast!"
- After exploring on both sides several times, pause. Take a *kinesthetic moment*.
- Come to standing by rolling to one side, gently pressing your hands against the floor to come to sitting, and then rising to standing. Pause. Look around.
- Notice your arms supported by your whole body. Move your arms in some simple movements, such as reaching for an object, smoothing your hair.
- Take a walk around the room, noticing yourself, your arms, and your whole body. See the space – practice *inclusive attention*. Pause.
- *Spy back*. How did your awareness of your arms shift through this Practice, beginning to end? Were there differences in your walk at the beginning and end of the Practice? If so, what were they?

This exploration allows you to sense the continuity of your whole arm structure supported by your body.

REVISIT PRACTICE 9.4   VARIATION: ARM JOINT PLAY

In this exploration, you can expand on Practice 9.4, as you take an "arm tour" by *initiating* movement in many directions through your arm joints.

- Stand. Pause. Take a *kinesthetic moment*.
- Allow the fingertips of your hand to lead your arm upward. Follow the movement *sequence* as it travels through the joints of your arm, eventually including your collarbone and shoulder blade.
- Reverse the *sequence*, letting your collarbone and shoulder blade release as your arm lengthens downward by your side. Pause.
- Repeat with the other arm. Pause.
- Repeat with both arms moving simultaneously.

- You can also reverse the *sequence*, beginning with your collarbones and shoulder blades.
- Other options: play with this *sequence* by *initiating* the movement at your elbows, your wrists, your thumbs. Where else might you *initiate* movement?
- Allow your arms to explore a wide range of actions: reaching up, down, side to side, forward, back, spiraling.
- You can also create patterns in space, like a figure eight or waves. Allow different parts of your arm to create the patterns.
- Play with rhythm and timing, connecting your arms with your whole body as they lead you around the room.
- Pause. Stand. Take a *kinesthetic moment*.
- *Spy back*. What did you discover about the dynamic connections between your arms and your body as you explored space?

Variations

- Repeat the above Practice, taking a "leg tour." You may want to begin by lying on the floor for this Practice, eventually moving to standing, crawling, or other actions.
- Or repeat, taking a "head–spine–pelvis tour."

PRACTICE 9.5 WALKING EXPLORATION

Walking is a powerful action of locomotion through space.

When you practice *kinesthetic awareness*, you can sense a subtle *sequence* of movements through your body and your unique personal rhythm. Everyone's walk is different: in this exploration, you can explore the unique qualities of your walk.

Warm up before you begin.

- Pause. Stand. Breathe. Take a *kinesthetic moment*.
- Walk through the room, exploring a range of different pathways in space.
- Begin to sense your personal rhythm. Become aware of this inner rhythm guiding your walk.
- Notice how your inner rhythm subtly orchestrates the timing of your stride.
- Then notice how your inner rhythm guides your whole coordinated body as the movement *sequences* through your body.
- Gradually begin to exaggerate your rhythm in time and space, allowing the pattern to become more visible and energized. Avoid forcing – allow the *sequence* to move through your whole body.
- If you are in a group, become aware of other people, and enjoy interacting with them.
- Gradually return to a simple walk through the space.

- Pause. Breathe. Take a *kinesthetic moment*.
- *Spy back*. What did you notice about your own walking pattern? What did you notice about other people's walking patterns?

Variations

- Play with your walk, exaggerate its rhythms and connections. Then begin to improvise and play with creating a variety of walks, finding the inner rhythms, and allowing their full physical expression. Allow yourself to interact with others, each from your own walking pattern.
- Explore the inner rhythm of a character you may be portraying; embody this walk, and let the pattern influence your interactions with other movers, as they explore their own character's walk.
- Return to your signature walk and pause. What is the difference between your character walk and your personal walk?

Partner Practice: Section II

Reminder: when touch is involved in an exploration, take a moment to stand face to face. Then take hands and pause, sharing a moment of connection, commitment, and safety before moving into the Practice.

In the exploration below, the person touching their partner's back is providing information about this area of the body. Let your touch be light, gentle, and receptive. Sense your partner's back and sense their back touching your hand.

Warm up before you begin these explorations.

PRACTICE 5.4 **HANDS ON YOUR PARTNER'S BACK**

Wake up your back as you explore your head–spine–pelvis connection.

- Stand. Pause. Take a *kinesthetic moment*. Breathe.
- Partner 1 stands behind Partner 2 and places their hands on 2's back.
- Partner 2 closes their eyes and begins to move through their head–spine–pelvis, while Partner 1 simply follows and subtly changes the position of their hands as needed. Allow your whole body to respond to these movements.
- At some point during the duet, Partner 1 and Partner 2 gradually change roles, while continuing the journey of their duet.
- At the end of the second duet, both partners pause, and each person steps back into their own space.
- Breathe. Take a *kinesthetic moment*.
- Take a walk around the room, noticing your whole *3-D body*.

- *Spy back.* How does this practice affect your awareness of your back within your whole body? What was it like to move with awareness of your back?

PRACTICE 6.5 LEADING WITH HANDS

- Pause. Stand. Breathe. Take a *kinesthetic moment*.
- Partner 1 and Partner 2 stand opposite each other.
- Partner 1 closes their eyes. Partner 2 takes 1's hands.
- Partner 1 allows Partner 2 to move their hands – gently exploring movement through their whole arm structure.
- After exploring for a few minutes, Partner 1 allows Partner 2 to move them through the space.
- Each person in the duet listens with their whole body, as one person guides the other, offering and receiving.
- At the end of the duet, Partner 1 opens their eyes; without speaking, both partners pause and release hands. Take a *kinesthetic moment*.
- Have a walk around the space. *Spy back* with your partner.
- Reverse roles and repeat the practice above.

PRACTICE 6.6 TOUCHING FINGERTIPS

- Pause. Stand. Breathe. Take a *kinesthetic moment*.
- Stand opposite your partner, with arms at ease, each of you sensing your whole body.
- Lightly join the tips of your index fingers.
- There is no leader/follower relationship in this exploration. With eyes closed, create a mutual duet with your partner, allowing movement to emerge from the fingertip connection.
- When you feel this exploration is complete, find a mutual moment to pause, release your fingers, and step back from each other.
- Pause. Breathe. Take a *kinesthetic moment*.
- *Spy back.* What was it like to sense another's movement and respond through this point of contact? Share with your partner.

REVISIT PRACTICE 9.5 VARIATION: WALKING EXPLORATION: PARTNER/ GROUP

- Revisit Practice 9.5, Walking Exploration, from Appendix I above, with this change: walk side by side with a partner; one partner begins to fully embody the inner rhythm of their walk, allowing it to gradually become more visible, and the other partner gradually allows themselves to take on this pattern as they walk together.

- Then reverse roles.
- *Spy back.* What did you discover when you embodied your partner's walk by taking on their inner rhythm?

Group Practice: Section II

Remember to warm up before beginning these Practices.

PRACTICE 9.8   CASTING SPELLS

When you free your body, you free your creativity. Explore joint action, *initiation*, and *sequencing* and the ways it can support you in creative movement.

- Stand. Pause. Breathe. Take a *kinesthetic moment.*
- Stand in a circle with the group.
- Warm up your whole body by *sequencing* through your joints (Practice 4.1).
- Pause. Breathe. Take a *kinesthetic moment.*
- Imagine that you have a large cauldron in front of you. There is a magic potion brewing. Play with stirring movements, beginning with wrist action, then your elbow, then your shoulder joint. You can move around your cauldron, playing with stirring from different angles.
- Allow the movements to *sequence* through your whole arm and into your body. Pause.
- Repeat with the other arm.
- When you have stirred on both sides, pause and set your imaginary cauldron aside. You are a magician. Use your arm joint action to cast a variety of spells.
- As you cast spells, allow your movements to *sequence* through your arms and your whole body.
- Play with large and small movements *initiating* from different places: wrists, elbows, fingertips.
- From these initiations, carve out patterns in space, and create timing changes (quick sparks of light, slow, large circles, etc.). Pause.
- One at a time, each person takes a turn to cast a spell.
- Everyone echoes that spell. The leader passes that spell to the next person. That person transforms the first spell into a new spell for the whole group.
- The process continues around the circle until everyone has cast their spell for the group.
- Then everyone casts a spell simultaneously.
- Pause. Breathe. Take a *kinesthetic moment.*
- *Spy back.* What did you discover about *initiation, sequencing,* and your joints as you moved in a creative activity?

PRACTICE 9.9 **ROUND ROBIN**

In this exploration you can practice *initiation* and *sequencing*. Put on some music, such as "Respect" by Aretha Franklin or "I Heard It Through the Grapevine" by Marvin Gaye. "See You Again," Charlie Puth and Wiz Khalifa, is an interesting mix of rhythms and tempos.

The group stands in a circle. Pause. Breathe. Take a *kinesthetic moment.*

- One person steps into the center of the circle and begins to *initiate* movement via different *body leads.*
- Three to four people join the leader and move with them, varying the leader's choices, as they feel inspired.
- The people in the larger circle echo the choices of the movers in the center, in smaller, more subtle ways.
- When the lead person has completed their exploration, they catch the eye of a person in the larger circle.
- That person takes the lead, entering the center of the circle. The first group returns to the circle, and others join the new leader.
- Continue to repeat the above process until each person has had a turn as leader. Then pause. Breathe. Take a *kinesthetic moment.*
- *Spy back* with the group.

Section III: What You Think Is What You Get

Individual Practice

PRACTICE 12.3 **STIMULUS, RESPONSE, AND YOUR PRIMARY COORDINATION**

Your body is instantly responsive to the world around you. Even imagined circumstances can affect your whole coordination as you will discover in the Practice below.

- Sit on a chair. Pause. Take a *kinesthetic moment.*
- Sense your sit bones. If you need to, rock side to side to help you find them.
- Feel the support of the chair through your sit bones. Allow the support to move up through all four curves of your spine right up to the top of your head; sense the gentle balance of your head at your A-O joint.
- Notice your breath and your relationship to the room around you.
- Now imagine you've received a piece of bad news, such as, you didn't receive a coveted role you were sure you were going to get.

- Let your body shrink inward, shoulders roll forward, chest and spine collapse. Notice your breath and your relationship to the room around you. Sense the downward pressure in your body.
- Now, imagine that it was all a mistake. You got the role! Allow your body to do whatever it wants to express the joy you feel.
- Notice your breath, your whole coordinated body, and your relationship to the room.
- Pause. Take a *kinesthetic moment*. Have a walk around the room.
- *Spy back.* What did you notice about your body's responses to a strong stimulus? What did you notice about your body's flexibility in response to change? Did it take a long time or a short time?

You can create other scenarios that affect your whole coordination. Learn how *stimulus* and *response* affect your whole body.

Section IV: Claiming Your Inner and Outer Space

Individual Practice: Section IV

PRACTICE 15.8 **AN EXTRA SET OF EYES**

To develop a sense of your *3-D body in the 3-D space*, Lenard Petit, master teacher of the Michael Chekhov Technique, encourages his students to imagine an extra set of eyes in their shoulder blades as they move about the space. Try it. You may find that this image expands your awareness of your *Kinesphere* and your whole *3-D body.*[2]

Section V: Progression Toward Presence

Individual Practice: Section V

REVISIT PRACTICE 17.4 **VARIATION: CONNECTING ROLL-DOWN WITH THE 5 CUES**

As you begin your day, or prior to movement class, a rehearsal, audition, or performance, you can practice joining the *5 cues* with the *roll-down* (Practice 9.2).

- Pause. Breathe. Take a *kinesthetic moment*.
- Begin by simply thinking the *5 cues*: *grounding*, *centering*, expanding, *poising*, flying.

- Repeat these thoughts, allowing the energy of these directions to build from the ground up, until your whole body responds and your arms "fly" forward, up, and out from your whole back.
- With your arms still "flying," pause. Breathe. Be aware of your whole energized body.
- Gently release your arms at your wrists, then elbows, and then shoulder joints, allowing your arms to return to your sides.
- Your awareness of the *5 cues* can energize you, as you begin a *roll-down*.
- Follow the *roll-down* to completion, pause, and breathe.
- Return to standing.
- Pause. Breathe. Take a *kinesthetic moment*.

You are "ready for anything, prepared for nothing."

Group Practice: Section V

REVISIT PRACTICE 17.1 **VARIATION: MAKING CONNECTIONS**

Actors sometimes lose their sense of 3-dimensionality when sharing text. We can get so focused on the person in front of us, we forget our *3-D body in the 3-D space*. In this variation on Practice 17.1, a gentle reminder from a partner can change your perception of yourself and your audience.

After warming up, the class divides into two groups. One person from Group A partners with one person from Group B. Group B are the speakers/receivers.

Group A will place a hand on their partner's back, about the level (between) of their shoulder blades. The intention of Group A is to provide a gentle awareness of the speaker's back. A soft, receptive hand is most effective. Think of your hand touching your partner's back, and their back touching your hand.

After exploring Part I of Practice 17.1, go on to Part II, using the variation below.

- Stand with your partner. Breathe. Take a *kinesthetic moment*.
- Group A, place your hand on your partner's back.
- Take a walk around the space together. Practice *inclusive attention*.
- After a few minutes, Group B begins to share their line – or other text – with the people they meet, enjoying the support of their partner's hand. Pause.
- Group A removes their hand from their partner's back. Group B thanks their partner for their support.
- Everyone takes a walk around the space. Pause.
- Return to your partner and switch roles.
- Pause. Take a *kinesthetic moment*.
- *Spy back.* Did your partner's hand on your back support your interaction with others? In what way? How might this exploration serve you as an actor?

Section VI: Authenticity and Commitment

Individual Practice: Section VI

PRACTICE 18.1   AUTHENTIC IMPULSE – SOLO VARIATION

If you do not have a partner, you can still experience the joy of connecting with your *authentic impulses* by moving on your own. Alone, you become both the mover and the observer as you experiment with allowing your body to move naturally: pause, listen to your breathing, the subtle shifting of weight in your body as you ground and center yourself in relationship with gravity.

Small movements will begin to happen naturally, due to the dynamic qualities of your body. Your muscles rhythmically shorten and lengthen, and your many joints are alive with possibility for change.

Warm up before you begin.

- Stand. Pause. Breathe. Take a *kinesthetic moment.*
- Lie down, allow the back surfaces of your body to connect with the floor.
- Close your eyes, breathe, and listen to the rhythmic movement of your breath.
- Begin to notice any small movement changes taking place in your body; perhaps your head is delicately moving from side to side, or maybe you feel some movements of release in your back.
- Continue to notice your breathing, and any small movement impulses in your arms and legs.
- Allow these movement impulses to guide you into fuller movement through your body. Open your eyes for safety as needed.
- You may feel that your body wants to move and change shape. You can recognize when the movement happens naturally and when you are "making" it happen.
- No judgement is necessary as you allow movement to *sequence* through your body.
- Your relationship with the floor may change; you can recognize the inner impulse that *initiates* any spontaneous movement.
- You can roll or change shape. Follow your *authentic impulses*. Open your eyes for safety if you begin to make large movements.
- Pause. Breathe. Take a *kinesthetic moment.*
- *Spy back*. What did you experience as you connected with the floor and began to listen to your body's natural movements?

You can sense the flow of life through your body: your breath, your heartbeat, and small changes that pass through you as you connect with the floor. These small impulses can guide and direct you into larger movements that are authentic and grounded in your unique expression of character and text.

Partner/Group Practice: Section VI

REVIST PRACTICE VI.1   VARIATION: CROSSING THE THRESHOLD

We encountered this Practice in a class with Chekhov master teacher, Joanna Merlin.

- After establishing the initial group circle, stand. Pause.
- "Breathe in your natural rhythm with a feeling of ease. As you breathe, imagine that you are breathing in a sensation of openness which flows through your body. On the exhalation imagine you are opening the space around you."[3]
- Turn away from the circle and take a private moment for yourself. Stand. Pause. Breathe.
- When you are ready, turn back to face the rest of the group in the circle.
- When everyone is facing the inside of the circle, the group Pauses, breathes, takes a *kinesthetic moment*.
- When everyone is ready, the whole group takes a step forward at the same time, *crossing the threshold* together.
- Pause. Breathe. Take a *kinesthetic moment*. See the others in the circle: you are ready for class, rehearsal, or performance.

This group Practice can be done at the beginning of a class or rehearsal. At the end of the class, the group can step back across the threshold as a group, and the actors return to their daily activities.

REVISIT PRACTICE 20.6   VARIATION: A FEELING OF WHOLENESS

This exploration builds on Parts I and II of Practice 20.6. Practice *inclusive attention*, and trust that a *feeling of the whole* will support you.

- Revisit Parts I and II of Practice 20.6.
- Move about the space, meeting and greeting others, maintaining your *feeling of the whole*. Sense the wholeness of your body as you shake hands, hug, or high-five someone. As your bodies touch, you create a new sense of wholeness. Sense the wholeness of the group within the room and your place within it.
- After a few minutes, have a walk around the space.
- With an awareness of a *feeling of the whole*, share the first line of a monologue, as you meet another person.
- You can maintain a *feeling of the whole* as you become an audience for their line. After a moment, move on and repeat the process.
- At some point, you may choose to share your whole monologue, maintaining a *feeling of the whole*.

- Be receptive as you allow others to share their monologue as well. Recognize the *feeling of wholeness* as actor and audience share this moment.
- Pause. Take a *kinesthetic moment*.
- *Spy back.* What was your experience of interacting with others with a *feeling of the whole*?

This Practice can be repeated with an emphasis on each of the other *brothers* and, of course, with all *four brothers* at once.

PRACTICE 20.7 GIVING AND RECEIVING: GROUP VARIATIONS

We encountered these games in workshops at the Michael Chekhov Association, the Great Lakes Michael Chekhov Consortium, and in master classes with Lenard Petit and Mark Monday at Florida Atlantic University.

A Koosh ball or hacky-sack work well for these Practices. You may find it helpful to sense your *life-body* make the movement before you follow with your physical body.

You can learn so much when you allow *the four brothers* to inform your movements as you practice giving and receiving. Throw with a *feeling of ease*, use your *whole* body, recognize a clear *form* in each movement – beginning, middle, and end. Throw the ball underhanded – and aim for the receiver's heart.

Appreciate the beauty in your movement and your interactions with others. *Fire the Judge, Hire the Witness*: you can learn a lot when you drop the ball – continue to practice *the four brothers*, as you retrieve the ball, return to the circle, and make eye contact with the thrower.

Staccato-legato is a great warm-up for these Practices.

The group forms a large circle.

Names

- Say the name of the person you are throwing to as the ball leaves your fingers.
- Learn everyone's nickname and say your receiver's nickname as the ball leaves your fingers.
- If you are practicing with the company of a play, you can say the character's name as the ball leaves your fingers.

Patterns

- To establish a repeatable pattern, everyone in the circle raises a hand. When you receive the ball, lower your hand. Only throw to a person with their hand raised. Remember who you received from and who you threw to.
- Everyone takes a moment to point to the person they will receive the ball from. Then point to the person you will throw the ball to.

- The first person throws the ball, following the pattern you established.
- After throwing one ball in the pattern for a while, the first person can introduce a second ball, then a third, each time following the same pattern.
- Stay focused, breathe, and practice *the four brothers*.
- After several minutes, the first person collects the balls as they come to them. Pause. Take a *kinesthetic moment. Spy back.*

Intention

- There are an infinite number of variations on this Practice – one of our favorites is to practice throwing with a particular intention: "lovingly," "grandly," "sexily," "coolly." It's fun to ask the other members of the group what they thought your intention was.

Section VII: Foundations

Individual Practice: Section VII

PRACTICE 22.4 **TIME PRACTICE**

This exploration builds on a Key Practice, 4.1 *Moving Through Your Joints*, by adding *initiation* and *sequencing* via *body leads* (Practice 9.4). In addition, you can explore a third factor, the two ends of Time *continuum*: Sustained and Quick.

- Stand. Pause. Breathe. Take a *kinesthetic moment*.
- Begin to slowly move through your joints. Enjoy exploring each joint and luxuriating in the sensations of each movement.
- Now begin to play with *initiation* and *sequencing*: allow the movement impulse to pass from one joint to another in your body in a leisurely way.
- Now focus specifically on your hands and fingers and allow the movement to *sequence* all the way through to your collarbones and shoulder blades and then, back to your fingers.
- Begin to *initiate* and *sequence* movement from other *body leads*: your feet/legs; your head, spine, pelvis. Take time to savor and linger in each moment of your exploration.
- Travel through the room with Sustainment as your guide.
- Pause. Take a *kinesthetic moment*. Breathe.
- Now begin to explore the opposite end of the Time *continuum*: Quickness.
- Allow movement to *sequence* through your body in a spark-like, staccato manner, starting with your hands and arms.
- Allow this instantaneous, exciting quality of movement to *initiate* from anywhere in your body and follow its path until another part of your body takes the lead.

- Travel through the space with Quickness as your guide.
- Play with Sustainment and Quickness, *initiation and sequencing* as you continue to travel through the space.
- Pause. Breathe. Take a *kinesthetic moment.*
- *Spy back.* What did you notice about your relationship to Time, as you explored Sustainment and Quickness? What did you discover about the interplay between them as you traveled through space? How does Time affect *sequential movement?*

PRACTICE 25.2   COMFORT ZONES

Get to know your comfort zone for each of the *Efforts.* Warm up before beginning this practice.

- Explore the Crossings Practice (Chapters 21–24) for each *Effort* and discover your comfort zone for each one. Pause.
- Then play, explore, interact with others, speak some dialogue from within each comfort zone. Pause.
- Combine *Efforts* and continue to explore. Pause.
- *Spy back.*

As you go about your everyday activities, notice how your comfort zones create your unique movement.

Partner/Group Practice: Section VII

PRACTICE 24.4   RED-LIGHT, GREEN-LIGHT

You can play with Flow through this children's game. Warm up before you begin.

One person is "It." They stand at the front of the room, facing the group standing at the other end. The object of the game is for someone to reach "It," and touch them, without being caught moving by "It." It's important that there be enough space for everyone to move without running into someone.

Be sure to keep breathing as you practice!

- "It" takes their place at one end of the room. Everyone else is at the other end.
- Stand. Pause. Breathe. Take a *kinesthetic moment.*
- "It" faces the group and says, "red light." Then "It" turns their back and says, "green light." This is the cue for everyone to try to reach "It," without being caught moving.

- When "It" turns around – saying "red light" – everyone stops still. If "It" sees someone moving forward – or several people – they send them back to start over.
- The first person to reach "It" without being caught moving, wins. They take "It's" place, and the game begins again.
- After several rounds, pause. Take a *kinesthetic moment*.
- *Spy back*. What did you discover about Bound and Free Flow in this Practice? What did you sense in your body when you were moving? Standing still?

PRACTICE 24.5   DISCOVERING FLOW

In this Practice, imagine that you are at a high school reunion. Notice how Flow is affected by each scenario and vice versa. Warm up before you begin.

- You have lost touch with your best friend from your school days and then you see them.
- Someone you think you remember, but when you meet, you realize you are mistaken.
- Someone you need to make amends to.
- Someone you really loved as a boyfriend or girlfriend, but you haven't seen them since high school.

You can have fun playing with the other *Efforts* in each of these scenarios as well.

REVISIT PRACTICE 25.2   VARIATION: COMFORT ZONES – PARTNERS

You can explore your *Effort* comfort zones with a partner. Though this exploration resembles the Crossings Practice you experienced in Section VII, the difference is that you and your partner are exchanging comfort zones. You are not exploring the entire *continuum* in this Practice.

If you and your partner seem to be in the same comfort zone, you can simply meet and dance. Or each partner can shift slightly toward one end of the *continuum* or the other end, until there is a discernible difference between you.

- Choose an *Effort* and go to the opposite end of the room from your partner.
- Begin to move from one end of the room toward the other, moving any way you like within your comfort zone. Your partner does the same.
- When you reach the other end of the room, pause.
- Begin to across the room again. When the two of you meet, create a "transformation dance," by taking on each other's comfort zone.
- At some point, part from your partner, moving around the room in their comfort zone.

- After some minutes, meet your partner, create another dance, returning to your comfort zone. When the dance is complete, pause. Breathe. Take a *kinesthetic moment*.
- Have another walk around the room. Pause.
- *Spy back* with your partner.

When you explore character movement, it is very helpful to know your comfort zone, and to give yourself permission to move beyond it. It's also helpful to "live" in others' comfort zones for a period of time, because you expand your array of movement choices.

Section VIII: Your Responsive Body and Imagination

Individual Practice: Section VIII

REVISIT PRACTICE 26.1 VARIATION: MOLDING, FLOWING, FLYING, RADIATING

In this variation on Practice 26.1, you can explore the *qualities of movement* and add sound.

- Follow the steps in Practice 26.1, and allow sounds to emerge as you explore each *quality*.

After exploring, you can pause and *spy back* or:

- You can allow the sounds to inform you vocally as you speak, sing, shout, whisper text. Play with sound, text, and the *qualities of movement*.
- *Spy back*. What sounds arose from each exploration? How does sound affect the movement and vice versa? Did emotions arise with the sounds and movements? How might this Practice inform your acting work?

REVISIT PRACTICE 29.1 VARIATION: DIMENSIONAL SCALE AND THE AFFINITIES

Laban noted that each direction in the *Dimensional Scale* created a certain response in our *body-mind*, a "mini-storyline" that relates to each of the *Efforts*. He called these connections between the *Efforts* and the directions, Affinities.

Reaching up, we can sense Lightness; down is associated with Strength. Reaching across ourselves, we close with Directness, and when we reach outward, we open with Indirectness. We back up, or retreat, with Quickness and we advance (move forward) with Sustainment.

Think about scenarios that suit the affinities: if you reach out to pet a dog and she snaps at you, don't you retreat with Quickness? If you are happy, you may feel lighter and throw your arms up in the air.

After warming up, practice the *Dimensional Scale* with an awareness of the Affinities.

- Stand. Pause. Take a *kinesthetic moment.*As you move in each direction, you can speak the following phrases, and allow your body to express the *Effort* that you name:
  Rising with Lightness
  Sinking with Strength
  Enclosing with Directness
  Spreading with Indirectness
  Advancing with Sustainment
  Retreating with Quickness.

- Repeat the Practice a few times, sometimes with your attention on the Affinities, sometimes with awareness of your pathways in space.
- *Spy back.* What did you discover about the directions and the Affinities? How did your body respond to the Affinities? How might this information serve you as an actor?

Partner/Group Practices: Section VIII

PRACTICE 27.1 **VARIATIONS: INTRO TO SHAPE AND SHAPING**

In these variations you can explore shaping with a partner or in a group. Enjoy the experience of creating a group 3-D shape in the 3-D space. Warm up before you begin.

Each Practice begins with the group standing in a circle, pausing, breathing, and taking a *kinesthetic moment.*

Shaping in Groups of Four

- Person 1 creates a shape, Person 2 joins them, creating their own shape in relationship to Person 1. Then 3 repeats the process, followed by 4, forming a group shape.To undo the group shape, Person 1 leaves first, followed by 2, then 3, then 4. Pause. Breathe. Take a *kinesthetic moment.* Repeat until each person has created the first shape. Complete the Practice by taking a walk around the room.

Shaping in a Large Group

- The whole group numbers off. The person with #1 starts the shape and then each person follows, as in the Practice above. To undo the shape, #1 leaves first, etc.

Pause. Breathe. Take a *kinesthetic moment.* Complete the Practice by taking a walk around the room.

Run, Meet, Shape

- Two people run toward each other, meet and create a shape together. Pause. Radiate. Release the *shape* and return to your starting place. If you are in a class, change partners and repeat. Pause. Breathe. Take a *kinesthetic moment.* Complete the Practice by taking a walk around the room.

Spy Back

- How does *shape* affect your awareness of your *3-D body in the 3-D space?* How can *shape* serve you as an actor?

PRACTICE 27.5   SHAPING WORDS

Below are word-shaping games for a group. We first encountered group-shaping Practices with Cathy Albers at the Great Lakes Michael Chekhov Consortium (used with permission).

Allow these shapes to come alive from the inside out, initiated from your *life-body.* Warm up before you begin.

- Stand. Pause. Breathe. Take a *kinesthetic moment.*
- Draw a word or a phrase from a hat – wait for an inner impulse, and allow the word/impulse to lead you into a *shape.* Others try to guess the word. Pause. Breathe. Take a *kinesthetic moment. Spy back.*
- Divide into two groups. Group A draws a word or phrase from a hat. They assume a group "sculpture," each person responding with their own shape, but also connecting with the group's shapes. Group B gives the sculpture a title or a phrase that describes what they see.
  Variation on the above: one person draws a phrase or a situation and allows their body to respond by moving into a shape. Though they don't know the word, the other members of their group join them, forming a group *shape,* based on what they see and sense. Pause. Breathe. The other group offers feedback. Take a *kinesthetic moment.*
- *Spy back* with the group.

REVISIT PRACTICE 28.1   VARIATION: DISCOVERING NEAR-, MID-, AND FAR-REACH SPACE

- As a variation on this Practice, you can revisit the scene at the ATM machine, Practice 15.5, choosing a spatial relationship – *near, mid,* or *far.* Begin the scene in that spatial relationship. Allow your relationship to change, as the scene unfolds. *Spy back*.

Part III: Creative Practice

REVISIT PRACTICE 30.1   **VARIATION: *STACCATO-LEGATO***

Name the Direction

- It can be energizing, and also add clarity to each movement, if you say the directions, "up, down, right, left, forward, back" as you move.

Opposites

- As a warm-up for an ensemble working on a play, the cast can develop three pairs of words, opposites that represent the oppositional forces within the script. After the cast determines the opposites, they say one of each pair as they move in each direction. For instance, in a production of Aristophanes' *Lysistrata*, the cast chose: Athens/Sparta, war/peace, and uh-huh/uh-uh (meaning "yes to sex" or "no to sex") as their oppositional forces.

When using the pairs of words, first practice *staccato-legato* in its original form, then repeat a few times with the "opposites."

REVISIT PRACTICE 31.3   **VARIATIONS**

Personal Movement Monologue

- A powerful variation on the *movement monologue* is to create a *personal movement monologue*. In our classes, students keep a journal, and a couple of times each semester, they choose an aspect of their movement journey to share with the class as a personal journal response. This Practice is another way of processing (and celebrating) our movement struggles, discoveries, and triumphs.

  You can also make a list of questions or topics for movement monologues: best piece of advice you've received in the last six months and how it's affected you; what scares you about acting and how it's affected you; why you act, and how that has affected your acting journey.

  You can build your personal movement monologue from the elements of movement you've explored in *YBK*.

Other Approaches to Movement Monologue or Duologue

- Ask "Who am I?" at the beginning of the monologue or scene and assume a shape or move the line, following your inner response to the text. Then "Who Am I?" in the middle. Then "Who Am I?" at the end. Develop the *movement monologue* or *duologue* from there.
- You can choose a sentence or phrase from the text – just pick one – whatever comes to mind is usually the right one. Begin to move in response to the text; if there is imagery in the phrase, explore the images' texture, color, shape (one at the time).

  Explore moving your phrase: how does it inform the beginning, the middle, and the end of the monologue or scene? Allow this overarching thread to guide you, as you create a *movement monologue* or *duologue* around the different aspects of this phrase and your character's arc.
- Explore subtext, different aspects of the character, or images. Music can be very helpful – although we highly recommend exploring without music as well.
- *Duologue*: explore staying apart and coming together – a spatial exploration. Then add in *qualities of movement*. Discover the tensions and resolutions of the arc of the scene through these powerful movement tools.
- *Duologue*: develop three lines/statements that express the beginning, the middle, and end of the scene. Each actor explores movement that expresses their character's connection with each statement. Then put them together and discover how your relationship to the statements is shaped by the other character.

There are as many ways of working as there are people: discover your own!

REVISIT PRACTICE 31.4   **VARIATION: PART II – THE DYNAMIC SPACE BETWEEN CHARACTERS**

You can discover subtle (and not-so-subtle!) impulses by playing in the "opposite" spatial relationship required by a scene:

- Play an intimate scene in *far* space.
- Play a scene in which the characters are very cold toward one another in *near* space.

REVISIT PRACTICE 32.1   **VARIATION: PLAYING WITH STAGE SPACE**

More explorations for entering and exiting:

- As you play with entering and exiting the stage, explore the *Efforts* one at a time. You can significantly change your entrance or exit by changing your relationship to Time, Weight, Flow, or Space. Experiment with entering at various points on the *continuum*.
- Note that making a specific choice changes your entrance or exit. Get feedback from the audience. As you change your relationship to each *Effort*, how does the audience perception of your character change?

REVISIT PRACTICE 33.6   VARIATION: PART II – RELATIONSHIPS

Group portraits, placing different characters at the center, can be informative about changing relationships throughout the play.

- After everyone enters and gives Irina her gift, the group can move into a group portrait, as if facing a camera.
- Group portraits for Acts II, III, and IV could also be an exploration of changing relationships.

REVISIT PRACTICE 33.7   VARIATION: THE LONG GOOD-BYE

- Repeat the Practice, this time saying good-bye to the character you feel most distant from in the play.

Short Open Scene

I can't believe it
I know what you mean
Just make a decision
I'm going

Long Open Scene

I made it
Obviously
You weren't here a minute ago
Neither were you
True
True
It's good to be here
We did it
And now
Next step

I can't
I can
Wait
It's time
I'm not ready
But you came
So did you
And we're moving on

Notes

1 Chekhov, Michael. *Lessons for the Professional Actor*. New York: Performing Arts Journal Publications, 1992. p. 67.
2 Petit, Lenard. *The Michael Chekhov Handbook*. New York: Routledge, 2010. p. 35.
3 Used with permission from Joanna Merlin. Personal correspondence, April 13, 2019.

Appendix II
The Movement Pioneers

Movement Pioneers are innovators who change the way we look at our bodies in motion. They base their theories in the facts of our body's design, and they offer unique ways of accessing freedom, ease, and authenticity in our movement.

Their discoveries also support and awaken an authentic creative approach to the artistic aspects of movement. The Movement Pioneers offer us the gift of deeply connecting with our instrument, liberating our creativity, and realizing powerful artistic expression.

The three movement pioneers whose work most influenced *YBK* are F.M. Alexander, Michael Chekhov, and Rudolf Laban. We've included short bios of each of them below and resources where you can find more about their work. In addition, we wish to acknowledge Laban's student Irmgard Bartenieff and the creators of *body mapping*, Barbara Conable and Bill Conable. We've also added a list of other pioneers whose discoveries have impacted our teaching.

F.M. Alexander (1869–1955): The Alexander Technique

Frederick Matthias Alexander was an Australian actor, movement theorist, and educator. He was a premature baby, which caused breathing issues early in his life. A very curious child, he was even sent home from school for asking so many questions! His probing mind was a key factor in developing his theories in later life.

In his twenties, Alexander moved to Melbourne to become an actor. Though he found some success, he developed chronic laryngitis caused by his breathing issues. With his career threatened, he focused his curiosity and his powers of observation on the problem. He watched himself speak in a three-way mirror, and he discovered a strong pattern of tension when he spoke. Over many months, Alexander learned to free this tension and bring his body into balance, which solved his vocal and breathing issues. He was able to return to the stage.

Other actors noticed the change in Alexander's voice and sought his advice. There were so many who asked for lessons that he eventually gave up his acting career to teach his method. He developed an educational process that became known as The Alexander Technique, and he moved to London and established a studio. There he taught actors, musicians, and other performing artists.

As his fame grew, many notable figures took lessons in the Alexander Technique: playwright George Bernard Shaw, writer Aldous Huxley, Nobel laureate Sir Charles Sherrington, and the great American educator, John Dewey. Alexander and his students realized that the Technique was effective not only for performers, but it also could be applied in therapeutic and educational situations. Over time, the Technique was studied by equestrians, athletes, business people, physical therapists, and others.

In 1930, Alexander established a teacher training course in London. He also taught his Technique and trained teachers in the US. He wrote a number of books on his discoveries, among them *The Use of the Self* and *The Universal Constant in Living*, which promoted the spread of his Technique throughout the world.

After his death, Alexander's students continued to train teachers, and there are now teacher training programs throughout the world. Teachers are certified through two International organizations, Alexander Technique International, and the Alexander Technique Affiliated Societies (ATAS). Today, Alexander's process is still taught to young artists – actors, musicians, and dancers – at the Juilliard School, Carnegie Mellon University, the Royal Academy of Dramatic Art, University of California at San Diego, and many others.

For further information:

The Complete Guide to the Alexander Technique: www.alexandertechnique.com
American Society for the Alexander Technique: www.amsatonline.org
Alexander Technique International: https://alexandertechniqueinternational.com

Sources:

Barstow, Marjorie. "Preface," in F.M. Alexander, *The Use of the Self*. United States: Centerline Press, 1984.

Bloch, Michael. *The Life of Frederick Matthias Alexander*. Great Britain: Little, Brown, 2004.

Jones, Frank Pierce. *Body Awareness in Action: A Study of the Alexander Technique*. New York: Schocken Books, 1979.

Michael Chekhov (1891–1955)

Michael Chekhov was a nephew of the great Russian playwright, Anton Chekhov. He trained as an actor with Stanislavski, becoming a member of the legendary ensemble acting company, the Moscow Art Theatre. Later, he was appointed director of the Second

Moscow Art Theatre and School, where he could experiment with his quest for "inspired acting." His theories linked movement with freeing human imagination and the psychology of the character: he sought to awaken the "soul of the inner artist." Chekhov's productions were wildly imaginative, his acting inspired, and he was much beloved by the Russian public.

However, his methods were too daring for the Soviet regime, and fearing arrest, Chekhov and his wife fled Russia in 1928. He performed and directed across Europe, becoming widely recognized as one of the great actors of his generation. In 1935, Chekhov performed on Broadway in *The Inspector General*. Actress Beatrice Straight saw his performance, and she and her parents invited him to establish the Chekhov Theatre Studio at Dartington Hall, Devonshire, England. Then in 1939, as war with Germany loomed, Chekhov and his benefactors moved the school to Connecticut.

In the US, Chekhov and his actors toured as the Chekhov Players. With the advent of World War II and the scarcity of gasoline, he moved to Hollywood. He became a film actor and was nominated for an Academy Award for his performance in Hitchcock's *Spellbound*. He also held acting classes and taught his acting methods to many Hollywood stars of the day. Among his students were Ingrid Bergman, Marilyn Monroe, Anthony Quinn, and Yul Brynner. He also published *On the Technique of Acting*, which describes his technique in detail.

Of his acting training, actress Joanna Merlin has said,

> Chekhov opened the door to our most creative space. He stimulated our minds, hearts, and bodies – gave us permission to freely explore, to surprise ourselves. He allowed for all impulses – he would not criticize or judge; he would only suggest alternatives that would take us in a different or better direction. No one ever felt foolish or fearful, though we were using ourselves in new and different ways. We were safe because we could not fail. We learned to trust in the power of our intuition and imagination.

After his death, his students established the Michael Chekhov Acting Studio in New York City; they trained a generation of teachers, who carry on his legacy. Many books are available on the Chekhov Technique, including Chekhov's *To the Actor* and *On Theatre and the Art of Acting*, Lenard Petit's *The Michael Chekhov Handbook*, and *Directing with the Michael Chekhov Technique* by Mark Monday.

You can read more about Michael Chekhov at www.michaelchekhov.org, also known as MICHA, where you can see videos of classes and find other resources. The Great Lakes Michael Chekhov Consortium and MICHA offer classes and teacher training in the Michael Chekhov Technique, as do many Chekhov studios throughout the world.

Sources: www.michaelchekhov.org/our-story

Powers, Mala. "The Past, Present and Future of Michael Chekhov," in Chekhov, Michael (ed.), *To the Actor*. New York: Routledge, 2002. pp. xxv–xlv.

Rudolf Laban (1879–1958)

Rudolf Laban was an Austro-Hungarian dancer, teacher, choreographer, and movement theorist. As a young man, his father placed him in a military academy, but Laban left the school to study architecture in Paris. There he pursued his passion for the theatre, dance, and mime.

Laban moved to Germany and opened a dance school, and later a summer school in Switzerland. He began training teachers in his methods, and his influence spread through Germany and beyond. Laban thought everyone should dance, and began to teach workers, teachers, and others, creating great public dances he called movement choirs. He also wrote books and developed a dance notation, known as Labanotation. His influence was widespread, and he lectured throughout the country, teaching his methods and his philosophy that the mind and body are inseparable.

As Hitler rose to power, Laban was placed in charge of dance throughout Germany, and he was invited to develop a movement choir for the opening of the 1936 Olympic Games in Berlin. However, when Hitler and his Minister of Propaganda, Joseph Goebbels, attended the dress rehearsal, they saw that the work was in opposition to Nazi ideals, and the performance was cancelled. Laban was placed under house arrest, and he eventually fled Germany with the help of friends. His books and dance notation system were banned.

Exhausted and ill, Laban moved to England, where he, like Michael Chekhov, was welcomed to Dartington Hall. Though he was too ill to teach, Laban wrote a book on his theories, *Choreutics*. Eventually, he was able to find work in Manchester, advising factory managers on how to improve worker efficiency through movement. His work contributed to England's war effort by dramatically improving factory output.

While in Manchester, he and his long-time student and collaborator, Lisa Ullman, began teaching in the basement of their home. Soon, they outgrew the basement, established the Art of Movement Studio and began teaching the Art of Movement in the schools. Laban published a book in English, *Modern Educational Dance*. Actors also sought training in Laban's movement methods. The Art of Movement eventually moved to a larger studio in Surrey, where Laban wrote the *Mastery of Movement* and trained dancers, actors, and teachers in his theories until his death.

Laban's students, among them Lisa Ullman, Irmgard Bartenieff, and Jean Newlove, carried on his legacy, teaching his methods, revising his books, and writing about his work and its application in the modern world. Movement certifications – such as LMA, Laban/Bartenieff Movement Analyst, and CMA, Certified Movement Analyst – have developed from his theories. His movement system and techniques are taught in acting and dance programs and conservatories throughout the world.

For further information:

www.labaninstitute.org
www.trinitylaban.ac.uk

Books by Laban and his students, some of which are listed in the bibliography.

Sources:

Newlove, Jean. *Laban for Actors and Dancers*. New York: Routledge, 1993, pp. 7–17.

Newlove, Jean and Dalby, John. *Laban for All*. New York: Routledge, 2004, pp. 11–16.

Other Movement Pioneers

Irmgard Bartenieff (1900–1981)

As a young dance student in 1920s Germany, Bartenieff trained with Laban and then began to teach dance on her own. She introduced her students to Laban Movement Analysis. She and her husband also formed a dance company, which flourished until they were forced to leave Germany in 1936 after the rise of Hitler.

They fled to the US; Bartenieff trained as a physical therapist and began to work with polio patients. She chose not to focus on isolating and working specific muscle groups, which was the standard treatment at that time. Instead, she emphasized connecting muscle groups through *initiation*, *sequencing* and spatial intent (clarifying our spatial pathways). To support her work, she developed a unique series of movement *sequences*, The Bartenieff Fundamentals.

Gradually, Bartenieff rebuilt her connections to the dance world. She worked with the Dance Notation Bureau in New York, and, in 1978, opened the Laban Institute of Movement Studies. She was also a founder of the American Dance Therapy Association. Today, the Fundamentals are used by dancers/movers/therapists all over the world.

Throughout her life, Bartenieff explored ways to support "continuous movement and change with stability and delight." Her book, *Body Movement*, published in 1980, has been reprinted many times over. Her students carry on her legacy through the Laban/Bartenieff Institute of Movement Studies (www.labaninstitute.org) and through books and publications, including *Making Connections* by Peggy Hackney.

Source:

Irmgard Bartenieff. *Body Movement: Coping with the Environment*. New York: Gordon and Breach, 1980, p. ix.

Barbara Conable

Barbara Conable is a senior teacher of the Alexander Technique, and the author of *How To Learn the Alexander Technique* (with Bill Conable). She is the founder of Andover Educators, a training program and a network of *body mapping* teachers, dedicated to "saving, securing, and enhancing musical careers with accurate information about the body in movement."

Barbara has further developed Bill Conable's theories of *body mapping* in her books *What Every Musician Needs To Know About the Body* and *The Structures and Movement of Breathing*. In addition, her students have written a series of *body mapping* books for musicians and one for dancers. Barbara is now retired but continues to write, and she acts as advisor to Andover Educators. To read more about *Body Mapping*, visit www.bodymap.org.

Sources:

www.bodymap.org

Conable, Barbara and Conable, William. *How to Learn the Alexander Technique*, Portland: Andover Press, 1995.

Bill Conable

Dr. William Conable is a senior teacher of the Alexander Technique and Emeritus Professor of cello at Ohio State University. Bill developed his theory of *body mapping* by observing cello students' movements as they played. He saw that their mistaken ideas about the way their bodies moved interfered with their playing.

As he introduced them to the Alexander Technique, he began to include information on the *friendly facts* of their anatomy. He called this experiential anatomy lesson *body mapping*. He discovered that the combination of Alexander's work and an understanding of their anatomy helped his young musicians develop a sense of ease as they played: they moved in partnership with their body-instrument, as well as their musical instrument. Dr. Conable wrote *How To Learn the Alexander Technique* with Barbara Conable. He lives and teaches in Spokane, WA. To read more about Bill's career and his approach to *Body Mapping*, visit www.alexanderworkshops.com/Bill/

Sources:

www.alexanderworkshops.com/Bill/

Conable, Barbara and Conable, William. *How to Learn the Alexander Technique*, Portland: Andover Press, 1995.

The pioneers below are from the worlds of dance, voice, and human potential. Their work has influenced our teaching and the material in *YBK*:

Cicely Berry (1926–2018), Voice Coach – Royal Shakespeare Company; Author: *Voice and the Actor*, *The Actor and the Text*, and more.
Irene Dowd, Dance faculty – Juilliard School, Hollins University; neuromuscular re-education; Author: *Taking Root to Fly*.
Jean Houston, PhD, human/cultural development, UN Development Program; Author: *The Possible Human* and 25 other books.

Kristin Linklater, Voice Professor Emerita, Columbia University; Author: *Freeing the Natural Voice* and *Freeing Shakespeare's Voice*.

Lulu Sweigard, PhD (1895–1974), Dance faculty – Juilliard School, NYU; Ideokinesis; Author: *Human Movement Potential*.

Mabel Todd (1880–1956), physiology and the psychology of movement; Author: *The Thinking Body*.

Mary Starks Whitehouse (1911–1979), Authentic Movement; Author: *Authentic Movement: Essays by Mary Starks Whitehouse, Janet Adler and Joan Chodorow*. Ed. Patrizia Pallaro.

Bibliography

*Titles marked with an asterisk are particularly recommended.

Alexander Technique

Alexander, F.M. *The Use of the Self*. London: Orion Books, Ltd., reissued 2001.

Carrington, Walter and Carrington, Dilys. *An Evolution of the Alexander Technique*. London: Sheildrake Press, 2017.

Conable, Barbara. *Marjorie Barstow: Her Teaching and Training*, 3rd ed. London: Mouritz, 2016.

*Conable, Barbara and Conable, William. *How to Learn The Alexander Technique*. Portland: Andover Press, 1995.

*Crow, Aileen. "The Alexander Technique as a Basic Approach to Theatrical Training," in Lucille S. Rubin (Ed.) *Movement for the Actor*. New York: Drama Books Specialists, 1980, pp. 1–12.

Dimon, Theodore. *Neurodynamics*. Berkeley: North Atlantic Books, 2015.

Fisher, Jean M.O., Ed. *The Philosopher's Stone*. London: Mouritz, 1998, p. 94.

*Gelb, Michael. *Body Learning*. New York: Henry Holt and Company, 1994.

Jones, Frank Pierce. *Body Awareness in Action*. New York: Schocken Books, 1979.

McDonald, Patrick, *The Alexander Technique As I See it*. Brighton, UK: Rahula Books, 1989.

Nicholls, Carolyn. *Body, Breath, and Being*, East Sussex: D&B Publishing, 2008.

Park, Glen. *The Art of Changing*, London: Ashgrove Publishing, 2000.

*Polatin, Betsy. *The Actor's Secret*. Berkeley: North Atlantic Books, 2013.

Walker, Elisabeth. *Forward and Away*. King's Lynn, Norfolk: Gavin R. Walker, 2008.

Wolf, Jessica. *Jessica Wolf's Art of Breathing: Collected Articles*. New York, 2013.

Anatomy

*Hale, Thomas Beverly and Coyle, Terence. *Albinus on Anatomy*. Mineola: Dover Publications, 1988.

Dimon, Theodore. *Anatomy of the Moving Body*, 2nd ed. Berkeley: North Atlantic Books, 2008.

*Conable, Barbara. *What Every Musician Needs to Know about the Body*. Portland: Andover Press, 2000.

Bartenieff Fundamentals

Andrews, Meade with Boggs, Carol. "The Bartenieff Fundamentals: Mobilizing the Dancer's Resources." *Contact Quarterly*, vol. 11, no. 2, Spring/Summer, 1986, pp. 14–18.

*Bartenieff, Irmgard. *Body Movement: Coping with the Environment*. New York: Gordon & Breach, 1980.

*Hackney, Peggy. *Making Connections: Total Body Integration Through Bartenieff Funda-mentals*. New York: Routledge, 2002.

Laban

Adrian, Barbara. *Actor Training the Laban Way*. New York: Allworth Press, 2008.

Adrian, Barbara. "An Introduction to Laban Movement Analysis for Actors," in Nicole Potter, Mary Fleischer and Barbara Adrian (Eds.) *Movement for Actors*. New York: Allworth Press, 2016, pp. 92–104.

Andrews, Meade. "F.M. Alexander and Rudolf Laban: A Symbiotic Relationship," in James Jordan Ed. *The Conductor's Gesture: A Practical Application of Rudolf Von Laban's Movement Language*. Chicago: GIA Publications, 2011. Companion DVD with Meade Andrews and James Jordan, pp. 278–279.

*Bloom, Katya, et al. *The Laban Workbook For Actors*. New York: Bloomsbury, 2018.

Dell, Cecily. *A Primer for Movement Description*. New York: Dance Notation Bureau Press, 1970.

Laban, Rudolf. *A Life for Dance*. Braintree, MA: Macdonald and Evans, Ltd, 1975.

———. *The Language of Movement*. Boston: Plays Incorporated, 1976.

———. *The Mastery of Movement*. Alton, UK: Dance Books Ltd., 1980.

———. *Modern Educational Dance*. Boston: Plays Incorporated, 1974.

*Newlove, Jean. *Laban for Actors and Dancers*. New York: Routledge, 1993.

Newlove, Jean and Darby, John. *Laban for All*. New York: Routledge, 2004.

Studd, Karen and Cox, Laura. *Everybody is a Body*. Indianapolis: Dog Ear Publishing, 2013.

Michael Chekhov Acting Technique

Chekhov, Michael. *Lessons for the Professional Actor*. New York: Performing Arts Journal Publications, 1985.

———. *On the Technique of Acting*. New York: Harper Perennial, 1991.

*———. Transcribed by Deirdre Hurst du Prey. *Lessons for Teachers*. Ottawa: Dovehouse Editions, 2000.

———. *To the Actor on the Technique of Acting*. New York: Routledge, 2002.

Petit, Lenard. *The Michael Chekhov Handbook*. New York: Routledge, 2010.

Other Books on Movement, Voice, Creativity, Acting, and Human Potential

Berry, Cicely. *The Actor and the Text*. New York: Applause Books, 1992.

Dowd, Irene. *Taking Root to Fly*. Northampton: Contact Editions, 1981.

Hodge, Francis. *Play Directing*, 5th ed. Boston: Allyn and Bacon, 2000.

Houston, Jean. *The Possible Human*. New York: Jeremy P. Tarcher/ Putnam, 1997.

Linklater, Kristin. *Freeing the Natural Voice*. New York: Drama Book Publishers, 1976.

Moss, Larry. *The Intent to Live*. New York: Bantam Books, 2005.

Pierce, Alexandra and Pierce, Roger. *Expressive Movement*. Cambridge: Perseus Publishing, 1989.

Potter, Nicole, Ed. *Movement for Actors*. New York: Allworth Press, 2016.

Stough, Carl and Reece. *Dr. Breath*. New York: William Morrow Company, 1970.

Sweigard, Lulu. *Human Movement Potential*. New York: Harper and Row, 1974.

Todd, Mabel. *The Thinking Body*. New York: Paul B. Hoebner, Inc., 1937.

Zeder, Suzan with Hancock, Jim. *Spaces of Creation*. Portsmouth: Heinemann, 2005.

Index

Page numbers in italic type refer to information in figures.